RADICAL SELF-CARE

Inclusive Tools for Overcoming PTSD, Heartbreak, Conflict, Anger, Anxiety, Addiction, and Other Trapped Emotions

SAGE LISKEY
ILLUSTRATED BY TARA CHÁVEZ

Copyright © 2023 by Sage Liskey
Published and distributed by Sage Liskey and Rad Cat Press 2023.
All rights reserved.

Printed in the United States of America
1st Edition

Edited by:
Tara Chávez, Tessa Angelica, Heather T. Campbell, Mysti Frost, Christina Appleby, Ashley Wright, Thuy H. S. Nguyen, Autumn Hummell, Lauren Appell, Alanna Sowels, Tonya Marie, Lela Copeland, Larissa Varela, Rosalie Sermak, Savannah Rose, Sieglind Gatewood, Erika Hauptman, William C. Parham, JR Worley, Sonya Marie, Zoe Werthamer, Alex Renirie, Marcella Dean, and Madelaine Au

Illustrated by Tara Chávez

Cover and Interior Design by Sage Liskey

E-mail correspondence may be sent to RadCatPress@gmail.com

www.SageLiskey.com

ISBN-13: 978-0-9862461-8-0

Table Of Contents

Feedback Please, Medical Statement, Personal Disclaimer, How To Use This Book, Special Thanks

1. Foreword - 1

2. Trapped Emotions - 7
2.1 Trapped Emotions (8), 2.2 Individual, Repeated, And Attachment Difficulties (11), 2.3 Subtle Stressful Experiences Can Be Detrimental (11), 2.4 Resilience (11), 2.5 Learned Behaviors (14), 2.6 Ancestral Trapped Emotions (14), 2.7 Recovery Increases Your Safety (15), 2.8 Creating A Better World (15), 2.9 How To Release Trapped Emotions (16), 2.10 The Time It Takes To Heal (20), 2.11 What Healing Looks Like (21), 2.12 Make It Work For You (24), 2.13 Radical Self-Care (24)

PART I - IDENTIFYING AND COPING WITH TRAPPED EMOTIONS

3. Identifying Trapped Emotions - 29
3.1 Emotionally Stressful And Abusive People (33), 3.2 Emotionally Mature And Loving People (35), 3.3 Symptoms Of Trapped Emotions (35), 3.4 Attachment Styles (41), 3.5 Dissociation (42), 3.6 Separating Trapped Emotions From Your Basic Biology (44)

4. Reducing Stress And Building Resilience - 51
4.1 Motivating Yourself (52), 4.2 Go Slow (59), 4.3 You Already Have Resources (61), 4.4 Removing Stress And Abuse (62), 4.5 Establishing A Safe Space (65), 4.6 Visualization (67), 4.7 Finding A Therapist, Co-Counselor, And Other Allies (70), 4.8 False Self-Help (77), 4.9 Basic Self-Care (78), 4.10 Self-Care For Oppressed Communities (86), 4.11 Increasing Your Income (92), 4.12 Establishing A Higher Power (95), 4.13 Medicines (96), 4.14 Releasing Tension And Correcting Posture (99), 4.15 Increasing The

Window Of Tolerance To Stress (99), 4.16 Addressing Shame And Denial (100)

5. Learning How To Experience Emotions - 103
5.1 Mindfulness And Reconnecting To The Present (106), 5.2 Neurofeedback (108), 5.3 Identifying Emotions (109), 5.4 Experiencing Emotions (111), 5.5 Fake It Till You Release It (114), 5.6 Emotional Mastery (116), 5.7 Emotional Dysregulation (117), 5.8 Healthy Angering And Asserting Yourself (118), 5.9 Awareness Of Thoughts And The Critics (122)

PART II - TRANSFORMING STORIES

6. Stories And Self-Limiting Beliefs - 129
6.1 Memory And The Imagination (129), 6.2 Placebos And Nocebos (130), 6.3 Self-Limiting Beliefs And Stories (131), 6.4 Renegotiating Memories (140)

7. Basic Story Reframing - 145
7.1 Somatic Therapy (145), 7.2 Your Life History And Reclaiming Memories (147), 7.3 Ritual (148), 7.4 "Imaginary" Friends (149), 7.5 Dreams And Nightmares (150), 7.6 Role-Playing And Theater (152), 7.7 Hypnotherapy (153), 7.8 Exposure Therapy (153), 7.9 Prolonged Exposure Therapy (155), 7.10 Narrative Exposure Therapy (157), 7.11 Journaling (158)

8. Communication - 161
8.1 Nonviolent Communication (NVC) (163), 8.2 Making NVC Sound Natural (165), 8.3 Apologizing With NVC And Making Amends (166), 8.4 Handling Conflict With Conversational Receptiveness And Curiosity (168), 8.5 Supporting Others (168), 8.6 Repairing Relationships With Clarification And Imago (172), 8.7 Effective Communication (175), 8.8 Non-Judgmental Language (179), 8.9 Knowing The Source Of Your Need (179), 8.10 If Your Request Is Rejected (180), 8.11 Not Communicating (181), 8.12 Delaying Communication (182), 8.13 Misdirected Communication And Complaining (183), 8.14 Incompatibility (184), 8.15 Unavailable People (184), 8.16 More About Communication (184)

9. EMDR (Eye Movement Desensitization And Reprocessing) - 187
9.1 EMDR With A Therapist (189), 9.2 Solo EMDR (192), 9.3 Accelerated Resolution Therapy (194)

10. Inner Family - 197
10.1 Externalizing The Inner Family With Sandbox Therapy (198), 10.2 Parental, Adult, Child, Future, Ancestral, and Cultural Selves (198), 10.3 Right And Left Brains (201), 10.4 Initiating Contact With Your Inner Selves (202), 10.5 Inner Child And Playfulness (203), 10.6 Inner Loving Parents And Reparenting To Ideal Guardians (205), 10.7 Future Self (207), 10.8 Ancestral Self (208), 10.9 Cultural Self (208), 10.10 Birth And Death (209), 10.11 Creating Inner Selves (209)

11. Psychedelic Therapy And Integration - 213
11.1 Legality (214), 11.2 Risks (216), 11.3 Possible Effects (217), 11.4 Tripping With Others (219), 11.5 My Trips (219), 11.6 LSD (220), 11.7 Psilocybin Mushrooms (222), 11.8 MDMA (223), 11.9 Preparing For And Going On A Safe Psychedelic Journey (225), 11.10 Navigating A Bad Trip (228), 11.11 Trip Sitting And Guiding (228), 11.12 Integration (229), 11.13 Microdosing (231)

PART III - BEHAVIORS, MINDSET, RELATIONSHIPS, AND ENVIRONMENT

12. Habits And Addictions - 235
12.1 Habits (235), 12.2 Addictions (241), 12.3 The Big No List (249)

13. Reforming Mental States - 253
13.1 Healthy And Regulated Nervous System (253), 13.2 Ego, Awe, And Developing Or Diminishing The Self (254), 13.3 Control (257), 13.4 Confidence Through Intelligence, Hormones, And Dopamine (260), 13.5 Guilt, Shame, And Resentment (265), 13.6 Blame And Identifying How You Reinforce Your Suffering (266), 13.7 Developing Compassion And Empathy (267), 13.8 Self-Compassion (269), 13.9 Self-Love (269), 13.10 Positive Self-

Talk And Affirmations (270), 13.11 Positive Energy And Creating Defining Moments (272), 13.12 Happiness (274), 13.13 Forgiving Yourself And Others (275)

14. Healthy Relationships - 283
14.1 Friendships (285), 14.2 Romantic Relationships And Secure Attachment (291), 14.3 Breaking Up With Someone (309), 14.4 Being Broken Up With (310), 14.5 Community And Individualism (313)

15. Changing Your Environment - 321
15.1 Personal Environment (321), 15.2 Businesses And Community Groups (321), 15.3 Creating A Less Stressful Culture And Society (322), 15.4 Discrimination (323), 15.5 Stopping Discrimination In Yourself (332), 15.6 Law Enforcement And Restorative Justice (343), 15.7 Media (345), 15.8 Capitalism And Mutual Aid (347), 15.9 Gender (349), 15.10 Good Parenting (353), 15.11 Healing The Natural World (356), 15.12 Culture (357)

16. Becoming A Changemaker - 363
16.1 Effective Change In Grassroots And Mass Movements (364), 16.2 Reminders For Activists (368), 16.3 Communication For Activists (370), 16.4 Persuasion (374), 16.5 Beyond Blame, Victimhood, And Cancel Culture (375)

PART IV - RELEASING TRAPPED EMOTIONS

17. How To Release Specific Trapped Emotions - 383
17.1 Where To Start (384), 17.2 Major Parts To My Healing (384), 17.3 Pulling Yourself Out Of A Triggered Space (386), 17.4 Right After You Have A Life-Or-Death Experience (387), 17.5 Unaddressed Single Past Incidents And PTSD (388), 17.6 Attachment Wounds And Complex PTSD (388), 17.7 Stress, Overwhelm, And Anxiety (391), 17.8 Anger, Judgments, And The Outer Critic (392), 17.9 Zooming Out And Disrupting Hyperfocus (392), 17.10 Workaholism (393), 17.11 Health And Fearing Death (394), 17.12 Self-Blame And Self-Hatred (394), 17.13 Loss And Grief (395), 17.14 Rejection (396), 17.15 Insecurity And Jealousy (396), 17.16 Feeling Empty

Or Numb (397), 17.17 Sounds (397), 17.18 Religious And Spiritual Abuse (398), 17.19 Ancestral Trapped Emotions (398), 17.20 Appearance (399), 17.21 Touch (17.21)

18. Moving Forward With Radical Self-Care - 405

19. Works Referenced - 409

19.1 Trauma And PTSD (409), 19.2 The Inner Child And Parts Of Ourselves (410), 19.3 Psychedelics (411), 19.4 Meditation, Spirituality, And Buddhism (411), 19.5 Addiction, Alcohol, And Dysfunctional Families (411), 19.6 Relationships (412), 19.7 Money, Business, Creativity, And Finances (412), 19.8 Gender, Race, And Social Justice (412), 19.9 Social And Communication (413), 19.10 Miscellaneous (414)

20. Further Resources - 415

20.1 Finding A Therapist (415), 20.2 Addiction And Dysfunctional Family Resources (415), 20.3 Podcasts (416), 20.4 Meditations (416), 20.5 Confidential Emergency Hotlines (416)

21. Bibliography - 417

About The Author, About The Artist

Feedback Please!

Feedback is welcome for corrections, clarifications, and additions, especially as it relates to fighting various forms of discrimination. The contents herein cover many sensitive subjects and I want to make sure to be releasing information that is as beneficial as possible to readers. Please reach out at radcatpress@gmail.com if you would like to share your thoughts. Thank you!

Medical Statement

While the contents of this book are thoroughly researched and I have successfully used many of the techniques discussed, I do not guarantee the accuracy of the information herein and I withhold any liability for the effects it may have in your own life. Please use this information at your own risk. If possible you should work with a therapist or other psychiatric professional while addressing your mental health. You should also always talk to your doctor before ingesting anything mentioned.

Furthermore, these techniques are meant for adults. While some are equally beneficial for children and teenagers, they may have to be learned or applied in ways specific to younger age groups that go beyond the scope of this book. For help raising a healthy child, I suggest reading John Gottman's *Raising An Emotionally Intelligent Child*. To release trapped emotions in children, read *Trauma-Proofing Your Kids* by Maggie Kline and Peter Levine, *What Happened To You* by Bruce D. Perry and Oprah Winfrey, or *The Boy Who Was Raised as a Dog* by Bruce D. Perry.

This book primarily deals with trapped emotions and attachment wounds that form the roots of PTSD, complex PTSD, heartbreak, anxiety, conflict, anger, jealousy, sadness, and other states of suffering. While the techniques covered can be effective for some forms of depression and will benefit anyone wishing to become more resilient in life, it should be known that there are many more causes of depression that can be explored in *The Depression Sourcebook* by Dr. Brian Quinn. The *Huberman Lab* podcast also has some great episodes on depression. Please read other resources or see a doctor if you believe your symptoms have proliferated from more than just life events and thinking patterns. Among these include inflammation, malnutrition, diet, lifestyle choices, hormonal shifts, gut health, chemical poisoning, genes, chemical imbalances, and events that happened to your ancestors.

There are also brain wirings such as bipolar, autism, ADHD, and high sensitivity that create extra considerations for your mental health. When undiagnosed or untreated, these conditions can make self-help information ineffective or difficult to apply. Keep in mind that many doctors are not well-trained in treating mental health struggles and you may need to seek out someone who is specifically researched in trauma, psychiatry, gut health, nutrition, and traditional psychiatric medications. At the very least, if a doctor prescribes you an antidepressant, they should also prescribe you a therapist. People dealing with chronic illnesses or conditions may also benefit from finding emerging and time-tested treatments in Tony Robbins's book, *Life Force*. That said, chronic illnesses can also be caused by or worsened by trapped emotions.

The contents of this book can bring up a lot of emotions in readers, so please take care of yourself as necessary. Chapters 2 and 3 may be especially difficult for some readers learning for the first time about how certain difficult events formed their behaviors and personality. It is okay to go slow or skip over information that is too triggering to handle right now. Many coping tools can be found in Chapters 4 and 5, especially Section 4.9. If you have thoughts of killing or harming yourself, or know someone else who is, please call the National Suicide Hotline at 800-273-8255. You can also call or text 988. Remember that things will get better with time and that change can happen very quickly.

Personal Disclaimer

This information summarizes and adds important additions to titles like *Complex PTSD*, *The Body Keeps The Score*, *What Happened To You*, and *My Grandmother's Hands*. While these books are great and include compelling narratives, they neglect to mention many aspects of healing. With so much important information to include, storytelling in *Radical Self-Care* is fairly minimal. That said, I share some snippets from my personal journey and have done my best to keep information concise and easy to understand. Chapter 17 also includes specific examples of using the techniques described. I do not typically go into the science behind the techniques I talk about, however, you can read any number of the sources mentioned to learn more if this interests you. Most of the techniques I have written about I have tried myself or have friends who have successfully used them.

I do strongly believe that the skills covered throughout this book will help anyone, no matter how marginalized, depressed, or economically disadvantaged they are. However, due to various forms of discrimination, many groups lack certain privileges or inherently feel unsafe in society. It may be harder for them to utilize some of the information provided. For these groups, deep healing will be difficult until larger cultural and structural changes happen, but increasing one's resilience to stress is still attainable with these techniques. I also conclude with a guide on becoming an effective changemaker to create a more equitable world. Beyond that chapter, readers should know that this book also illuminates how their oppressors started acting out in abuse and hatred. Understanding and dismantling trapped emotions is one of the greatest things people can do to fight against injustice socially and environmentally.

I have done my best to include the lived realities of marginalized communities and as part of the editing sought out a racially and gender-diverse group of readers to comment on this work. That said, this is not a comprehensive guide to oppression, but I hope it can act as a very solid summary for readers to uproot oppression in themselves and society. I am not perfect and acknowledge having internal biases to still work through. I had the privilege of growing up in the body of a White man without a disability in the United States of America and with a family who gave me support when in need. While I have been on the brink of suicide, have spent most of my life living well below the poverty line, was subjected to body shaming, had a speech impediment, do not fit into the mainstream norms of what a man is "supposed" to be, and was raised within a dysfunctional family, the difficulties I have experienced were made much easier because of my privileges. There are struggles I can empathize with but can never fully understand. Please contact me at <radcatpress@gmail.com> if you have thoughts on how I can improve this dialogue in healing humanity. More about how this book is being made accessible can be found at <www.sageliskey.com>.

How To Use This Book

Radical Self-Care guides readers through how to overcome any past emotional difficulty. Starting at the end of Chapter 3, there are also questions to help you reflect on the reading. A lot of information is presented here, so it is recommended to keep a journal, highlight or underline passages of interest, and use sticky notes to mark content you would like to return to later. This will help you integrate and keep track of the pieces you find valuable. Take what you need and leave the rest. Just know that simply reading may not be enough. Some of these techniques must be performed dozens or hundreds of times as a regular practice to see the most benefit.

If you are struggling with more severe trapped emotions or have been diagnosed with PTSD or complex PTSD, you may benefit most by reading this book in chronological order and trying the exercises along the way. The contents build on each other in the following order: understanding trapped emotions, learning how to regulate your nervous system, building resources to handle your emotions and memories, learning to experience the present moment and your body, tools for renegotiating stories and releasing trapped emotions, and lastly, creating changes internally and externally to improve your life.

Even sections that do not seem to pertain to you may offer unique insights. After your initial read-through, go back and focus on the techniques and exercises that felt especially relevant, or do further reading that I mention in the Works Referenced. Of course, you may have already started on your healing journey and wish to focus on whatever areas feel most beneficial to you right now. If you want some practical tools for immediate use, the basic self-care information in Section 4.9 is a great place to start.

Otherwise, many readers will want to use this book as a reference guide for things like improving their communication, dealing with anger, or transforming self-limiting beliefs. In this case, you can refer to the Table Of Contents or Chapter 17 for ways of dealing with specific trapped emotions. I do suggest beginning with reading the first two chapters though to understand some of the basic concepts used throughout the book.

Special Thanks

Many friends and acquaintances pitched in their insights to help edit this book and give feedback on the cover design. I want to thank Tessa Angelica, Heather T. Campbell, Mysti Frost, Christina Appleby, Ashley Wright, Thuy H. S. Nguyen, Autumn Hummell, Lauren Appell, Alanna Sowels, Tonya Marie, Lela Copeland, Larissa Varela, Rosalie Sermak, Savannah Rose, Sieglind Gatewood, Erika Hauptman, William C. Parham, JR Worley, Sonya Marie, Zoe Werthamer, Alex Renirie, Marcella Dean, and Madelaine Au. You made this work a million times better! I also want to give an extra big thanks to my childhood friend Tara Chávez for her amazing illustrations, dedication, and wonderful suggestions along the way.

Chapter 1

Foreword

Before the introduction, I feel that it is important to explain the inspiration for this book. I use the terms trauma and post-traumatic stress disorder (PTSD) in this foreword, but only to describe how I find these terms problematic and confusing. In some ways, this book is all about trauma, PTSD, and complex PTSD, but through the perspective that even seemingly small difficulties can have long-term negative impacts on anyone. I believe that any event or unresolved emotion can be traumatic or cause alterations in behaviors. These include heartbreak, conflict, anger, discrimination, and many types of depression and anxiety. While the terms trauma and PTSD can be useful for many people seeking specific types of support, they won't appear much later on because of how misleading they are. Allow me to explain.

As a young child, I experienced a lot of stress surrounding my parents, my body, and society at large. These difficulties were simply the norm; I did not know anything else. Together they resulted in deep anxiety, depression, anger, and a constant sense of abandonment which prevented me from trusting others. In reaching adulthood, I was finally able to address many of these feelings, but something important was still missing from my healing. After an extremely difficult relationship ended in 2019 and at the suggestion of a therapist, I began looking more deeply into how being the child of an alcoholic impacted my brain. I quickly realized that I had *complex PTSD* and started to broaden my knowledge on the topic through my local library's free audiobooks. It blew my mind, yet also made me realize how words like PTSD and trauma are deeply misunderstood.

While I believe labels can be very useful for addressing symptoms of various mental health conditions, and I pride myself in being fairly open about my mental health struggles, I had never thought of myself as traumatized. Trauma felt too extreme to describe what I had experienced growing up, even though I now understand those events caused me many difficult symptoms correlated with PTSD. I began to realize that this stigma often holds people back, and it's not their fault considering that PTSD started as a word to describe the symptoms of war veterans and sexual assault survivors. Even though it is now understood to be caused by many other circumstances, this association often prevents people from getting a proper diagnosis or the help they need. Even the five therapists I had over the years never mentioned that I might have PTSD.

I did benefit greatly from the books I read about PTSD, more than what any therapist had ever done for me. However, I also found that most of this literature is not very accessible or useful to the casual reader. The writing often disregards many forms of trauma, never discusses how to change maladaptive behaviors, relies on expensive therapy practices, ignores the power of healthy communication, entirely neglects marginalized and underprivileged individuals, disregards psychedelic therapies, or misunderstands the true breadth of trauma and PTSD in society.

Just like many doctors, researchers, and therapists do when speaking about mental health, these books tended to dissect a complex issue away from its whole form.[62] I'll share more about the limitations of the mental health and therapy industry in Section 4.7. While I had not planned on writing another mental health book for quite a while, I found it imperative to do so as I began discovering ways to heal. So what are trauma and PTSD really?

Trauma and PTSD are often used interchangeably, but they are different. *Trauma* in Greek means "wound." It is simply an event that your mind or body experiences as negative, dangerous, or deadly. It is an energetic protective mechanism, and everyone reacts differently depending on their resilience, symptoms, past, and the event itself. Traumatic experiences most often cause sadness, anxiety, depression, PTSD, or complex PTSD. An official PTSD diagnosis is given when a person has intrusive and avoidant symptoms, changes in mood and thinking, an alteration in their ability to regulate their nervous system, as well as changes in how they react to external stimuli.[132A] These correlate to parts of the brain being shut off or greatly diminished. More generally, PTSD is a traumatic energy that remains unresolved and trapped in the body even months after happening. This causes a wide variety of pervasive symptoms meant to protect oneself from the event happening again.

Simple PTSD refers to a single difficult incident, such as an injury or deeply frightening experience. *Complex PTSD* occurs from attachment wounds, especially from caregivers, paired with repeated traumatic incidents, like growing up with an abusive, alcoholic, or neglectful parent.[218] While both types throw a person into an overly fearful and emotional state, complex

PTSD also distorts their basic sense of self, drastically altering their personality and relational behaviors. Simple and complex PTSD are most frequently triggered when confronted with a memory or stimulus similar to the initial event, but may show up in all parts of one's life in things like anxiety and depression. That is all to say that PTSD is not necessarily a disorder; it is a natural protective response to unresolved emotions and stress.

The symptoms of trauma are immense. Doctors like Bessel van der Kolk, author of *The Body Keeps The Score*, believe that if the *Diagnostic and Statistical Manual of Mental Disorders* (DSM) was actually based in real science, the majority of the conditions described would be designated as symptoms of trauma and PTSD.[97A] This includes many cases of anxiety, depression, narcissism, and addiction. Trauma can even result in symptoms that mimic bipolar, ADHD, and autism. The thing is, all of these symptoms can be treated with similar techniques when we understand that they are the result of trapped emotions that were left unresolved. In fact, many Indigenous groups, such as the Māori, see things like depression, trauma, sleep issues, and drug abuse all coming from the same source.[132B]

While psychological differences do exist between different traumas, traditional healing has always involved community connection, dance, music, songs, stories, spirituality, and plant medicines.[132C] These correlate with the *neurosequential model of therapeutics* for handling PTSD. You do not start with trying to fix a person's symptoms. Instead, you first regulate the nervous system, relate to the person, and then reason with them to fix the symptoms.[132D] While people with severe traumatic experiences may need to go slower, deal with dissociation, integrate experiences like empathy, heal attachment wounds, and unlearn more maladaptive behaviors than others, the essential steps to healing are still similar.

Typically when we talk about traumatic events, we think of extreme situations, but behavioral and emotional changes can happen from things that seem fairly benign, especially in children. Breakups, an argument, falling on the ground, being bitten by a dog, a scary clown, failing a major test, a hospital visit, the death of a loved pet, witnessing something traumatic happen to another person, verbal abuse, an embarrassing situation, or having parents who are frequently unavailable can all be traumatic, cause maladaptive behaviors, or result in PTSD. This is especially true when no one is there to help support us through the emotions that arise or when we have already experienced past unresolved difficulties.

Some people try to distinguish between traumas with little t (small incidents), big T (really intense incidents), or not traumatic, but these designations sometimes ignore the complexity of emotions and PTSD. Any event, even a very subtle one, can cause a difficult emotion to become trapped in the body and create painful changes in thinking and behavior. Naturally, the symptoms differ depending on the event, and some events, especially repeated ones, are likely to cause more severe trauma responses and PTSD. However, there is no way of knowing for any given individual or instance what symptoms, if any, will arise. This is because each person responds according to their unique personality and the amount of resilience they have to difficult experiences. These symptoms can also appear almost immediately or years after a traumatic event. For instance, some of the more prominent signs of complex PTSD appear only once a person has entered into a romantic relationship. This is because relationships mimic many parental and familial dynamics, thus triggering any abuse or neglect experienced as a child.

Furthermore, many symptoms that are quite detrimental to individuals are commonly accepted or even celebrated by society, such as workaholism, perfectionism, alcoholism, aggression, or being overly giving and submissive. This often results in trauma being covered up and unaddressed no matter how much suffering it causes people and society. There are also many trauma symptoms like various forms of discrimination, sadness, depression, and anxiety that the mainstream health industry explains as cognitive or chemical problems rather than trauma. While some of it is cognitive or chemical in nature, a lot is caused by past experiences.

In other words, we may completely ignore the severe trauma someone experienced because they do not exhibit the "correct" symptoms. The thing is, any difficult experience can cause long-term negative impacts on a person's life, and no one can know for certain if recovery will happen naturally or require intentional action. When unaddressed, even small traumas can grow into bigger and bigger problems with increasing amounts of anxiety, depression, and maladaptive behaviors.

For these reasons, I strongly dislike the words trauma and PTSD. They are confusing, intense, and prevent many people from seeking help. In their book *What Happened To You*, PTSD specialist Bruce Perry tells Oprah Winfrey, "The language [of trauma] is getting in the way of progress."[132E] On one hand, we could create a broad understanding that any difficult experience can create maladaptive behaviors and that most diagnoses in the *Diagnostic and Statistical Manual of Mental Disorders* are symptoms of trauma. However, at this point, I think attempting to change the cultural understanding of trauma and PTSD would be excruciatingly difficult. In my book, *You Are A Great And Powerful Wizard*, I explore through metaphor how using the correct words and other forms of communication is essential for succeeding in life and getting your point across. To increase understanding and accessibility, I've decided to refer to PTSD, or the unresolved emotions and behaviors caused by difficult experiences, as *trapped emotions*. CPTSD is now *attachment wounds, childhood abuse, repeated highly stressful experiences, being in a long-term abusive relationship,* or *growing up in a dysfunctional family*. Trauma is *difficult experiences, highly stressful experiences, abusive experiences,* or *near-death experiences*.

Am I saying that you should change your use of PTSD and trauma? No. I'm merely trying to use words that will help more people understand the nature of their difficulties and be able to find healing from big, small, and complicated struggles. Especially with the shame that many people have after experiencing trauma, I wanted terminology that is easier for people to approach without potentially feeling even more shame. PTSD and trauma will occasionally be used throughout the book too, typically to refer to pieces of research. Above all, I want you to know that your emotions and past difficulties matter and deserve your attention. Thank you for hearing me out. I hope you enjoy.

Chapter 2

Trapped Emotions

2.1 Trapped Emotions, 2.2 Individual, Repeated, And Attachment Difficulties, 2.3 Subtle Stressful Experiences Can Be Detrimental, 2.4 Resilience, 2.5 Learned Behaviors, 2.6 Ancestral Trapped Emotions, 2.7 Recovery Increases Your Safety, 2.8 Creating A Better World, 2.9 How To Release Trapped Emotions, 2.10 The Time It Takes To Heal, 2.11 What Healing Looks Like, 2.12 Make It Work For You, 2.13 Radical Self-Care

The standard guide for living a fulfilling life given to newborns might go something like this: Welcome to the human race! You are about to be blessed with many problems no one tells you how to handle, resulting in many confusing feelings. Good luck!

For some reason, our parents, teachers, and government believe this is adequate information to succeed and be happy. It's not. Likely the reason why you are reading my book is that at some point you realized that someone messed up, things are hard, and you'd rather they be different.

Let's start again. Welcome to the human race! This guide documents the greatest tools humans have discovered in living fulfilling and happy lives. I care about you and believe you deserve the truth. The truth is not always easy, but it does come with great benefits like insurance against despair and doom.

First of all, you are a badass. You are a human being. How cool is that? You can survive in more environments than any other creature. You are capable of creating and using sophisticated tools to protect yourself and stimulate amazing sensations. With modern medicine, you can heal almost any physical or mental wound. The options for changing your life and defying fate are nearly limitless - you can grow, be a better person, become a leader, and learn to be content with what you have. However, there will be hurdles along the way.

Many of these hurdles come in the form of present or past difficult experiences such as breakups, disagreements with friends, injuries, unavailable parents, discrimination, abuse, feeling judged, living in an unfair society, witnessing something difficult, or making a mistake. I have encountered many of these hurdles myself and want to share a few things that I discovered in my healing journey. My goal is to condense what I learned from over sixty books, a lifetime of experiences, and countless research papers into an inclusive and easy-to-understand guide exploring the many facets of recovering from emotional and traumatic events.

One of my most important discoveries was learning that what happened to you in the past often creates *trapped emotions*. Books like *The Body Keeps The Score*, *In An Unspoken Voice*, *My Grandmother's Hands*, and *Complex PTSD* explore how the severity of difficult experiences translates into a certain amount of emotional energy entering the body. This energy can immediately hinder you by taking the shape of sadness, anxiety, anger, or several other physical and emotional reactions. After a few seconds to a few months, the energy will either leave your body, or it will become trapped inside of you.

2.1 Trapped Emotions

Trapped emotions cause a wide variety of symptoms and are a large source of depression, maladaptive behaviors, addictions, discrimination, and abuse. Symptoms may appear shortly after an incident or without warning years later. These are the body's attempts to protect you from anything similar to the stressful experience happening again. However, this safety mechanism tends to be unhealthy by overgeneralizing what is dangerous or by creating a reaction that does not actually protect you. These energies show up in many ways and the same incident can make two people react entirely differently. That said, consider events and outcomes like these:

- *Heartbreak* - You avoid your ex and it hurts to even drive down the street you used to take to get to their house
- *War* - You have a panic attack when hearing loud sounds like fireworks or barking dogs
- *Conflict* - You are unable to forgive a friend for something they did that angered you and now frequently think about it
- *Injury* - You always feel distressed driving after recovering from a car accident
- *Growing up with alcoholic or unavailable parents* - You have trouble trusting people and constantly feel abandoned or have difficulty maintaining relationships
- *Discriminatory media* - You avoid certain racial groups or view

some body types as unhealthy
- **Experiencing racism** - You feel stressed being outside or sharing space with people of a different skin color
- **Abuse** - You dislike touch and struggle to trust others
- **Regularly witnessing or hearing about atrocities** - You feel depressed or want to quit your job

This list just scratches the surface of the long-term impacts that difficult experiences can have on your life. Trapped emotions fundamentally create a feeling of not being safe. In my research, I found three components that tie together almost every therapy modality dealing with trapped emotions:

1. **Unexpressed emotions** - These can include stress, grief, or anger. True anger is the innate response we use to physically defend ourselves from immediate harm. However, behind most of what we perceive as anger and stress is actually grief or the desire for a basic need to be met. All humans have needs such as sustenance, safety, love, empathy, rest, community, creativity, freedom, and purpose.[127]
2. **Distorted stories and beliefs** - All trapped emotions perpetuate through a story that hyper-focuses on the negative aspects of an event. This story may then evolve into self-limiting beliefs you have about yourself, or beliefs that you have about objects or other people and how they relate to you. For instance, *I am unlovable, all dogs are dangerous, people who touch me are going to hurt me, they did it intentionally,* or *I cannot protect myself.* Trapped emotions are also often accompanied by a story of shame which may make you believe that you are alone in your experiences and cannot share what happened. You may not be consciously aware of these stories and beliefs, as they become integrated as a normal part of your reality. These beliefs may also stem from what someone said about you.
3. **Wanting resolution** – To the body, the initial incident never was resolved, so it continues to seek solutions to protect you from impending harm. These solutions may work temporarily but tend not to resolve the incident and actually are *maladaptive behaviors.* For instance, you may obsessively think about what you could have done differently, or start addictively consuming media, alcohol, or other substances. Many people also subconsciously recreate the incident. You may date people similar to your abusive parents hoping that they will give you the love you so desperately wanted, or put

yourself in dangerous situations after getting into a car accident. In these ways, the difficult experience or experiences that created the trapped emotion continues to persist as something happening right now or about to happen instead of a memory that occurred in the past.

In combination, these components of trapped emotions cause people to be unable to get over present or past hardships and have *flashbacks*.[184] Flashbacks are the various symptoms of trapped emotions that appear when stimuli similar to the original incident occur. A common example is the noise of fireworks bringing war veterans back into battle. This flashback may just involve the emotional memory, but can also include acting out the behavioral memory as well, such as hiding or lashing out in violence against others. These emotions and actions can seem like a natural part of your existence and you may struggle to understand why most other people do not respond in the same way that you do. Symptoms can also show up in all aspects of your life even without a trigger as you pick up protective behaviors, use coping mechanisms, or constantly feel distressed.

Some days are easier than others. Even with more severe trapped emotions, things like happiness, meaningful friendships, creativity, and success are still often available. However, these may be periodically interrupted by your triggers and flashbacks or cause an unhealthy obsession with them. For instance, you may find yourself too angry to effectively communicate through conflict or you hide your emotions by working too much and consuming addictive substances.

It can be exceptionally difficult to see the impact that trapped emotions have if you belong to a culture that supports unhealthy behaviors or were raised under difficult circumstances. This is especially true if you experienced painful events before forming memories, or if you have lapses in memories from dissociation (see Section 3.5). You may also attempt to logically explain the three parts above with things like *I just don't like fireworks*, or, *my coworker is inconsiderate*, when, in fact, these feelings are unconsciously formed from past hardship. However, as you learn about healthier ways of being you will start to become aware of your trapped emotions. Most importantly, working on any of these three parts will help disrupt the others and make them easier to transform. Consciously working on one part may even bring you to naturally find resolution with the others.

2.2 Individual, Repeated, And Attachment Difficulties

Any difficult experience can become trapped in the body and cause undesirable outcomes. Typically however, trapped emotions will be more severe the more intense that experience is, the closer it brings you to death, the longer it lasts, the less able you are to react to the situation, the more times it repeats, or the more it derails your sense of secure attachment. Especially with unresolved events that happened in childhood with neglectful or abusive caregivers, a grownup will have adopted a large set of protective behaviors that seem entirely natural to them. These include workaholism, addiction, being avoidant or anxious in relationships, aggressive behaviors, codependency, a lack of self-compassion, and putting the needs of others first. Incidents that make the body believe it is going to die such as war, assault, or car accidents tend to create the strongest immediate reactions. These can include nightmares, debilitating panic attacks, severe depression, and even bodily pains or headaches.

2.3 Subtle Stressful Experiences Can Be Detrimental

Stressful energies can also become trapped very subtly. For instance, if you trip and fall in front of friends, you may feel very ashamed and not speak for some time. An experience may have also been so normalized growing up that you did not think of it as stressful. If you're raised by a parent who gives most of their praise to your sibling, you might believe you are dumb or unattractive. You might also become a perfectionistic workaholic, where nothing you do feels like enough. If you had a painful dental procedure as a child, you may avoid medical facilities now.

The media you consume will also increase your stress response to different cultures and bodies. Consider how the media has historically depicted Black people as criminals or side characters, and how the fashion industry only models one type of body while shaming others. Things like this perpetuate discrimination against people of color and the great diversity of bodies that exist in the world. In general, keep in mind that **any small or large amount of stress can create long-standing negative consequences**. That said, a person may also naturally recover or be unphased by a difficulty normally seen as severe because of their resilience to trapped emotions.

2.4 Resilience

Your *resilience* to trapped emotions is how well you can recover from emotionally stressful situations and prevent them from becoming trapped in your body. It is dependent upon many factors and is constantly changing. Having less resilience does not mean you are incapable of healing; it just means that trapped emotions are more likely to stick around and you have fewer resources to handle them with. At a baseline, your resilience and much of your personality are determined by:

- Your genetics, which rule a large number of traits including extroversion, agreeableness, openness, conscientiousness, neuroticism, and various physical and mental conditions[136]
- Your gut bacteria, which recent studies show have a huge impact on mental health[115]
- How you were raised, especially if it was with abuse or neglect, or with supportive empathy and stability
- How young you are - difficult experiences will impact your brain more severely the younger you are, especially in the first two years of life[132F]
- Being an introvert or extrovert, with introverts much more likely to have their needs ignored in extrovert-driven cultures like the USA[18A]
- Your peer group and the surrounding culture
- The trapped emotions already inside of you
- Your positive experiences in life
- How much stable support and acceptance you have or believe that you have
- The amount of difficulty you have experienced and overcome in your life - people who grew up in dysfunctional families often have an amazing capacity for putting up with stress, but not necessarily for preventing it from becoming trapped in their bodies
- Your *heart rate variability* (HRV), which is a good measure of how well parts of your nervous system are working - it is increased by things like mindful breathing and exercise and can be read with simple devices and phone apps[97B]

During an incident, your resilience is decreased by:

- Tiredness and stress
- Low or unbalanced hormone levels
- How present you are with your surroundings, with dissociation or a drunken state decreasing the intensity of an experience, but with many drawbacks[97Q]
- How many of your basic needs are not met

- Not having an emotional release (see Chapter 5)
- Being frozen and not moving your body with shaking, shivering, or running away (see Chapter 5)
- Lacking the tools to cope with stress (see Chapter 4)
- Delayed or nonexistent support from community, professionals, or loved ones

A person with healthy relationships tends to have more resilience than someone isolated. Someone who exercises will have more resilience than someone who sits all day. Someone who feels safe and comfortable with their appearance will have more resilience than someone who doesn't. A person who grows up with a speech impediment may have less resilience than someone who can speak a language according to mainstream standards. Someone who has grown up with a healthy family will have more resilience than someone who has been surrounded by abuse. A person who faces oppression due to things like their race or gender may have less resilience than someone who has privilege in these areas.

In the days and weeks following an incident, how stress moves through your body is dependent upon having community, securely attached relationships, self-care practices, skills to overcome distorted thinking, and various tools to release stress like communication, grieving, and calming techniques. This is why everyone's emotions are valid. Not only can the same incident drastically impact two people differently, but how one handles the trapped emotions will vary widely as well. In other words, comparing your emotional response to someone else's, or shaming someone for struggling after an incident will not help anyone get better - in fact, it will probably make them worse.

Especially for those of us highly sensitive souls out there, emotional energy will become trapped due to almost anything. According to Dr. Elaine N. Aron, about 20% of the population is born highly sensitive.[6] Highly sensitive people are more empathetic but also more reactive to stress and external stimuli, which in turn makes them have special considerations in healing, therapy, and relationships. Most notably, high sensitivity requires a person to spend more time regulating their emotions while being careful not to take on an amount of stress or stimulation that would cause overwhelm. This group includes introverts, extroverts, and all genders. To better understand yourself and your peers, check out one of Dr. Aron's books such as *The Highly Sensitive Person's Complete Learning Program*.

People who have recently had a difficult experience or have a lot of trapped emotions may also take on certain characteristics of highly sensitive people. A fall in front of friends might be laughed off by one person but make another hide away and cut off social contact. When one person gets into a car accident it might simply be an annoyance of insurance agents and replacing the vehicle, but for another, it might make it excruciatingly difficult to drive at all. For yourself or when considering a loved one, never assume how emotionally difficult something is. It is okay if something seemingly very small is very upsetting, it is still an emotional energy that must get moved and processed through the body.

Regardless of the incident, take good care of yourself and stay aware of how your reactions and emotions change. Whatever difficult events happened to you, you are capable of healing. This healing looks different for everyone and does not necessarily mean you will never again be triggered or have a flashback. Overall though, you will be able to live your life with an increased sense of security and joy without having to worry about what happened in the past.

2.5 Learned Behaviors

Separate from the hardships you experienced, you may mimic the maladaptive behaviors and beliefs of your parents, peers, or culture. This often comes out in unhealthy communication, being deeply critical of oneself or others, discrimination against groups of people, workaholism, and addiction to various substances. Many people believe they have successfully rejected their parents only to later realize that they actually adopted similar behaviors or date people like them. Even though there was no specific incident that hurt you, learned behaviors can still exist as trapped emotions or prevent healing from trapped emotions. Identifying and transforming them is vital for healing and is also covered throughout the book, especially in Part III.

2.6 Ancestral Trapped Emotions

While parents with unresolved trapped emotions often raise their children in problematic ways that perpetuate those same energies, trapped emotions can also be inherited between generations at the chemical level.[26] For instance, regardless of their upbringing or home environment, the children, grandchildren, and great-grandchildren of people who survive atrocities like the Holocaust have a higher risk of being depressed or anxious. These *ancestral trapped emotions* are caused by *epigenetic* changes. They are changes that do not permanently alter DNA, only how the DNA is read and expressed. This means that your parents or grandparents can pass their trapped emotions onto you, and until you weed it out of yourself, it may become passed onto your children as well. To identify this type of energy, you'll need to know the history of your parents, grandparents, or culture.

Ancestral trapped emotions help explain the greater incidence of depression in marginalized groups and people whose parents or grandparents suffered severe hardships. Epigenetics is still a relatively new field and there is much to be learned. For instance, mice studies have shown that specific stress responses such as a smell paired with an electric shock can be passed on between generations, with the mice children of the first generation exhibiting greater sensitivity to that smell, but not to others.[33] It also seems as though the epigenetic changes disappear after a few generations if the stress is removed.[232]

In his book, *The Embodied Mind*, Dr. Thomas Verny explores memory networks that exist outside the brain and has some anecdotal stories about specific memories being transferred to offspring.[67] On the other hand, researchers like Dr. Andrew Huberman believe that humans can only pass on generalized characteristics, like an increased stress response or heightened desire for dopamine.[74,232] While there is much to learn about it, dealing with ancestral trapped emotions is relatively similar to others that we'll explore later on. It is also unlikely to be the only cause of a person's difficulties as parents with unresolved trapped emotions are likely to act in ways that cause difficulty to a child.

2.7 Recovery Increases Your Safety
Some people fear that dealing with their trapped emotions will prevent them from identifying dangerous situations, but this is not how recovery works. Decreasing your hypervigilance to stressful stimuli helps protect you by maintaining a calm and rational mind that can accurately assess a situation. For instance, just because you release the trapped emotions surrounding an abusive ex does not mean that you are going to start dating them again or ignore the healthy boundaries you established. Instead, it will mean that you stop having obsessive thoughts and no longer feel unsafe or emotionally out of control when confronted by things you associate with that ex.

2.8 Creating A Better World
Trapped emotions are not just an individual problem, they are an important element to understand in creating a world without greed, discrimination, toxic masculinity, White supremacy, abusive behaviors, and other social problems. People with trapped emotions tend to hurt themselves and other people. This is why we need to lift up everyone across demographics like age, gen-

der, ability, and race.

Unfortunately, most self-help, spiritual, and activist literature neglects to mention trapped emotions as a facet of the human experience. Even many therapists ignore it in their work. They instead focus on the rational mind, arguing that a person can become happier or stop being a racist simply by how they think. The rational mind can certainly help, but much of the time, a person's trapped emotions must be released before they are able or willing to change their thinking and behaviors.

Even when trapped emotions, trauma, or PTSD are discussed, it tends to be quite limited or unscientific. That is why this book is based on an immense collection of research (see the Works Referenced and Bibliography) and concludes with a psychology-informed activist guide. Addressing the cultural, societal, and individual patterns that reinforce trapped emotions will do a great deal toward uplifting humanity and all organisms we coexist with.

2.9 How To Release Trapped Emotions

Everyone's trapped emotions must be uniquely dealt with, but in general, healing involves six stages:

1. Identifying that you are regularly having undesirable behaviors or emotions.
2. Finding a place of safety away from any triggering people or things.
3. Calming down from stress or overwhelm enough so that the rational mind is available and emotions can be mindfully experienced.
4. Having an emotional release.
5. Transforming self-limiting beliefs and stories.
6. Changing your behaviors, mindsets, relationships, or environments to increase your resilience, fix maladaptive behaviors, and develop parts of the brain that never got activated growing up.

When trapped emotions are caused by conflicts with others, certain types of nonviolent communication are often the easiest tool for quickly transforming your anger, getting your needs met, and reestablishing safety. This may include:

1. Taking space to sort out your thoughts and calm down any aggressive anger or extreme emotions.
2. Figuring out your unmet needs and objectively understanding why the conflict happened, including your role in it.

3. Communicating your feelings and needs using empathetic and non-judgmental language, but only if it is safe to do so.
4. Listening to the other person and asking questions to understand the source of their feelings and needs. Even if it is frustrating, it does not mean you have to agree with them. Often a person's true needs are hidden behind an initial conflict, so be sure to explore what may be lacking in terms of attachment needs like touch or safety as well.
5. Adjusting your expectations of the other person and understanding that it is easiest to change your own behaviors rather than control those of another person. Another person's way of doing things can be equally valid to your own.
6. Figuring out a solution, whether that is to meet in the middle, ask for an apology, cut out a person altogether, make an ultimatum, or get these specific needs met by someone else.
7. Moving on with your life, creating new memories, and not ruminating on the past too much.

These communication strategies are more thoroughly explored in Chapters 8, 14, and 16. Healthy communication is often accompanied by emotional releases and a stronger sense of safety. However, conflicts frequently bring up deeper wounds that arose from an unresolved stressful experience, especially from childhood. To understand your feelings, needs, and your role in the conflict, you may have to dive deeper into your healing before you can communicate. It may also be unsafe or impossible for you to communicate with the source of your stress. That is okay. Whether or not you can interact with it, the following methods are for releasing trapped emotions caused by repeated stresses, attachment wounds, or growing up in a dysfunctional family:

1. Understanding the maladaptive behaviors you are playing out, or recognizing that something needs to change. See Chapter 3.
2. Creating a safe space by getting away from stressors and anything that acts as a trigger or associated memory to a difficult experience. See Sections 4.4 and 4.5.
3. Regulating your mood with relaxing activities, sleep, releasing present emotional energy, getting your basic needs met, and other coping strategies. See Chapters 4 and 5.
4. Reconnecting with your bodily sensations through mindfulness or a movement practice such as yoga.

5. Developing at least one supportive ally that helps you co-regulate your nervous system such as a friend, therapist, or support group member as explored in Sections 4.7 and Chapter 14.
6. Becoming triggered and inquiring, "What is this experience reminding me of from my past?" By doing so you become aware of patterns you have been repeating time and time again such as dating abusive individuals. See Chapter 3.
7. Coming out of isolation and breaking away from any shame you carry by beginning to write and speak about what happened within a safe container. This is done at your own pace, do not force it out. See Chapter 7.
8. Releasing the energy that never got to be expressed from the incident with crying, shaking, and other somatic techniques. See Chapter 5.
9. Resolving whatever was left unfinished from the incident. This may take the form of changing the story you have about the incident (see Chapter 6), using visualization to mentally prevent the incident from happening in your imagination (see Sections 4.6 and 6.4), or communicating with your inner selves (see Chapter 10). This process is sometimes known as *renegotiation*.
10. Fixing any inaccurate or distorted beliefs created from the difficult experience. See Chapters 6 and 7.
11. Remembering the bigger picture and dismantling your hyperfocus and stuck ego with things like friendship, nature, art, meditation, a higher power, love, and community. See Chapter 13.
12. Understanding how you reinforce or cause yourself and others suffering. See Chapters 3 and 4.
13. Learning healthy habits and thinking patterns you may have missed, avoided, or distorted because of a difficult experience. See Part III. This work also includes healing your avoidant or anxious attachment style that prevents secure relationships from forming as explored in Section 3.4 and 14.2.
14. Healing your attachment wounds, especially those caused by your parents during your childhood. See Section 14.2 and Section 17.6.
15. Helping change the cultural and societal norms that perpetuate suffering in the world. See Chapters 15 and 16.

While these are ideal trajectories, we do not live in an ideal world and all of the previous steps may take place in a different order or even happen simultaneously. For instance, you may not be able to escape an unhealthy relationship immediately, but you could start learning the third step's coping strategies. Or, you may be unprepared to start this work until after you have at least one secure relationship, overcome an addiction, or join an exercise program. Many people reading this book will also have already started on their healing journey and be focused on areas they have yet to tackle.

Trapped emotions from a one-time incident can be handled through practices that allow the memory to be worked through in the body. This might involve:

1. Creating a safe space away from any triggers. See Section 4.5.
2. Becoming aware of your body and finding where the emotions you feel are located. See Chapter 5 and Section 7.1.
3. Exploring an emotional sensation such as the texture, voice, and story attached to it. See Section 7.1.
4. Allowing that sensation to transform into emotions and bodily movements. See Chapters 5 and 7.
5. Allowing that sensation to transform into thoughts and memories that complete the safety response you were previously unable to at the time of the incident, such as fighting or running away. See Chapters, 5, 6, and 7.
6. Reframing any self-limiting beliefs you have that supported the story. See Chapters 6 and 7.

These steps may have to take place several times before the body no longer exhibits symptoms of trapped emotions. Just keep in mind that immediately opening up your most painful emotional wounds is often not suggested, so you might first connect with some new allies, develop a better sleep regimen, or find a social activity to participate in. In general, move slowly enough when opening up these trapped emotions that you do not become debilitated by an emotional flashback. You need to build up the resources you did not have when the incident occurred to handle it now. Your healing may also partly require larger cultural and societal changes to take place first, but know that you can still learn skills to substantially improve your well-being.

Care has been given to making all techniques in this book for releasing trapped emotions as accessible as possible, including both traditional therapy modalities and solo or communal equivalents. The book is outlined in four parts:

1. ***Identifying and coping with trapped emotions*** - In Part I, Chap-

ters 3 through 5, you will learn how to identify trapped emotions, destress your life, create a safe space, practice mindfulness, and healthily experience grief and anger.
2. ***Transforming stories*** - Part II, Chapters 6 through 11, dives into methods for renegotiating memories and overcoming self-limiting beliefs. This starts with learning basic ways to reframe your experiences and how to use healthy communication, then follows with techniques from somatic, prolonged exposure, EMDR, Internal Family Systems, and psychedelic-assisted therapies.
3. ***Behaviors, mindset, relationships, and environment*** - Part III, Chapters 12 through 16, details how to change your world internally and externally to learn and integrate the essential aspects of a fulfilling life you may not have been exposed to. Simultaneously, you transform problematic behaviors copied from caregivers, unhealthy relationships, and cultures. It includes things like letting go of control, making friends, building healthy relationships, healing attachment wounds, dealing with addictions, understanding guilt, fostering self-love, and forgiving others. Part III finishes with a guide on creating healthier environments and transforming the world around you by becoming a changemaker. This includes an exploration of how society, culture, the government, and big business reinforce trapped emotions and cause things like discrimination, poverty, bad parenting, individualism, and abusive law enforcement.
4. ***Healing specific trapped emotions*** - Part IV, Chapters 17 through 20, finishes this guide by showcasing ways of overcoming different trapped emotions with techniques explored throughout the book. After the conclusion, I share the many resources I used to compile this information together including books, podcasts, websites, and emergency lines.

2.10 The Time It Takes To Heal

The time it takes to heal differs widely depending on the incident that caused you distress. These factors include how young you were when it happened, how severe it was, how often it happened, how much care was received, how difficult your past was, how many sources of healthy regulation you have now, how much stress was experienced during and right after the incident, and whether the event stemmed from neglect, abuse, injury, loss, or something else. The emotional energy that becomes trapped from brief and isolated difficult events, such as an injury or argument, can mostly be dealt with over a few days or weeks.

Trapped emotions may even release naturally without any intentional work from the individual, especially if they have a supportive community of loved ones and good self-care practices. According to the *National Institute of Mental Health*, this typically happens within 90 days after an incident.[125] Of course, certain tactics are important to use to heal faster, learn from the past, and prevent the incident from repeating, but you might find some relief in knowing that the pain experienced from things like heartbreak or bad grades will usually dissipate given time. That said, a trapped emotion may increase in severity the longer it sits in the body, especially if more stressful experiences happen before the initial energy is released. Each time you become triggered by a similar incident, the emotional energy grows. Even if someone dies, the suffering they caused you may persist until you take action to release that pain.

Difficult experiences that take place over an extended time, happen in childhood, or repeat regularly, such as growing up with an alcoholic or abusive parent, will require months or years of work. This is because events like these drastically alter one's basic understanding of reality, shut off parts of the brain, and proliferate many maladaptive behaviors. While these behaviors are an attempt to protect you from experiencing danger when triggered, they tend to make functioning in daily life and relationships very difficult and can easily lead to trapping additional emotions within the body. That said, you can still make vast improvements within a short amount of time; there are just many more steps involved in fully releasing these complex energies.

2.11 What Healing Looks Like

Releasing trapped emotions and healing the damage they caused your psyche is hard work, but absolutely worth it. You will find yourself with increasing amounts of joy, empathy, meaningful friendships, love, financial stability, and contentment. Take it slowly though; it is okay to rest. Sometimes you will find yourself overwhelmed and seemingly backtrack in your progress, but that is all part of the journey forward. Healing is messy and not a linear path, but that is why we learn to have compassion for ourselves and make allies to help us through it. I cannot begin to describe how beautiful life can be, but know that whatever you have experienced, there is ever-deepening goodness available beyond the veil of your present emotions. With action, change can occur very quickly.

So long as you dedicate yourself to an effective method for releasing trapped emotions, healing will come. You may even experience what psychologists Richard Tedeschi and Lawrence Calhoun call *post-traumatic growth*. These are the positive influences of a difficult experience and may include: "greater appreciation of life, greater appreciation and strengthening of close relationships, increased compassion and altruism, the identification of new possibilities or a purpose in life, greater awareness and utilization of personal strengths, enhanced spiritual development, and creative growth."[91] These can translate into things like being more empathetic, quitting an addictive substance, accepting your body, becoming better at romance and friendship, learning how to communicate through anger, finding meditation, dedicating to an activist cause, or picking up an artistic passion.

It is important to remain realistic. According to Professor Sam Vaknin, true closure promised in many self-help circles is not actually possible.[175] That is to say that suffering usually does not suddenly go away, but instead slowly eases and transforms. Hardship is a natural and healthy part of life that integrates into who we are. Things like expecting a quick fix or an apology may considerably slow down your healing and act as a way of avoiding difficult emotions. Pauline Boss expands on this topic in her book, *The Myth of Closure*.

You cannot forget the past, but you can make new associations that help you renegotiate what happened to you. Some things are going to hurt for a long time, and that's okay - it is part of being human and often helps you grow. Of course, these difficulties which are dealt to us are often not fair, especially in the case of oppression, but they are a reality we must contend with nonetheless. Fortunately, healing yourself, finding a supportive community, and changing the status quo are all quite possible.

Dr. Bessel van der Kolk believes that the most important part of healing is being able to tolerate what you feel in your body and what you know in your memories.[97C] With all incidents, this means zooming out from the difficult experience, seeing that it was something that happened in the past, and knowing that it does not define how you step through the future. It was a *part* of your life, not your *whole* life. Instead of getting triggered into an emotional flashback, you say "This reminds me of a difficult experience I once had."

Healing can look several ways with more severe trapped emotions, especially from growing up in a dysfunctional family. This includes being able to maintain mobility and cognitive processing when confronted by something you once feared, obtaining at least one healthy social connection outside of therapy, diminishing judgmental attitudes, reducing dissociative behaviors, sharing your beautiful gifts, and developing compassion for yourself and others.[106D,184B] You learn how to self-soothe and co-regulate with trusted allies, which helps you recover from hard places and be more resilient from falling into them. While the past was painful and might still make you emotional thinking about it, you do not allow the incident to dictate your life. For some, this translates into developing healthy romances in which you and your partner can communicate through conflict, support each other, and feel securely attached. This also means ending the legacy of abuse and neglect that may have been passed down through your family for generations. You can make the future a better place by stopping this cycle from spreading to your children, community, friends, and culture.

It does not matter how old you are, you are capable of rewriting your story at any age. If you practice healing, you will start feeling a reduction in symptoms. Symptoms may not leave altogether, but you will be able to reduce the severity and frequency of panic attacks, addictions, anger, sadness, and other parts of trapped emotions. For some people, it is something that can be accomplished in a few days, whereas others may spend their entire life dedicated to a practice that helps manage their emotions.

How far you take your recovery is up to you. For instance, I have spent a period of no contact with a partner after an emotional breakup and then reestablished a friendly connection. I want most people to ask before touching me, but I still love physical contact. I sometimes binge on media or food when I'm stressed out, but I know how to break those cycles of addiction and return to things that regulate my nervous system in healthier ways. If I quarantine due to sickness, I can start feeling abandoned by friends, but once I'm better I still reach out to make plans and trust the connection again. I'm warier around men, but that does not stop me from working with or becoming friends with them. I also don't really care to let go of my fear of snakes having grown up with deadly ones, or to forgive and put myself around verbally abusive people. That said, I also don't become emotionally out of control and run away when confronted by these things.

Part of this work is identifying those fears that are actually protecting you and those which are holding you back. What makes you have extreme emotional reactions? Who do you judge harshly for no particular reason? What unhappy relationships are you putting up with? What is preventing your dreams from becoming true? Some triggers you will leave alone, some you will learn to manage, and others you will fully overcome and reestablish as safe. Things don't have to be good or great. Feeling "just okay" is still worthy of celebration.

You are allowed to create contentment and happiness moving forward.

That does not mean that you become perfect or continue putting up with unhealthy dynamics with friends or family. The goal is to repair *your* nervous system and put yourself around healthy people who have done the same. You might have recovered from your trapped emotions but still have bad days, not speak to your family, or be single. That is all okay because healing and the pathway there truly look different for everyone.

2.12 Make It Work For You

All of the techniques presented in this book can be modified as you see fit. For instance, drawing or writing out certain components may be very beneficial for some. Others may be able to strictly use their imagination and have meaningful internal conversations. Virtual reality is presenting a lot of amazing possibilities as well now too. When you really start diving deep, you begin to get clear on what is best for you. Follow your intuition and do not be afraid to experiment. As some Twelve Step programs say, "Take what you need and leave the rest." Adults tend to repeat patterns rather than break out of their comfort zone, so if something is not working after a few attempts, force yourself to try something different. Make it work for you.

2.13 Radical Self-Care

The popularity of self-care practices has grown massively in recent years. Unfortunately, most of the techniques offered are ineffectual at treating the real source of one's difficulties. At its worst, traditional self-care can act as a form of escapism that only provides temporary relief from strong emotions. Radical self-care takes a different approach by acknowledging six things:

1. Many forms of stress, distorted beliefs, and unhealthy behaviors are the result of trapped emotions that must be released in yourself or another person before change can occur.
2. Community and allies are essential for healing; you cannot do this alone.
3. While some short-term stress is a healthy part of life, most long-term stress is needless and created by cultural traditions, distorted beliefs, income inequality, and governmental laws.
4. Your behaviors, mental health, group dynamics, and culture are formed from both rational decisions and chemical processes. While humans can control their moods and behaviors with thinking to a certain extent, those behaviors and thoughts often have an evolutionary motive driven by biochemistry and animalistic instincts. Some of

these basic processes stay fairly consistent across the human race, but others vary widely between individuals and make some people have easier access than others to certain mental states, emotions, and beliefs. That all said, how your genes express themselves is greatly influenced by your upbringing.
5. Healing does not, and should not require money, but it does help.
6. Being discriminated against creates special considerations for healing.

Unlike many self-care guides, I want to affirm that, yes, your problems are caused by other people, but also by your personal life decisions. Throughout this book, I will be covering how to transform yourself, your peers, and society itself. However, because changing others is slow, hard, or sometimes impossible, we're going to be focusing primarily on what you can do yourself. After all, you have the most power over your own thoughts and actions. Healing your personal suffering first also makes changing others much easier. As *The Luckiest Club's* mission statement says so clearly:

- It is not your fault.[112]
- It is your responsibility.
- It is unfair that this is your thing.
- This is your thing.
- This will never stop being your thing until you face it.
- You can't do it alone.
- Only you can do it.
- You are loved.
- We will never stop reminding you of these things.

The goal of this work is to take care of yourself so that you can use that strength to better take care of your communities, the natural environment, and people less privileged than you. Remember, as you do this work for yourself, you are inherently helping your family, friends, culture, and society do it too. By rooting out your trapped emotions, you are ending a vicious cycle of suffering from spreading to others. However, nothing will change until you put knowledge to practice. Read this book and apply what you learn. I'm positive you'll thank yourself later.

PART I

IDENTIFYING AND COPING WITH TRAPPED EMOTIONS

Chapter 3

Identifying Trapped Emotions

3.1 Emotionally Stressful And Abusive People, 3.2 Emotionally Mature And Loving People, 3.3 Symptoms Of Trapped Emotions, 3.4 Attachment Styles, 3.5 Dissociation, 3.6 Separating Trapped Emotions From Your Basic Biology

Everyone has at least some trapped emotions in their bodies, even people perceived as very successful. The severity of these energies varies between completely debilitating to something that a person and society can mostly ignore. However, these energies can be quite difficult to see unless you know what you are looking for. This is because you may have experienced difficulties before you started forming memories, your trapped emotions are blocking your memories, you have been made to believe that what you experienced should not be so hard, or, you struggle to realize that your behaviors are coping mechanisms for stress. Understanding why you behave a certain way though will give you greater control and empathy with how you react to your triggers. You can also use this chapter to help choose what you want to work on in yourself. Here are four methods of identifying trapped emotions:

1. Remembering a difficult experience that caused you great stress.
2. Having a strong negative reaction to specific stimuli. Sometimes you will be able to connect this to a past event or be able to vaguely know what could have happened if your memory is foggy. What makes you defensive? What do you complain about?
3. Understanding the symptoms of trapped emotions.
4. Noticing a recurring pattern in your behavior, such as dating the same abusive personality type, and recognizing where this attraction stems from.

Please be aware however that it may be overwhelming and even dangerous to recall difficult life experiences until you have the proper skills and safe space. Even if you rationally believe you can handle it, recalling atrocious events can throw you into a deep depression that makes the trapped emotion stronger. This is because each time you recall an emotionally difficult event, you are literally re-experiencing it in body and mind. With many techniques, it is not even necessary to fully remember the original incident, so for now just keep reading or make a small mental note until we dive into creating a *life history* in Section 7.2.

If you start feeling overwhelmed, take a break, or consider reading some of the basic self-care strategies in Chapter 4. You could also skip over parts that you feel might trigger you. Another option is reframing these contents from "These are all the reasons why I am broken" to, "These are all the reasons that I have to be angry at my family and society." As a heads-up, this chapter in particular can be difficult for people to read. With that warning out of the way, the following sections list common experiences that may trap emotional energy. The younger and more frequently you experience these, the more likely it is that they will impact you as an adult, but they can create trapped emotions at any age and any number of occurrences.

Trapped emotions caused by general life experiences:

- Breakups and heartbreak
- Having a disagreement or conflict
- Not getting your basic needs met
- Physical injuries from accidents
- Getting a chronic or terminal illness
- Being in a romantic relationship with someone who has an avoidant or anxious attachment style and is unwilling to work toward secure bonding
- Hospital visits, especially if you needed to be strapped down or put under anesthesia as a child
- Having a bad reaction or experience with a medicine or medical procedure
- Performing poorly in school, or being forced to learn in a way that is not conducive to your personality or neurotype
- Losing a loved one, including pets
- Moving locations against your will, especially if it results in not being able to see your friends again
- Near-death experiences like car crashes and war
- Being deeply embarrassed or making a mistake

CH 3 – IDENTIFYING TRAPPED EMOTIONS   31

Trapped emotions caused by abuse:

- Verbal abuse such as being yelled at, bullied, lied to, manipulated, called demeaning names, or threatened
- Avoidant communication in which a person withholds information or leaves to prevent discussion
- Physical abuse such as slapping, spanking, or being hit in any other way
- Sexual abuse or harassment
- Spiritual abuse such as being raised under fear of an angry, violent, and omnipotent God whose judgment is dictated by a hierarchical system
- Scientific and medical abuse in which research is applied to you that was poorly conducted or did not include your gender, age, or race
- Toxic sarcasm and teasing
- Being shamed for your appearance, abilities, or expressing emotions

Trapped emotions caused by discrimination:

- Growing up in a culture that discriminates against a group of people
- Growing up being discriminated against including in race, culture, ability, housing, gender, jobs, schooling, religion, and relationships
- Consuming media that portrays marginalized communities in demeaning ways or does not include them at all
- Consuming media that only portrays one race, gender, or ability type being successful, especially if it does not represent you
- Being forced to uphold specific gender norms, especially when that gender norm prevents you from fully experiencing your emotions, personhood, and autonomy
- Being poor

Trapped emotions caused by primary caregivers and neglect:

- Having primary caregivers who do not showcase healthy attachment and parenting such as making you feel safe, being attuned to your needs, soothing you when you're upset, expressing delight about your life and existence, and supporting your curiosity and creativity[227]
- Having a primary caregiver who is an alcoholic or addicted to any other substance

- Having a primary caregiver who is generally unavailable, gone, distracted with technology, or multitasking
- Having a primary caregiver who is arrested
- Having a primary caregiver who is overly protective or excessively controlling
- Having a primary caregiver who gives little or no physical affection
- Having a primary caregiver who is not empathetic to your feelings or physical boundaries
- Having a primary caregiver who introduces a new partner too quickly[132G]
- Having primary caregivers who divorce, granted it is better to get children away from abusers or high-conflict environments[132H,123]
- Having one or both parents with PTSD, but especially if the mother does[97BZ]
- Not having reliable consistency in spaces or secure relationships, especially in the first year of life[132I]

Trapped emotions caused by culture:

- Growing up in an economic and education system where your success depends on competition instead of cooperation as is the case in capitalism
- Growing up where individualism is celebrated
- Being observed and punished by a militant and oppressive system of law and policing
- Having a culture that discriminates against certain demographics of people
- Growing up where anger, violence, and revenge are celebrated

Trapped emotions are also caused by:

- Any other experience creating intense emotions or making the body think it might die
- Witnessing or hearing about someone else have these experiences - this is especially common in therapists, social workers, and medical staff[110]
- Being restrained or unable to move during any of these experiences will trap a much greater amount of emotional energy[106A]
- Having genetic markers influencing DNA which are inherited from

ancestors who experienced great hardship such as genocide, war, or stolen land
- Worry about future events such as with climate change[41]

3.1 Emotionally Stressful And Abusive People

Our parents typically have the greatest impact on our psyches, so I want to discuss their roles in more depth. In *Adult Children of Emotionally Immature Parents*, Lindsay C. Gibson identifies several common problematic personality types and behaviors from guardian figures that cause trapped emotions and attachment wounds in children. These include the emotionally unstable, busy perfectionist, emotionally avoidant, and rejecting parent.[46A] Guardian figures like these often:

- Lack emotional affection but instead provide material comforts and literal thoughts
- Are inconsistent or contradictory
- Are highly defensive
- Shame and tease
- Use coercion to get their way
- Fear feelings in themselves and others
- Fail to celebrate a child's happy moments
- Are emotionally intense and reactive
- Do not accept "no" as an answer
- Adhere to toxic religious and spiritual ideologies that instill shame and fear
- Are obsessed with intellectual reasoning
- Are silent, do not communicate, or are generally not present
- Require that a child acts and thinks the way they do
- Force adherence to traditional gender norms
- Use manipulative tactics like gaslighting
- Is constantly distracted with media, multitasking, or work

It may or may not be difficult for you to see that these are all forms of abuse that can be carried by parents, lovers, co-workers, teachers, or friends. Generally, these behaviors are insensitive and unempathetic to an individual's emotional states, wants, needs, and personal development. They are the opposite of love. However, as John Gottman points out in *Raising An Emotionally Intelligent Child*, almost all abusive parents are well-meaning and believe their actions are helping their child grow. Most people who perpetrate these acts genuinely feel they are justified and are using healthy forms of parenting. They are unaware of how severely damaging their behaviors are, especially if the abuse is culturally ingrained in the case of things like spanking.

Physical and emotional abuse are both damaging. However, it is possible that some acts are incidental, rooted in a cultural tradition, or required by trying to survive in a capitalist society. Some people with trapped emotions may also perceive entirely normal actions as abusive. Any of the previously listed characteristics are signs of unaddressed trapped emotions in the parents that will spread to the children by creating insecurity and emotional detachment. Abuse can even negatively impact a developing fetus.[15]

Please note that as children we often idealize and put one or both parents on a pillar regardless of how they treated us. This may involve that parent also being abusive or enabling your other parent's abusive behaviors. As you do this work you will be better able to objectively see the role both of your parents had in developing your current stresses and take appropriate action. This does not mean you have to hate or reject these people, but perhaps you create better boundaries that advocate for your emotional safety.

Know that emotional abuse is harder to see than physical abuse, but is often just as detrimental if not more so because of the difficulty in identifying and escaping it. This is especially true if you grew up with emotionally abusive or neglectful parents and now experience emotional abuse as the norm. Furthermore, while physical abuse is generally understood as problematic, many forms of emotional and verbal abuse are still accepted parts of most cultures.

Gibson organizes the adults raised in these environments into two categories - internalizers and externalizers of problems.[46B] Externalizers seek outside validation and comfort for their difficulties with addictions, anger, and being dominant. Internalizers have difficulty speaking up for themselves, struggle to seek help, excuse abusive behaviors, and do most of the emotional work in relationships. Generally, externalizers are more likely to inflict abuse upon others, and they are less likely to read a book like this or to identify their behaviors as problematic. Their trapped emotions will need to be dealt with by alternative methods we will explore later in this book.

Someone with a regulated nervous system will be able to step away from abusive people, but depending on your parental upbringing you may not be able to identify abuse or you may even seek it out. This is because your notion of love became associated with abuse. Furthermore, children and adults alike in toxic relationships generally believe an abusive individual's behaviors will change for the better, that "This will definitely be the last time." Victims of these behaviors take on roles to attempt to end the emotionally immature individual's behaviors, or use these roles to attempt to receive an unmet need like love or safety.[46B] These roles are wide-ranging but are often expressed through aggressive communication, temper tantrums, ignoring personal needs, acceptance of emotional or sexual abuse, or staying quiet and out of the way.

3.2 Emotionally Mature And Loving People
Gibson also shares the signs of emotionally mature people.[46C] These include consistency, reliability, not taking things personally, respecting boundaries, not going to emotional extremes easily, honesty, apologizing, laughter and playfulness, supportiveness, empathy and compassion, saying nice things about others, having the willingness to change, and responsiveness when communicated with. This list is a great starting place when considering the health of your close relationships, especially lovers and guardian figures. The majority of the listed qualities should be present in the people you keep closest, otherwise, they are good candidates to create boundaries with or remove from your life. We'll discuss more about stress, abuse, boundaries, and cutting people out in Chapters 4 and 5. You may also lack some of these qualities in your own life, and we'll explore ways of implementing them throughout the book, especially in Part III.

Love shares these same qualities. Many people confuse love with obsession, sexual attraction, or codependency. However, healthy love requires vulnerability, presence, and the ability to love yourself independently of another. Being in a relationship of course helps foster self-love, and might awaken a part of ourselves we previously lacked, but we cannot rely on a single person for our happiness. Healthy relationships are further explored in Chapter 14.

3.3 Symptoms Of Trapped Emotions
Another way to identify trapped emotions is from the symptoms they inflict. While having one of these symptoms does not specifically mean it is caused by trapped emotions, it is very likely if the symptom can be attached to your past or is triggered by specific stimuli such as a loud noise, holiday, or personality type. As previously described, these symptoms are sometimes referred to as *flashbacks* because your body is subconsciously remembering the original difficult experience that instilled the trapped emotion. Flashbacks will appear entirely normal, indistinguishable from reality unless you bring awareness to your stress responses. The related symptoms are almost infinite but always form in direct correlation to protecting oneself from a specific difficult expe-

rience. These can be broken down into common feelings and actions.

Feelings and mental shifts:

- Depression, anxiety, anger, shame, blame, insecurity, greed
- Low tolerance to stress
- Developing a strong critical inner voice that judges yourself or others
- Nightmares
- Lack of purpose in life
- Overwhelm or panic attacks, especially from unexpected or spontaneous events and conditions
- Difficulty enjoying positive emotions
- Difficulty being cared about
- Mental states that mimic things such as manic depression, ADHD, or autism spectrum disorder
- Borderline personality disorder (BPD), which is highlighted by emotional instability and swings between anger, depression, and obsessiveness, especially around interpersonal relationships - may change their sense of identity very quickly
- Dissociation, or disconnection from the present moment to the extent that you do not remember doing certain things, feel foggy, or do not feel your emotions
- Short and long-term memory difficulties
- Believing that you do not deserve fair compensation or treatment for the things you do in the world
- Have friends but feel lonely or invisible
- Various bodily pains like a sore neck, migraines, and upset stomach
- Autoimmune diseases and chronic pain
- Difficulty feeling close with people, trusting others, or experiencing love
- Fear of strangers
- Inability to enjoy touch or sex from a significant other
- Lack of empathy and compassion
- Increased thoughts about violence and sex
- Inability to experience one or more emotions around things that should be sad, happy, etc.
- The belief that you are a victim whose problems are more important than others
- Hear a person's needs expressed as a personal attack

- A basic belief that others will hurt you emotionally or physically

Actions:

- Suicidal thoughts or attempts
- Self-harm through deliberately treating yourself poorly, losing sleep, or cutting
- Perfectionism in which you harshly critique your work often or are unable to show what you create
- Immobilization or limited mobility in certain body parts
- Specific body language like fidgeting, wide eyes, or collapsed posture
- Diminished tone of voice
- Excessive eating or purging
- Workaholism in which you work more than necessary and prefer work over relaxing
- Need for control over an environment or people
- Difficulty with play, spontaneity, humor, and fun
- Inability to move your body in certain ways without becoming anxious
- Using language or consuming media that reflects violence and trapped emotions
- Thrill-seeking behaviors such as sex with strangers, drugs, or risky outdoor adventures
- Sexualizing oneself for attention
- Addictive behaviors with food, media, exercise, drugs and alcohol, sex, and other avenues for escape from your emotions and the present moment
- Difficulty working with others or deep independence - granted that introversion is a valid personality trait, it does not mean you totally avoid people
- Recreating the initial difficult experience such as getting into abusive relationships or engaging in life-threatening activities

Interpersonal dynamics:

- Anxious, avoidant, or anxious and avoidant attachment behaviors when engaging in romantic or intimate relationships
- Cheating on a partner or engaging in dangerous sexual behaviors
- Trauma bonding, or forming relationships with people who use

abuse in a way that you confused for love growing up
- Seeking out or avoiding conflict
- Avoidance of touch, sex, or being close to others
- Hypersexuality, or, having sex but not enjoying it
- Codependency in which you caretake abusive or manipulative individuals, do anything possible to control a situation or person's behavior, are unable to be independent, are addicted to love, have difficulty speaking up about your feelings or needs, have a constant need for approval, or seek to fix a sense of self-hatred through the love of other people
- Becoming self-righteous and excusing your toxic behaviors or ignoring the suffering of others
- Feelings of abandonment or upset to any kind of real or perceived social inconsistency
- Forgetting about the good times and barely recognizing friends or loved ones as people you have spent years with
- Putting others' pleasures and basic needs before your own
- People-pleasing in which you change your opinion or personality to avoid a potential disagreement or conflict
- Fearing anyone with more perceived privilege or power due to race, class, or job position such as law enforcement
- Discriminating against others in which you have a blatant or subconscious dislike of a group based on their appearance or culture
- Holding negative stereotypes or judgments on others based solely on their interests or consumption patterns, such as disliking a person because they drive a truck or drink beer
- Being highly argumentative or aggressive in conversation
- Violence towards others or having the desire to harm others
- Passive aggressive behaviors
- Compulsive lying
- Inability to communicate your needs or feelings
- Oversharing thoughts, feelings, or explanations
- Sociopathy, or being manipulative, unempathetic, spontaneous, rule-breaking, violent, antisocial, a compulsive liar, and unfeeling of guilt for wrongdoings
- Narcissism, or being entitled, having a big ego, inflating the truth, belittling and taking advantage of others, and being unable to empathize

In Chapter 6 of his book, *Complex PTSD*, Pete Walker splits these symptoms into several primary personality types, although a person may express multiple types and the symptoms can belong to several categories. The types include:

- ***Fight Type*** - Aggressive, argumentative, conflict-oriented, and often verbally or physically abusive
- ***Flight Type*** - Avoids conflict, emotions, and stress, focusing instead on work or various numbing stimuli
- ***Freeze Type*** - Avoids human contact, shuts down and cannot process information, struggles to make decisions
- ***Fawn Type*** - Helps others instead of themselves, apologizes a lot for things that aren't their fault, enters into codependent relationships - Also known as the *Friend Type*
- ***Flop Type*** - This is not included in Pete Walker's original list and is similar to the freeze type, but involves complete dissociation and bodily shutdown, with the muscles becoming floppy[169]

At the moment when activated, these five responses deactivate a person's ability to rationalize or connect with their narrative memory.[132J] The specific science behind why these responses happen can be learned by reading *The Polyvagal Theory in Therapy* by Deb Dana, *The Body Keeps The Score* by Bessel Van Der Kolk, or *What Happened To You* by Bruce D. Perry and Oprah Winfrey. Pete Walker also explains specific familial dynamics that create the various *F-types* in *Complex PTSD*.

All of the *F-types* are healthy in the right situation. A person with a regulated nervous system will actually first use a *flocking* response to check in with the reactions of others in the area surrounding a dangerous event.[132L] Seeing the visual cue that "I'm safe" or "you're safe with me" helps calm our nervous system.[97D] The five *F-types* may be activated based on what is witnessed or simply with what the subconscious deems appropriate for self-preservation. When confronted by danger you can fight, run away, stay motionless in hiding, or act friendly so as not to agitate the threat further. For example, you stand up for yourself, leave abusers, avoid uncomfortable people, or casually help strangers or people who you have mixed feelings about because it makes you feel good.

However, people with trapped emotions tend to be stuck applying these behaviors at inappropriate times when they become triggered into flashbacks. This automatic reaction has likely caused you or others a great amount of suffering. While emotional energy often becomes trapped from situations out of our control, we are still responsible for our actions and cannot use it as an excuse for hurting others. Poor communication, violence, breakups, getting easily upset, or an inability to adequately perform a job are all difficult side-effects of having these energies unresolved.

Build a *mental map* by listing how these triggers are activated and what feelings they create in you. Starting in the next chapter, you can also include what helps you return to a calm and regulated space. Your list will help you realize that depression, anxiety, or anger are usually not random and uncontrollable feelings, but a cause and effect. Over time you can start individually working through the items on the list with a therapist or with the techniques outlined in this book. While I do not suggest doing so yet, once you begin working in a specific area, it can be beneficial to attach it to a particular cause and the times you've experienced that, especially the worst or first times. For your emotional safety, this shouldn't be detailed but just a few words. You may not know the source though, and it's okay if you never do. It can just be helpful for some of the techniques outlined later. For example, my list includes things like:

- Loud men - Anxiety - Father
- Preference for being around workaholics - Parents working
- Inconsistency or a long time apart from friends or a partner - Abandonment - Parents working
- Not getting enough physical affection from a partner - Abandonment - Lack of touch from parents

It is important to note that people with narcissistic or sociopathic tendencies (often fight types) may use the contents of this book to further bully or demean people around them. These personality types frequently overlook their role in conflict and suffering, instead placing the blame on others. While it is less likely for these personality types to be reading a book like this, I want to bring it to their attention. Other personality types may also similarly become hypervigilant in their reading and begin seeing everyone as problematic or dangerous. In both cases, I suggest slowing down and asking yourself how you are enabling certain behaviors or your own suffering. It is important to get away from abuse and triggering individuals, but it's also possible to ignore our own roles and cut out entirely healthy relationships. Know that it is very difficult to change or control others, so we primarily focus on transforming ourselves. Simultaneously, no one is perfect and we live in cultures and societies that perpetuate harm. Everyone has healing to do, so try to find empathy for yourself and those who are still hurting.

3.4 Attachment Styles

Your *attachment style* is how you connect with others, especially as it relates to your romantic life. In general, you gravitate toward what is familiar, which can be really unhealthy. Attachment is primarily determined by how you were raised by a caregiver.[41] However, it can also be impacted by things like divorce, your relationship with your siblings, gender norms, your genes, discrimination, moving, how safe and nourishing your environment is, how secure your friendships are, fears about the future, the death of a loved one, your needs not getting met, and the attachment style of your partner.[217] These experiences culminate into four types of attachment:

1. ***Anxious or preoccupied attachments*** - Usually get into relationships very quickly, caregive for their partners, do things they don't really want to, need a lot of reassurance, or generally become codependent and always believe that people will leave them. They are constantly aware of their partner's supposed emotional states but tend to make it about themselves or guess incorrectly.
2. ***Avoidant or dismissing attachments*** - Shy away from communication, intense conversation, and intimacy. They often believe they are securely attached, withdraw into work or hobbies, want to be seen as strong, tend not to share their emotional states, desire closeness but get easily overwhelmed by it, are highly independent, and struggle to meet the emotional and intimacy needs required in a healthy relationship.
3. ***Anxious-avoidant or disorganized attachments*** - Oscillate between both anxious and avoidant characteristics. They are fearful of others even though they desire closeness. They may use others for their personal benefit and have a very fragmented sense of self.
4. ***Secure attachments*** - Are not emotionally avoidant and do not feel anxious about the health of the connection when together or apart. That said, there is a normal level of dependence and independence in each relationship. It is okay if a person needs a little more space or a little more closeness, within reason. Securely attached people may still have trapped emotions and become triggered, but know how to regulate their nervous system and repair conflicts with loved ones. They are also able to identify and step away from abusive people, make big

life transitions, and are generally flexible with how they manage day-to-day.

Attachment wounding is the main cause of severe trapped emotions and primarily stems from growing up with emotionally stressful, neglectful, inconsistent, or abusive parents as explored previously in this chapter.[218] Anxious, avoidant, and disorganized attachment styles carry abusive behaviors that deeply hurt any platonic or romantic relationship, but all of them can also become securely attached or form secure relationships. On the other hand, even two securely attached people could become insecure if their basic relationship needs are not being met. A person may also initially be anxious or avoidant around a new relationship, but as a bond grows they become secure. People can quickly move between attachment patterns in reaction to specific stimuli and triggers though.

Please keep in mind that it is often difficult to determine your attachment style and the attachment styles of your relationships. This is because these behaviors are happening subconsciously. They may therefore require the help of a therapist or other outside observer to help determine the exact patterns playing out. Specifics on healing attachment wounding and building healthy relationships are covered in Sections 14.2 and 17.6.

You can also learn more about attachment styles and healthy relationships by reading *Your Brain On Love* by Stan Tatkin or *Polysecure* by Jessica Fern. Even though *Polysecure* is a book for polyamorous partnerships, at least ninety percent of the information applies to monogamous couples as well. There are also many podcasts and articles online exploring these topics in depth, such as various episodes of the *Therapist Uncensored Podcast*.

3.5 Dissociation

One of the most helpful and difficult symptoms when dealing with trapped emotions is dissociation. Dissociation is an entirely normal function in healthy people as they cycle in and out of being aware of the present moment throughout the day. In people with trapped emotions though, it can become a dominant experience that prevents them from being aware of the positive aspects of life. Dissociation helps protect people from their past and present experiences by distancing themselves from the intense feelings they would otherwise be having. This makes sense until a person can find a safe space to start healing, but dissociation may continue even in these safe spaces. A dissociated person is only partially capable of experiencing reality and cannot always access their emotions, an essential part of getting better. Dissociation takes on several forms including:

1. Using distractions like media or people to avoid emotions.
2. Always speaking or thinking about a subject logically without experiencing the associated feelings.
3. Medications or drugs like alcohol dulling the senses.
4. Being entirely disconnected from the mind's mental processes.
5. Constantly doing and thinking.
6. Other behaviors that distract from reality like oversleeping.
7. Using certain spiritual or meditation practices to ignore the emotional self. This is especially common in the practice of calming oneself by focusing on the breath or other physical sensations. Mindfulness is a very helpful technique, but it must be used appropriately.

I know when I am dissociated because reality seems fuzzy or fake, I'm upset but not having an emotional release, I'm angry and obsessively thinking bad thoughts about a person, or I get stressed out when I take a pause in my schedule. On any given day, being tired, consuming too much media, or not interacting with enough people will exacerbate my dissociated mind. A nap, going out to nature, or socializing can help, but I often remain dissociated until I get a night of sleep. This does not just impact me, I have said really awkward things and made conflicts much worse by not being able to use my words thoughtfully.

To the extreme, dissociation prevents a person from knowing what is happening around them and can cause memory problems. After severe incidents, a person may slip in and out of this dissociated state when confronted with any kind of stress. There are cases when a person "wakes up" hours later unaware of where they are or how they got there. In this way, a person may unknowingly put themselves in dangerous situations and face more and more difficult experiences that cause even worse trapped emotions. Alongside lacking self-awareness, a person's sense of purpose may also be disrupted.[97E] These extremes of dissociation are most common when someone experiences maternal neglect.[97F]

When working with a therapist or tackling bigger trapped emotions, dissociated individuals will have to first learn how to come back into their bodies and stay present with what is happening. This may need to happen slowly though. Breaking down the wall of dissociation may initially be intense, bringing with it awareness of strong emotions and abuse. Dissociation is a protective mechanism that happened for a reason, so it is important to be prepared with new physical, mental, emotional, and relational resources that can handle whatever is on the other side. This is essential because becoming present, aware, and open to painful sensations allows an individual to work through those feelings and create a healthier life. As we will explore in the next chapter, slow and safe is fine as you build a strong community and self-care practices to support you.

Becoming more present will be aided by establishing a safe space, managing stress, getting regular massages, starting movement exercises like yoga, and practicing forms of mindfulness meditation. *Neurofeedback* therapy will especially help. Medication or medication changes may be required as well. These are all covered in Chapters 4 and 5. For people with dissociation caused by a deep distrust in others, animal therapy will help rebuild socialization, trust, and compassion. Dissociated people also benefit from taking more control over their lives.[60] This is covered in Section 13.3 and may mean a person becomes empowered to choose their meals, schedule, or cancel plans if they are feeling overwhelmed.

Many coping mechanisms are also dissociative and prevent connection to the present moment. You may have to remove certain activities like watching television, or at least do therapy and self-work before indulging yourself in your soothing hobbies. Stepping away from dissociative activities can also simply be a choice as we become aware of our subconscious tendencies and instead choose something that will either maintain our presence or at least benefit our growth. Chapter 12 explores how to change habits and overcome addictions. Just keep in mind that it is generally easier to stay present earlier in the day since the nighttime brings tiredness and decreases hormones associated with confidence.[87] This is partially why we are more likely to succumb to depressive states and consume dissociative materials at late hours.

3.6 Separating Trapped Emotions From Your Basic Biology

While trapped emotions can mimic symptoms of various mental conditions, it is important to separate trapped emotions from your basic biology. These include personality traits like extroversion, agreeableness, openness, conscientiousness, and neuroticism.[136] They also include conditions such as high sensitivity, bipolar, autism, depression, anxiety, ADHD, and the overlap between them. These create a lot of variability in how different people function and cope in the world. Please keep in mind that there is mounting evidence that at least some of these are also influenced by your gut flora as explored in Section 4.9.

Recently figuring out that I am a highly sensitive extrovert with ADHD helped me understand that although my childhood was difficult, it impacted me much more than a person without my chemistry might otherwise experience. This gave me more empathy and availability to forgive my parents. It also made me accept that certain things will never be comfortable or safe for me to do, like being around some personalities, watching horror films, or being able to remember things well.

This does not mean I never challenge myself or cannot put up with stress, but it does allow me to celebrate my strengths, focus on healing my actual wounds, and build a life in which I do not constantly feel agitated. Accepting these labels also helps connect me with others struggling with similar problems and gives me a lot more potential support to cope in life. Through that awareness, I can then use willpower, rationality, various tools of civilization, or safe spaces to overcome my perceived limitations and work through tasks that do not otherwise come easily.

Separating your basic biology from your trapped emotions does take quite a bit of time, self-reflection, or help from doctors or psychiatrists. For me, this involved observing that some of my behaviors could not be explained through my past experiences and were not getting better through my healing work. Even medical professionals often get diagnoses wrong, so it is important to remain open-minded.

For more common personality traits, taking personality tests may help, especially the *Big Five Personality Test*, which specifically tests for the five previously mentioned genetic personality traits. You may also find insight through journaling, asking friends about your personality, trying out different activities, taking tests like the *Myers-Briggs Type Indicator* or *Enneagram*, and of course understanding your trapped emotions.

Again though, trapped emotions can considerably distort personality test results and it is important to remember your ability to transform and overcome challenges. For instance, as a teenager, I hated people, but am now quite extroverted, albeit also sensitive to who I spend my time with. This change required discovering people I felt safe around, dealing with my social anxiety, and overcoming my addiction to media. Proclaiming oneself an introvert may be an excuse to avoid vulnerability and emotional intimacy, when, in fact, introverts need meaningful and regular social connection as well. On the other hand, supposed extroverts may seek out stimulation to hide from their thoughts, emotions, and the reality of their life. This is, of course, not always the case, but personality can substantially evolve as we find safety and work on ourselves.

The following list is a basic description of some of the most commonly undiagnosed brain wirings. Please keep in mind that some of these are labeled as disorders but usually create some benefit as well, especially as it relates to creativity and the ability to see the world from a unique angle. Many famous individuals have these. There is also a lot of variability with how various brain wirings present themselves, especially between people assigned male or female at birth. Most importantly though, once they start, they are lifelong. A person can also have multiple of these at a time. While beyond the scope of this book, there is a lot that can be done to cope with and improve these conditions:

- **Highly Sensitive People (HSP)**: More sensitive than the average person in body and mind to various stimuli and stresses – explored in Section 2.4
- **Major Depression**: Lack of interest in everyday activities and general feelings of sadness which may disrupt all aspects of life – generally, major depression is at least partly caused by or intensified by trapped emotions, but the risk is increased by genetic factors
- **Bipolar Disorder (BPD)**: Switches between periods of abnormally high energy levels (happy, cleaning or rearranging frenzy, very energized without sleep, sexually motivated) and depressive episodes – typically the depression is more common than the manic episodes and is often misdiagnosed as depression
- **Hypomania**: A less severe form of bipolar disorder that may involve only low-level manic episodes which are not as self-destructive or out of control as bipolar disorder – more a happy high that can be really productive but still involve compulsive behaviors
- **Autism Spectrum Disorder**: Often struggle with reading social cues and emotions, overwhelmed by certain sensory stimuli and doing something differently, or may only understand very direct forms of communication and have obsessive behaviors
- **Generalized Anxiety Disorder**: Has an increased amount of worry and stressed overthinking around everyday situations, conversations, and events
- **Attention Deficit / Hyperactivity Disorder (ADHD)**: May struggle with paying attention, keeping plans, multitasking, remembering things, or have compulsive and hyperactive tendencies with the ability to hyper-focus that increases the risk of things like addictive behaviors and workaholism

I do want to caution against holding onto a label too strongly. For instance, if you identify as a person with a lot of social anxiety or sensitivity to stress, you may greatly limit what you think you are capable of. The goal is to be aware that this is an influence in your life but it does not have to be your main story. For instance, with work, anxiety can be reframed as general excitement and having more energy. Many brain wirings have also been traditionally considered more spiritually attuned.

Genetic personality characteristics are controlled by several factors. For instance, as we'll explore in Section 13.4, your levels of testosterone and estrogen impact your confidence and empathy. These hormones also fluctuate throughout the day, week, month, year, and over the course of your life, which then alters some of your personality along the way. Everyone also has a different baseline level of dopamine, which controls things like confidence, motivation, and pleasurable feelings.[257] For the *Big Five Personality Test*, each characteristic is graded on a spectrum between high and low. Again, there is a lot of flexibility in how these are expressed or how you can challenge yourself on a given day. The traits include:

- **Openness**: Open to experiences and creative versus closed-off and cautious
- **Conscientiousness**: Good with scheduling and structure versus inattentive to others and struggles to complete tasks
- **Extraversion**: Gains energy socializing versus loses energy socializing, prefers fewer people, and dislikes small talk – introversion is different than social anxiety or shyness though
- **Agreeableness**: Empathetic and interested in people versus unempathetic and uninterested in others
- **Neuroticism**: Frequently anxious and stressed versus emotionally stable and calm

Many other characteristics are pushed by your biology too. For instance, people who believe in conspiracy theories often have higher levels of free dopamine in their brains, which increases the risk of false pattern recognition.[224] This fictional belief is then reinforced through fear, feelings of helplessness, confirmation bias, others who believe in the conspiracy, and not taking accountability for what they can personally change. Political conservatism is also marked by a greater fear response and is partly linked to inherited genes.[179] It is likely that ancestral trapped emotions impact personality characteristics like these as well by increasing the base level of stress experienced as discussed in Section 2.6.

***
Chapter Reflections

1. What are the behaviors you exhibit from your trapped emotions?
2. What are your learned behaviors that reinforce your trapped emotions?
3. What does healing mean to you?
4. Was there anything that your ancestors experienced that may have been passed down to you as a trapped emotion?
5. Do you tend toward exhibiting a fight, flight, fawn, freeze, flop, or flock response?
6. Do you experience any forms of abuse in your relationships today?
7. Do you experience forms of love in your relationships today?
8. In what ways do you dissociate?
9. What are your dissociative activities protecting you from?
10. Is there evidence that your brain is wired differently from a neurotypical brain? How can you know for certain? How would this brain type change the ways in which you maneuver social situations and work tasks?
11. What results do you get by taking the *Big Five Personality Test*? In what ways does this impact how you can accept yourself and cope with stress? How can you use the results to help build a life of ease and flow for yourself? In what ways do the results change how you might go about achieving your goals?

Chapter 4

Reducing Stress And Building Resilience

4.1 Motivating Yourself, 4.2 Go Slow, 4.3 You Already Have Resources, 4.4 Removing Stress And Abuse, 4.5 Establishing A Safe Space, 4.6 Visualization, 4.7 Finding A Therapist, Co-Counselor, And Other Allies, 4.8 False Self-Help, 4.9 Basic Self-Care, 4.10 Self-Care For Oppressed Communities, 4.11 Increasing Your Income, 4.12 Establishing A Higher Power, 4.13 Medicines, 4.14 Releasing Tension And Correcting Posture, 4.15 Increasing The Window Of Tolerance To Stress, 4.16 Addressing Shame And Denial

While a certain amount of stress is healthy and natural in life, too much can cause overwhelm or increase the likelihood of being triggered into a painful flashback.[66] When stressed, triggered, or experiencing a flashback of intense emotions, you are actually unable to access your rational mind and may struggle to communicate or act effectively or at all.[25] As Gabor Maté explores in his book, *The Myth of Normal*, chronic stress also increases inflammation and deactivates the immune system, leading to various illnesses and making healing even harder. Many of these stresses are perpetuated by society and culture, requiring that you intentionally regulate your nervous system more often. In Chapters 15 and 16, I also explore how to make a more safe and relaxing world, but until then, let's learn what you can do right now.

In states of high stress and suffering, it may not be a good time to have a difficult conversation, confront your past, or do something that requires much willpower. Instead, it is a great time to de-stress. The goal is to get your nervous system regulated, and then keep it there.

With a regulated nervous system you will be able to handle stresses and triggers, create more resilience in your life, and learn new coping strategies. Even small moments of joy can help return the nervous system to a regulated state, so whatever you do, do something.[25] Calming techniques are especially important for releasing trapped emotions. The body needs to be shown that what happened in the past is no longer a threat and the present moment is safe, or at least manageable.

As you do more of this work, you will become attuned emotionally and rationally to how much you can handle on a given day or week. Everyone has a different *window of tolerance* to stress, and when you get close to or reach over your tolerance, you'll know it is time to implement one of the techniques I share in Chapters 4 and 5. That said, overwhelm can sneak up on us or daily obligations can override our self-care, so it may be important to establish a rule of intentionally checking in with and regulating your nervous system at least every three days. It is also important to note that you can handle a lot, often more than you think you can, and this information is not meant to dissuade you from challenging yourself in work, school, love, or being vulnerable to experiencing life.

4.1 Motivating Yourself

As Oprah Winfrey and Gary Zukav say, all decisions start with an intention.[132S] Releasing trapped emotions is not easy work. Even identifying that your feelings and behaviors are causing problems can be a struggle, but so long as you develop the intention of healing, your pathway is clear. By holding onto this intention, you will know right from wrong and be able to correct your actions if you become distracted or lost. Your intention will help you face struggles you might otherwise avoid, take on activities that you find uncomfortable, or cut out people who do not align with who you are becoming. Try writing out your intention and comparing it with the life you are living.

Your healing will usually only begin when you prioritize and seek out healing. You may be waiting for the motivation first, but often motivation comes after you begin taking action. Many people already have all the resources they need to heal, it's just a matter of identifying and putting them into practice. What is the specific outcome that you want and what is getting in your way? Do you want to feel happier, have deeper friendships and intimate partnerships, be able to handle stressful situations, remove toxic people from your life, and generally feel fulfilled? Probably, so what's holding you back?

4.1.1 FOMO

We often get stuck in what we have now, fearing we will never have it again, even if it is hurtful. The fear of missing out (FOMO) sucks. For instance,

CH 4 – REDUCING STRESS AND BUILDING RESILIENCE

many people struggle to separate from emotionally abusive parents or unhealthy partners. This is a form of codependency. These relationships may guilt you into maintaining contact because they have created no other emotional support. You can acknowledge four things here:

1. Each individual is responsible for their own life. The fact that your parents or partner have isolated themselves to the extent that you are their only emotional support is not your fault and not your responsibility. While relationship repair, community care, and supporting those in need are important, if your assistance is being ignored or if you are unable to care for yourself, creating boundaries or entirely removing yourself from a person is the better option.
2. The world is abundant. There are more friends, more lovers, and more communities if you are willing to put yourself out there, change locations, or explore new interests.
3. Healing yourself first will give you the option to one day return to these unhealthy relationships and help them with their problems much more effectively, if you want to. Remember, it is not your responsibility to fix anyone.
4. Codependent and abusive relationships hold each person back from creating healthier patterns. Until you break this cycle, no one will get help and no one will be truly happy.

In general, know that:

- You owe nothing to abusive friends, family, or partners
- You owe nothing to people or situations that frequently stress you out
- You deserve happiness, contentment, and relaxation
- Everyone shares basic needs including sustenance, safety, love, empathy, rest, community, creativity, freedom, and purpose - lacking or being deprived of any of these causes stress
- Your needs are just as important as anyone else's
- Removing yourself from people who make you feel bad is a form of self-love
- You have a right to establish boundaries and to end relationships that do not comply with your boundaries
- You have a right to heal your suffering

4.1.2 Rock Bottom

Many people only choose to change their life around when hitting some version of rock bottom. Of course, this isn't a place you are likely to intentionally find, but know that some of the greatest motivation is found at our lowest points. Humans are naturally resilient, even when we've descended to a place so low that we can't even imagine staying alive, or have lost all of our friends and loved ones. In these moments we can say to ourselves "I never want to feel that way again. I know beauty and love and happiness exist in this world and dammit I deserve those things. I will do whatever it takes to heal." Then curiosity takes over, and we dedicate ourselves to finding healthier friends, quitting an addiction, seeing a therapist, getting a better job, starting to exercise, and so on. Breakdowns often lead to breakthroughs.

I've been at rock bottom several times. When I moved back to my home base after a year of being away, seven friends unrelated to one another no longer had time for me. I was devastated, but kept going and decided to do anything the world presented to me that seemed like it would help me escape that rejected and lonely misery. One acquaintance suggested a group immersion program centered around deep connection and authentic relating. Another suggested attending co-counseling classes. Both of these programs allowed me to grieve the loss of old friendships but also make new ones that still exist to this day.

When you give up hope, you let go of the control you wish you had over a situation and can move on to more practical or healthier goals. This may be especially important for oppressed people who have felt obligated into activist roles rather than taking care of themselves (see Chapter 16). Letting go of control is further explored in Section 13.3.

Breakdowns don't have to be so cataclysmic either, because every failure is an opportunity to learn and grow. Motivation often comes from a typical low point or a difficult interaction with an emotionally stressful loved one. It can also arise from moving cities, traveling abroad, or attending an event that takes you out of your comfort zone like a week-long camping or meditation retreat. This same experience may be felt when transitioning out of a depressive episode. You'll have a lot of energy to say "I don't want to feel that way anymore" and strengthen your resources in friendships, activities, support groups, therapists, reading materials, and cutting off abusive relationships.

It is unfortunate, but it is rare that anyone is going to come and save you. Sometimes there are friends or lovers who will lift you up a little bit, to give you some small glimmer of joy in the darkness, but in the end, it is you who must change. As poet June Jordan wrote, "We are the ones we have been waiting for." You may go through a period of feeling angry and bitter about this, about how your friends or family or government did not do enough, but it is the only way. However, once you start taking those steps, there will be so many people excited to celebrate and support who you are becoming, including yourself. Healing can take place at any point in your life regardless of how young or old you are. Every moment is a new chance to begin anew and change things for the better.

4.1.3 Trust Your Process
Know that it is hard to predict the future, and impossible to truly know what something is like unless you personally experience it. You cannot know the beauty at the top of a mountain through a book or video, you must climb the mountain yourself. Healing is a practice, so more than anything, trust your process. While feeling bad, you might give up hope that these techniques work. You may try them and they won't work immediately, or you may even initially feel worse, but often you'll suddenly realize after an hour, "Oh, I feel okay now." Healing after using a technique might also come after sleeping or after a few weeks of integrating what you learned.

Remember that wounds take time to heal and your reality can flip upside down in a single moment. You are likely wanting to heal but also attached to your suffering and needing to rewire some old brain patterns. This is a learning process, you will discover that some of your coping mechanisms actually make you feel awful, and things you never thought of trying are actually really enjoyable. It will take believing that other ways of being could create a better life than what you have now. If you feel stuck, journal about the type of life you want and create a detailed list of steps to get there - this can help clarify your direction forward and the skills you need. Change is always possible!

4.1.4 Suffering Creates Suffering
While you may not be aware of it, your unaddressed stresses may have directly or indirectly hurt the people around you. This includes your physical and mental health. Trapped emotions make us act out in difficult or unreasonable ways, cause us physical health problems, reduce our lifespan, and are a central cause of abuse, manipulation, discrimination, toxic communication, anger, attempts at revenge, and ruined hangouts. This alone is a great reason to address your past experiences because it's not just you being affected, it's also your family, friends, romantic partners, co-workers, medical personnel, and all of society. Taking it a step further, you are intricately connected with the web of life and share breath with all organisms on Earth. Even if you haven't

directly harmed people, your ability to gain greater emotional regulation and understand the nuances of healthy relationships will allow you to improve your relationships with others. Your healing will allow you to spread joy and fight to improve conditions for all beings.

4.1.5 The Easiest Person To Heal Is Yourself
While there may be factors slowing your ability to heal, recovery is still possible. It certainly helps when allies reach out, people we communicate with agree to change, or the random events of the universe support us, but more often than not, no one is going to save you unless you put in the energy. People frequently feel that they must heal their parents or society before they can heal themselves, but this is untrue. Even if you get revenge, a person dies, or someone reforms their behaviors, your trapped emotions may still be present. Sometimes these things create a safer space that allows healing to begin more easily, but you still have to do the work. Furthermore, even if you communicate with a person, they won't always change, and culture takes quite a while to transform.

The world is not always fair. You must get past this unfairness as you may be using it as an excuse to not heal at all. Keep in mind that two people in the same situation can have entirely different experiences, and much joy can still be found in dire times. You may not believe it yet, but you are capable of creating a new narrative for your life.

Even for people who experience deeply rooted discrimination, there are many ways to grow more resilient to the atrocities created by cultures, society, and the government. While in the long-term we must transform discriminatory institutions, finding moments of peace is essential. Mindfulness, grieving, healthy angering, resting, quitting addictions, creating community, and so many of the other techniques outlined here will greatly benefit the well-being of anyone. More about coping with and building resilience to discrimination is covered in Section 4.10.

4.1.6 Who Are You?
While doing this work, some people strive to discover their *true self*, but there are many versions of you that can be content or happy. Keep in mind though that it is not necessarily possible to become someone you idolize because you have been given a unique set of conditions as explored in Section 3.6. That said, you can still achieve a lot and your pathway to success may simply be different than someone else depending on your biology and upbringing.

Once you know your basics, imagine a few different ideal lives for yourself including your job, house, emotional state, relationships, family, income, and so on. Now, add in a little bit of realism based on your basic personality. What would you have to do to reach those goals based upon where you are now? This will be a gradually changing process and one that I like to journal about every few years. Moving towards an ideal version of yourself can be challenging as it is difficult to separate your coping mechanisms, fear responses, culture, and learned behaviors from what brings you genuine fulfillment. Therefore, this is not a plan to necessarily actualize and conquer, but one that can be used to identify general roadblocks or contradictions in how you want to be.

4.1.7 Media
While media consumption can become an unhealthy addiction that I cover in Section 12.2, I've also used it to motivate myself. This is especially true with movies where I resonate with the characters. Unlike with books or TV shows, with movies I can experience a complete emotional arc in one sitting. Often I would become jealous of these characters succeeding, finding happiness, and falling in love. It reminded me that I wanted those things too and gave me the hope that I could obtain them. It also helped me distance from my intense emotions and gave me unique ideas about how to approach my own life.

Of course, movies are often not inclusive and you may find better resonance with the story and characters in other mediums such as comics, TV, books, and fanfiction. Each person will resonate with different media, but for me, I have found some inspiration in movies like *Everything Everywhere All At Once*, *The Matrix*, *Amélie*, *Everything Is Illuminated*, *The Barkley Marathons*, *Eternal Sunshine Of The Spotless Mind*, *JoJo Rabbit*, *Princess Mononoke*, *The Wind Rises*, *Your Name*, and *After Life* (1988). In general, try to connect with your inner world of sensations before and after consuming media, and do not allow media to take up more than a few hours of your time a day.

4.1.8 Avoiding Healing
There are many ways in which we become avoidant of healing, one of which is comparing our experiences to the difficulties of others. This minimization of ourselves often comes up in fawn type trauma responses, codependents, and people disconnected from their emotional body. It's also proliferated in toxic masculinity and US culture. If you're having a hard day, that's okay. Convincing yourself otherwise (as many abusers and spiritual practices have you do) is going to bury your feelings in unhealthy ways. Your emotions are

energies that need to be considered with compassion and released. Crying, healthy angering, communicating, and making changes to your life are much more helpful than stuffing your feelings down. Remember, the healthier you are, the more you'll be able to help others. Deeper trapped emotions do not go away on their own; you have to be proactive about them.

You may also struggle giving up certain addictive behaviors and the communities they connect you with. For instance, people giving up alcohol, tobacco, or video games often initially struggle with establishing new ways of creating friendships, participating in social activities, and being involved in family gatherings. Remind yourself that the world is abundant and there are many other enjoyable activities and friendships that are healthier for your well-being and relationships. Generally, know that you can be much happier with a different set of conditions, hobbies, lovers, and allies. We will cover the specifics of how to deal with addictions in Chapter 12.

Lastly, you may believe you are improving your life but actually are doing the same thing over and over again. For instance, you may replace one isolating behavior with another, or break things off with an abusive relationship just to establish a different one. Remember, nothing will change unless you break the cycle and go down a whole new route. As adults we became grooved into patterns, trying to reiterate solutions that we once thought worked.[134] It's a conservation of energy and makes it tough to apply novel ideas to old problems. Establishing a new direction may then take time and a willingness to try something uncomfortably new that your emotional mind severely questions.

To begin this work it is good to ask yourself, "How am I reinforcing my suffering?" Your various triggers or unhealthy behaviors may be preventing you from connecting with loved ones and caring for yourself. These include your communication, hobbies, social connections, self-limiting beliefs, and behaviors that limit your sleep. Removing trapped emotions can be hard, but it can also be really easy as we learn that immense happiness arises from simply stopping certain behaviors. We realize that many of our difficult emotions are not caused by other people, but rather by our attachment to certain outcomes. Throughout your reading you may notice yourself being resistant to some of these methods, initially thinking it is stupid or childish. However, part of your journey is opening up to possibilities rather than following what you have been led to believe your whole life.

A huge turning point for me was realizing that I expected others to save me. I was bitter and angry at people for not being better friends, reaching out, changing behaviors, or understanding my plight. I finally decided that I could no longer rely on individuals, and instead committed myself to connecting to communities of people and finding nourishment in nature. I joined the rock climbing gym, attended meditations, devoted myself to a support group, started writing in the woods, and stepped away from stressful people, media, and nighttime computer usage. When I stopped needing people to be a certain way, I became happier and as a result was a better friend when people did show up.

4.1.9 The Regrets Of Dying
Sometimes it can be good to compare your life pathway with your elders, especially if you are struggling with finding an intention to direct you. According to Bronnie Ware, a nurse who for twelve years recorded the regrets of those soon to pass away, the top five regrets of dying are:

- I wish I'd had the courage to live a life true to myself, not the life others expected of me.[163]
- I wish I hadn't worked so hard.
- I wish I'd had the courage to express my feelings.
- I wish I had stayed in touch with my friends.
- I wish I had let myself be happier.

4.2 Go Slow

Transforming your life is typically not something that happens overnight, especially when you have attachment wounds from childhood. Instead, you make incremental improvements that gradually uplift your mood and empower your resilience. It may take several years to develop new habits, remove toxic people, form healthy relationships, and discover new activities to participate in. The goal is to move slowly enough that you do not trigger an emotional flashback while re-engaging your senses and changing your stories. Even after you've removed some trapped emotions, they can sometimes return later, causing you to regress into old patterns. That is okay though, it will be easier the second time to release.

It is best to focus on one difficult experience at a time while releasing trapped emotions. Your successes will make future work much easier, so it does not necessarily matter where you begin. However, typically you will be focusing on your immediate stresses first and sometimes find them attached to some childhood incidents. After you do feel settled about a particular incident, it can be beneficial to give yourself a week or two before moving on to your next target. This gives you time to integrate what you have learned and decreases the chance you relapse into past behaviors. Spending all your time dealing with these energies can also be hard on your relationships and yourself, so enjoy your newfound freedom a little bit. You are not a project, you are a human being with a lot of wonderful things about you already.

While doing this work, it is difficult to know that you are making progress unless you pause and self-reflect. What skills have you learned? Did you successfully implement a coping skill? Have you removed a source of stress or made progress in doing so? Are the number of days that you feel relatively okay increasing compared to a year ago? The smallest victories are big accomplishments and deserve celebration. This is especially important in realizing that instead of trying to eliminate a negative feeling altogether, you can ask yourself, "How do I relieve the stress by ten or twenty percent? How do I feel just a little bit better?" Know that even by reading books like this one, you are making progress as your awareness increases.

Some trapped emotions may initially feel quite overwhelming to take on, so it's good to break them up into more manageable steps. Congratulate yourself after you complete each step. For instance, "Today I am going to search for therapists with open schedules, tomorrow I will contact a few to see their availability, then after an interview with each next week I'll select one." This greatly increases motivation and is much easier than "I have to get a therapist."

It can also be beneficial to have small victories to prove to yourself you are capable of taking on larger tasks, even if they are unrelated. For instance, the sense of accomplishment in completing a drawing, cleaning your room, or reading through a book can be very empowering. As previously mentioned, I sometimes use digital media in this way too, especially in stories with characters that I relate to who go from an average or downtrodden person to an accomplished individual. These growth arcs can provide empowerment and instill a sense of "yes I can." While I have to be sure to eventually step away from these activities, or at least regulate how much I am doing them, they provide a safe starting point to rebuild my ego from.

After finding a new place of contentment, it is easy to forget the great suffering we experienced even a week ago. However, the opposite is true as well. When we become triggered or stressed, it may color our entire history, friendships, and anything we recently experienced as good in a negative light. You're going to make progress forward, and sometimes you will make progress backward - so have compassion for yourself, it is all part of the healing journey. Hard times are also a healthy and natural part of the human experience and are essential for happiness and love to exist. You're not trying to eliminate stress altogether, but rather address that stress which is trapped within you and holding you back from life.

Note that you may initially feel entirely fine confronting some of your past difficulties, but then suddenly find yourself triggered or depressed a few hours later or the next day. This is because people often dissociate into the rational mind when thinking of the past. Even though it is still impacting you, there is a delayed effect. De-stressing and increasing your resilience to stress helps you to cope with the symptoms of trapped emotions and release them more easily. Just go at your own pace, and take breaks to stabilize your stress levels.

4.3 You Already Have Resources

Likely, you already have many strengths, even if you don't know them yet. What allowed you to start reading this book? What got you to your job or school today? What allowed you to complete an art project or sign up for a therapist? What moments in your lifetime or healing journey are you proud of? Even the things that a person considers undesirable about themselves often directs them into really fulfilling passions such as service work, creating community, art, or research. The fact is, humans are resilient creatures and can survive or even thrive in dire situations.

Mindfully use your hobbies and memories as grounding points to empower yourself. What activities do you enjoy? What times have you laughed, felt safe, or loved something? That might include things like reading, dancing, being in nature, spending time with friends, playing sports, gardening, or gathering together for games. Even if you do not currently have one of these hobbies, you can identify things you might be interested in like making art or taking care of animals. The goal is to create stable places of joy and connection that you can go to in times of difficulty.

It is okay if you have certain hobbies typically seen as addictions or unhealthy, but know that in the process of healing from deep childhood wounds, you'll probably have to change your relationship with them or quit them altogether. Although they often depress the mind overall, compulsively consuming certain substances and media provide a quick boost to the brain's happy chemicals. Addictive behaviors are typically formed as a way to dull the immense stress and uncomfortable feelings of trapped emotions. However, that dulling often destroys our ability to exert mastery over our emotions and meaningfully deal with our stresses. We'll discuss how to better regulate or quit addictive behaviors later in Chapter 12, but keep in mind that addiction is primarily the result of stress, culture, and your peer group.

Trapped emotions can also be beneficial when moderated properly. For instance, people who have experienced deep mental wounds tend to have the capacity for greater emotional intelligence and empathy. They know when something is wrong and can act on it. Critical judgment and love for one's work lend to being a respected leader. Being emotional makes releasing trapped energies a lot easier. The goal is not to destroy your inner demons, but rather to befriend and work with them. The suffering you have weathered is a sign of strength, not weakness.

Keep in mind that humans have been dealing with trapped emotions since the beginning. Many spiritual beliefs and cultural traditions deal with releasing these energies through dance, ritual, plant medicine, storytelling, and more. Reconnecting with the practices of your ancestors may provide a powerful way of both creating community and navigating your difficult feelings.

4.4 Removing Stress And Abuse

You can only handle so much stress at a time before becoming overwhelmed. Generally, it is healthy to remove certain stresses from your life, or at least reduce them to reasonable levels. The caveat here is that people with severe trapped emotions may find almost anything stressful. It can be difficult to separate healthy stress and stress caused by triggers, intentional abuse, and unintentional abuse.

Normally people have no interest in putting up with abuse, but many people with trapped emotions do not know what abuse looks like or lack the motivation to stand up against it. In fact, they may seek it out to recreate unhealthy childhood dynamics that they confused for love. Identifying the difference between love and abuse is already covered in Chapter 3, but let's further break these behaviors down. Just keep in mind that it is possible to communicate through your problems and repair certain relationships as I explore in Chapters 8 and 14.

Healthy stress involves things that provide a long or short-term benefit. This includes things like going to school, working out, processing with a partner, having your opinions challenged (to a point), earning money, completing a project, socializing, or traveling abroad. Since your stress tolerance is limited, these things may still sometimes need to get removed or at least paused to allow you to recover. For instance, if you're feeling overwhelmed or tired, your ability to handle additional stress will be limited. That said, according to psychologist Alia Crum, stress will impact you differently depending on your mindset.[180] Stress that you reframe as something beneficial to your growth or education actually increases your ability to handle it. This power of mindset is covered in Chapter 6.

Triggers are anything that activates your trapped emotions and can include loud sounds, certain types of people, or physical touch. Discovering your triggers can be a very important part of healing as things you once thought were entirely normal are actually the causes of your anger, anxiety, or depression. In general, your goal is to reduce the reaction you experience when confronted by triggers that are otherwise healthy. However, healing may require totally removing specific types of triggers for a time.

Intentional abuse includes name-calling, violence, racism, sexism, threats, and actions that are repeated over time to manipulate a person. Intentional abusers do not show empathy and do not attempt to change their behavior when asked. If they do, it is temporary and used as a means of gaining power over you again.

Unintentional abuse falls into two categories. One is when a person does something abusive but is willing to shift that behavior and is empathetic that they hurt you. It may take them quite a while and many reminders to shift this behavior, but they are willing to try and seemingly make progress. This is common in people still learning about love who repeat patterns from their parents.

Unintentional abuse secondly appears when a person fails to do something, such as communicating, frequently flaking out on social engagements, or never doing any relationship work like making plans or initiating conversations to process issues. These people will not necessarily change their behavior. There are also cultural norms that could be considered abusive such as abrasive or passive-aggressive communication styles (think communication on the East Coast versus communication on the West Coast of the USA). A person who is different from you or was raised with different cultural norms doesn't necessarily mean they are abusive, but it can mean that you're incompatible, and that's okay too.

Rather than figuring out if something is abusive or not, get used to asking yourself, *is this stress worth my time and energy? Is this person willing to learn?* No? Well, it's time to move on or create some strong boundaries. Let go of trying to get approval, understanding, or love from people who are incapable of providing that for you. Keep in mind that abusers are full of trapped emotions themselves, and often will not change until shocked out of their routines - you are doing them a service by leaving or taking back control over your time. Their well-being is not your responsibility and the world is abundant with people who you will enjoy more. Of course, how quickly you leave is up to you. Consider establishing a boundary, whether secretly or shared aloud, such as:

- After communicating a want or need (if it's safe to), I expect change to happen within a month
- Three strikes and they're out
- If it is stressful more than 20% of the time then I'm leaving
- If ____ ever happens again, we're through

Boundaries can be difficult to uphold, especially if the threat of physical violence, moving homes, or a child's health are in question. Just remember, this is for your well-being and happiness. Each person is responsible for their own needs and you alone cannot fill in the void this person is experiencing. If you are a caretaker, codependent type, or have strong family values, you may struggle with this concept, but you deserve to be treated with love and respect. Being someone's savior is not love. Constantly having to take care of a person's emotional and physical needs is not love. Having a one-sided relationship is not love. Abuse is not love. Your being miserable is not love. Being deprived of your basic needs is not love. If you find yourself constantly forgiving a person for repetitive misdeeds, start keeping a list as a reminder of how much you put up with. How to assert needs and boundaries are detailed in Chapter 8.

It is an unfortunate reality that we often stay in abusive and unhealthy relationships much longer than necessary. We make all kinds of excuses as to why, hoping that the behaviors will change or things will start feeling okay. They rarely do. Yet, many people need inexplicable proof. It might take dozens or hundreds of times of getting hurt by someone before finally we can see that the relationship is not serving us. This is the same for any addiction. Even if friends tell us "You need to take space" or "That's really unhealthy," we find it hard to believe - our friends may have an objective point of view, but our emotional world is wrapped up in fear, love (or what we mistake for it), empathy, and desire.

While people are capable of increasing their resilience to stress, it often becomes more difficult to tolerate many behaviors as you become mindful of abuse. You frequently see this in people who start reading literature on feminism, racism, and love. Unfortunately, this may substantially limit romantic and platonic relationships as you more easily discern who is healthy to be around. Even for people who are willing to learn, you will likely have to spend a decent amount of time educating them. Just remember that everyone has to start somewhere and you were not always so aware yourself. In a society built on toxicity and abuse, awareness can be a privilege most have never had access to. Many types of abuse deserve zero tolerance, but if you otherwise like a person, you might at least try communicating the problem to see if transformation is possible.

Abusive situations may be dangerous to leave. In this case, it is important to do so quickly and preferably with the assistance of allies to protect you. The *Joyful Heart Foundation* website or *National Domestic Violence Hotline* may be able to help give guidance at 1-800-799-7233. Teenagers at least 16 years of age can file for emancipation. School counselors may also guide youth to important resources for securing safety.

There are situations where you have done everything you can and know that the source of your stress is leaving, but they're still there for a few weeks or months. Maybe this is with sharing space with an ex, putting in your 30 days notice for a job, or waiting for a toxic housemate to move out. I wish time machines existed, but I'll try to offer some alternatives:

- While you may feel like you are submerged in negativity, try remembering the positive and regularly creating gratitude lists
- Try to reframe negative statements towards your stresses into an empathetic understanding of why they act the way they do
- Create temporary safe spaces as explored in Section 4.5
- Communicate some boundaries as explored in Chapter 8
- Spend as much time outside of your house as possible
- Avoid complaining about the source of your stress, do not let it consume your energy any more than it has to

4.5 Establishing A Safe Space

It is extremely difficult to release trapped emotions unless you first establish a safe space. This space should not trigger any stressful memories or feelings, at least for the difficult experience you are currently working with. When we remove stressful triggers from our lives, our minds and bodies will naturally begin healing. Some people may therefore only need the steps covered in this chapter to make profound shifts in life, especially if their mental wounds are too painful to confront more directly right now.

Some healing modalities and therapists push you to process things you are not ready for yet but know that resting in a feeling of "safely okay" is a great place to be for as long as you want. After all, the goal is to improve your life, not to be perfect. Just know that the trapped emotions may continue to impact you in unforeseen ways until the emotions, self-limiting beliefs, and maladaptive behaviors are transformed. Healing often requires some discomfort and vulnerability, but it is typically small compared to the suffering experienced by not addressing the hurt at all. A safe space may involve:

- Staying somewhere other than your house
- Putting yourself around people who you trust, will hold you, or can speak empathetic words to you
- Breaking up with a partner or friend
- Cutting contact and phone calls with a family member, or at least creating specific boundaries with them
- Blocking a person and their friends on social media
- Removing, deleting, or destroying objects from your house and social media that remind you of a difficult experience (give them to a friend for safekeeping if you'd rather not destroy them)
- Quitting a job
- Practicing mindfulness and returning to the present moment rather than thoughts of the past or future
- Moving to a house where you are surrounded by more nature and enjoy your neighbors or housemates[62]
- Stopping the consumption of all news media
- Logging out of all of your social media accounts and turning your phone off
- Giving your mind a break with a nap, going to sleep, or watching a movie
- Stepping away from any additional stress once you begin feeling overwhelmed and releasing the emotions as explored in Chapter 5
- Growing old enough to move away from a difficult parent or guardian figure or obtaining a legal right to emancipate early
- Learning some basic skills to cope with anxiety and depression
- Using an antidepressant or anti-anxiety medication
- Cutting out anything or anyone that is causing you anger, stress, or sadness more than 20% of the time or more than once or twice a month - adjust these numbers to whatever level seems reasonable for you
- Communicating your needs and creating boundaries about what you want and do not want as covered in Chapter 8

Creating a safe space may be difficult if you live with stressful or generally unlikable people, or if you are financially insecure and scared of losing a job. In these situations, it will be important to find other ways of relieving stress such as by taking on less responsibility or asserting boundaries. For instance, if you caregive for a family member or friend, assert times that you are reserving for yourself or establish that you cannot be their only friend. This is discussed in more detail in Chapter 8.

Safe spaces may initially be experienced as unsafe because of how unfamiliar environments can be stressful, or you still feel triggered by a recent experience. Safe spaces may also be considered boring. People who grew up in stressful environments can become addicted to excitement, dissociating into drugs, sex, work, games, parties, and other activities to push away their emotions. It can therefore take a few hours to a few days to adapt to and appreciate being in a new environment, so allow enough time for this transition to take place even if it is an emotional one.

Establishing a completely safe space may also be almost impossible for people who face discrimination based on their gender, race, or other factors. If you can move, there are locations where certain forms of discrimination are not as bad or that have more supportive allies. Even in difficult areas though, or when you are impacted by systemic forms of discrimination, you can still make progress; it is just going to be harder. Self-care and building resilience for oppressed communities are discussed in more depth at the end of this chapter.

4.6 Visualization

Visualization is a powerful imagination technique that may be used to practice skills, calm the nervous system, renegotiate painful memories, and heal wounded parts of ourselves. For instance, you could conjure your favorite superhero to speak empowering words to you, imagine a golden light to protect your heart from pain, or enter into a difficult memory and overcome what happened. Each visualization is unique to the individual. You can create a desired outcome beforehand, or allow the outcome to unfold as you progress through your thoughts and mental images. This allows you to create a resilient mental landscape. Try using visualization practices for 5 to 10 minutes daily. Just make sure you are emotionally resourced and feeling relatively safe. For visualizations you create beforehand:

1. Choose a desired outcome such as winning a competition or protecting yourself from evil energies. Try to keep it positive rather than negative - "I will..." instead of "I don't want to..."
2. Find a calm space free of distractions and close your eyes. Alterna-

tively, wear headphones and play music or white noise to mask out the rest of the world.
3. Use mindfulness and deep breathing while releasing the tension in your body as explored later in this chapter and Chapter 5. This helps the body enter into a state of self-hypnosis in which it is more able to handle stress and rewrite narratives.[140]
4. Imagine yourself performing all of the actions involved in reaching your desired outcome.
5. As you imagine this, make sure you are also imagining all of the associated sensations. Writing the visualization out or making a vision board with images will help create the world surrounding your goal. What emotions will finishing that goal create? What do you do about the obstacles that might obstruct your way? What will the weather and lighting be like? Imagine these things in vivid detail.
6. Repeat the visualization multiple times to increase the likelihood of success. This is mental practice. Of course, a reasonable goal will also increase your chances of success. What are you capable of now? And with a little more practice, what could you be capable of?
7. Consider using a mirror to help. Mirrors give you direct feedback for your movements, emotions, and appearance. Dressing up, making silly faces, and doing other visual experiments will expand your self--awareness and allow you to practice who you want to be seen as while acting out a visualization.

Here are a few visualization exercises you can use:

1. **Positive thoughts** - Many therapists use Peter Levine's *oscillation* technique in which you move between focusing on the intense emotions created by your trapped emotions and grounding in a positive memory or positive sensation in your body.[105] With memories you want to viscerally experience them so that you can feel the energies they previously created. Perhaps it is a time you felt loved, happy, or safe. Perhaps it is a stuffed animal or hat that you cherished. Remember as many of the associated sensory details as possible (sounds, smells, sights, textures, tastes, and emotions). Perhaps there are also words such as "I love you" or "You are appreciated." These memories can exist prior to our difficult experience or from more recent times.
2. **Loving-kindness meditation** - In Buddhism there is *loving-kindness meditation* which promotes positive emotions towards oneself

and others.[197] This is a practice in which different people are thought of with loving-kindness and given words such as "may you be happy and well." Many guided versions of this practice may be found online, but I'll share a quick summary. You start by relaxing and finding a sense of peace, kindness, and love within yourself. If this is difficult you can recall a time in which you have felt or witnessed this from another person, and apply those sensations to yourself. You then bring your awareness to a person who you care about and love, followed by a person you are struggling with emotionally. Lastly, you bring your awareness to each of these people in loving-kindness, including yourself, and expand it to your community, your city, nature, the Earth, and the Universe. You can end with, "May we be happy and well," while sitting with the warm glow of positive regard for all beings.

3. ***The memory vault*** - If certain thoughts or memories are tormenting you or endlessly reiterating, you may need to give yourself some distance from them. Instead of just distracting yourself, you can create a memory safe. Imagine a container that not even sound can escape from. Perhaps it is guarded by strong creatures whose immense love for you makes you confident they will keep that memory locked away until you are ready to confront it. Imagine yourself placing the memory into the container and sealing it away. Repeat this visualization as needed. When the memory tries to intrude, you can recall that it is in your memory vault.

4. ***The safe space*** - Imagine or think about a space you feel safe within. I've used thoughts of my room as a container of safety, complete with warmth, cleanliness, my blankets, and the click made when locking the door. I can then instruct certain emotions and memories that they're not allowed in. Alternatively, visit a happy and magical world. I once conjured the image of jumping between giant colorful Skittles. Even though I don't eat Skittles, I found this strangely soothing.

5. ***The guardians*** - Think of compassionate and powerful beings who will keep you safe and guard against unwanted energies. These are preferably non-human entities or fictional characters and are great for guarding your safe place.

6. ***The remote*** - Visualize a remote control that has power over your memories. With it you can mute, slow down, speed up, pause, take out the color, zoom in, or zoom out any thought or image that comes to mind. This can be especially useful when confronting difficult

memories.

If you have trouble visualizing anything, you can also illustrate your imagination on paper or in a sandbox, write out the story in a journal, look at a photo of a finished product, edit yourself into a photo scene, or create a physical manifestation of the visualization by performing a ritual. Emerging digital tools like drawing software combined with virtual reality can also help you experience a powerfully immersive version of your creation. There are also more advanced visualization techniques we will discuss starting in Chapter 6.

4.7 Finding A Therapist, Co-Counselor, And Other Allies

There are many allies who can help you regulate your nervous system and deal with your trapped emotions. While it may initially be difficult to find your perfect match, you are simply looking for someone "good enough." You will discover better allies along your journey. Any healthy friend, therapist, pet, motivational speaker, author, community, or spiritual guide will naturally empower you and help bolster your ability to regulate and co-regulate your nervous system. Whoever it is, establish at least one non-judgmental ally who you enjoy and can speak with openly about your struggles. That is, someone who you feel safe around and is capable of actively listening to and empathizing with your difficulties.

For actually dealing with trapped emotions, it is useful to have a mental health professional trained in Eye Movement Desensitization and Reprocessing (EMDR), Somatic, Psychedelic-Assisted, Internal Family Systems (IFS), Neurofeedback, Hypno, Attachment-Focused, or Narrative Exposure therapy. Websites like *GoodTherapy* and *PsychologyToday* have directories of locally available therapists who are easily searchable. Online therapy is also available through *BetterHelp Online Counseling* and *Talkspace*.

People who reflect on our words and actions tend to be better at seeing and naming our patterns than we are, so you may find some great insights from therapy.[68] However, it can require quite a lot of privilege to get a good therapist. They may be too expensive, not readily available in your area, or don't take your insurance. It can also be quite stressful and time-consuming finding a skilled therapist. This is part of the reason why I felt it important to write this book, to help decentralize the mental health industry and make therapy techniques more accessible to underprivileged individuals and the general public. It can still be helpful simply having a therapist who can empathetically listen, but their usefulness will vary for dealing with trapped emo-

CH 4 – REDUCING STRESS AND BUILDING RESILIENCE   71

tions.

I've worked with five different therapists practicing various modalities over the years, and while each has given me certain skills or relieved some day-to-day difficulties, none have felt truly safe or capable enough to deal with my suffering, even ones specially trained in the previously mentioned modalities. As mentioned in Chapter 1, none of them ever even mentioned that I might have PTSD. Thus, my healing did not begin until I stopped relying on the therapy industry as the only road to feeling better. As therapist Omar Hill says, there are many issues within the institution of therapy, and most therapy actually happens outside of the therapy room.[65]

Great therapists do exist and can be important for people with severe trapped emotions, extreme dissociation, or difficulty managing their time. I'll discuss finding one later in this section, but I do want to note how problematic mainstream therapy can be, especially for oppressed communities. This starts with there being little to no oversight in therapy work. Some therapists enter into the field for entirely the wrong reason, are emotionally struggling themselves, or take on clients they are unable to help simply to fill their schedule. Most sessions are less than an hour long each week, making it take a long time to form a trusting relationship or find the roots of a person's struggles.

Many therapists lack the cultural intelligence to understand the oppression faced by groups like people of color, the LGBTQ+ community, Native Americans, or Black people. Very few even identify in these groups, which may be essential for certain people seeking services. In combination with this, the research and training behind therapy techniques often call for specific modalities that lack the cultural nuance to work for many groups of people.

Typically therapy is also not holistic in its approach, neglecting the many aspects of basic self-care found in the next section. Furthermore, insurance companies and doctors often refer clients to therapists who use techniques that are relatively ineffective for many types of trapped emotions. Clients may rely on therapists to act as a healthy relationship, but this will always be limited by the existence of money as the basic entry point to the connection and with therapists being trained not to share their emotions and experiences.[65]

As a result of these problems, you may need additional allies who are more accessible and helpful. These may come in the form of:

- Authors and artists
- Books and other literature that dive deeply into your difficulties
- Your inner selves
- Support groups or a sponsor through a Twelve Step program

- Personal growth seminars
- An accountabilibuddy, or a friend or partner who is doing similar work
- A co-counseling relationship
- A life coach
- Animal companions
- A doctor or doctors who specialize in nutrition, gut health, hormone regulation, inflammation, and psychiatry

4.7.1 Authors And Artists

Authors and artists like myself can act as allies and mentors - you can begin doing a great amount of work on your own simply by reading books, listening to podcasts, or following creators online. While media can be an addiction that fosters avoidance of your problems, the arts can also help you tap into your emotions and put your life into perspective. Consider reading poetry, listening to lyrical music, or visiting an art museum. The only thing is that you have to practice what you learn or feel inspired by as it is rare for any change to take place by simply consuming knowledge.

Please see the end of this guide for the literature I read to write this book. Much of my education about trapped emotions came from the local library. With a library card, I gained access to the digital catalog of *Hoopla* and was able to listen to many audiobooks for free as I worked jobs or drove. Educating yourself will also help you choose a good enough ally and know what to expect from certain therapeutic techniques.

4.7.2 Your Parts

As we will explore in Chapter 10, your greatest ally may be versions of yourself including your past, present, and future selves. Similarly, a character from a fictional story, a famous actor, or a historical figure may also empower your ability to deal with life's difficulties.

4.7.3 Support Groups And Adult Children Of Alcoholics And Dysfunctional Families

Many types of support groups meet regularly to deal with every form of mental suffering and addiction. You can search online for ones happening locally, on the phone, through chat, or over video conferencing. Twelve Step programs are the most well-known, though are often criticized for being demoralizing and shaming, not based on current science, too religious or spiritual, and kind of cultish. They are, however, the most broadly available support group happening all hours of the day. At the very least, these groups can be a great starting point, allowing you to hear from people who have gone through similar difficulties, get free one-on-one support through a sponsor or fellow member, and make friends. They also give you something to occupy your time with when you might otherwise seek out a toxic behavior or have no one to get help from.

I want to note that many people misunderstand the use of a higher power in Twelve Step programs - this higher power can be anything such as a community, nature, a Christian god, or a deity of your choosing. You might even think of it as a mentor instead. It does not require you to be religious or believe in a god in the traditional sense. You also do not have to fully commit yourself to a program to benefit from it, although often the more you do, the better the results.

Of Twelve Step programs, joining an *Adult Children of Alcoholics and Dysfunctional Families* (ACA) group will be greatly beneficial for anyone who grew up with stressful, abusive, controlling, or unavailable parents. Many of the criticisms garnered by Twelve Step programs are remedied in ACA, especially when using Tony A's version of the Twelve Steps or doing *inner child work* (see Chapter 10). It is still not perfect, but ACA holds strongly to the ethos of "take what you need and leave the rest." It also provides community and structure to find healing through, and each meeting is a little different so you can find ones that feel best for you. The goal of ACA is to come out of isolation and obtain *emotional sobriety*.

After a year of regularly attending online and in-person ACA meetings, I realized that it was the first time in my adult life I had unconditionally felt cared for and loved. Knowing that I could attend a meeting at any time created a stable trust as if a friend were always there. Simultaneously, knowing that the founders had created this program purely for the loving benefit of others without any monetary gain made me feel very safe. Honestly, I do not attend meetings regularly anymore, in part because I found that constantly hearing people talking about the negative sides of their families made it harder to find forgiveness for my own. I do think hearing this dialogue is initially a really important part of healing, but it needs to be balanced with doing the practices and a lot of self-care. I am happy to know ACA is there when I need it though and am sure I will revisit the workbooks at some point.

Harm reduction is also a valuable model that meets a person where they're at in their drug usage and establishes healthy goals that do not necessarily equate to abstinence. Finding a therapist or support group that practices harm reduction may be a better fit for some people. We'll discuss this model in Section 12.2.

Aside from Twelve Step programs and harm reduction, there are also day-long to week-long personal growth seminars and authentic relating groups. These can be expensive, are less regular, and can be based around ineffective techniques, but sometimes do provide a space to practice skills and develop deep connections. You might also find a lot of healing in attending open mics for musicians or poets. While this may be a less direct form of personal growth work, it is a space to share your story and hear others.

Another option is meditation and yoga groups. Please keep in mind that Western versions of these both are derived from Eastern traditions and most often Indian people. Western versions are very different and lack much of the supporting spirituality, mindset, awareness, and practices true to the original.[139] That said, both Eastern and Western versions of these practices are effective for a variety of purposes, and people with lots of trapped emotions may need a trauma-informed version of yoga or meditation to be able to handle the emotions that arise. For everyone else though, consider supporting the creators of these practices - that is, seeking out teachers who are not White, are trained from minds familiar with more traditional forms of the practices, or at least give credit to the history of practices now taught. Meditation is explored more deeply in the next chapter.

4.7.4 Friends

Friends who are doing similar work are great to have around. People healing often congregate in personal growth communities such as spiritual groups, addiction support groups, meditation circles, yoga, art or music festivals, and the like - establishing a friendship with one of these people may be easiest by going to special day-long or weekend retreats. You might also find them by creating a self-help book club that reads empowering literature and discusses it weekly in person or through video chat. Surround yourself with encouraging people who love what you love and are supportive of your passions. More about making friends is covered in Section 14.1.

You can also ask for support on social media. Just be sure that this is not a passive-aggressive swing at friends you felt have wronged you. That means no belittling others and being careful about sharing inaccurate stories created in your suffering. Remember that you are not the center of the universe and that everyone has their own struggles and distractions they are facing. State specifically what you are feeling and wanting. While this can be a very serious, vulnerable, and authentic share, it may sometimes be more productive if you can make it funny and playful, or just neutral. Each direction will attract a different response and group of people. I've personally noticed that being vulnerable can be quite cathartic and start some really sincere conversations. Then again, the more fun and playful posts tend to attract more connections. Just try to steer clear of anything along the lines of "everyone has abandoned me" or "no one likes me."

4.7.5 Co-Counseling
There is also the option of establishing a co-counseling relationship. Co-counseling is a form of DIY therapy in which two people switch between being the *client* and the *counselor*. The client primarily directs the session and can ask for anything within reason including touch or simply being witnessed. The counselor mostly provides a safe space for the client with active listening, reflecting in summary what the client said, and asking open-ended questions. Sessions typically last anywhere from 15 minutes to an hour, with a short break before switching roles. There can even be three or four people in a group taking turns in the role of client. You can learn co-counseling through books and online or in-person classes. Co-counseling has several great benefits including learning how to empathetically support others and allowing you to receive as much therapy as you want for free. You can establish co-counseling relationships with friends, through your co-counseling classes, or by asking in mental health forums and support groups. Make sure that you create a consistent schedule for these appointments, as otherwise, it is unlikely that you'll utilize this resource.

4.7.6 Life Coaches
Some people benefit from having a life coach for learning skills to succeed in life and keep on track with their goals. Typically a life coach helps you achieve various personal and professional goals, whereas a therapist works on your mental health and past, but the roles can get blurry. Life coaches tend to be more direct and open than therapists are, but there is also quite a lot more variability between how different life coaches operate compared to therapists. This is because while some life coaches become certified through a training program, no formal education is required. Life coaches do sometimes benefit people more than therapists do, but they may charge considerably more than therapists and do not accept insurance.

4.7.7 Animal Companions
Animals can help you rebuild socialization, regulate your nervous system, and experience love. For animals, I think that dogs are the most beneficial because

they closely emulate human relationships. They bond deeply with their caregiver and protest if they are not feeling safe, nourished, or taken on walks. Not only are they lovely companions, they also force you to go outside and get exercise. Even more, they give purpose to your existence and provide a great excuse to be in spaces that might otherwise cause you anxiety. That said, dogs can require a lot of responsibility. Cats are probably the next best option, but people also enjoy rabbits, hamsters, snakes, birds, and so on. There are also horse therapy programs and many volunteer opportunities in animal shelters.

4.7.8 A Good Therapist
For all the reasons that I think the therapy industry is problematic, it is possible to find a good therapist and is an important step for many people attempting to address their trapped emotions. This is especially true for people who grew up in a dysfunctional family or have attachment wounds. A therapist can showcase what a stable and trusting relationship looks like and help identify healthier friends and romantic partners. They can also reflect the way your body moves as information for your trapped emotions. Their regularity and support provide a certain level of unconditional love and emotional regulation for the client. Over time through self-reflection and relational support, a therapist helps rebuild basic interpersonal and self-regulation skills that may have been missed growing up. Many therapists accept insurance or sliding scale payments if you ask. Beyond finding a therapy modality that fits your personal healing needs, you can determine to stick with or leave based on three factors:

1. Even before meeting up, interview your potential therapist and ask them specific questions related to your recovery. If they do not have experience in an area like addiction or PTSD, it's time to move on. It is also ideal if they understand or share your lived experiences in race or gender, or have personally recovered from the thing you are dealing with.
2. After six weeks, does the therapist feel like a trusted friend that you are comfortable with and glad to see? Or is there the potential for this to develop? Feeling safe is one of the most important factors in a beneficial therapeutic relationship. This includes the therapist's personality as well as the space that they meet you in.
3. Has the therapist been meaningfully helpful or insightful? If not, it's probably time to try someone else.

Naturally, each person will form a relationship with their therapist differently, and it may take some people ten to twenty sessions, if not longer, to form a trusting connection.[132L] I even had a therapist I didn't like at all because of how emotionally rigid she was, but that ended up being my friend's favorite therapist. Some people will find single-session therapists beneficial as well, as they may give you helpful resources, tools, and advice much faster than a traditional therapist would. Follow your feelings and know that there are many options out there if one person does not work out.

If you are a therapist reading this, consider upgrading your practice by reading *The Wounded Healer* by Omar Reda, *Trauma Stewardship* by Laura van Dernoot Lipsky, and *The Practitioner's Guide to the Science of Psychotherapy* by Richard Hill and Matthew Dahlitz. Episode 170 of the *Therapist Uncensored Podcast* with Dr. Laurel Parnell also has a great commentary on adapting therapy techniques to the cultures of various groups.

4.8 False Self-Help

The world has become inundated with self-help information, but not all of it is very useful. Even when it is, if a technique is not taught or used correctly, then the benefits won't be experienced beyond temporary relief or a placebo effect. At its worst, self-help and pseudoscience can reinforce your suffering and promote escapism. Some people use self-care as an excuse to never challenge themselves in being vulnerable. Meditation practices can be used to dissociate and ignore dealing with your problems and the suffering in the world. Astrology can be used to discriminate against others and limit what you think you are capable of. Toxic positivity and spiritual bypassing can be used to blame others for your hurtful words and actions.

Most spiritual and religious practices like Christianity promise to alleviate suffering in one form or another but may do so through guilt, shame, intolerance, or escapism. Furthermore, spirituality and religion tend to be best at helping a person change their story, but may not be the best at helping a person create a safe space, release their emotions, or alter unhealthy behaviors. Any of these modalities can aid in a person's healing, but whether or not they will help address your specific problems is fairly random and you have to be careful with how you are using them.

For example, a popular tool people use is *manifesting reality*, even though manifestations can increase anxiety and depression.[84] This might involve repeating "I will be rich" while visualizing that event. According to the mental health treatment center, *Newport Institute*, manifestations may make you neglect difficult feelings, believe that you should have complete control over your thoughts, that negative thoughts will always come true, blame yourself for the outcome of a situation, and avoid taking practical action to improve your life. Done properly though, parts of manifestation can be healthy such as visualizing what success looks like, embodying an empowered mindset, and setting the intention of what you want to focus on.

Even science-based methods can be problematic. For instance, when research does not include certain demographics of people, a study is too small, or the methodology is poorly conducted. As previously stated, people also often just focus on a single research study that ignores the whole person. In this way, the application of science can often forget the importance of empathy, compassion, morals, spirituality, and interpersonal connection.

In reading this book you will hopefully be able to distinguish between effective and ineffective strategies for addressing your emotions. Generally, look for research-based approaches that integrate multiple methodologies and treat you as a human being. Be wary of quick fixes or huge upfront costs. Know that many therapists are unskilled or incompatible with your specific problems. There are lots of options though with any type of self-help, so keep trying until you find something that feels safe and uplifting. If you do not start seeing results, try something else.

4.9 Basic Self-Care

Stress, anxiety, depression, and other feelings take over your life in ways that prevent you from regulating your mood and energy. While these forms of suffering may control your life from a subconscious place, you can consciously apply certain techniques to regain some of your power. Calming your emotions also has the added benefit of calming those around you.

Most often these skills will help decrease the intensity of stress, anxiety, sadness, and anger. While they may be highly beneficial for dealing with depression as well, please keep in mind the many dietary, chemical, hormonal, and nutrient sources of depression as mentioned in this book's medical disclaimer. Some forms of trapped emotions also make it difficult to be aware of stress, so it can be important to establish a basic self-care routine that regularly calms your nervous system at specific times of the day or week. Self-care is a dedicated practice that creates resilience to difficulty and helps regulate your nervous system after an emotion arises or you have a stressful experience.

This self-care list is quite long, but of these, getting enough sleep, nutrients, social time, safety, exercise, time in nature, and mindfulness meditation with breathing are often the most impactful. You can abbreviate this list with the acronym **MENDSSS** (**M**indfulness, **E**xercise, **N**ature, **D**iet, **S**afety, **S**ocialize, **S**leep). These are covered below, but if nothing else, you should figure out how to regularly get better sleep. To help you decide which strategies to utilize, you can rate your current emotional intensity from 1-10 and then ask yourself, "How can I decrease this number?" When one thing works a little, you might then try another strategy to get your score down even more. This will become easier or even intuitive as you see what is effective for a given situation. You can add these to your *mental map* as discussed in Section 3.3.

Not all of the larger list will be relevant to you and you may learn them before, during, or after your healing process. Just devote yourself to a few that resonate with your needs or interests. Trying to control too many aspects of your life can increase your stress or prevent you from connecting with people, so make sure your routine is actually beneficial! See Chapter 12 if you need help forming new habits or cutting out old ones. Also please remember that not everyone will respond well to some of these protocols and you should talk to your doctor before incorporating them, especially if you have any known health concerns.

4.9.1 Skills
1. **Schedule** - Schedule out your week in advance, filling it with a balance of work, play, socializing, healing work, and relaxation. If you have too much open space in your life, start a project or join a group. Prioritize a minimum of 15 minutes a day to the techniques discussed in this book, especially in the morning or before going to sleep. Participate in at least one activity around other people outside your house. If you are struggling to start a project or healthy behavior, split it into smaller tasks and get specific about each part. I personally love my weekly paper planner and crossing things off along the way, but some people benefit from an electronic calendar.
2. **Create systems** – Set up systems for your success. Make your self-care options visible and know your *mental map* for coping with triggers as they arise. Find online groups, friends, or therapists who you can reach out to any time for support instead of engaging in addictive behaviors. Have healthy meals ready to eat. Join activity groups that make you feel obligated to get out of your house.
3. **NVC** - Learn how to use Nonviolent Communication (NVC) to settle conflicts and identify your needs. This is covered in Chapter 8.
4. **Journal** - Start journaling regularly, especially to sort out your problems and emotions. Unlike thoughts that easily repeat over and over again, written words are concrete and can be built upon to explore an

idea rather than flounder in it.
5. ***Science*** - Understand the science behind why something is healthy or not healthy to help get past the flavor, discomfort, or general desire for a thing.
6. ***Habits*** - Learn how to form and deform habits as covered in Section 12.1.
7. ***Useful information*** - Ask yourself if you are simply consuming new knowledge that you will quickly forget or that will stress you out. If so, how could you transform that time into space for practicing healing? For instance, instead of listening to an informational podcast or the news, listen to a meditation.

4.9.2 Body
1. ***Breathing*** – Use calming breathing techniques. Breathe in as much air as you can, deep and slow, through the nose, into the belly, then release it outward at equal timing.[198] Breathing is one of the few things that allow us to consciously control the part of the nervous system tied to our emotions.[97R] It also lowers your heart rate, which improves resilience to depression.[216] This is especially powerful when we intentionally focus on the full sensation of the breath as explored in Chapter 5. Since the breath is always with us, I often use controlled breathing as my first tactic for dealing with overwhelming emotions and stress.
2. ***Sleep*** - Get enough sleep by limiting screen exposure at night, eating your final meal several hours before bed, sleeping on a decent mattress, blocking out all light with a sleep mask or curtains, reducing your stress, and burning off excess energy by exercising during the day at least 6 hours before bed. Avoid caffeine, THC, and alcohol, at least anytime after the morning. Create a quiet space by using earplugs, white noise, or a fan. Keep your room at 60 to 67° Fahrenheit.[192] 7 to 9 hours of sleep a day is ideal, but you can also incorporate napping into your routine. Lost sleep negatively impacts the body in ways that you cannot make up for later on in the week. Sleep apnea is also a common condition that interrupts sleep, so consider getting tested if these suggestions do not improve your wakefulness. If your thoughts are loud, do a small activity in dim lighting like reading instead of fighting them. Exposing yourself directly to 10 to 30 minutes of natural light shortly after you wake up will help set your sleep rhythm for the rest of the day.[82] Sleeping and getting quality

sleep are two different things as many substances can disrupt the different components of sleep.[72] Many sleep supplements such as melatonin and valerian have very little evidence showing that they work. Consider getting a sleep tracker that can record your sleep cycles. Read *Why We Sleep* by Dr. Matthew Walker.

3. ***Exercise*** - Exercise for at least 30 minutes each day, preferably with something that gets your heart pumping and makes you break a sweat.[36] Team exercise is especially potent as it helps motivate you to be consistent and acts as a social outlet. Even a 5-minute walk is quite beneficial though, so start where you can. Generally, the more you exercise, the more you decrease your risk of diseases later in life, and the more you increase your lifespan and mood. We evolved with exercise as a natural part of our day, so it is a vital aspect of the human body fully functioning. I've even benefited from just doing 30 seconds of jumping up and down swinging my arms when in an emotionally tumultuous space. Transform your feelings into motion!

4. ***Inflammatory foods*** - Avoid or limit foods and medications that inflame your body. These include bread, dairy, sugar, alcohol, excessive salt, and fried foods. Overeating or eating foods you are allergic to can also cause inflammation.

5. ***Anti-inflammatory foods*** - Eat nutritious and anti-inflammatory foods. Fish oil (omega-3 fatty acid with DHA and EPA), zinc, and vitamin B12 are common deficiencies great for helping treat depression. Two to four grams of omega-3 fatty acid a day seems ideal for optimizing health.[73]

6. ***Gut health*** - Eat foods that support good gut bacteria such as fiber, fish, nuts, fruit, colorful vegetables, prebiotics, and fermented foods which are refrigerated and not made with vinegar.[189] Address conditions like irritable bowel syndrome (IBS) that interrupt digestion and increase the risk of depression.[20,96]

7. ***Chemical tests*** - See a naturopath and get a nutrient and hormone test. Most doctors do not order tests that are extensive enough to show deficiencies or absorption problems caused by poor gut health or genetic abnormalities.[117] For instance, some people have a genetic error that prevents them from breaking *folic acid* down into *L-methylfolate*, which then results in treatment-resistant depression.

8. ***Nutrient deficiencies*** - According to naturopathic doctor Maria Shaflender, all mental health conditions have a nutrient deficiency attached to them - while it may not be the main cause, addressing the

deficiency may help other conditions which are causing you stress. For instance, depression is frequently associated with several deficiencies, such as Vitamin D, that do not help treat the depressive symptoms but are still good to supplement for the functions they do benefit.[129]

9. **Nutrient sources** - Ideally get your nutrients directly from whole foods, but supplement if necessary. Keep in mind that supplement absorption varies widely depending on what the vitamin or mineral is compounded with, so do your research. Multivitamins often use the cheapest and least absorptive compounds. Note also that even whole foods may be lacking in nutrients if the soil they were grown in is deficient. Check out <https://examine.com/> for comparisons and research on different nutrients and supplements.

10. **Cannabis dangers** - Avoid consuming cannabis regularly, especially before the age of 25 when your brain is developing the most.[212] While used by some people to treat anxiety and depression, regular cannabis use (two or more times per week) is actually associated with increases in anxiety and depression as well as some cognitive decline. It is still uncertain if this is true only for THC-heavy strains or all strains.

11. **Touch** - Get healthy consensual touch with hugs, cuddling, sex, or petting animals - platonic touch is often most easily found in dance, acroyoga, and spiritual communities. As family therapist Virginia Satir says, "We need four hugs a day for survival. We need eight hugs a day for maintenance. We need 12 hugs a day for growth." This is why normalizing platonic touch with friends and family is so important. I find that longer and tighter hugs are most beneficial for me. Hugging yourself or a pillow may also be comforting, especially when paired with affirmations.[231] Alternatively, try using a weighted blanket or large stuffed animal.

12. **Blocking sounds** - Use white noise, a fan, earbuds, or bone conduction headphones if you are stressed by sounds in your home or out and about.

13. **Chronic illness** - Find ways to alleviate or cure your chronic illnesses and conditions. As many doctors are not aware of effective protocols for certain people, Tony Robbins collected a vast trove of emerging and time-tested treatments in his book, *Life Force*. In general though, changing your exercise, diet, mindset, and sleep routines can have a huge impact. Healing trapped emotions also often helps and may be at the root of some chronic illnesses.

14. **Calming sounds** - Listen to calming music and sounds such as lo-fi, classical, nature clips, or a voice you find soothing. Alternatively, listen to music or motivational speakers you find uplifting or cathartic.
15. **Dance** - Connecting with a dance group can be a great community to create friendships, get platonic touch, and reconnect with your body. I especially like ecstatic dance spaces for being improvisational, sober, and silent.
16. **Singing** - Find a space away from others or in your car and sing loudly whatever comes to mind.
17. **SAD** - Especially for people who experience *seasonal affective disorder* (SAD) during the Winter months, socialize and get outside more or purchase a light therapy lamp or an ultraviolet B (UVB) light. Listen to podcast episode 68 of the Huberman Lab for specifics.[82]
18. **Health** - Discover a healthy lifestyle, whatever that means for you personally. Avoid the stress of becoming militant about only eating "healthy" food though - continue enjoying your treats, sweets, and comfort foods within the range of what feels good.
19. **Massage** - Get a massage. For people with trapped emotions causing sensitivity to touch, finding someone trained in trauma-informed massage may help re-introduce touch more safely.
20. **Hormones** - Remember that everyone, regardless of their sex, has hormonal fluctuations that decrease their tolerance to stress. Testosterone is lowest each evening and estrogen's most pronounced shift is monthly - sometimes you just need to sleep or give it a few days for the hormones to rebalance themselves.
21. **Sauna** - Sauna four or more times a week for at least 20 minutes at 170°F or hotter.[73]
22. **Intentional stress** - Intentionally expose your body to short periods of stress as explored later in this chapter.

4.9.3 Mind

1. **Mindfulness** - Learn a form of meditation or exercise that incorporates mindfulness such as yoga, tai chi, or qigong. If these feel intense, seek out a group that is trauma-informed and understands that some people need to go very slowly when exploring movement and breathing so as not to become triggered by past physical abuses. If you choose an activity, try committing to doing it at least two to four times a week. The best benefits of meditation are seen by doing it for at least 13 minutes daily for 8 weeks.[11] That said, you may have to

build up to these numbers, so start with whatever feels manageable to you, even if that is just a couple minutes once a week. More about meditation is covered in Chapter 5.
2. **Socialize** - Go socialize or put yourself in a social environment. This can be in a gym, dance, open mic, support group, or through a sponsor or fellow member found in a Twelve Step program. You can also ask for affirmations about yourself or hugs.
3. **Nature** - Get into nature or at least outside into natural light. The fewer signs of humanity there are though, the better. Even just laying under a tree and staring up into the canopy of leaves is calming.[248] In one study, veterans with PTSD taken out camping in nature for a week experienced a 30% reduction in symptoms.[248] If nature is limited around where you live, decorate your space with house plants, hang up art of plants, and watch nature documentaries. Learn how to propagate houseplants with cuttings from a branch. Growing a garden can also be quite therapeutic.
4. **Calming environments** – Beyond nature, place yourself in environments that calm you down. Some ideas include having good lighting, warmth, quiet, loved ones, and no stressful people.
5. **Do nothing** – Especially for people who are constantly busy, it is important to periodically stop and do nothing. Stare out the window. Look at some trees. Let your mind wander. Give yourself space to enjoy your alone time and not be productive. Practice JOMO, the *joy of missing out*. Connect your success to your well-being instead of what you accomplish. Keeping too rigid of a self-care routine can become exhausting and counter-productive. Check in with what you need right now. The Dutch practice this concept in what they refer to as *Niksen*.[258]
6. **Self-affirmation** - Use self-affirmation by reminding yourself of what your strengths are and what core personality traits you pride yourself in upholding, such as courage or dedication.[233]
7. **Secure attachment** - Establish at least one securely attached connection that you are not anxious around or avoidant of. This may start off being an animal or plant but ideally can be a human connection (see Chapter 14).
8. **Give** - Volunteer for a cause or give a gift to a person you care about for a burst of joy that will last longer than just giving to yourself.[34,8] That is, so long as you already have your basic needs met. Gifts can include things like funny memes, money, food, or an expression of

gratitude. More tips for creating happiness are covered in Section 13.12.
9. ***Calm spaces*** - Seek out a calming environment or just take a break.
10. ***Curiosity*** - Approach everything with curiosity – why is this thought appearing? Why do I get into these kinds of relationships? Why is this so distressing? Why did this argument come up? Curiosity leads to developing a growth mindset that allows for change to happen.
11. ***Novelty*** - Have novel experiences.[107] Keep life interesting by traveling, visiting new places, or trying new activities. Experiencing nature is also great because it is never quite the same.
12. ***Beyond you*** - Believe in something other than or greater than yourself such as a community, religious or spiritual pathway, activist cause, or animal companion.
13. ***Good memories*** - Recall the positive and beautiful moments of your life. You can assist your memory by writing down your good memories and storing them in a box, or keeping a file folder of photographs with faces of friends and good times.
14. ***Pause your media consumption*** - Do a digital detox as explored in Section 12.2.
15. ***Mindfully consume empowering media*** – Music, movies, TV, art, informational guides, and fiction can be empowering and fun if they are balanced with building a healthy life. I love fantasy, cartoons, comics, and video games, but consuming more than an hour or two of them a day goes from nourishing fun to escapism.
16. ***No news*** - Stop consuming all news media, or at least only consuming news that you are going to do something about.
17. ***No social media*** - Limit your social media usage, delete it altogether, or only use it for events and messaging friends.
18. ***Laughter*** - Laugh by watching something funny, creating a joke, making faces in the mirror, or drawing something silly.
19. ***Journal*** - Journal to sort out your thoughts and emotions.
20. ***Gratitude*** - Write three things you are grateful for each day, or even just three things that are going right, even mundane things like air existing.
21. ***Creativity*** - Express yourself creatively - draw, paint, dance, garden, build a house, or write a story.
22. ***Relax*** - Relax and enjoy one of your hobbies. If life is especially overwhelming, consume media to dissociate from the intense feelings

until you can stabilize or reach out to an ally. Just be careful not to allow this to become an addiction and know that there are often more effective ways to regulate your nervous system.
23. **Suicidal ideations** - If you start having suicidal ideations, know that these intense feelings will pass with time and can be remedied with some of the techniques throughout this book. If you need support call the National Suicide Hotline at 800-273-8255. You can also call or text 988.

4.10 Self-Care For Oppressed Communities

People who face discrimination have some special considerations for bolstering their self-care and resilience. This is because experiences of discrimination and the witnessing of discrimination are built into the very fabric of society and are a daily occurrence for certain demographics of people. These may create trapped emotions in individuals, or just make life more difficult.

Discrimination is the act of treating two groups of people differently in a way that causes harm to one of those groups. This may include violence, verbal attacks, leaving people out, unbalanced hiring practices, harmful stereotypes, or viewing people as less than another group. Oppression then is similar, but specifically is acted out by those with more power or privilege upon those with less power or privilege. While there is a difference in that everyone can discriminate but not everyone can oppress, this book uses these words interchangeably with the play of power in mind.

The oppression that many groups face is part of a system intentionally created to treat certain people as less than human. It makes life harder, increasing the risk of emotions becoming trapped in the body with devastating results to mental and physical health. People who have historically faced discrimination may also be more sensitive to certain triggers due to ancestral trapped emotions as previously mentioned in Section 2.6. Dealing with these epigenetic changes is explored in Section 17.19.

4.10.1 Disclaimers
This is a very sensitive topic, and as a White man, I want to acknowledge that I can never fully understand the lived experiences of many oppressed communities and am no expert on these topics. However, as I have a diverse readership and the topic of oppression is completely ignored in most mental health literature, I felt it important to include. Research was conducted through books written by authors belonging to several races, genders, and sexualities. This includes *My Grandmother's Hands* by Resmaa Menakem, *Black Fatigue*

by Mary-Frances Winters, *Native* by Kaitlin B. Curtice, *Healing Racial Trauma* by Sheila Wise Rowe, *How To Be An Antiracist* by Ibram X. Kendi, *Patriarchy Blues* by Frederick Joseph, *Trans Like Me* by CN Lester, and *The Unapologetic Guide To Black Mental Health* by Rheeda Walker.

Please keep in mind that this section summarizes information that requires many books to fully explore, so see the materials I reference for a deeper exploration of these topics. Considering the diversity of ideas on how to tackle oppression in society, every resource also has at least some criticisms, so read reviews to get a more complete perspective of the content. There do however seem to be some generally agreed-upon ideas. Debate exists around whether or not "White people" should be capitalized, but following that it refers to a specific demographic of people who have benefited from racism, it will be capitalized within this book.

Methods of creating social change and uprooting oppressive patterns in oneself are explored in Chapters 15 and 16. If you feel like something is missing, it may be further elaborated on later, but again, this is an introductory guide. I also cover most of the specific tactics explored in this section in more depth elsewhere in the book such as on mindfulness, identifying what you can control, accepting your body, and changing your internal story.

4.10.2 Forms Of Discrimination
Many forms of discrimination exist, but some people are impacted by it more than others. In the United States, discrimination most negatively impacts people along the lines of race, gender, sexuality, ability, religion, and income. This includes Black people, Indigenous people, people of color, people living with a disability, women, poor people, non-binary people, and the LGBTQ+ community, especially trans people. When a person belongs to more than one of these identities, it increases the likelihood they will experience discrimination. When combined with a person's privileges, Kimberlé Crenshaw calls this *intersectionality*.[195,89]

A White homosexual woman is oppressed along the lines of gender and sexuality but is privileged along the lines of race. A rich Black man with a disability is oppressed along the lines of race and ability, but privileged with income and gender. Someone who grows up with a healthy family has more privilege than someone who has trapped emotions from growing up with an unavailable, abusive, or dysfunctional family.

Discrimination is maintained at the individual and societal level through things like culture, law enforcement, government, capitalism, media, and ignorance. White, cisgender, able-bodied, rich, and heterosexual men benefit the most from the oppression of others and also have the most power to change it.[120A] *Cisgender* means that a person identifies with the gender they were assigned at birth. In contrast, *transgender* applies to people who identify with a gender other than the one they were assigned at birth. Non-binary people are those who do not identify with any gender.

We'll discuss ways in which people with more power and privilege, particularly those who are White, can help take a stand against discrimination later, especially in Chapters 15 and 16. In his book, *Patriarchy Blues*, Frederick Joseph makes the case that even if you are oppressed in one way, it is your moral duty to stand up for those who lack the privileges that you have.[89] While discrimination needs to be tackled with the help of many hands, there are many tactics people facing oppression can use to improve their situation.

4.10.3 Community

Find a community of people that shares your identity, culture, and history, and also celebrates your existence. This is by far the most important factor for improving mental health conditions for people facing discrimination.[186,147,24,118,103] Come out of isolation; you need allies. This might come from, for example, support groups, elders, reservations, *Historically Black Colleges and Universities*, drag shows, queer bars, or spiritual and religious communities. In *Trans Like Me*, CN Lester shares that at least during childhood, family support of trans identity is more important than community support for positive mental health outcomes.[103] If there is only a small number of people sharing your identity where you live, connect with people online, with other people who face oppression, or with people who treat you well and listen to your needs. You can also create your own support or interest group that shares your identity, such as in addiction recovery or a book club.

To expedite your healing, finding community may also involve, at least temporarily, removing yourself from commonly oppressive forces such as White people and men. Ideally, as you create more resilience and heal some of your trapped emotions, you can engage with allies from these groups who have educated themselves on your oppression and do their work to repair any triggering behaviors they might act out. Please see Section 2.4 for how this book defines *resilience* in relation to trapped emotions.

It is not your responsibility to educate people ignorant of your history and the discrimination you face.[195] However, as Dr. Anton Treuer says with his work teaching people about Native Americans, it is helpful when you can, but it should not come at the cost of your well-being.[118] You could also ask people to act as allies by educating themselves or supporting you in becoming more financially or emotionally secure. As we will explore later in the book, part of fighting discrimination requires healing the relationship between cultures that are often oppressed and those that oppress.[120] You are not required to take on that role though, heal and open up at your own pace.

4.10.4 Spirituality And Religion

For those like Black and Indigenous people who have a history of belonging to a spiritual or religious community, health outcomes seem to further improve by engaging with those spaces.[147,186,24] Rheeda Walker explains that having a higher power helps a person no longer feel responsible for everything that happens to them. As previously mentioned, it also creates a strong sense of community. The faith usually has to represent a person's cultural heritage or predominantly be attended and led by people with a shared identity.

Frederick Joseph does point out in his book, *Patriarchy Blues*, that many religious and spiritual groups reinforce forms of discrimination such as sexism, homophobia, and racism. It is important to either find a more inclusive faith or work to uproot these practices in your place of worship. The book *Native* by Kaitlin B. Curtice explores ways of transforming some of these problematic power structures, connecting with your people's traditional spiritual beliefs, and discovering your identity.

4.10.5 Establish Identity

Become secure and proud of your identity by developing a positive sense of who you are. Come out to your friends and family if they are supportive of LGBTQ+ identities.[149] Transition genders.[103,193] Label yourself with your race such as Native American or Black. As a Black person, connect with your African roots.[186] As an Indigenous person, learn about your Native American history and traditions during and before the colonization of the United States.[173] Your heritage is not just slavery or colonization.[186]

It is complicated who is accepted into a gender or racial identity. If some people do not accept you into a particular group, find others who do based around a shared sense of culture, interest, or oppression. That, or fight for the rules to change, such as what percentage of blood a person is required to have to be officially accepted into certain Native American tribes. Anton Treuer explores this in his book, *Everything You Wanted To Know About Indians But Were Afraid To Ask*.[118,173]

More and more people are accepting that racial and gender identity do not have to be defined by your hobbies, clothing, or having a high percentage of blood from a particular race.[88] For example, it could instead be defined by growing up in a particular culture and facing discrimination along the lines of race. Someone saying "That isn't something that Black people do" or "That's a White person thing" may hurt a person's mental health by barring them from certain activities while simultaneously reinforcing White power. Being forced to comply with the language, beliefs, or interests of a more privileged group will negatively impact mental health.[186] On the other hand, it is perfectly fine to enjoy whatever hobbies and interests will benefit you or you feel drawn toward like going on hikes, seeing a therapist, or watching cartoons.

4.10.6 Celebrate Identity
Celebrate your identity.[24] Know your history before your people faced oppression, but also know the figures who have fought valiantly for your freedom or taken on significant roles in the arts and sciences. Learn about how to cook the foods your people historically have eaten, play their music, sing their songs, dance their dances, and dress up with their clothing and hairstyles. Speak their language or accent as something equal to any other language or accent.[186] Rename yourself or be given a name that connects more deeply with your gender or racial identity. Read books and watch shows created by and featuring characters that you identify with. Explore your cultural identity further with new iterations of music, food, and dress that incorporate the modern world. This does not mean you deny your personal interests, or the advancement of culture, but perhaps this celebration of identity is something that helps you connect with your community and ancestors a few times a year.

4.10.7 Self-Care
Practice the self-care skills that I share in this chapter and the next.[120,186,147] Self-care can be a radical act, especially when you have felt obligated to participate in activist spaces or constantly speak up against oppression. Find the belief that you deserve rest and relaxation, that it is an ethical obligation to yourself. Break the idea that you always have to present as "strong" or unmoved by upsetting things. The discrimination you face is hurtful and it may be necessary to take time off to recover from triggering news or oppressive actions from others. If you need support, Rheeda Walker points out that going to the doctor or seeing a therapist is not just a White person thing, but it is important to find health professionals who either share your identity or at least are culturally competent. Stop consuming media that constantly portray your identity in a negative light. Get off of social media and news sources that

feed you constant reminders about your oppression. Stop using language and consuming music that preaches anger, violence, and self-hatred.[120]

Resmaa Menakem distinguishes between "clean pain" and "dirty pain." Dirty pain harms others or yourself with anger and violence, while clean pain supports your growth and healing through things like grieving and quitting addictions. Learn breathing techniques and choose self-care over hypervigilance. Take some time in the bathroom, under headphones, or on a walk to create a temporary safe space to decompress intense feelings. Understand your triggers and plan or practice how you will or will not respond before being confronted by them.[147] Identify how some of your coping mechanisms like media consumption or revenge fantasies may be holding you back from healing and being happy. One study showed that, at least for Black women, avoidant coping strategies like using addictive substances increased depressive symptoms associated with perceived racial discrimination, whereas solution-oriented coping like journaling or seeking support helped to relieve those symptoms.[191]

4.10.8 Talk About It

Black children who are *racially socialized* by their parents tend to have better mental health and academic outcomes.[4] Racial socialization involves promoting cultural pride, celebrating history, creating awareness about discrimination and how to cope with it, as well as instilling the belief that even though racism exists, the child can still find success and happiness in the world. On the other hand, convincing your children to mistrust people from other races leads to worse mental health outcomes. Regardless of what messaging you received as a child, you can still practice forms of self-talk to integrate these healthier lessons into your reality. You might also consider talking to your *inner child* about them as discussed in Chapter 10.

4.10.9 Renegotiating Stories

Change your story.[186] Are you trying to control something you cannot control? Identify what you can control. *Microaggressions*, or unconsciously acted out oppressive acts, do happen, but it is important to consider your mood. The more depressed or negative your mood is, the more likely it is that you will perceive something as a microaggression.[108] Was it a racially charged microaggression, or was it someone having a bad day, being introverted, or feeling depressed? Take a break or use some self-care before reacting in a regrettable way.

Identify any ways in which you believe that you are less than another group of people and establish how that simply is not true. Find the story of how resilient your people are, or of the great accomplishments and wisdom within your ancestral roots. Trust that your ancestors are proud of you for relaxing and enjoying yourself. Write out your strengths and ways in which you have overcome obstacles. Know that being discriminated against has given you empathy and awareness to what a healthier society could look like. Understand how White supremacy and privilege harm both privileged and White people as explored in Chapters 15 and 16.

If experiences of discrimination cause you to believe you are worthless or less than others, can you instead focus on the objective truth, such as that someone ignorant or hateful said something that you and your peers do not acknowledge as truth? When seeking support or attempting to change institutionalized oppression, keep in mind what a person can and cannot do; an impoverished White person and a White corporate CEO have entirely different types of power to enact change.[147,195] Use the tips in Chapter 6 to renegotiate self-limiting beliefs, and Section 13.3 to understand what you can and cannot control.

4.10.10 Internalized Oppression
People who are oppressed may still discriminate against others or reinforce their own suffering. For example, women can uphold the power held by men, and Black people can judge other Black people based on their hobbies and how light or dark their skin is. Ibram X. Kendi says that calling all White people bad does not help dismantle oppressive institutions.[93] That said, White people, and especially men, are historically the root of racism and have the most power to change discriminatory institutions. These topics and methods of uprooting discriminatory patterns in oneself are explored further in Chapters 15 and 16.

4.11 Increasing Your Income

The notion that money does not equate to well-being is an absolute lie.[95] A lot of people are unable to leave stressful situations due to a lack of money. Money is time, health, social activities, travel, rest, stability, political power, and so much more. Unless an addiction to money prevents you from having meaningful relationships, or you are unhappy in your job, then earning more money is generally a good thing. Unfortunately, systems of greed, discrimination, and capitalism prevent many people from climbing any kind of income ladder. We'll talk about dismantling capitalism later, but I want to provide some basic advice for becoming more economically resourced, whether or not you have the privilege to switch careers.

4.11.1 Start A Side Hustle Or Solo Business
Independent, local, and solo businesses are becoming really popular and don't have to require a lot of money to start. You might even already have the supplies needed to do basic yard maintenance or house cleaning, or maybe your city has a Saturday Market to sell products at. Open-air markets are a great place to gather ideas about the types and qualities of products that sell well. If one doesn't exist yet, starting an artisan's or farmer's market can help bolster your local economy and create a great community hub. Etsy, Shopify, and eBay have helped start millions of successful online businesses too.

Many cities have a *Small Business Development Center* (SBDC) through the *U.S. Small Business Administration* (SBA). This group provides free business counseling. There are often similar groups for aspiring women, Black, and other marginalized business owners too. For instance, Shopify teamed up with Operation Hope to help start a million new Black-owned businesses by 2030. Search online for these programs. Similarly, the UpFlip podcast and Youtube channel provide practical strategies for turning minuscule startup investments into big earnings. If you know what you want to start, there are also free business plans online that will help guide you through the process.

There is also Creative Live, which makes business or art school for many people entirely unnecessary. For less than the cost of a single college class, you can get a year's subscription which has immensely more practical advice for aspiring creatives and business owners. I strongly suggest listening to the founder's podcast as well - Chase Jarvis interviews successful creatives from many fields, providing great insights and inspiration. His book, *Creative Calling*, is helpful for people wanting to get started in a creative profession. More than anything when starting a business, remember that failure is just a form of learning that will help you succeed better in the future and that most "successful" people have failed a lot.

4.11.2 Connect With Community
Living in a community or with friends can save a lot of money. You can share expenses on food, toiletries, gadgets, and utilities. Some places like certain farms even let you work trade for rent. I'll discuss how to create communities in Section 14.5. You can find communities through the *Foundation For Intentional Communities* website <www.ic.org>, farm work trades at the *Worldwide Opportunities on Organic Farms* (WWOOF) website <https://wwoof.net/>, and other international work opportunities at the

Work Away website <www.workaway.info>. The community you choose to live in can also alter your monetary outcome as the number one factor for breaking out of your parent's income class is making friends and allies who are in higher economic classes.[214]

4.11.3 Learn Skilled Trades
While college is not for everyone, may be off-limits due to time or money, and is sometimes a complete scam, there are many one-year or two-year degrees available through community colleges that can lead to immediate jobs on the other end. Apprenticeship positions also exist that may pay for your education and earn you a wage while you learn. Check out <www.coolworks.com> for paid positions with certification training and affordable or free housing. Quite a few scholarships and loans exist as well to help fund your education, especially if you are poor, a person of color, a single parent, or returning as an older student.

4.11.4 Cook At Home
Learn how to cook for yourself and create your own fancy beverages. While many people eat out to save time, you can actually save a lot more time by cooking for yourself. Just cook large batches of food and freeze a portion of it. I boil a whole chicken with sweet potatoes, onion, kale, broccoli, and cauliflower which is good for 3 weeks of lunches. Seasoned with hot sauce and salt before eating with a side of tortilla chips, it's a great combination of health, affordability, tastiness, and laziness. If a proper grocery store is not readily available nearby, there are lots of emerging food delivery options for groceries and meal kits.

4.11.5 Control Your Purchasing And Find Free Things
There are many things people can do without or regulate by creating a monthly "fun budget." For instance, consider cutting out alcohol from your life, buying from a thrift shop instead of new, or putting off purchasing an item for several days to avoid spontaneous money spending. There is also a lot of opportunity for obtaining things for free through online groups, Craigslist, government welfare, and asking friends. You can host clothing swaps, create a communal tool library, or build a culture of borrowing items rather than buying them new.

4.11.6 Vote, Strike, And Unionize
Sometimes your income has to be increased or protected by more radical

means. Getting your co-workers to formally unionize or strike for better working conditions may be essential. Introducing laws or voting for politicians who support rental protections and increasing the minimum wage can help too. Part IV of the book covers tactics for being an effective changemaker.

4.11.7 Read Money Management Books
There are many more strategies for saving money that go beyond the scope of this brief guide. For a deeper look at your finances, I suggest reading alternative money management books like *I Will Teach You To Be Rich* by Ramit Sethi or *A Cat's Guide To Money* by Lillian Karabaic.

4.12 Establishing A Higher Power

Many Twelve Step programs strongly encourage a person to establish a connection to a higher power, whatever that means for them. As previously mentioned, if you dislike this term, you could use *mentor* instead. This relationship is very valuable as it creates a permanent ally to speak with, reminds you that the world is bigger than pain and struggle, and interrupts the hyperfocus often placed on ourselves and our peers. Atheists and people who have suffered religious abuse may struggle in separating this concept from a religious god but know that it does not have to involve any kind of religion or unscientific belief. It also does not mean that you are giving up your power as an individual, but it will help you recognize the things that you need support with or cannot control.

More than anything, a higher power is something you believe can help with your struggles. Your higher power should probably not be any individual living organism like your friend or dog though. Consider things like nature, a community gathering, a support group, the ocean, trees, the universe, a species of animal, or your inner loving parent that we explore in Chapter 10. You can also of course use more traditional monotheistic Gods, polytheistic gods, and spirits.

The truth is that life is unpredictable and people will sometimes let you down. Many of us with trapped emotions have high expectations of others and want to control situations so that we do not become triggered. However, due to the nature of reality, those expectations and desire to control are bound to fail, leading to sadness and anger. Connecting with a higher power will help soften these energies because you are reminded that it is more than your will that determines the events of the world. Your higher power is an anchor you can rely on, even when people disappoint you or things don't quite go your way.

When you are needing direction or company, you can pray to or visit your higher power if it has a physical manifestation in nature or a church. The only necessary thing on your part is to believe that this "entity" has power and is capable of helping you. This may first involve hitting a rock bottom in which you realize you are individually powerless over the circumstances in your life you are attempting to control. That could be a pervasive sense of abandonment, an addiction, dysfunctional parents, or anger. Many people also experience a higher power after using psychedelics, which are discussed in Chapter 11. When first establishing this connection, it is important to regularly make contact to develop a relationship you trust. For me, this meant prioritizing time in nature with trees and attending my support group over making plans with friends or getting lost on the internet.

For those who grew up with family dysfunction, the *Twelve Steps of Adult Children Steps Workbook* can help with connecting to a higher power. However, much of the content is outdated so I recommend using Tony A's Twelve Steps in conjunction with the workbook, especially for anything past the third step. You can find a breakdown of Tony A's Twelve Steps by searching online. The concept of a higher power may also make more sense later in Part II as we cover "imaginary" friends and the inner selves. While connecting to a higher power is not necessary, it will make many parts of your recovery easier.

People dedicated to a religious or spiritual community are typically happier largely because of the social connections they create.[109] That said, you do need to be careful in regard to certain spiritual and religious traditions which are unhealthy or based on power, shaming, and control. Many groups also preach hateful messages to spread their distorted agendas. Your higher power should be a loving one who cares about you and knows forgiveness.

4.13 Medicines

Many medicines exist that can help relieve the intense emotions that difficult life experiences or brain chemistries create. Medications can treat things such as anxiety, depression, bipolar, and ADHD, especially when combined with other lifestyle changes and therapy. It is nothing to be ashamed of if you use medication to regulate your mental health, especially as it may be the easiest or only way to feel stable or focused enough to deal with your trapped emotions. Sometimes medication alone can relieve a person's emotional struggles as well, so long as they can find a good dosage or regimen when taking it.

Medications can help with trapped emotions, but there are some important things to keep in mind. First, I want to remind readers that this book and the following information is not about a person's natural biochemistry, but instead the suffering caused by difficult past experiences. According to Dr. Bessel Van Der Kolk, "Drugs cannot 'cure' trauma; they can only dampen the expression of a disturbed physiology."[97G] Some medicines can interfere with being fully in touch with your emotions, which is important for releasing trapped emotions. You want the medication to take you out of emotional extremes, but not so far that you become unable to experience your emotions. The benefits of most medicines are also temporary, ending soon after you stop taking them.

Since doctors may prescribe medication without therapy or knowing the source of a person's suffering, people become reliant on the medication and never treat the root cause of their behaviors and emotions. This is even more problematic as doctors frequently misdiagnose bipolar as depression, even though antidepressants are ineffective or even dangerous for people with bipolar.[61] Medications also may cause possible side-effects with energy levels and sex, and sometimes make feelings of anxiety and depression worse. Furthermore, it can take upwards of six weeks to have a positive effect, and that initial positive effect may dissipate within a few months.

Unfortunately, your primary doctor may be ignorant of effective strategies for treating the roots of mental health struggles. For instance, regular exercise is at least as effective as medication for treating most cases of depression.[207] While a doctor can help connect you to some resources, it is up to you to ensure that you receive a proper healing regimen. Medication can help and may be essential for some people, but it is often only needed temporarily or should be paired with many of the other self-care strategies outlined throughout this chapter. On the chemical level, you may actually need to alter your hormone levels or boost up a certain nutrient. If you can, obtain the relevant tests to know what is going on inside of you. If you want to understand different chemical processes in an accessible way, I suggest listening to the *Huberman Lab Podcast* or reading *Tools of Titans* by Tim Ferriss.

Some alternatives to antidepressants exist too. There are fast-acting anti-anxiety medications like *beta blockers* that can be a great middle-ground with a lower risk of addiction or withdrawal symptoms. Emerging medicines like the Stellate Ganglion Block give temporary relief from emotional extremes long enough to allow focus on creating healthy change as well.[138] In the near future, neural implants may be a viable option as well for easily curing treatment-resistant depression.[150] Talk to your doctor about what might work for you.

Herbal alternatives to traditional Western medicine, often with fewer side effects, also exist. These include kava, L-theanine (the active calming component of tea), saffron, ashwagandha, chaga, lion's mane, and St. John's Wort.[78,35,57,165,213] You should still check in with your doctor and review side effects before taking any of these though.

Recent research has shown that improving gut bacteria can help alleviate many mental conditions including anxiety, depression, and even autism.[115] The fastest way to alter this microbiome is through a fecal transplant, but this procedure, while highly promising, is still in development and can be dangerous. Diet impacts the gut as well, although there is still much that is unknown. Current studies show that increased fiber consumption will bolster the numbers of certain gut flora, but eating several servings of low-sugar live fermented foods per day will actually decrease inflammation in the body.[124,76] Both fiber and fermented foods are important for people who have taken antibiotics which destroy all healthy and unhealthy organisms in the gut. While not yet available everywhere in 2023, companies like *Microba* in Australia have begun offering testing for important bacterial strains alongside guidelines on how to correct your balance.

Another option is with substances that are still illegal in many parts of the world and potentially dangerous to use but are shown to be quite effective in studies for addressing trapped emotions. Ketamine may be able to help a person put a difficult experience into context as something that happened in the past rather than continuing to happen today.[148,162] Microdosing small quantities of psychoactive substances such as psilocybin mushrooms and LSD may help with anxiety and depression.[37] When taken in larger doses in a psychedelic-assisted therapy session or properly done in a more casual setting, these substances become one of the most powerful tools to fight against trapped emotions. We will explore psychoactive substances and their risks in Chapter 11.

While technically not medicines, some electrotherapies are showing promise and usually carry few side effects. At least one study has shown that electroconvulsive therapy is more effective than antidepressants for reducing depression and PTSD symptoms.[1] A much lighter electrotherapy known as *transcranial direct current stimulation* (tDCS) is also effective for a wide variety of brain conditions, including reducing symptoms of depression and PTSD.[2] These devices are compact, affordable, and can be used at home. It is unclear how long-lasting these therapies are, and just like medication may be better for managing symptoms while utilizing other strategies. Neurofeedback has also been making a lot of exciting headway as a non-invasive therapy and is discussed in the next chapter.

4.14 Releasing Tension And Correcting Posture

As you learn how to sense your body better throughout this book, you may notice a great amount of tension in your face, shoulders, stomach, and other parts. Often this tension is accompanied by stress, negative emotions, and difficult thoughts.[106C] While emotions often alter our facial expressions, the reverse is also true as facial expressions can dictate emotions.[98] This means that releasing your tension can relieve stress, emotions, and thoughts. Using this technique relies on your personal awareness though, which might not always be present. That's why regular massage, meditation, and various body-focused activities are good to practice.

When I begin feeling overwhelmed, I'll lie down on my bed, close my eyes, and focus into my body. Starting with my face I attempt to release any tension, letting go and melting into my mattress and pillows. Scan your body while checking in with your scalp, brain, forehead, eyes, mouth, jaw, neck, shoulders, arms, hands, fingers, stomach, pelvis, thighs, knees, calves, and feet. You can repeat this scan several times as you become more relaxed. Deep and slow breathing during this exercise will also help.

Researchers have additionally found that slouching your body can increase negative thoughts and the amount of time it takes to recover from the feelings associated with those thoughts.[182] Conversely, a straight posture seems to increase mood recovery beyond what a normal posture can. If I find myself ruminating on negative thoughts after laying down for a period of time, getting up and moving around or going on a walk outside often helps.

4.15 Increasing The Window Of Tolerance To Stress

Your window of tolerance to stress can be bolstered by creating brief periods of self-induced stress while in a safe environment. The body has important chemical reactions which only occur when it is under stress such as working out, fasting, intensely breathing, and exposing oneself to temperature extremes.[73] According to Dr. Andrew Huberman, this helps release stress as well as increases our stress tolerance.[74] When we deliberately expose ourselves to safe stress for short periods, we stop overgeneralizing all stress as dangerous. This rewiring is assisted when a trusted ally is present who helps co-regulate your nervous system and makes you know that you're safe.[245] It also helps to talk about your failures and how you learned from them.[234]

Huberman suggests five minutes a day of *cyclic hyperventilation*, which is intensive breathing, in and out for about a second each, for 25 breaths before exhaling fully and holding for at least 25 seconds, and then repeating. People who experience anxiety or panic attacks, or have heart problems, should not do this. Intense exercises, cold water showers, and ice baths can also help induce a healthy stress response. While cold exposure is normally done for minutes at a time, even 20 seconds in a shower at 49°F can have great therapeutic results.[73] For specifics, check out the Huberman Lab podcast episodes, *Using Deliberate Cold Exposure for Health and Performance* and *Dr. Rhonda Patrick: Micronutrients for Health & Longevity*. Again, cold exposure can be hazardous to your health if done incorrectly so be sure you are checking in with a doctor beforehand.

You can also use mindfulness as explored in Chapter 5 to increase your stress tolerance. With mindfulness, you begin to separate healthy stress from being in danger. You note that you feel uncomfortable but can keep going with your present awareness.[245] You keep in mind that pushing away distress creates distress. Maybe you self-regulate by breathing deeply or taking a little break. In this way, you learn how to stay within your window of tolerance while also challenging yourself. This is the practice of accepting that hard things happen and knowing that even though you might temporarily feel difficult emotions, you can handle them.

4.16 Addressing Shame And Denial

Shame and denial often accompany trapped emotions and prevent you from speaking up about your past experiences. You may believe it is too embarrassing to share, feel as though sharing would break your family's trust, or you blame yourself for not being able to get over something you believe should be insignificant. Being able to acknowledge and talk about your past is often essential for healing though. Breaking out of shame and denial may involve first hearing others sharing similar stories in a support group such as *Adult Children of Alcoholics and Dysfunctional Families*. It could also involve reading accounts in books, educating yourself on the roots of trauma and PTSD, discovering your anger at the people who hurt you, or meeting an ally who is safe enough to share with.

You are not alone, many other people have experienced what you have. Know that your suffering matters, and that when you break the silence, it helps others understand that their pain is deserving of healing too. Of course, this may be upsetting to family or loved ones, and you need to consider the repercussions it may cause. Perhaps you only share your story with people you know are safe, or you feel prepared to talk with and create boundaries with the people who caused you suffering.

***
Chapter Reflections

1. How do you know when you are outside of your window of tolerance? What are the warning signs that you are starting to feel dysregulated or dissociated?
2. How do you stay motivated with intentions, media, and passions?
3. How do you reinforce your suffering?
4. What is your personality like and what do you want to change about it?
5. What activities and spaces make you feel safer?
6. What are some sources of stress you can reduce or cut out of your life?
7. What visualization practices would benefit your healing?
8. Who are some allies or support groups that can help you do this work?
9. What activities help regulate your nervous system, and are there any you would like to try out?
10. How can you incorporate meditation, exercise, nature, healthy eating, socializing, and sleep (MENDSSS) into your daily routine?
11. Have you talked to your doctor about medication options or explored alternatives like improving your gut health and taking plant medicines?
12. Is there a higher power, mentor, or something you can passionately devote yourself to that would help you with your struggles?
13. In what ways do you incorporate healthy stress and vulnerability into your life?
14. How can you increase your window of tolerance to stress?
15. In what ways are you discriminated against or underprivileged?
16. How has oppression hurt your ability to heal from trapped emotions?
17. As someone who experiences oppression, what stories do you tell yourself about what you are capable of, what you are allowed to do, and what you cannot do?
18. What are some communities you can connect with or create that understand your culture and the oppression you face?
19. What is the story of resilience, strength, and hope of your ancestors?

Chapter 5

Learning How To Experience Emotions

5.1 Mindfulness And Reconnecting To The Present, 5.2 Neurofeedback, 5.3 Identifying Emotions, 5.4 Experiencing Emotions, 5.5 Fake It Till You Release It, 5.6 Emotional Mastery, 5.7 Emotional Dysregulation, 5.8 Healthy Angering And Asserting Yourself, 5.9 Awareness Of Thoughts And The Critics

Humans are emotional creatures and the full spectrum of emotions allows us to healthfully experience life. If you avoid difficult emotions like sadness, anger, or fear, it is much harder to experience happiness or love. This requires vulnerability. Emotional energy most often becomes trapped within us when we do not adequately feel the difficult emotions that arise from stressful experiences. This may include things that have happened to us, but also things that have not happened to us, such as not having an available parent or not getting enough quality social time with others. Trapped emotions perpetuate our avoidance of emotions in a self-protective feedback loop.

Expressing emotions releases energy. Without that release, the energy becomes trapped and festers within us. Even just a few seconds of releasing our emotions can move us out of overwhelm and back into a space where stress is manageable. Learning how to mindfully experience emotions is therefore the foundation of healing from many painful experiences. The contents of this chapter explore some of the techniques used in somatic therapy with research partly derived from Peter Levine's books and my experiences with various Buddhist meditation communities. With these, you can learn to fully experience your body and emotions.

There are several reasons why you may have difficulty releasing your emotions:

1. As a child, you were shamed for crying or otherwise told not to. This

can be quite subtle, such as not being consoled or your parents expressing stress whenever you emoted.
2. You do not feel safe enough around your housemates, spouse, co-workers, or friends to express difficult emotions.
3. Culturally you have been told that your gender is not supposed to cry, which is most common for men, or not express anger and assertiveness, which is most common for women.
4. You use various things to dissociate from your feelings including food, media, sex, drugs, medications, or thinking and explaining. Granted, these can also sometimes help a person connect with their emotions when used right.
5. You have been taught to feel your emotions in your body without an emotional release such as with certain mindfulness practices, or you have been taught to have an emotional release without focusing on your emotions.
6. You express emotions in ways that do not actually help you release your internal energy, such as violence or complaining. There are healthy ways to release these that we will cover later.
7. Spiritual teachings, therapy, and cultural ideas have wrongly taught you that you can heal simply by changing how you think. Informational solutions often won't solve your problems, you can only change how you think by first releasing the trapped emotions keeping you stuck.

For people with severe emotional blockages, you may have to use other techniques for releasing trapped emotions before your body will allow you to experience things like happiness, sadness, or anger. A therapist would be very useful for helping determine this. Many people can reconnect with their emotional body first, but others with severe blockages may require using some of the techniques explored in the later chapters. For instance, you may have to share your story with an empathetic listener, remember more of your past, or hear other people telling a story similar to your own in a support group. Peter Levine, the founder of *Somatic Experiencing* therapy, also believes that re-engaging an empowered posture and movement first through activities like stretching, massage, yoga, tai chi, or the suggestions mentioned in Section 4.14 may be essential to accessing emotions and transforming thoughts.[106C]

Some people will also find becoming aware of their bodily sensations too overwhelming. Mindfulness practices can even unlock dormant trapped emotions when a person has experienced life-or-death incidents or abuse in childhood.²²⁵ Be gentle with yourself. If you start feeling overwhelmed with painful emotions or feelings of self-hatred, try oscillating your focus back to a part of your body that feels good or take a break doing something nourishing. You may need to breathe deeply, release some emotions, try again in a few days, or use other techniques throughout the book to tackle your bodily sensations.

As stated in Section 3.5, dissociation happened for a reason. You first need the emotional, physical, mental, and relational resources to handle whatever you could not in the past. That doesn't mean you need to recall in detail what happened, because the memories are already activated in your body and can be worked through with somatic techniques as explored here and in Section 7.1. The goal is to be present with your physical, emotional, and mental worlds.

According to Bessel van der Kolk, yoga is a good alternative to mindfulness meditation and is more effective than medication for people who have PTSD.²⁴¹ As a movement practice, yoga provides a release that simply sitting and observing your sensations does not. While difficult, it shows a person that they are capable of overcoming challenges and teaches that sensations come and go. Ideally, this yoga practice is trauma-informed to help guide you through any difficult emotions that may arise.

Otherwise, you may just be too activated and need a little space from your thoughts before you can handle a sensation. Emphasis on little. A few minutes to an hour of distracting yourself with your favorite show or game can help calm you down a lot. With practice though, you learn to instead meditate, go to a support group meeting, journal, explore nature, visualize uplifting memories or thoughts, release your emotions, or call a friend. If you are ready, you need to attend to the feelings you are experiencing rather than distancing yourself from them.

I am also very easily distracted and staying present requires really specific spaces. Even in spaces that feel safe, I can have some parts of my guard up. Often my focus dissipates if I feel any sense of obligation, hear certain sounds, think I need to act a certain way, am tired, or feel uncomfortable with someone around me. What distracts you?

If you have been avoiding or dissociating from difficult emotions for a long time, take it slow and be sure to regulate your feelings as necessary. Unlocking this aspect of your humanity may initially be overwhelming, but quickly becomes healing. The release of tension, anger, sadness, debilitating anxiety, and the like, into tears or other outlets is very nourishing. Yes, I'm going to teach you how to cry and be angry, and you're going to love it. Let's begin.

5.1 Mindfulness And Reconnecting To The Present

Reconnecting with your emotional self is a practice that can be learned through forms of meditation, including mindfulness. Mindfulness is simply a non-judgmental awareness of what is happening in the present moment. In the mind preoccupied with thoughts of the past or future, these sensations may be muted or quite dull, so you'll need to learn how to see them. Mindfulness practice can also help you celebrate things as mundane as washing the dishes. Most beginning meditation methods focus on the mindfulness of physical sensations, especially the breath. Instead of maintaining continuous focus, the goal is to be able to refocus as you become distracted.[211] Unlike emotions, physical sensations are easily accessed and so are good training for experiencing deeper layers of yourself.

With even just a small amount of mindfulness practice, all of your senses will be heightened, creating a more vivid world. Further training will help you find acceptance for difficult events and diminish the need to judge everything. The world and its wild fluctuation will simply be. No need to worry or criticize, life just is. That is not to say you become tolerant or ignorant of abusive behaviors, you merely maintain awareness of your body when confronted by stress and can react in a healthy manner.

The intention of physical mindfulness is to become aware of your five senses. Thoughts and judgments will arise but know that you always have a choice to not think and instead experience. This is the true practice of mindfulness, learning to refocus after being distracted. You are not your thoughts, but you are this present moment, so gently return to your sensory focus. You can kindly thank your thoughts or let them float on like clouds. Your ability to remain focused will increase from brief moments to seconds or even minutes. In many ways, mindfulness is like watching a movie, except that you are also performing as one of the characters, fully immersed in the small details, conversations, and relationships.

Exercise: Find a quiet space you can be uninterrupted in for five minutes. If quiet is difficult to find, play some white noise on headphones or turn on a fan. Set a timer. Close your eyes and focus on the sensations made by your breathing, following the air as it enters your nose, reaches into your belly, and travels back out. Using a simple word with each in and out breath may also be helpful, such as "in" and "out."

Try to repeat this exercise every day, gradually increasing the time from three minutes to fifteen or twenty. As previously stated, the best therapeutic benefits begin after eight weeks of daily thirteen-minute or longer sessions.[11] You can use any point of focus or sensation such as your big toe, the smells of your house, or the flickering of a candle. I do find that mindfulness practices that change focal points are easiest because it is harder for thoughts to take over and become judgmental. For instance, when going on a walk practicing visual mindfulness, or focusing on deep breathing which moves through the entire body. I also find that if I keep getting lost in an emotion or thought, slow and intentional breathing is the fastest way to return to the present.

Focusing internally versus externally actually trains different parts of the brain, and for some people who struggle to control their thoughts, focusing inward may actually increase anxiety.[211] For instance, using the breath versus some visual cues. It can therefore be beneficial to note if your focus is more internal or external and practice the opposite.

As you develop the skill of mindfulness, start trying it out during random parts of your day, checking in with the present moment while walking, driving, or showering. One practice that Dr. Andrew Huberman suggests is to spread out your focus as wide as possible, trying to be aware of an entire scene rather than just a single point.[40] This has been shown to decrease stress and anxiety. Deep breathing also has the added benefit of creating calming chemicals in your body, and stepping away from thoughts of the past or future can relieve a great amount of stress.[131] You can even create *mindfulness bells*, associating everyday sounds like sirens or barking dogs as a reminder to check in with your present moment.

If you're really struggling to keep out of your thoughts, you can start naming off items in your vicinity or hold an ice cube. Another option is listing off all five sensations, plus feelings and thoughts you are presently experiencing - I see, I hear, I taste, I smell, I think, I feel physically, I feel emotionally. Mindfulness is a great technique for relaxing or falling asleep too - scan your body and release any tension you find, especially in your jaw and forehead as previously described.

Mindfulness can be difficult if your life is something you always are trying to escape from. Being present will be much easier if your surroundings are enjoyable. Just think about how captivating a sunset or pleasant aroma is. You want the physical spaces you inhabit to hold your attention to a similar level. Consider the lighting, art, cleanliness, smells, sounds, and so forth.

Being in nature or a calm and quiet environment generally helps our ability to be mindful. On the other hand, I've found that things like sleepiness and staring at a screen for too many hours prevent me from being mindful, sometimes for the remainder of the day. Many practitioners also use mindfulness to avoid reality and their emotions. This can help de-escalate an overwhelming emotion but also can bury an emotion deeper in the mind.

If you're anything like me, practices like mindfulness are hard to remember to do regularly. That's why I highly suggest joining an online or in-person meditation group or other exercises that incorporates mindfulness such as tai chi, qigong, or yoga. The *Clubhouse* app offers a lot of free meditation communities, and the *Liberate Meditation* app is specifically made for people of color. There are also many great meditation teachers online such as Tara Brach, Thich Nhat Hanh, and Jack Kornfield that give free guided meditations. Buddhism is another option.

Buddhism is one of the birthplaces of mindfulness. It should be known that when mindfulness is divorced from the teachings of Buddhism, it loses some of its original intentions. Try expanding your education in mindfulness by reading Buddhist texts. Also, if possible, find teachers who are not White, and give credit to the source of these ancient traditions from the Buddha and Indian minds.

In his book, *The Trauma of Everyday Life*, Mark Epstein explores how the Buddha likely developed his meditation practice to heal from traumatic experiences. In other words, Buddhism and mindfulness meditation are all about dealing with trapped emotions. To be clear, I am not Buddhist, but I have learned meditation through Buddhist communities, also known as *sanghas*. Learning in sanghas helped me commit to the practice of reconnecting with my body, especially with the discussions, reading, and safe container it created. These are donation-based spaces and so are accessible to people of a low income. I especially appreciated sanghas based upon the teachings of Thich Nhat Hanh, which I find more accessible for non-Buddhists than other traditions. Many Buddhist sanghas teach more out of secular philosophy too, so your religious or spiritual beliefs are not being questioned.

Experiencing physical sensations in Buddhism is known as the first of four *Foundations of Mindfulness*. While this level of mindfulness is very powerful and life-changing, most practices, including many Buddhist sanghas, stop here. To start releasing trapped emotions though, we need to fully experience our emotions. This second *Foundation of Mindfulness* is the real focus of this chapter.

5.2 Neurofeedback

If mindfulness is particularly difficult or you'd like to learn it faster, one more option is *neurofeedback*. This is a type of therapy that essentially gamifies the practice of mindfulness. Neurofeedback is great because it is a noninvasive therapy and does not require the client to recall difficult memories. Also, unlike medications, the results last. You do need to hit a certain threshold of sessions for the changes to stick though - the more, the better, but powerful results are often found with anywhere from 10 to 30 sessions.

In neurofeedback electrodes are attached to the client's head, which provide direct feedback from their mental states as they watch a screen or listen to sounds. The electrodes are moved around depending on what cognitive ability is being worked on. A focused or calm mentality creates a different visual or auditory effect than a dissociated or upset mentality. In this way clients gain mastery over their focus and emotions, witnessing in real-time the power to step away from ruminating thoughts, distraction, and upset. When paired with other modalities it becomes quite effective for releasing trapped emotions as well as greatly improving symptoms of things like dissociation, ADHD, and autism.[63]

Neurofeedback is best done with a trained professional, but several home systems are now available that can, to a limited extent, assist in a person's brain training. These are probably best for focus training and should not be used for severe trapped emotions. You can research home systems online or talk to your therapist for suggestions. Some neurofeedback therapists can also set you up with a complete system to take home and still work with you remotely.

5.3 Identifying Emotions

If you don't have emotional releases such as crying over things typically considered sad or upsetting, you likely have emotional blockages. Even if you sometimes or often have these releases, there are some important distinctions to make between healthy and unhealthy releases. Begin by reminding yourself that all emotions are a natural part of being human. Whatever people have told you about expressing your feelings being wrong or a sign of weakness, know that these words were informed by their own trapped emotions and fears of vulnerability.

The most important part of reconnecting with your emotional body is giving it enough space. Do not escape from your feelings in food, media, sex, drugs, or other distractions, but rather confront and work through the pain you are experiencing. Step away from dissociative activities and instead be mindful of the present moment. Knowing when you are practicing escapism can take time because you have associated feelings of pain with using these coping mechanisms. Check in with your body. Are you genuinely hungry, horny, or wanting to enjoy a TV show? Or is there a painful or stressful emotion there that you hope will go away? Typically a coping mechanism will only make you temporarily feel better before the difficult emotion returns.

Start practicing emotional mindfulness by focusing on positive emotions. After watching or reading something funny, or spending time with a friend, check in with your body. What qualities do you notice? Compare this with when you are feeling fairly neutral, or are experiencing stress around a deadline. Recognize that these emotions typically have a location and can move. Naming a subtle emotion can also help bring it out into the open. Even if this is a strong emotion, naming it can give you greater awareness and control over the sensation as well. You can also journal with tracking your mood daily or exploring the associated feelings that might be attached to various events. Here is a small list of emotions, but know there are many more! Say to yourself, *I feel*:

- *Happy emotions*: joyful, beaming, bright, content, fulfilled, grateful, loving
- *Sad emotions*: depressed, rejected, heavy, mournful, lonely, isolated, desperate, hurt
- *Angry emotions*: annoyed, irked, upset, violent, enraged, jealous
- *Anxious emotions*: confused, startled, insecure, frozen, flighty, shy, uncertain
- *Energetic emotions*: energized, stimulated, motivated, overwhelmed, tired, sleepy, focused, strong, powerful, successful, relaxed, peaceful, determined

None of these emotions are positive or negative, they are simply reactions your body is having to stimuli, attempting to help the brain make informed decisions. Each of these emotions has unique qualities to them. Know that one emotion may take on characteristics of multiple emotions. You can feel joyful, but that joy also feels overwhelming and stressful. These emotions also exist in different parts of the body at the same time. You can feel motivated in your brain, sad in your heart, and energized in your legs. Often one emotion will take center stage, but know that others can still exist, even contradictory ones.

As you develop the ability to identify emotions, you'll also begin seeing stresses that once appeared invisible throughout your day. They still impacted you, but you were unaware of their source. You do not need to avoid these subtle energies, and in fact, avoiding some of them would be problematic such as in the case of racial stresses. An awareness of them is important as you find ways of releasing the associated stress. Common invisible stresses include:

- Feeling unable to fully celebrate your culture in public
- People with different clothing, body types, or languages than you
- Dislike of people you perceive as more or less attractive than you
- Barking dogs and other loud and abrupt sounds
- General city sounds

Your awareness of a feeling like anger or fear allows you to separate from it in such a way that you can stop it from controlling you. When you feel overwhelmed or stressed out, a simple acronym that can help identify the specific feeling is *HALT*. Used by PTSD therapist Pete Walker and many others, HALT stands for hungry, angry, lonely, or tired. This is useful for meeting your unmet needs and resolving difficult emotions. It is also a good reminder to pause and check in with yourself before reacting to a trigger response - are you actually in danger? Or are you having a flashback to a time your body experienced as dangerous? Naturally, get out of danger if necessary, but if your body is simply remembering danger, you'll use the techniques we discuss next.

5.4 Experiencing Emotions

Experiencing your emotions is somewhat similar to experiencing your physical sensations, but instead of fully focusing on something like your breathing, you are checking in with your current emotional state. Emotions can be quite subtle or entirely overwhelming. To clarify, **feeling an emotion is very different from obsessing over what caused an emotion**. We fuel emotions with our thoughts, memories, external stimuli, and trapped emotions. According to brain scientist Jill Bolte Taylor, author of *My Stroke Of Insight*, without that fuel, emotions only last for 90 seconds.[143] That is why it is important to recognize that emotions are not facts, but rather temporary energies moving through our bodies; they can dissipate or change very quickly.

5.4.1 Creating Safety
As emotional releases can carry a lot of self-judgment, you must create a safe space to experience them. Perhaps that is your room, car, alone in nature, or at a support group. Using a pillow to mute your angry or sad sounds can also create a nice buffer between you and concerned ears.

5.4.2 Emotional Awareness

Once you identify a difficult emotion in your body as described in the previous section, check in with it. Your exercise is to stay present with the emotion, fully experiencing its shape, temperature, texture, location, movement, desires, and whatever other qualities it might have. The thoughts that arise in this case may deepen the emotion or give it new qualities. You still want to return to focusing on the emotion as much as possible, but you can sometimes use those thoughts to your benefit.

You'll notice that most intense emotions have a need attached to them - perhaps you are feeling overwhelmed and your body wants quiet alone time or sleep. Perhaps you are feeling sad and your body wants to cry. Perhaps you just got really scared and need to shiver and yell. In the same way that you eat when you are hungry, this is a natural and healthy biological urge that all animals use. In the case of emotions, performing the associated need helps prevent that energy from becoming trapped within the body.

Not all expressions are releasing emotions in a healing way. For instance, physical and verbal violence do not typically release anger, but instead amplify it by putting the body in danger. Even if you remove or scare off the source of your anger, that energy will still be contained within your body. Things might get substantially better and it will be easier to deal with your difficult energies as you no longer become actively triggered, but even the death of an abuser will not fully take care of the trapped emotions. To truly release this trapped energy, you will have to first discover its source. For instance, anger tends to be a misrepresentation of fear, sadness, or an unmet need you have. This is discussed later in this chapter in Section 5.8.

5.4.3 Using Art And Media

One helpful tool I used while learning how to reconnect with my own emotions was art media, especially movies and music. Using media that resonates with your current emotional state can help heighten the experience and immerse you deeper into the emotion. Your goal is to have an emotional release while staying focused on the emotion. For me, music videos like *It's Called: Freefall* by Rainbow Kitten Surprise act as a quick way to deepen my emotional state. Most people also seem to tear up to Studio Ghibli's *Grave of the Fireflies*. Forewarning though, both of these deal with very intense subjects like death and starvation. Works like these taught me how the body cries - tensed stomach and shoulders, pushing through the throat almost like a growl, squeezing of the eyes shut, and deep and intense breaths. This series of bodily actions is something I now use to more easily access that emotional release.

Creating art can also reconnect you to your emotional body. This is especially the case with music, but any medium that allows for a fast and free flow of expressions like drawing, painting, and poetry is good. It is often important that you learn to explore this medium on your own rather than copying images or playing the songs of others. Improvisationally singing songs is especially powerful.

5.4.4 Emotional Expressions
You'll notice that when given enough attention, most difficult emotions will eventually transform into tears. There may be other states you experience as well such as shaking, laughing, screaming, growling, roaring, singing, running, clenching your fists, or hugging yourself. This may require following the emotion as the energy transforms in different parts of your body. Mindfully stay present and see what it becomes.

5.4.5 Shame
Shame may arise, especially if you were belittled for expressing emotions while growing up. This can require some healthy angering about how you were treated before you can grieve properly. The shame will force you into being quiet or keep you tense. Breathe deeply and allow your body to move and release as loudly as it wants to. This is your human right. Once you have a release, you'll likely feel a little to a lot better, but check in with your body - where is the sensation now? How do you experience it? Does it feel settled for now or is it asking for another type of release?

5.4.6 Allies
This process can be much easier with a trusted ally such as a therapist trained in somatic therapy or grief work. Part of somatic therapy notes small movements in your body, changes in your vocal tone, and word choice. They will also periodically ask you, "What do you feel in your body now?" You can also have a friend do this inquiry as you process through a difficult experience with them. Having someone else mirror how you are feeling can be powerful in helping unlock these vulnerable releases. Therapists and friends may also not feel safe enough or be too distracting for you to access these emotional states, so find what works for you.

An ally can alternatively show empathy or express the emotions that you might want to be feeling. After sharing your story or stating your emotions without actually feeling them, your ally might reflect that what you went through sounds really hard, that they would be pissed off, or that what your partner, parents, or abuser did was absolutely awful. This kind of confirmation will help you break past the story that you were somehow responsible, wrong, or it wasn't such a big deal. It was a big deal, and no one should have to go through what you did. Hearing about others' stories and their related emotions can also be a huge help, such as in support groups.

5.4.7 Communal Grieving

Communal grieving can further strengthen your emotional releases and is quite common in many cultures throughout the world. This can involve an entire group of people getting together to emote around a tragedy through crying, yelling, screaming, dancing, playing music, and various rituals like burning trinkets or writing letters. It may also involve a single person being witnessed by the group as they move and speak without restraint for whatever is coming up for them. *ZEGG Forum* is one of the largest cross-cultural practices of this method.

ZEGG is a German acronym that translates into *Center For Experimental Cultural And Social Design*. As the person speaks, often surrounded by dozens of onlookers, one or more facilitators help them access what is authentic at that moment. Afterwards, individuals from the audience mirror what they witnessed - simplifying it into a body position and phrase such as "I'm scared" while curled up into a ball. To learn more you can visit <www.zegg.de/en/> or <www.zegg-forum.org/en/>. Many other groups incorporate aspects of communal grieving too such as the sharing period in Twelve Step programs and co-counseling sessions. However, this tends to be quite limited in comparison to what is practiced in ZEGG Forum or certain cultural traditions.

Connecting with your emotions can also be facilitated through some music and dance such as that found in an *ecstatic dance* group, or by simply witnessing other people cry. You can seek out therapists, spiritual forums, and personal growth groups who put on grief workshops as well. In Japan, there are rui-katsu, or grieving festivals. Or, maybe you feel emboldened to start a local group? Experiment and see what works for you. Can you access a tearful release right now?

5.5 Fake It Till You Release It

Similar to crying, you may have to learn other emotional expressions. You could start taking self-defense classes to learn how to protect yourself and express anger in healthy ways. Perhaps you enroll in an acting class to break down the basic facial and bodily movements that create an emotion. You could do this on your own as well, attempting to mimic actors in movies or animals in the wild.

If you watch animals that have near-death experiences closely, you will sometimes notice them have a freeze response and drop to the ground.[106] Consider a deer caught in the headlights. If the danger is still present when they come to, they may react with sudden aggressiveness, protecting themselves and startling their adversary. If the danger has cleared when they regain control over their body, they may start shaking for a time before rejoining their companions. All of these actions are releasing energy and ensure that energy does not become trapped in the body.

In general, mimicking the bodily expression you think might be appropriate for a given feeling will help deepen that emotion and assist you in releasing it. It is okay if it feels unfamiliar or forced, just give it a try - you've likely been conditioned your whole life away from having a natural response to releasing emotions. Practice by faking it till you make it. Emotional releases feel great and you will likely feel lighter, happier, and less burden on the other side of one.

The following is a list of normal reactions to common experiences. Know that this is by no means a definitive list, especially as these emotional reactions could arise in any situation you find difficult. It is simply meant to illuminate how an unblocked emotional system might work.

- *Shaking*: Something frightening happens, your life is threatened, or you have a fall
- *Crying*: You go through a breakup, a loved one passes away, or you feel overwhelmed
- *Anger*: Your boss or friend mistreats you, you are lied to, or you have an argument
- *Empathy and compassion*: Your friend or lover is emotionally or physically hurt

While emotional releases like shaking and crying are ideal, energy can still come out in other ways such as running, chopping wood, dancing, having sex, and so on. However, remember that many activities used to regulate emotions do not actually release the emotions. Generally, you need an intense physical action rather than a calming technique like meditation or yoga. You also need to stay present with the emotion while you are doing this activity. It needs to be activated.

Many people use media or certain thinking patterns to numb, dissociate from, or otherwise bury their difficult emotions. This is also very common in spiritual communities that use "spiritual bypassing" to explain difficult circumstances. Common bypasses include "Mercury is in retrograde," "The universe meant it to be," and "I don't see skin color because there's only the human race." Saying these to someone in distress is cruel and not helpful. For those that have survived on numbing techniques, you may have to unlearn some behaviors or distance yourself from certain communities to become fully present with your emotional world.

5.6 Emotional Mastery

In an ideal world, having emotional releases would be celebrated at any time, but in many cultures, they are not. Perhaps you are in a public space, releasing the emotion would make a difficult situation worse, or you simply do not feel safe. While it is ideal to release an emotion as quickly as possible so it does not become trapped in the body, you can withhold experiencing it until you are in a safe place. Stay in your thoughts, focus on your bodily sensations, practice calming techniques like breathing deeply, or distract yourself with media. This also involves learning to ask a person for consent before forcing your difficult emotions on them or launching into a stressful conversation.

Once you're in a safe space, even if the emotion has seemingly dissipated, check in with your body. If there are residual difficult feelings, give space to and experience them as quickly as you feel prepared. Even just excusing yourself to use the restroom can provide enough time to release emotions and calm your nervous system.

If the difficult emotion has increased in intensity after attempting a release, you may need to regulate your nervous system, seek out a friend or therapist, or somehow dissociate from the emotion and return to it at another time. Sometimes you can only experience an emotion once properly prepared. This may be much easier given enough time and space from a triggering situation. You're learning how to listen to your body.

Remember that you may not be able to resolve certain emotions until you are fully separated from the source of the difficult situation. You may have too many associations with the person who hurt your feelings, or they may be unwilling to alter their triggering behaviors. Establish a life separated from them, or find a way to communicate boundaries or otherwise meet your needs in another way. Healing is easier if the difficult experience came from someone who you love and trust, and who is willing to prove that they are a source of support and safety again.

In general, the body wants to heal if it is allowed to. There are many subtle ways that your body already releases emotions. For instance, you might feel angry and decide to go on a jog, you talk to your friends or parents about an incident, or loving individuals show you empathy and compassion. Even your dreams may assist with healing strong emotions. As such, a lot of emotional energy is resolved given time. As previously said, a trapped emotion may even slowly leave the body over three months as you overcome thinking patterns and form new behaviors. For instance, after an argument, you and a friend rebuild trust through apologies or just proving that you still care about each other. Alternatively, you quit a job with a difficult employer and can now see your boss for qualities other than your basic survival. Resolutions like these can of course be problematic in the case of lovers that break up, forget why it wasn't working out, then get back together and repeat this cycle again and again.

There is a gray area in this process of experiencing emotions. Just because you are crying, angrily jogging, or hitting a pillow, does not mean you are having a beneficial emotional release. First of all, you must be in a safe environment. Secondly, you cannot be fueling your feelings with self-deprecating thoughts around the incident. This is often a form of whining and is not helpful. For instance, your boss fires you and your mind insists you are worthless or incompetent. This is a catastrophized story you are telling yourself and should be reframed. "This job wasn't the right fit for my skill set," or "I didn't meet my boss's difficult expectations, but I am capable of learning and succeeding if I try again at a different job." Verbally and physically violent thoughts are generally detrimental unless used in a very particular way. Remember, stay with your emotions and bodily sensations, not your thoughts.

5.7 Emotional Dysregulation

Emotions can also become dysregulated in which you fall into intense emotional spaces without any particular reason, or you may have a fresh difficult experience that you mentally cannot escape from. These might be caused by a form of chemical depression like fluctuations in your hormones. In these cases, no emotional release is happening. It may be important to give yourself some space from your emotions so that you can function in life and find more effective ways of coping. You can either practice calming the emotion or dissociating from it. Review the contents of Chapter 4 for some ideas.

Emotional dysregulation can also come in the form of being addicted to instability and painful emotions. As you establish healthier behaviors and friends, you may experience a kind of withdrawal effect. You might feel this life is boring or question if you deserve happiness. This form of hypervigilance is a likely indication that you need to continue to work through some of the trapped emotions that persist in your body. Embracing your new life will become easier and easier as you let go of the past and find joy in health and stability.

5.8 Healthy Angering And Asserting Yourself

Anger is a protective mechanism. As previously mentioned, most animals have an aggressive fight response when they come out of a freeze response or are otherwise in danger.[106B] This greatly increases their chance of survival by scaring a predator and giving them a little extra time to escape. Anger plays other important functions too, like motivation, determining what is important to us, and helping us get what we want or need.

People opening up their trapped emotions often find anger as they finally identify a parent or other individual responsible for their suffering. This anger acts as a guard against the self-blame we may have experienced for years. It helps us differentiate between what we are responsible for and what is dangerous and abusive. This anger process can be necessary before grieving is possible.

Anger can of course come out in unhealthy ways. When we get angry at someone, we tend to start overgeneralizing what they are responsible for. We look for any evidence we can find that they are unlikable. We blame them for entirely unrelated things, or even how our lives are going. Through our anger, we also tend to ignore doing the things that would most readily get our needs met.

Anger is one of the most misunderstood emotions, likely because it arises from so many different factors and can deceptively feel good. Beyond its biological implications, anger also is learned from our culture. For instance, one study found that people from the United States tend to express anger and respond to anger more strongly than people from Japan do, but that response can be decreased or increased quite easily.[7,14]

Unfortunately, trapped emotions can cause a person to either shut down their healthy anger responses or become hypervigilant with anger and constantly respond to stressful situations with a fight response. A diminished anger response can mean you struggle to express frustration, never speak up for your needs and wants, or cannot defend yourself when verbally or physically attacked. These characteristics are common in people who grew up in situations that actively ignored their voice, especially in women who have

CH 5 – LEARNING HOW TO EXPERIENCE EMOTIONS   119

been culturally taught to be submissive. You may even turn your anger inward upon yourself, believing that you were somehow the one to do wrong.

For people who struggle to stand up for themselves, reconnecting with your anger may require empowering your voice with the techniques in Chapter 8 and learning about how unfairly you or your peer group were treated in the past. Many people find this in becoming educated about discrimination, corporate and governmental abuses, and environmental destruction. Learning about your ability to defend yourself or fight adversaries can awaken you to your powerful strength as well. You may start by feeling powerless, but then remember how unfair or terrible someone's actions were, and in that anger discover the ability to take rational action toward change. Take a class in martial arts, or bolster your ego and sense of control as explored in Chapter 13.

Aggressive hypervigilance may then make a person react automatically to stressful situations with name-calling, yelling, aggressive arguing, road rage, revenge fantasies, or physical acts of harm to attempt to get one's way. These are common with people who grew up experiencing or witnessing physical violence, especially if they were surrounded by a culture that promotes aggression like in the United States. These people are experiencing a flashback in which anger is the only tool they have to protect themselves. Both a shutdown and hypervigilant anger response are unhealthy except in rare situations of self-defense. We will therefore explore how to cultivate a healthy balance of anger.

According to the authors of *When Anger Hurts*, expressing traditional forms of anger like yelling, revenge, or violence only offers temporary relief, and actually reinforces aggressive feelings.[116] Even just punching a pillow or yelling to let off steam habituates aggressive reactions to anger because it is still dissociated from your body.[241] Some people believe that anger must be expressed as a biological force of nature, but we can actually transform our relationship to it with other techniques. The authors point out that behind anger are typically basic unmet needs and feelings of stress, fear, or grief. Healthy angering therefore may involve:

1. Creating a habit of stepping away from situations in which you start feeling overwhelmed. It's okay to say, "I'm feeling angry and need a little time and space to calm down." All aggression starts with stress, and you always have the choice to release stress instead of anger with the techniques in Chapter 4.
2. Lowering the total amount of stress you experience daily and choosing to maintain a regulated nervous system.

3. Journaling to understand where your stress is coming from or why a person took the actions that they did.
4. Identifying your unmet needs and voicing or acting on them in a constructive manner. This might involve asserting boundaries, breaking off a relationship, or simply not responding to words that aggravate you. You cannot expect anyone to know why you are angry at them unless you ask for specifically what you are needing. It is important to be focusing on the correct need with non-blaming language. Harriet Lerner's *The Dance of Anger* covers this quite well, but I also summarize it later in Chapter 8. Isolation also greatly aggravates anger, so healthy relationships and community are essential for diminishing feelings of anger.[70]
5. Identifying which of your values are being contradicted, and either communicating that or aligning your life in a way that better represents your values. For instance, supporting an activist cause as explored in Part IV.
6. Addressing your trapped emotions with the techniques outlined in Part II. This may involve mentally realizing you are now capable of using violence if necessary to protect yourself, but typically there are much healthier tools at your disposal.
7. Understanding how unhealthy aggressive anger is. Chronic feelings of anger translate into a decrease in lifespan and an increase in feelings of loneliness.[116] Holding onto anger prevents you from forgiving others, repairing relationships, or being listened to. Aggressive anger also often stems from a belief that you can control the behaviors of other people, when in fact you can usually only control your own response to other people. You can read more about this in Section 13.3. Ask yourself who benefits from your being angry.
8. Stepping away from the culture of anger. Especially consider the anger that is expressed in your music, movies, news, television, masculinity, revenge fantasies, language, and communication patterns. Consume things, put yourself around people, and repeat patterns that do not reflect anger or violence. Seek out games, movies, activities, and work that promotes cooperation, kindness, and forgiveness.
9. Having a neutral or positive experience with the person you are in conflict with. Often when I'm passive-aggressively avoiding a person, or cannot stand having them in my space, it can help a lot to ask them a question. Asking them how they are, what their new project is, or about their latest adventure can help prove to my instinctual body

CH 5 – LEARNING HOW TO EXPERIENCE EMOTIONS

that they are not a monster. Get curious when you're angry.
10. Understanding that the actions of others are usually not intentionally harmful or directed at you. Instead, the actions of others represent their personal needs, wants, culture, and reality. No one can read your mind. Frequently anger arises from misunderstandings. Breaking away from an automatic judgment may require asking yourself, "What is this other person experiencing?"
11. Detaching from the idea that you are required to help people who choose not to help themselves. For the most part, every adult is personally responsible for getting their own needs met. That means that you are not responsible for putting up with an abusive situation for the sake of someone else. For instance, you can free yourself from the stress of being your mother's only friend when she refuses to step away from an abusive relationship or seek help. That said, within reason, you should allow people to make mistakes and learn from them without ending the relationship. You can be supportive of the struggles others go through, especially oppressed communities and the elderly, but you should not ruin your own life in the process.
12. Setting a time limit for your rumination before putting a stop to it. This can help make space for you to correct damaging thoughts or use calming techniques like deep breathing.

Naturally, anytime that you need to defend yourself from immediate harm, anger is essential for acting quickly in physical or verbal defense. Angry rebuttals may also be appropriate when standing up for yourself or calling out a heinous act in public. Even asserting your right to say "no" or saying, "I don't like that, please stop" are healthy expressions of anger. Just know that more direct expressions of anger may activate a person's defenses in such a way that they are likely to anger back at you or simply not listen to your words at all. This is especially problematic with activists hoping to create change through angry conversations.

Just like other releases, anger is not something you dwell on forever. The hope is that the energy is released and potentially allows you to move on from, forgive, or even happily spend time with a previous source of stress. Naturally, this won't be possible unless your expectations about a person have changed, you never have to see them again, you have strong boundaries about how you interact, or they have changed their behaviors.

If you already have a healthy relationship with a person who wronged you in the past, you can separate them into their current and past selves so as not to harm your current relationship. It is even suggested while doing this work to visualize placing the good memories of a person into a safe container so that you can freely work on the ones that caused you suffering. Not all things need to be forgiven either, although carrying around hatred in your body can be quite taxing. I discuss more on how to establish boundaries with a person in Chapter 8, and how to forgive someone in Section 13.13.

Anger can also be stimulated or reduced through our biochemistry.[81] Contradicting popular belief, testosterone increases competitiveness and motivation, not aggression. That said, more testosterone will make already aggressive people more likely to act out. Anger is primarily stimulated by stress. It has been shown that things like caffeine and alcohol can increase the likelihood of expressing anger. On the other hand, omega-3 fatty acids, tryptophan, ashwagandha (used at most 2 weeks at a time), and getting more light earlier in the day can reduce aggression. You can listen to *Episode 71* of the Huberman Lab podcast to learn more.

If you want to dive deeper into the subject of anger, I suggest a few resources. For people who express anger too strongly, read *When Anger Hurts* by Matthew and Judith McKay. For people who need help expressing anger, read *The Dance Of Anger* by Harriet Lerner. This book is intended for people who identify as women, but anyone who struggles to speak up about their needs can benefit from it. Lastly, Black men dealing with anger, victimhood, or self-righteousness may be interested in reading *Tough* by Terry Crews. Crews has an excellent podcast interview on episode #587 of *The Tim Ferriss Show* as well. In it, he says, "You can have revenge or success, but not both."

There is one instance outside of physical defense in which violence towards others is acceptable, and that is in your imagination. Now, obsessively imagining violent acts probably isn't healthy or helpful. However, while renegotiating a past difficult experience, you can have yourself or a powerful ally step in to stop a horrible act from occurring. Perhaps the evildoer is killed or imprisoned and guarded by an army of your mental companions, or maybe you are angry enough to talk back to your nemesis or break free from a frozen state and run away - whatever you need to feel safe again. We will talk more about this imaginative renegotiation in Part II of the book. Next, we'll explore how anger shows up in your thoughts.

5.9 Awareness Of Thoughts And The Critics

Emotions and thoughts work hand in hand, but just like our emotions, we can use techniques to change our thoughts. You can use mindfulness for identifying thoughts as well. Instead of letting them control your emotions and actions, you can just let thoughts pass on through like clouds in the sky. Say, "I am aware that I am having this thought, but it does not define me or how I have to act or feel." Alternatively, I find it is easiest to slow my thoughts down and acknowledge that they are happening through journaling. Especially when my thoughts are reiterating over and over again, I can instead get curious about them, reflect on their truthfulness, and consider other possibilities.

Pete Walker, author of *Complex PTSD*, refers to the intrusive negative thoughts that arise in our minds as the inner and outer critics.[184] People with trapped emotions typically have especially strong critics that start speaking when triggered. These voices say painful things about you and others. The inner critic is often based on the voices and negative sentiments of your parents, while the outer critic stems from the anger you withheld towards them.[184E,184F]

The inner critic might proclaim, *I'm so stupid, there's no way I could succeed,* or, *no one likes me.* It can be a major cause of anxiety and depression by constantly repeating self-critical attacks. The outer critic says things like *you're not doing it right, everyone is dumb, the world is unfair,* or, *it's your fault this happened.* Your outer critic often judges people for things you are insecure about in yourself such as your appearance or quality of work. It can show up as doing activities that scare people away or being overly honest and perfectionistic. Passive-aggressiveness is common too such as avoiding contact, intentionally doing things that make people feel upset, or withholding kind words.

Both critics can also show up subconsciously as reactionary emotions and behaviors. There are still thoughts behind these emotions, but they may be buried deeply. For instance, you might not even think of asking for a raise because the inner critic does not believe you are worthy of one. Or, you might exclude certain people because the outer critic thinks poorly of them. There may also just be a pervasive feeling of anxiety or dislike present. Getting curious and reflecting on your emotions and behaviors may help reveal the thinking behind them. You can also take free online tests such as the *Implicit Assessment Test* or *Primal World Beliefs Survey* as explored in Sections 6.3 and 15.4. In this way, you go from being controlled by an emotional flashback to re-engaging your rational mind. What emotion is coming up? Why was the event hurtful? What need are you having? Naming your thoughts may require having an emotional release first as well, or at least calming down with self-care practices.

Walker believes that these critical voices prevent self-compassion and healthfully connecting with others, which are both essential aspects of recovery.[184B] The first step to diminishing your inner and outer critics is knowing that they are speaking for you. Use mindfulness or journaling. Ask what you have missed out on or given up due to these commanding judgments. Identify that this is not your true self, but rather a frightened part of you. As we will explore later discussing *the inner family* in Chapter 10, you can talk with the critics. Pete Walker does warn that as you become aware of them, the critics may initially speak even louder, but this is part of breaking out of dissociation.[184G] Move forward at a pace that feels safe.

Walker says that people who were traumatized by their parents need to first practice their healthy anger by denouncing the critics.[184A] You can say things like, *You've had enough time speaking, STOP, I don't believe what you are saying*, or, *Sorry, but your opinion is no longer needed*. Pete Walker calls this *thought-stopping of the inner critic*. This is essentially standing up for yourself against the voices of your parents or other abusers. Just know that this can be a very intense process and require many iterations as you reprogram your judging mind. Often grief will arise in the form of healing tears as you mourn the loss of your childhood and the thousands of times you have attacked yourself and others needlessly. Grieving for the way you were treated in the past that led to these voices taking over may also be essential before you have the emotional strength to use thought-stopping.

However, thought-stopping can become a form of avoiding your emotions and intuition. You never fully get rid of the critics because they are an important part of keeping you safe and moving you along in life. Thus, some therapists alternatively suggest asking the voices questions from a place of compassion. You can get curious about what the inner critic is scared about behind its words, or hear when the outer critic is genuinely protesting something dangerous or abusive. For instance: *So you feel alone? Where is that coming from? What are you worried about? I am not going to outright agree that this is true, but I am here to listen. How can we improve this situation?* I will discuss these inner dialogues more in Chapter 10.

Many other techniques are explored throughout the following chapters to help correct and replace damaging thoughts with ones that are neutral or positive. For instance, quieting the outer critic can be aided by practicing gratitude, making daily lists that highlight the good qualities in others, noting the things that bring you pleasure while walking around, and telling people directly what you appreciate about them.[184G] You can also shut off the judgmental part of your brain by using mindfulness, being present, and experiencing awe. People with a strong inner critic will want to bolster their ego and create secure relationships. These topics are explored throughout the book such as the previous healthy angering section, Sections 8.8 and 8.13 on judgments and complaining, Chapter 13 on building a healthier mindset, and Sections 14.2 and 17.6 on healing your attachment wounds. Pete Walker also offers several free resources on his website exploring the critics in more depth at <www.pete-walker.com>.

***
Chapter Reflections

1. What options do you have for practicing mindfulness or activities that incorporate it - online or in your city?
2. What is the best time and place for you to stay present?
3. What things make mindfulness harder for you?
4. If you cannot currently connect with your emotions easily, how did that come to be?
5. How can you start a practice to identify your emotions at least once each day?
6. How do you access big emotional releases such as crying, growling into a pillow, or movement activities?
7. How do you express anger?
8. Has your expression of anger in the past hurt people, and if so, how could you have communicated your needs in a more nonviolent manner?
9. Do you experience any forms of emotional dysregulation? How do you know you are in one of these states?
10. When you check in with yourself, what is it that you're feeling, needing, or avoiding?
11. What does mastering your emotions look like for you?
12. How do your inner and outer critics show up in your life? What do they say? Is one more dominant than the other in your life? What works for you to diminish their voices?

PART II

TRANSFORMING STORIES

Chapter 6

Stories And Self-Limiting Beliefs

6.1 Memory And The Imagination, 6.2 Placebos And Nocebos, 6.3 Self-Limiting Beliefs And Stories, 6.4 Renegotiating Memories

Now that we've explored how to reduce stress and release emotions, the third part of handling trapped emotions is changing your story and self-limiting beliefs. The goal is to recognize that you do not have to believe your thoughts, and in fact, can transform them into more empowering mental messages. Just remember that these stories can be hidden deep inside your subconscious or physical body rather than your rational mind.

Even when a story is accessible to your rational mind, your cognitive abilities can be limited while triggered in an emotional flashback. Finding a safe space, moving your body, breathing deeply, and having an emotional release may be necessary before you can change your thoughts. This chapter introduces these concepts and the more rational side of transforming stories, while Chapters 7 through 11 discuss the subconscious and bodily workings of your inner narratives.

6.1 Memory And The Imagination

One way that our bodies hold onto trapped emotions is through memories. Even though a person may not be able to remember their past or the details of a difficult experience, some memories may return as the techniques in this book are used. These memories may be very troubling, and it is important to take care of yourself as you reclaim your past.

Memories are also quite complicated. Two people can remember the same moment entirely differently, and memories can be created that never happened. This is why history is such a problematic field - cultural lenses, emotional states, what we are focusing on, and what details we remember can color a retelling of events quite differently. This said, according to PTSD specialist Dr. Daniel Brown, traumatized individuals are actually much less likely to create false memories because adverse experiences make people less trusting of external influences.[218]

At the same time, trapped emotions do complicate memory difficulties, as focusing on positive stimuli is almost impossible when being triggered or feeling unsafe. Often there is a hyperfocus on the difficult memory and everything else is muted. Many people also experience dissociative memory blockages surrounding an adverse experience, especially sexual assault survivors. Even after the initial event, this forgetfulness or unawareness may become a regular occurrence, blocking out portions of the day and leading to questionable or dangerous decisions as explored in Section 3.5.

Even though memories can be unreliable, they are still part of our identities and can help us feel healthy and fulfilled. In fact, the unreliable nature of memory is quite useful for releasing trapped emotions. Not only does forgetfulness protect us from fully re-experiencing the pain of a triggering memory until properly prepared, but it also allows us to *renegotiate* a difficult memory into something safer and more positive. This is possible because our bodies react quite similarly to the stimuli found between our waking life, dreams, and imagination. As a result, our emotional world can be influenced heavily by dreams, our greatest ally may be a fictional character, and memories from each of these states may mix together to become our reality.

6.2 Placebos And Nocebos

The power of your mindset is immense. Consider the *placebo effect*. Researchers have found that simply believing something is good for you will impart small to significant healing benefits in the mind or body.[176,42] This effect is amplified the more intense the treatment is. For instance, an invasive surgery will impart stronger benefits than a massage. This is also why many unscientific treatments are accepted by the masses - even though they may not cure the long-term symptoms, the person's belief in the healing modality still makes them feel better. Mindset can decrease the amount of stress you experience, increase the success rate of medications and medical procedures, change how hungry you feel, lower pain perception, and drastically improve the health benefits of even small amounts of exercise.[180,126] In fact, health outcomes improve simply by being told by a doctor that the food you are eating is good for you or that you are getting enough exercise.

The opposite is true as well with the *nocebo effect* when a person does not believe in a treatment. Things like chronic stress can hurt your performance and immune system functioning.[152] People can come to believe that they are being bitten by insects or that their coworkers are glaring at them. As Malcolm Gladwell describes in *The Tipping Point*, a person can even experience very real nausea after being convinced their food is poisoned. Many times I have quickly pulled back the shower curtain in fear there was a monster hiding behind it after watching a scary film. This effect is especially worrisome when groups of people collectively believe something that ripples out in detrimental ways like discrimination and stereotypes. Imagining negative outcomes will naturally make you feel much worse about that thing. The brain is amazing, and sometimes terrifying. Be careful about what you focus on.

In another example spanning two studies, Asian American women's test scores in English and math either increased or decreased simply by announcing their gender or ethnicity before the test.[156,114] This activated the stereotypes these women held regarding how they were "supposed" to perform in English and math. Similarly, children raised with positive reinforcement consistently do better in life than those not given this affirmation.[178] This also plays out at the neighborhood, city, and cultural levels. Do your surroundings inspire creativity, beauty, and inclusion, or are they a concrete jungle steeped in oppression and individualism? Your thoughts are very powerful and create significant changes to your biology and self-confidence. Find the people and places that make your mind flourish in positive self-regard.

Knowing about the nocebo effect makes it even more important to deal with your trapped emotions, as your past difficulties may be informing a negative mindset with things like medicines, exercise, or your ability to learn certain subjects in school. This is why going at your own pace and accepting your healing process is so important. You stressing too much about getting better, feeling guilt over what you eat, or never enjoying your personal time may be hurting your ability to recover. While change may require a certain amount of healthy stress, you have to balance this with knowing when that stress is holding you back and simply creating additional stress.

6.3 Self-Limiting Beliefs And Stories

Depression, anxiety, anger, and other difficult emotions are often characterized by self-limiting thinking patterns.[52] Known as *cognitive distortions* or *self-limiting beliefs*, they fuel a distorted sense of reality. These beliefs can be wedged into you very deeply because they are often developed in childhood and have been repeated through your inner and outer critics as explored in Section 5.9. Identifying and changing how you think can be an essential step to stopping trapped emotions from controlling your life.

6.3.1 Self-Limiting Beliefs

Self-limiting beliefs include:

1. Minimizing how bad it actually was. Any stress or suffering can negatively impact a person and everyone is worthy of healing. Never compare your pain to anyone else's.
2. All-or-nothing thinking by making an event all good or all bad, even if there was a mixture of feelings or the possibility of misunderstandings.
3. Making conclusions without any direct proof. Ask people directly what is going on before believing your assumptions.
4. Taking everything personally, even if it has nothing to do with you. This often arises either when you are in a depressive episode or when friends are struggling with their own difficulties.
5. Thinking about what *should* be done rather than what you *can* or *want* to do.
6. Assuming the worst or catastrophizing the future without actually knowing what will happen or how you will feel.
7. Comparing yourself to others, especially people who have been doing something for years longer than you or have had many more privileges than you. Everyone is uniquely capable and intelligent.
8. Thinking that your feelings are facts, or, that you can rationally predict how you will feel about something. Feelings are ever-changing, and there is no way to know for sure how you will feel in the future.
9. Believing that you have or had control over a situation that you are actually powerless over.

It is especially important to be on the lookout for self-limiting beliefs when you are feeling depressed or are otherwise upset at someone. Write about what you're feeling and the possible cognitive distortions that are getting in your way. Rewrite your thoughts with the distortions corrected. You might also use logic to clarify reality. Can you zoom out from your limited perspective to look at the wider world and discover that things are actually just fine? Is there any tangible proof that something is true? Or are you making assumptions? It is easy to misread facial expressions and make unrelated things be about ourselves. Ask a person directly what their words meant. If they do match what you thought, it opens a great opportunity to resolve whatever conflict existed. Paranoia and silence get us nowhere.

As previously mentioned, emotions only last for about 90 seconds if they are not refueled with thoughts, memories, or external triggers. That is why it is important to transform self-limiting beliefs because it gives you a more positive aspect of an experience to focus on. This is also why taking some space from an experience and gaining control over intrusive thoughts can be good so you can regulate your emotions and consider the positive aspects of the experience.

This does not mean you are avoiding what happened though, you still need to spend a reasonable amount of time releasing those feelings and integrating them into the larger context of your life. Simultaneously, it is a balance, and some amount of rumination can be expected after a difficult experience. Thoughts fuel our emotions, and emotions fuel our thoughts. Addressing either will help your body quiet both intense feelings and painful mind chatter.

What is actually true? Is the story you've been telling yourself a fact or are you protecting a frightened part of yourself? During any given moment many truths can exist. Truth is also layered. You might be angry or depressed, but with a slight change in thinking, that can become happiness or love. In one frame of mind you might believe that your friend does not care about you, but with a slight change in understanding come to realize that they have been immensely stressed and busy themselves. What are you hyperfocusing on and what are you ignoring?

6.3.2 Choice Of Words
Even if it is not a self-limiting belief, your choice of words and how you define them have a huge impact on things like your gender, mental health, and reality.[201,202] For instance, certain cultures do not have a concept of the individual. In his book *IntraConnected*, Dr. Dan Siegel writes about how we have deluded ourselves into believing that the self only exists within us. He instead argues that the self exists within our relationships, environment, and the whole universe. Switching to this broader sense of self gives us more compassion for how we treat our neighbors and the environment.

The book, *Lost In Translation* by Ella Frances Sanders illustrates and describes words that do not directly translate into English. One of my favorites is the Japanese word, wabi-sabi, or the ability to find beauty in imperfection. This is why preserving languages is so important because they each hold unique ways of seeing the world around us and transforming our stories. My book, *You Are A Great And Powerful Wizard* invites readers to explore the power of words by reimagining every thought, word, movement, and emotion, or lack thereof, as a magic spell creating change in the world.

According to psychologist Alia Crum, even just giving healthy vegetable dishes more exciting names greatly increases how often people order them.[180] Language is not static; you and your culture can change how you relate to, define, and use words in very impactful ways.

Jonah Berger, the author of *Magic Words*, further illuminates the power of language. He shares that when speaking to yourself or others, action is much more likely when there is an identity to live up to.[255] For instance, people will vote more often if you ask them "Will you be a voter?" instead of "Will you vote?" The opposite is true as well. If you identify as a smoker, then quitting is much harder. You have the choice to identify as a failure or recognize that you failed once. Start identifying as the person you would like to become in the world.

Berger has also found that speaking to yourself in the third person is more effective than using "I" statements. For example, instead of saying "I love myself" say "You love yourself." This may be the reason why speaking to the inner selves explored in Chapter 10 is so effective.

6.3.3 Focus And Attention
Humans can only keep their focus on one thing at a time, so where do you want that to be? Your attention is a precious resource, so use it wisely. This means that just because you are participating in an activity, it does not mean that you are learning the lessons it provides. For instance, in martial arts, you might learn how to punch and kick, but if you look deeper, there are lessons of mindfulness, mental discipline, resolve to overcome adversity, and believing in yourself. You have all the hardware you need to succeed, but it is a matter of discovering the software, technique, word, or mindset that will help you use that hardware effectively. You can be focused on a moment but still distracted from its true depth and meaning, because you filter out anything you are not aware of. This is part of why the meaning of a book can change so much across the span of your life. Where is your attention and focus? Is it on the trees or is it on the trash? What else could you be learning or experiencing from a moment? What lessons or affirmations do you want to be scanning for? You have the capability to see the world as a more beautiful, righteous, kind, artistic, and interesting place.

6.3.4 Stories And Reframing
Self-limiting beliefs also commonly show up as *stories* that we tell ourselves. Stories are how we construct our reality and how we feel about it. The objective reality of what happened cannot change, but our feelings and the mean-

ing of that experience can. For instance, a person dying is the objective reality, but then cultures have various traditions to change what emotions arise and what it means through reincarnation, the afterlife, spirits, karma, celebration, and mourning. Multiple stories can also simultaneously be true. You can both be perfect the way you are and still need to do work to create the life you desire. I was once upset for being too sensitive to maintain a relationship but remembered that our belief systems were also incompatible.

What do you believe about yourself or other people that is a story? Has someone actually confirmed that this story is true? Even if one or two people have said something that has hinted at it, does that mean the whole world believes it? These stories may be subconscious, and so the first step to changing them is simply naming the story and acknowledging it is there. Then, can you:

- Reframe that story to be positive instead
- Imagine the opposite of the story being true
- Find acceptance of a situation and believe that *everything is actually okay and I am going to make it*
- Replace *I will never____* with *I have not yet____*
- Get curious and replace *I will have a bad experience* with *I've never experienced this before so want to try it out*
- Reframe your anxiety as energy and excitement to complete the task at hand
- Saying "Wow, you're really good at this" instead of "I'm bad at this"
- Ask yourself, "Is this thought representative of something that has always been true or is it just a temporary experience?"
- Challenge the thought or allow the thought to complete itself in acceptance, like, "What if I am all alone" or "What if no one likes me right now" - can you still find joy or find ways that these are not true forever?
- Identify the beliefs you have and find the strength to look at the bigger picture surrounding an incident
- Believe that your boss is just having a bad day instead of believing that you are a bad person or focusing on how much you wish they would change
- Believe that even through your hardships you still have some beautiful gifts to offer the world
- Replace *I am a bad person* with *I am having the thought that I am a bad person*

- Expand your focus to be about more than just you, for instance by buying a gift for your friend or writing them a letter about how much you appreciate them
- Find the belief that you have more to learn and that your past does not define your future
- Believe that a person who is different from you is an opportunity to learn
- Believe that your losses are actually wins

Reframing stories may be used with your appearance, physical and mental abilities, social activities, or relationships. For instance, I've always been sensitive about my face - I have blemishes and scarring from growing up with acne. Over time though, I've been able to see that people are still attracted to me, and I've begun thinking that I kind of look like a wizard which is pretty cool. In another case, telling myself that I was born for a reason was probably the only thing that kept me alive through the years of suffering that I endured growing up. The anger I felt toward the system I had been born into gave me plenty of reason to fight on so that I could help others. Stories almost always have a positive and negative way of being told. I could have easily believed that I was being punished, the world was against me, and that I had no purpose. Instead, I found a story that allowed me to have a beautiful gift to offer.

A father you remember as showing disapproval may be renegotiated in your memories as showing concern and worry. An embarrassing experience might instead become something you learned a lot from. A friend who you felt betrayed by may become someone who was reacting from their own suffering. A time you publicly cried could be realized as an act of strength and vulnerability.

There are many ways to transform stories. Sometimes the easiest is by having a profound experience like becoming a parent, having a spiritual breakthrough, taking a psychedelic, or falling in love. Understanding the cultural, historical, or political forces that have caused you or others to be a certain way can also provide a lot of motivation to change your stories. Creating a family history as explored in Section 7.2 may be essential to finding empathy, forgiveness, or understanding for your parents. It can also assist you in identifying where a story first arose or continues to be reinforced such as a community group, news source, or family member.

Separating what you are personally responsible for from the burdens of others can help you make big transitions toward the life you want. Maybe you need to write a message for yourself you read every morning, or research the science behind why some gross-tasting food is good for you. You could also test out a belief as a visualization. Ask yourself, "I wonder what it would feel like if I wholly believed that I am inherently a lovable person worthy of kindness and success?" Framing it like this can help get past the inner critic too.

What do you want to believe? Rewrite your story so that it benefits your growth and healing. For some incredible examples of reframing, read *Man's Search For Meaning* by Viktor E. Frankl as well as *The Gift* and *The Choice* by Edith Egar. These Holocaust survivors share how stories can be transformed and help a person survive even through the most horrific of situations.

6.3.5 Integrating Stories
Finding an alternative story is not too difficult, but integrating it as something you actually believe can be challenging. Often your emotions may be blocking you from letting go of an old narrative or believing in a new one. Therefore, you may have to employ various methods of extinguishing the emotions you have to an old story. The goal is to be able to bring up the story and say, "Oh, this isn't actually scary or dangerous, and I can handle the challenges that may arise." Ketamine therapy, as mentioned in Section 4.13, is especially effective at this by allowing the user to experience a memory or thought without their usual trigger responses arising, but the techniques throughout the next few chapters are all helpful. I often have to journal using logic to rationally compare the new story to what I have experienced before or know factually. Generally, the more you study and experience the unknown, the more stories you will have to draw upon for your reality. Then, the more times you experience something like love, friendship, or success, the more easily accessed stories attached to those things will become, like, *I am lovable*, or, *I have meaningful friendships*.

What do you do when you have not yet personally experienced something? You can still draw upon facts, science, and observations from the world around you to integrate a story as a possibility for yourself. For instance, maybe you haven't made any friends in a long time, or have not yet experienced love, but you can still see that other people, when they act a certain way, have. Then you find the story that obtaining these things is a skill you can learn with effort. Alternatively, many people can first believe something when it is talked about by a person they respect with a level of power behind their name. For instance, an author, spiritual figure, doctor, or politician.

You may also change the scope of the story to be smaller. In the past I changed *I have friends* into *I have people I enjoy being around*, which was a much easier positive reframing to integrate at the time. Maybe instead of being loved, it's being appreciated for what you do, or maybe instead of human friends, it's animal and plant ones. Find the story that you can believe. Even the smallest shift in the direction of empowerment, taking action, or learning can disrupt a depressed or stuck mental state.

That's not to say that all stories that make you feel upset are untrue. You may have to change things about yourself to believe your stories. If you want to believe something different about your appearance, you can dress up in ways that feel empowering. If you want to bolster the trust in your skills, practice and take classes in a particular area like art, or use the skills in Section 12.1 to form new habits. Maybe you need to volunteer or care for an animal to start feeling important. You may have to communicate your needs to a person if you want to change your story about them being incompetent or unloving. Many people believe that math or writing is hard because they had a bad or mean teacher growing up - is there a different method or a more compassionate teacher who can help alter this story? Section 13.4 also discusses how to bolster your confidence.

6.3.6 Your Core Story And Internal Working Models
Most of your preferences, mindset, behaviors, and the way you respond to emotional situations were developed in childhood. Beyond genetic factors that we discussed previously, these are typically based on what you witnessed or experienced from your caregivers. Think of things like your cleaning preferences, touch needs, communication style, mindset, walking speed, and what relationships you engage in. Psychologists refer to these as *internal working models*.[237] Alternatively, I like thinking of them as your *core story*, because they heavily influence all your other perceptions and self-limiting beliefs.

Healing attachment wounds and many interpersonal conflicts requires transforming some of these core stories. That, or at least becoming aware of them and communicating that they are the source of your behavior or feeling. Completing the narrative of why you behave a certain way allows you to, for instance, stop blaming people for being slow, and instead remember that your mom walked fast and dragged you along while growing up.[238]

What is your first memory attached to adopting a core story? Who said the words? What incident made you decide? Knowing this isn't always easy though, since these behaviors may seem entirely normal to you, inseparable from your basic personality and how people should act. These adaptive behaviors can develop even before conscious memory forms. As such, you may get defensive when someone calls out the behavior as difficult. With abusive or neglectful parents, you may also shut down certain parts of your memory. The first goal may then be to simply acknowledge, "I have a stronger reaction to this thing than others do." This alone can help open up compassion and understanding in conflicts with others.

Core stories are responsible for a lot of upset feelings. This is especially the case when the stories of two separate people contradict each other. For instance, someone who is messy and someone who is clean, or a romantic couple with one person having anxious attachment and the other having avoidant attachment. Many parts of the following chapters are dedicated to transforming your core story.

6.3.7 Primal World Beliefs
Psychologist Jer Clifton identified 26 *primal world beliefs* that everyone operates from.[247,250] These determine your main primal world belief of whether the world is a fundamentally good or bad place. They can also be split into three main primal world beliefs. Do you see the world as:

1. **Safe or dangerous** – These include pleasurable vs. miserable, regenerative vs. degenerative, progressing vs. declining, harmless vs. threatening, cooperative vs. competitive, stable vs. fragile, and just vs. unjust.
2. **Enticing or dull** – These include interesting vs. boring, beautiful vs. ugly, abundant vs. barren, worth exploring vs. not worth exploring, meaningful vs. meaningless, improvable vs. too hard to improve, and funny vs. not funny.
3. **Alive or mechanistic** – These include intentional vs. unintentional, needs me vs. doesn't need me, and interactive vs. indifferent.

There are also five neutral primal world beliefs that do not influence your view of good or bad. These include interconnected vs. separable, changing vs. static, hierarchical vs. non-hierarchical, understandable vs. too hard to understand, and acceptable vs. unacceptable. Primal world beliefs greatly alter your personality. For instance, a person who believes that the world is a just place tends to be happier and work harder but also blames victims more for the suffering they experience. Children who are raised to believe that the world is a dangerous place tend to have worse outcomes in life.

Clifton's research does not yet show where many of these primal world beliefs arise from or how alterable they are, but I believe that they share many of the same qualities as the core stories I previously discussed. They are likely changeable through dedicated effort working with trapped emotions and speaking to the inner selves. Even if you don't change your primal world beliefs at all, understanding your own and loved ones' beliefs can help you have more empathy and work through hard conversations. You can take the test for free at <https://myprimals.com>.

6.3.8 The Story Of Our Objects And Environment
We also relate to our surrounding environment and the objects in our lives with stories. For better or worse, some objects and environments hold stronger stories than others. These might include objects that are gifted to us, that are handmade, have a family history, or that we create ourselves. Or for environments, places that we grew up, had ancestors previously living, have spent a lot of time in, had significant experiences in, or have heard a lot about as being beautiful, historical, or spiritual.

While you can change the story about an object or environment with similar techniques to those previously explored, I believe that it is more important to be mindful of what objects and environments you are surrounding yourself with. Do these environments fill you with joy, neutrality, or feelings of discontent? How can you start replacing or transforming these objects and environments to empower you? Consider the color, artwork, view of nature, architecture, lighting, and how your surroundings make you feel. Could you craft it yourself or make it a collaborative experience with friends? I cover this topic in more detail in Chapter 15.

6.3.9 The Story Of Our Emotions
According to Dr. Lisa Feldman Barrett, author of *How Emotions Are Made*, emotions are largely cultural.[254] While energetic states exist such as pleasant, unpleasant, calm, or aroused, how we relate to these states can be changed. This is why sometimes people suggest transforming anxiety into excitement, or why behind anger can be grief or stress. None of these states are bad, they're just energy moving through you. What reframing would help a difficult emotion become easier to process?

6.4 Renegotiating Memories
Memories can also be directly altered by using your imagination and visualization techniques. Remember how there is little difference between the imagination and real life? Each time you recall a memory or tell your story, your body is literally reliving it and experiencing the stress over again. Thus, if you can alter the events of a memory with your imagination, your body will expe-

rience it differently. Perhaps you stop a car that was about to hit you, create a force field around your loved ones, or call the cops on someone who hurt you. What would have to change in the past for you to believe something different? Which trustworthy person could tell you a healthier perspective and reassure you?

Part of the reason why the brain hyperfocuses on difficult memories is to know it can handle the incident in the future. Therefore, changing those memories is not lying to ourselves, it is letting the brain know that we have conquered our fear and are now safe from the threat we once experienced. Luise Reddermann explores this in her book, *Who You Were Before Trauma: The Healing Power of Imagination for Trauma Survivors.*

One option is to apply the opposite reaction you normally have in a situation. Perhaps you froze when a dog was barking at you and got bitten - in your renegotiated imagination you might now either run from the dog, fight it, or do both in separate imaginations instead. Using Pete Walker's four F-types, either through visualization or in real life:

- **Fight types** - Can you pause and listen, run from, or help?
- **Freeze types** - Can you flee from the situation, defend yourself, or tell a person to stop?
- **Flight types** - Can you stand your ground, breathe deeply, or assert your needs?
- **Fawn types** - Can you put your needs first and say what you want?

You can also make more subtle alterations to a difficult memory. For instance, playing it backward, muting it, giving everyone a different voice, or changing the colors.[241] This helps stop the constant replaying of the same events in your imagination. Instead, the memory becomes something that happened in the past. It may also reveal new details surrounding the incident.

Renegotiating memories will be easier if you have a stable source of positivity to draw resilience from. This could be from any positive source of energy such as a good memory, but Peter Levine has his clients empower themselves by connecting to their bodily sensations.[105] When in a triggered state a person often becomes tense. Perhaps their stomach is tight, or they have their arms crossed. This sensation can be explored with curiosity. What are you protecting? Where is the sensation and what are its attributes? As previously described, you can oscillate to other parts of the body which feel okay or strong. Feel into those parts and know they always are there for you to access and power through difficulty.

Levine also has clients create visual resources using a positive memory associated around the time of an incident. These can include a favorite article of clothing, an animal companion, or a skill. These resources often arise out of probing around the felt sense. The client instills this visualization by imagining its textures, smells, sounds, tastes, and how it made them feel emotionally. The resource is then brought along in the difficult memory and can be accessed anytime things become troubling. Perhaps you touch your jacket, eat some of your favorite food, are cheered on by characters from Sesame Street, or feel how powerful you were defeating the main boss in a video game.

***
Chapter Reflections

1. What are some self-limiting beliefs and stories that you hold?
2. What are some alternative stories you could tell yourself about the things currently upsetting you?
3. What emotions are holding you back from being able to believe a different story?
4. Where is your attention focused and how is it limiting the reality you have access to?
5. Who do you identify as? What identities would help you become the person you want to be?
6. How does your story change when you take a step back and look at the bigger picture?
7. How can you access more possible mindsets and beliefs? How can you come to discover more of the unknown?
8. Who are your fictional, imaginary, or media allies?
9. How could you reimagine your memories to change your core stories?
10. What are your positive anchors you can recall, touch, or visually see to oscillate back to a positive space?

Chapter 7

Basic Story Reframing

7.1 Somatic Therapy, 7.2 Your Life History And Reclaiming Memories, 7.3 Ritual, 7.4 "Imaginary" Friends, 7.5 Dreams And Nightmares, 7.6 Role-Playing And Theater, 7.7 Hypnotherapy, 7.8 Exposure Therapy, 7.9 Prolonged Exposure Therapy, 7.10 Narrative Exposure Therapy, 7.11 Journaling

Many specific techniques can help you reframe stories and overcome self-limiting beliefs. This chapter will introduce a few, with the next few chapters then diving into communication, EMDR, inner family work, and psychedelics.

7.1 Somatic Therapy

As previously stated with more severe trapped emotions, your story and what is preventing it from changing is often not available to your rational mind. However, even though you may not remember, your body language, posture, breathing patterns, skin temperature, and vocal tone are access routes into the difficulty you once experienced.[241] Somatic therapy involves becoming aware of your body with mindfulness, identifying the story it is holding onto, and expressing your emotions through movement and sound. In this way, you work on the *current* pain rather than the memory of it. Dr. Peter Levine, the author of *In An Unspoken Voice*, combines body scanning techniques with creating imagined resources to help oscillate you between overwhelming feelings and a place of safety. As discussed in Section 6.4, these could be good memories or visualized allies.

Somatic therapy is most easily accomplished with the help of a therapist to witness the small changes in your body and voice. They also act as a healthy relationship to help regulate you. Somatic therapy by itself is most effective for treating single incidents like injuries, car accidents, and witnessing deeply troubling events. That said, learning somatic releases is also often essential for healing repeated trapped emotions and attachment wounds as it allows unexpressed emotions to release from your body.

As you become more mindful of your body, you can use some of the practices from somatic therapy. Establish a safe environment. Identify how you are holding yourself and get curious about that. Using a mirror or taking a video of yourself may help. You can also establish a co-counseling relationship as explored in Section 4.7, going back and forth with a friend stating the sensations in your own body and what you see depicted in theirs. You are looking for patterns in how the body moves when it is activated by the memory of a difficult experience.

When you recall a difficult memory or experience an emotion, where in your body can you feel it? Is there a way your body wants to move? Or maybe your body is immobilized in some way? Does it collapse? Can you slowly move that body part and mindfully witness it? What is it saying? Is it protecting you? Is there a memory there? Are thoughts, images, or feelings appearing? Do your words match up with how you emotionally respond when telling the story? The goal is to keep the rational and present mind activated while simultaneously releasing any emotions that arise. If you start to slip into a dysregulated or dissociated state, oscillate to your good memories or place of safety as necessary. This said, it is important to explore the sensation for as long as possible for it to complete its unexpressed movements or emotions.[242]

Part of this practice requires that you accept the expressions your body wants to make. Giving your body permission to move may require some work. One thing that can help is practicing an exercise. This can also be directly linked to a somatic therapy practice. For instance, yoga, tai chi, cycling, swimming, or running. Ideally, this is done in a social setting, and as previously mentioned, may require being trauma-informed to meet the specific needs of people with deeper trapped emotions. Nonetheless, exercise is healing, good for you, and should be part of your routine in at least the form of a daily walk.

While big emotional expressions are sometimes ideal, emotional releases may also be quite small in sighs, deep breaths, walks, dreams, twitches, or crying just enough to dampen your eyes.[132] These releases may come out more easily when you are in the presence of an ally who helps you feel safe, or a support group that opens you to be vulnerable to your emotions. The hundreds of micro-releases that take place over a few weeks or months help a person heal as they can move slowly through recovery without triggering a flashback.

Whatever you are working on, it needs to be emotionally activated - rationally talking about it won't be enough. Somatic activities seem to become even more effective though when paired with sharing your difficult experience verbally or through writing.[97J] Try ten minutes of a movement exercise followed by ten minutes of writing about a difficult experience. Include the details, how you feel about it, and how you think it is impacting you now. More about the power of journaling this way is covered in Section 7.11.

7.2 Your Life History And Reclaiming Memories

When you have childhood trapped emotions, it may sometimes be necessary to create a *life history* to help reveal the sources of pain rooted in your past. This can be a very intense process so it is only suggested to do so if you feel adequately well, or in the company of a therapist. Remembering everything is typically not essential to your healing, so take it slowly. This history might require several years to write as you collect new pieces of information and find different ways of relating to it. More memories will appear as you develop safety and heal. Section 4.6 and Chapter 10 also offer some visualization exercises that can make memories easier to handle.

It is important to be careful because each time you recall a memory, it is physically experienced. This can be good if you are ready to renegotiate it but otherwise may make the difficult experience and the symptoms you have because of it even worse. There was a reason why you dissociated from this experience. Do you have the resources and community to help take on this overwhelming energy now? It can be helpful to distinguish that it is not necessary to retell a story like a car accident in which everyone already knows the details to.[241] On the other hand, it can be a really empowering part of healing being able to break the silence around abuse that you were told not to share, no one believed you, or you felt unsafe telling anyone. Memories that impact you are also already active in the body. Thus, instead of talking about them, memories can be worked through with somatic techniques as already explored.

With those warnings out of the way, your life history can start with surface-level details and quick notes. Include your major life events such as relationships, illnesses, family feuds, and times your basic beliefs about the world changed. You may not remember everything yourself, but photos, videos, and stories from your family might help fill in the gaps. If it is safe to do so, ask your parents and relatives specific questions about how you were raised.

Ideally, you can create a similar history about your parents, grandparents, and their ancestors to further illuminate the source of your suffering and the healing that must be done. Include each person's time of birth and death as well to see if these overlapped with any major changes in other family members. These lists may reveal patterns of addiction, abuse, toxic relationships, attachment wounds, and more that you have subconsciously recreated in your own life. While this knowledge may initially fill you with feelings of blame toward your family, the same information may help you feel empathy and compassion for what they experienced. More about forgiving your family is explored in Section 13.13.

While reclaiming all your memories can be intense, a much easier practice to start with is highlighting the nice parts of your past. Negative emotions are very loud and often drown out anything good that happened. Intentionally finding the positivity that existed during that time can help loosen self--limiting beliefs. Try writing out all of your positive experiences, especially as a child.

For me, I had blocked out much of my childhood. I could remember some details, but generally avoided doing so and labeled the whole thing as a bad experience. However, one day while in a support group, I became inspired to write a list of all my positive memories as a child unattached to the outcomes. I remembered my favorite foods, my best friend, and little activities that excited me. Most importantly I realized that I had been holding back these good memories because I expected my family to be a part of them. They weren't, and that was oddly freeing. However, by doing this exercise my disdain for my family also nudged itself into a kind of neutrality. I could recognize that I had been cared about and not everything was bad. It felt as if I had reclaimed a small part of myself that was capable of childlike play and joy.

7.3 Ritual

Rituals are physical manifestations of visualization practices. They may incorporate metaphor, prayer, objects with specialized meanings, meditation, magic spells, celestial phases, group activities, and interactions with deities or imaginary figures. Many rituals will not appear sensible to outside observers, but that is fine - accessing trapped emotions can require doing some very strange things. Most spiritual and religious practices use rituals for healing, community bonding, personal empowerment, and deepening faith.

Rituals are extremely powerful for releasing trapped emotions. This is why many people find themselves drawn to existing ritualistic practices such as astrology, tarot, magic, crystals, chakras, oracle cards, and a wide variety of monotheistic and polytheistic traditions from around the world. While sciencey folk may scoff at these practices, people who belong to a religious or spiritual group are typically happier than non-believers primarily because of the community and shared culture they create.[187,109] They also may help limit the number of choices you have to consider, make you see the world beyond yourself, and share inspiring stories of growth and redemption. Of course, as previously discussed, these practices can also be very toxic, especially by preaching discriminatory messages, convincing you that you are incapable of changing certain aspects of yourself, or by offering solutions for trapped emotions that do not actually provide a proper release.

You can create your own rituals. Right before I left home for college, I found a need to eradicate my troubled childhood. I was born and grew up surrounded by the forest, a place that became a safe place for my words and intense feelings. The trees were a sort of guardian spirit for me, an entity that had witnessed my entire upbringing. One day I snuck out with the photo album of my birth and youth, burying it underneath the firs and pines, allowing them to devour those memories. In this way, I started to see the natural world as my family more than my parents

After departing for college, I essentially cut off all communication with my biological family for five years. During that time I did a lot of healing and later did return. I now have a decent relationship with my biological family, although my relationship is based on them being friends rather than a family I am obligated to. I do not support anyone putting up with abusive behaviors, and I would quickly cut off communication again if that friendship turned toxic or if I could not have strong boundaries. Upon returning, I also dug up that photo album. Thousands of tiny roots had grown through the pages, and the photos were a colorful and blurry wash of the unrecognizable past. I now keep this album in my room, a reminder of the ritual that *reparented* myself to a healthier family. We'll discuss reparenting more in Chapter 10.

7.4 "Imaginary" Friends

One especially powerful use of the imagination is to create kind allies to assist you through your suffering. Many people, especially children, develop "imaginary" friends that provide a deep sense of support in difficult times. These may be experienced as a spiritual phenomenon or as something that feels natural. Believe what you will, the result is the same - they are friends who can include historical figures, characters from fiction, someone looked up to, animal companions, deities, or fantastical creatures. While these entities may be entirely conjured from one's imagination, they can provide profound insights and listen to your greatest difficulties. This is because to the brain the voices, images, and emotional bonds are quite real. You may think of it as weird and something only people with certain mental conditions would experience, but these friends are actually very common and may greatly assist with one's troubles. These friends can also be toxic and unhealthy, but the goal is to create healthy ones.

Anyone can develop a friendship with an "imaginary" ally. This is simply another part of yourself. Just like an actor steps into various roles, you can visualize or write out the qualities of an idealized friend. These are "compassionate beings" as Luise Reddermann calls them in *Who You Were Before Trauma: The Healing Power of Imagination for Trauma Survivors*. They love you unconditionally. You just have to regularly spend time with them, like a few minutes a day. What questions do you have for these entities? Does Oprah Winfrey or the wizard Gandalf have special advice for you? Would your home feel safer with a dragon or pack of wolves guarding it? Can your ancestors create a wall between you and something that triggers you? These are all forms of positive energy to help you better handle your trapped emotions. We'll explore your internal world of selves more in Chapter 10.

7.5 Dreams And Nightmares

Your subconscious world of dreams can illuminate quite a lot about your waking life. Stressful, nightmarish, or recurring dreams are often signs of trapped emotions. While reality impacts your dreams, dreams can also directly impact your relationship with reality. Just think about when you wake up from a good dream, you feel more awake and joyful. My favorite is falling in love in dreams. These are not just random images but a collage of your memories, feelings, and thoughts. Whatever you put into your mental space can enter your dream world, so be careful not to add more stress than necessary. Do you have to watch the news or scary films every night?

Dreams are capable of processing trapped emotions too. Shortly after I left home and cut off contact with my father, I began having dreams about him. It was a series of three recurring dreams, but once the next series started, the previous one stopped. In the first dream, I was fearful of him attacking and hurting me (although to be clear, I was never physically abused in real life). In the second, I began defending myself and retaliating back. In the third, we began hanging out like a father and son should, going fishing and enjoying each other's company. This was quite healing for me and probably took place over the course of a year, but it still took me four more years before I would return to my birth home. We're now on decent terms, although I maintain plenty of boundaries for my emotional well-being. There are ways to increase your attention to important dreams including:

- Writing down anything you remember from your dreams as soon as you wake up no matter how boring or strange the details are
- Telling yourself before sleeping to dream
- Learning techniques for lucid dreaming
- Stopping the consumption of substances that prevent dreams such as cannabis and alcohol
- Consuming substances that promote dreams, like mugwort tea
- Cutting back on sensationalistic media like horror films, action flicks, and the news and replace them with things that actually resonate with you emotionally and spiritually

Once you have formed a good relationship with remembering your dreams, start taking note of things that specifically bother or enliven you. Are you missing the bus? Feeling cluttered? Falling in love? Around lots of people? Failing assignments? Confronted by ghoulish figures? Dreams do not always have meanings, sometimes they may just be random cyclings of your memories, so I like to focus on the recurring themes. I have never had much faith in dream interpretation books myself as I think it is important to consider how you personally relate to the images. What desires, insecurities, or lifestyles are your dreams whispering to you? A therapist or friend may help see how these various aspects connect to your life in themes like control, insecurity, or safety.

For several years I had a recurring dream about being late for the bus with all my stuff scattered around. While I never intentionally tried addressing these stressful dreams, they all but went away once I got a car. I believe growing up poor made me quite attached to my possessions, each essential to my ability to survive. Simultaneously, a car gave me a sense of security about reaching my destinations and doing so on my own time.

How can you empower yourself in your waking life to settle your fears in your subconscious? You can even use visualization practices to confront the uncomfortable aspects of a nightmare. For instance, when you wake up after a nightmare, try to imagine fighting off or standing up against whatever menace was plaguing your sleep. This may require that you resource yourself first by connecting with your abilities and support networks to keep you safe, or slowly working through the meaning of the dream and identifying how truthfully it reflects the reality you actually live in.[257] What do you need to resolve the dream?

Lucid dreaming, the act of using your conscious awareness in the dream realm, can help you go even deeper into this practice. Check out some guides online if you want to experiment. I've also had a friend successfully overcome nightmares in a very short period with the help of a neurofeedback therapist as explored in Section 5.2. Alternatively, you can use other techniques for dealing with trapped emotions such as EMDR covered in Chapter 9.

7.6 Role-Playing And Theater

Instead of visualizing possible scenarios in your imagination, your conflicts and trapped emotions can be acted out by others. Usually, this involves a therapist or co-counselor *role-playing* your parents or partner, allowing you to speak to them in a safe environment.[99] The role-player may also act out an idealized version of these characters in which they say something compassionate or empathetic about the hardships they have caused you. These people may or may not be a current part of your life, but the technique can be fairly effective at helping you rewrite self-limiting beliefs and expel any trapped emotions holding you back.

Group role-playing sessions also exist. For instance, in *The Body Keeps The Score*, Bessel Van Der Kolk explores *Pesso Boyden System Psychomotor* (PBSP) therapy.[971] These groups are led by a facilitator who may reflect your emotional states or ask questions. You select and position members of the audience to role-play your mother, father, sibling, friend, bully, boss, and so on. These individuals can play the parts with lines, facial expressions, or movements, and you can interact with them by standing up for yourself, hugging them, yelling, or whatever else is reasonable for the experience you are attempting to resolve. You can also call upon your ideal versions of these people to play through lines and actions that may have been more supportive and healing.

Kolk believes that therapies like PBSP can help you develop empathy and love even if you did not experience these things as a child. The language used is very specific to reduce the potential for being triggered. For instance, the facilitator might reflect on your emotional state by saying, "A witness can see how sad it makes you when talking about your father." You might say "I enroll ____ as my ideal mother." The ideal mother might say, "If I had been your ideal mother, then I would have treated you with love and honesty." Find video examples of this technique online, check out <pbsp.com>, or read Chapter 18 of *The Body Keeps The Score*. Spaces that practice psychomotor therapy are unfortunately quite limited, but similar groups exist, or it would be possible with a little training to get friends together to create a scenario as described above. That said, many therapists and personal growth seminars incorporate role-playing into their work.

A more dynamic form of role-playing is theater. Kolk explores this in Chapter 20 of *The Body Keeps The Score*, saying that it can help traumatized individuals explore other ways of being by acting as characters in an alternative story. By doing so they remove themselves from the dangers of their own life and can freely embody things like courage, strength, hope, and empathy. Some theater programs are specifically made for individuals with PTSD, helping them incorporate aspects of their story into a script, learn teamwork, study acting, and then collectively challenge what previously traumatized them through the performance. The tabletop role-playing game, Dungeons & Dragons, can be used similarly if established with therapeutic intent.

7.7 Hypnotherapy

Hypnotherapy helps create a calm and relaxed state in the mind and body that is suggestible to new ideas. This state can even prevent dissociation while confronting triggering memories and is an effective technique for dealing with big and small trapped emotions.[97S,101,174] Self-hypnosis is similar to the visualization technique previously described in Section 4.6, but working with a hypnotherapist will generally allow you to tackle larger issues.

Visualization and self-hypnosis can also be powerful tools for instilling self-confidence and training your brain to be able to handle challenges. There are many self-hypnosis apps and guided videos available online such as at <www.reveri.com>, but a hypnotherapist will often give you the tools to take the technique home with you as well. You can also read *The Heart and Mind of Hypnotherapy* by Douglas Flemons.

7.8 Exposure Therapy

Normal exposure therapy uses small doses of stimuli you find stressful to normalize the experience and eventually establish it as safe. This can be applied to visual stimuli, touch, memories, movements, and more. However, in its simplest form, exposure therapy is generally ineffective for treating PTSD, but it can be useful for overcoming simple anxieties and unfamiliar experiences.[97T]

Exposure therapy is typically best when you can control the difficult stimuli within a safe space. You should always start at the easy end of your difficult trigger. For instance, I struggle with human-based conflict. While I can have healthy communication with loved ones, hearing people arguing or being criticized for long sends me into a freeze or flight response. This made me avoid most activism, politics, movies, strongly spoken individuals, and even board games. Interestingly, this trigger did not typically appear around videogames or animated shows, just around real people. This is perhaps why I became a bit of a nerd.

I knew that avoiding these things was not healthy and I wanted to play boardgames with my friends. Board games were an ideal place to introduce healthy conflict into my life because I determined when the conflict happened and for how long. Not only that, but I was also among friends. I could welcome this insecurity around conflict when I felt mentally well enough, and opt out of playing or suggest something other than board games when I was already feeling overwhelmed. Initially, I only played cooperative games, but slowly introduced competitive ones too. I wouldn't be able to play for long before feeling overwhelmed, and typically could only finish one round before calling it quits - but I got better.

7.8.1 Affirmations
What especially helped while building my tolerance to board games was reframing affirmations. Whenever I felt attacked or bad about my self-worth, I started to think to myself "I'm not losing, I'm learning," or "I'm excited my friend is doing so well." This positive reframing can provide an alternative to the nagging negativity that distracts the mind from a good experience. I share more affirmations in Section 13.10.

7.8.2 Simplify The Stress
When exposing yourself to a stressful trigger, take it slow with simplified and controllable versions of the difficult experience. Always empower yourself with good memories and deep breathing. Remember, if you start to feel triggered, stop the activity, mindfully experience the emotion or resource yourself with a positive memory. Only return to the activity when you feel emotionally settled, and only if you want to. It is okay to take a break and return at a later time, or even excuse yourself to use the bathroom.

7.8.3 Re-Experience It In A Positive Light
Soon after a stressful incident, it can be very therapeutic to re-experience the objects and people who were involved again in a positive light, so long as they are normally safe and positive for you to be around. You may need time, emotional releases, or a safe ally to accompany you, but just know that the longer you wait, the more likely it is for the experience to become a trapped emotion that generalizes similar people and objects as stressful. For example, a person who gets into a car accident might want to get into a car again. Or, a person who just had an intense conversation with their partner might benefit from going on a date with them the next evening rather than a week later. Again,

take it slow - exposure can be uncomfortable. It may require multiple sessions or the use of more advanced techniques in this book to feel right.

7.8.4 Practicing For A Stressful Event
Normal exposure therapy can also help relieve anxiety before experiencing something new. I deal with a lot of performance anxiety and sometimes have trouble being in spaces where I don't know anyone. If you want to participate in a group activity but feel too anxious, watch a recorded version of one of their meetings to normalize the environment and protocols. You can also learn the basics of a skill online for activities like tai chi or yoga before attending your first in-person class. Video meetings are also great for dropping in anonymously to observe different groups while being able to control the volume and whether or not you interact. Virtual reality is opening many possibilities for safely exposing people to triggers as well. Of course, the goal is to eventually move beyond the practice spaces and connect with activities in real life.

7.8.5 Triggering A Difficult Emotion
Exposure therapy techniques are also great at activating a charged feeling that then can be used with the emotional release and renegotiation techniques outlined in Chapters 5 and 6. For instance, you might bring up part of a memory or read a note an ex-lover sent you. You can directly work with these feelings, or, you may realize that there was a time in your past that something similar triggered you, such as a parental figure, and then work on the core source instead. There are also more advanced versions of exposure in therapy used to resolve very severe forms of trapped emotions.

7.9 Prolonged Exposure Therapy
Therapists trained in *prolonged exposure therapy* start by establishing a therapeutic relationship with the client and teaching them calming techniques, especially with deep breathing.[137] Sessions then involve the client relating memories of a difficult experience from beginning to end in the present tense. These are recorded to listen to at home. The client is instructed to fully experience their emotions, not using any kind of avoidant thinking or withholding. Each retelling in the course of a session and consecutive meetings attempts to dive deeper into the details and emotional qualities of the experience. Sessions are 90 to 120 minutes in length. Between each retelling, specific points and contradictions might be highlighted for the client such as "How did this person make you feel?" or "Do you still believe that about yourself?"

This process both normalizes the event as something in the past and slows it down in such a way that the client can reprocess the incident. As trapped emotions are often a hyperfocus on very specific memories, expanding the details of a memory can loosen its grip on the mind.

Prolonged exposure therapy can be quite intense and goes against the ethos of many practices which avoid digging up a whole difficult experience. In *The Body Keeps The Score*, Bessel Van Der Kolk does not see it as particularly effective for PTSD because it does not integrate the experience into the past.[97K] On the other hand, Andrew Huberman of the *Huberman Lab Podcast* believes that integration can occur in prolonged exposure therapy so long as positivity is attached to the former experience.[74] He uses as an example that a person's bicycle incident is explored over and over again to diminish the fear response. Then a new narrative is learned that creates a positive association with bicycle riding. Lastly, this positive association is integrated into the past, that "I am enjoying riding my bicycle even though I had a difficult experience with it in the past."

Prolonged exposure therapy, if done correctly, is effective and safe. Well-resourced people can even apply some of these principles without a therapist, though it is only suggested to do so with your smaller wounds. Try it out with these steps:

1. Start by grounding yourself in positive memories, meditation, or deep breathing.
2. Write out a difficult experience, your emotions surrounding it, as well as how you relate to it now.
3. As emotions arise, witness them, allowing grief and anger to surface.
4. Read the passage several times and practice self-care as necessary, but do not try to withhold your emotional release.
5. The next day, return and read the passage again. You may notice the intense feelings are no longer present, but if they are, dive deeper into the story. Note the details of the rooms, what people were wearing, and the smells and sounds. Consider the intentions of the people there, the self-limiting beliefs you are holding, and why a person acted the way they did.
6. Continue re-reading and adding to this story daily until you feel resolved with the events and characters involved.
7. You may find yourself reframe a basic belief about yourself you formed due to the incident. Perhaps "I always feel unsafe" becomes "I am capable of discerning danger from normal situations and protect-

ing myself when necessary." Perhaps you recognize that an ex did not mean you harm, but your expectations or need to control situations made you incompatible. Or, perhaps you recognize you are no longer in danger from someone who previously harmed you. It may be helpful to write these realizations out or repeat them as affirmations.

This form of exposure therapy was quite powerful for me while sharing my personal stories throughout these pages. Sometimes the trapped emotions are only partly resolved or return later. Repeat the practice as necessary with the new feelings and details that arise. You may also need to do work in other ways before being able to fully renegotiate or access a difficult energy. These might include techniques I cover in other parts of the book such as creating a safe space, meditating, doing neurofeedback, or using EMDR.

7.10 Narrative Exposure Therapy

Narrative exposure therapy builds on prolonged exposure therapy with some key differences.[160] This technique works by organizing disjointed memories into a cohesive chronological narrative, which helps establish a difficult experience as something that happened in the past instead of something that is still happening. This is done by first creating a personal history as described in Section 7.2 up to the point of a difficult incident. Exposure to the triggers and full emotional releases then begins while continuing to record the events. Strong emotions are translated into words and also become part of the story. The narrative is then continued with all the events after that time up to the present day.

The personal history helps the client know that their difficult experience does not define the rest of their life and was not something that happened out of nowhere. Rather, the difficult experience was one event with a specific time in the past that was part of many other experiences. It reminds the individual that there is a future after the incident and that the emotions and experiences before the incident are still available.

According to psychologist Todd Kashdan, a softer approach to narrative exposure therapy can also involve identifying and focusing on the things that you find pleasurable in life.[233] Instead of thinking about a difficult experience, you identify and pursue your primary goals, purpose, enjoyable hobbies, and commitments. This is different than escaping from your suffering in a distraction because you are specifically doing things that are nourishing and essential to your overall success and joy in life. For instance, spending time with friends, challenging yourself physically, or working on a creative project. People who do this tend to have better health outcomes after distressing events, because they decrease their focus on the original stress and get reconnected to the bigger picture. Of course, you may have to find activities that are healthy and pleasurable first. Refer to Chapters 4 and 14 for some ideas.

Once again, you can use these techniques for yourself. It won't go quite as deep as working with a therapist, but you may discover some profound insights. Journaling frequently can help correct distorted thinking. Be sure to question your narrative by asking questions like: What elements are you ignoring? Are you focusing only on the bad experience you had? What were the good times like? What is true without your judgment?

7.11 Journaling

Journaling is powerful because it allows you to concretely build on ideas rather than repeat the same thoughts over and over again. Writing in my journal is often the first place that I go when I realize I am stuck in a negative emotion. Get curious. For instance, answer questions like, *Am I in danger? Am I at fault? How did this happen? What can I do to fix this situation? Have I done everything I can to make things better? How can I prevent this from happening in the future? What is the worst possible outcome of this feeling and how likely is my worry to manifest into reality? Even if it does happen, are there similar situations I have gotten through before, or, can I trust that love, stability, and calmness still exist in my future?* Laura Davis, co-author of the book, *Courage to Heal*, also offers writing workshops with some great prompts to help explore your memories and perspective around family. For instance, instead of journaling about just your mom, you might reflect on her wardrobe or the time spent driving together.

Bessel Van Der Kolk cites research showing that journaling about a traumatic experience decreases symptoms of PTSD.[97L] This is essentially a form of exposure therapy. It was important that those sharing included the details of the event, their feelings and emotions about it, as well as how they thought that event now influenced their life. Just retelling the details of the event had no beneficial health outcomes. This act helps put the event within the framework of the rest of your life. Journaling sessions were 15 minutes each for four consecutive days. These journal entries were also read by researchers, which may have had some influence on the outcome with the participants knowing their words would be witnessed. Kolk notes that for journaling to be most effective it must be done for yourself and because you want to without any outside influence causing you to hold back your words or emotions.

***
Chapter Reflections

1. Who are your fictional, imaginary, or media allies?
2. What are the positive anchors you can recall, touch, or visually see to oscillate back to a positive space?
3. What patterns show up in your dreams that you can learn from? What resources do you need to resolve your difficult dreams?
4. What difficulties of yours might benefit from simple exposure therapy and practice?
5. Which of your trapped emotions might benefit from narrative or prolonged exposure therapy?
6. How can you incorporate journaling into your daily routine?
7. Do you write about your emotions or how an event has impacted your life when you journal?

Chapter 8

Communication

8.1 Nonviolent Communication (NVC), 8.2 Making NVC Sound Natural, 8.3 Apologizing With NVC And Making Amends, 8.4 Handling Conflict With Conversational Receptiveness And Curiosity, 8.5 Supporting Others, 8.6 Repairing Relationships With Clarification And Imago, 8.7 Effective Communication, 8.8 Non-Judgmental Language, 8.9 Knowing The Source Of Your Need, 8.10 If Your Request Is Rejected, 8.11 Not Communicating, 8.12 Delaying Communication, 8.13 Misdirected Communication And Complaining, 8.14 Incompatibility, 8.15 Unavailable People, 8.16 More About Communication

Learning some general guidelines for communicating with the source of your stress can do a lot for dissolving difficult emotions. Communication is one of the easiest and most effective ways to create or reestablish a safe space and change a story you have about another person and your relationship with them. Clarifying a situation, apologizing for misdeeds, or asking for your needs to be met can be deeply soothing and heal damaged relationships. It can also help open up the true expression of your pain such as turning anger into grief and allowing the release of trapped emotions.

Unfortunately, communication is not always easy to accomplish. Even though speaking and writing well are paramount to obtaining what we want in life, most people simply emulate how their peers use words and nonverbal cues. While this might impress your parents and first crush, cultural language norms typically instill many antagonistic patterns toward yourself and others. In fact, I believe that most suffering is caused by poor communication. It is common to feel hurt by how others communicate or we do not get our needs met because we cannot adequately communicate what we want. While communication can be uncomfortable, not communicating is often very hurtful to you and any other parties involved. Learning these skills is also very powerful for learning how to lovingly talk to yourself, especially with the *inner family* explored in Chapter 10.

Communication skills are especially important to learn because humans tend to inaccurately read how a person's facial expressions and other behaviors relate to their true beliefs.[177] In other words, a person might leave a party early, be frowning, or cancel plans, and you might create a story about them disliking you that you hold onto for years. According to communications psychologist Tessa West, even if you "put yourself into another person's shoes" or live with another person for years, you are still likely to read their thoughts and emotions wrong. The only way to reliably know a person's inner mental landscape is by asking them directly.

Language creates the foundation from which we relate to reality. Everything is communication including our words, thoughts, actions, inactions, body language, fashion, decorations, and celebrations. My book, *You Are A Great And Powerful Wizard* is already devoted to this topic, so I'll simply share what I believe to be a few of the most important communication techniques. Just keep in mind as you learn these techniques that you typically cannot control how others communicate, only how you respond. Needing others to speak the same as you is typically not fair and can be discriminatory, although it is nice when people are on the same page. Exceptions can of course be made with people who repeatedly use toxic or abusive language.

Many people have trapped emotions to certain communication styles, especially ones that remind them of how their parents spoke to them as children. In Chapter 10 we explore the inner child, but for now, just know that you are often speaking to an adult *and* their hurt inner child. This is why using very specific language is often essential for healthy outcomes in conversation. This also applies to you and may mean that it is important that you can access your rational mind going into conversations, ask a person to change how they communicate, temporarily step away from people who utilize certain communication styles, or renegotiate the trapped emotions you have. Please be wary of using your triggers as an excuse to avoid communicating altogether though. Communication can be hard and feel very intense, but it is so much easier than sitting with unresolved upset for weeks, months, or years.

People who grew up in dysfunctional families or experienced repeated abuse as a child may have to rebuild their social skills from scratch by healing their attachment wounds as explored in Section 17.6. A therapist or support group will be especially helpful here, but the following contents and Chapter 14 provide some starting points. These skills may involve learning basic body language, observing healthy conflict resolution, mirroring the movements of others, experiencing a secure relationship through a therapist or animal companion, engaging in prosocial hobbies, and practicing active listening.

8.1 Nonviolent Communication (NVC)

Marshall B. Rosenberg developed nonviolent communication to help resolve religious and racial conflicts, but the technique is equally useful for everyday strife as well. NVC works by avoiding language that psychologically creates defensiveness and instead promotes language that nurtures open-mindedness and mutual understanding. It forces you to slow down, listen carefully, and think about how you are speaking before possibly making an emotionally uncomfortable situation even more stressful. NVC does have critics, but I have done my best to resolve commonly cited issues with several additions. There are also many thoughtful reads online, such as Ido Sternberg's Medium.com article titled *How To Get In Trouble While Learning Nonviolent Communication*. Most importantly, remember that NVC is a tool. It requires skill to use and just because you use it does not mean you are right. NVC can still oppress and abuse others, or ask for unreasonable things. Nonetheless, it is really powerful when practiced in the correct situations.

In Rosenberg's book, *Nonviolent Communication: A Language of Compassion*, he explains how to use observations, feelings, needs, and requests without judgment to navigate unmet needs you or others around you have.[145A] NVC is generally used for any emotionally charged conversation such as establishing boundaries, arguing with a person without triggering them, clarifying misunderstandings, or explaining a difficult lesson. The following sections cover the basics of NVC and some other communication skills, but for a deeper understanding, read the book, watch video tutorials, and seek out local workshops. It is a powerful and life-changing technique that I believe everyone should learn. The basic format of NVC goes like this:

1. **State an observation** - What is it specifically that you like or don't like that a person is doing or did?
2. **State your feelings** - How does the observed action make you feel? Does it make you feel happy, alive, afraid, bored, detached, angry, or calm? Remember that a feeling is not a judgment, do not use slander or make accusations. Make it an "I" statement as well. Instead of "you make me feel..." use "I felt..."
3. **State your needs** - Common human needs include sustenance, safety, love, empathy, rest, play, community, creativity, freedom, and purpose. What is your unmet need from this list or from things you

have identified as essential to your well-being? Why do you personally want this change? How does it benefit you? Does it create more order, improve your life, make work go faster, create a quieter space, or make a higher quality product? This could also involve having a need to take space and calm down feelings of overwhelm or anger.
4. **Make a request** - Make it clear, polite, reasonable, and preferably a "do" instead of a "don't." Remember, you are making a request, not a demand. "Could you please rewrite this with more action language," or, "Can you start doing the dishes after you finish eating?"

For example, "Alex, when you play your electric guitar past 10:00 PM (observation), I feel frustrated (feeling) because I need to wake up for work early (need). Could you keep your playing to before 10:00 PM (request)?

Please note that this is just a framework, it does not have to be followed exactly and often should not be depending on the context and culture being interacted with. The real power of NVC is unlocked when the principles behind this framework are integrated into how you communicate.[223] These include:

- *Using non-judgmental language*: Non-judgmental language avoids using words that attack the other person's character or beliefs such as dumb, bad, slow, or mean
- *Keeping the focus on your personal experience*: Part of maintaining non-judgment is by using "I" language and speaking only from your personal feelings and needs rather than what another person should do or should be
- *Knowing your feelings and why you are upset*: Perhaps you journal, use mindfulness, or reflect with a friend or therapist to really understand the situation
- *Leading with empathy*: Empathy is the ability to understand what another person is feeling and imagine what that experience is like – more about empathy is covered in Section 13.7
- *Being a strong listener*: Instead of only focusing on what you're going to say, listening and getting curious about what the other person is saying and the feelings behind those words allows you to maintain mutual respect between parties
- *Trying to reach a workable solution*: So many disagreements become aimless arguments, but the end goal of NVC is to repair the relationship, get each person's needs met, and move forward

Altogether, you can adapt to the situation at hand. The other person does not have to be using NVC or speaking kindly for you to use these techniques effectively. NVC principles create an alternative to destructive forms of communication like maintaining silence, using violence, and being passive-aggressive. Many of the stated principles are explored more throughout the chapter.

8.2 Making NVC Sound Natural

The biggest criticism of nonviolent communication is how unnatural it often sounds, which can then cause a person to hear the phrasing as condescending or annoying. Practice is essential, as people new to NVC often forget to use body language, or appear inauthentic in their delivery as they try and remember the four parts. The style used previously is most valuable for two people who agree to use it as their default mode of conflict resolution, but this greatly limits its application. The original *Nonviolent Communication* book does not cover how to adapt it to everyday speech, but it is possible. Through my experience, the previous steps can be split up and slowed down so that it becomes more of a conversation. For example:

Person 1: Hey can we talk about house chores?
Person 2: Sure.

Person 1: Well I've honestly been feeling kind of annoyed (feeling) because I seem to be the only person cleaning the bathroom (observation). It is really important to me that we each take turns doing the chores equally like we agreed (need). How can I support you in remembering to take your turn?

Person 2: Oh sorry, maybe if you texted me a reminder, that would help a lot in my busy schedule.

Person 1: Cool, thank you. I can do that.

We can also rephrase the example given earlier to flow more naturally: "Hey Alex, do you have a minute? I've been hearing you play your electric guitar late (observation), and while I appreciate that you are falling in love with music, I've been getting frustrated and cranky (feeling) because I wake up for work early (need). Could you keep your playing to before 10:00 PM (request)?" Remember, tone and timing are everything and it is better to approach a person in a neutral voice rather than an angry one. Calm yourself.

A person may still become triggered or defensive in these exchanges, in which case you will have to clarify or reiterate specifically what you are trying to say. The goal is to maintain a person's openness to change rather than turning them defensive and closed off. This may require that you listen to their side of the conflict, admit that you played a role in causing the situation to happen, or apologize for a misunderstanding. Stating your feelings is also not always necessary, but it humanizes the interaction and creates space for empathy to emerge. That said, not all cultures are open to vulnerability. In the example above I might leave out "frustrated and cranky" for simply saying "I'm not getting enough sleep as it is."

Conflict is messy, and tensions often increase before bonds can be healed or boundaries are agreed to. That is okay, just be sure to start somewhere, be empathetic, and be willing to meet halfway with a person. While you do have the option to not communicate, it may make releasing the trapped emotions or getting your needs met especially difficult, if not impossible.

8.3 Apologizing With NVC And Making Amends

Learning how to apologize can be deeply healing, including for things that happened years ago. Even if you don't believe that you were responsible, if you hurt someone else's feelings, then an apology can start the communication process and open a person to eventually listen to your side as well. Often an apology opens up a person to admit their role in a conflict or allows them to forgive you. I'm not suggesting you apologize or forgive heinous acts, especially if you are a fawn type. However, conflicts are rarely one-sided even though our defense mechanisms usually push us to believe otherwise. Admitting that you messed up can take a lot of courage, but it may be essential for healing.

Keep in mind that a person may not be ready for your apology or may refuse to accept it. That is okay, empathize that what you did was hurtful, or know that perhaps you did not apologize in a way that felt genuine. Regardless, it is often very healing to apologize by helping you forgive yourself and be able to focus on that your final act toward a person was a positive one. Nonviolent communication is a good model for framing an apology:

1. **Observe** - State the incident or words that you believe upset the person.
2. **Feelings** - State the feelings the incident caused or likely caused in the other person.
3. **Needs** - State what the other person was probably needing. Generally,

this involves some security that you care about them and will be more careful about what you did in the future.
4. ***Request*** - Ask what you can do to make it up to them and reestablish their trust.

For example, "I'm really sorry that I broke your guitar. I understand why you're upset with me, you can't play music right now and that guitar was really important to you. I promise I'll be more careful in the future and I want to do what I can to help you repair or replace your instrument. Are there any other things I can do that will help you forgive me?"

Be careful about trying to rationalize why you did something hurtful. This can come off as a really poor excuse that immediately negates your apology. If you do try explaining, be sure to add that you understand why those actions were still hurtful and you will not repeat them. Apologies are most effective when you are genuinely empathetic to a person's emotions and you fully embody how sorry you are in your facial expression and tone.

If there is something you need to explain about the incident, do so after a person has accepted your apology. Do not blame or point your finger at misunderstandings. Even if you feel wronged in some way, it is important to be present with one person's emotions at a time - focus on the other person who feels hurt first. Remember too that not everything needs to be said. The goal is to repair the relationship, not to prove someone wrong, so let go of any desire to be "right." More about relationship repair is discussed in Section 8.6.

For those of us who grew up with trapped emotions from childhood, it can be a powerful practice to create a list of people we have harmed in our life and make amends for the pain that we caused. This may be an apology, but it might also be an internal decision to change how we act and never repeat the harmful behavior. Remember, only make direct amends to people with whom it feels safe to do so and be careful about blaming yourself for things that were not actually your fault. An apology does not mean your actions were intentional, or even that you have to feel guilty or blame yourself for the incident. An apology just acknowledges that your actions harmed another person.

If you know you wronged a person, especially your child or a sibling, directly asking for forgiveness may help them know you have changed and want to make up for your past mistakes. How to forgive others and yourself is covered later in Section 13.13, but for now know that forgiveness can be a slow process and no one is obligated to forgive you. That is to say, if you hurt a person too deeply, or show any sign of still being a threat, they may not be willing to release the suffering you caused them. Typically it is best to ask for forgiveness after having apologized for your actions.

8.4 Handling Conflict With Conversational Receptiveness And Curiosity

Another framework that can be used together with or instead of NVC for handling disagreements is *conversational receptiveness*. This is a communication technique developed by researchers to calm a person down and reach a middle ground between differing beliefs.[210] The technique involves four parts:

1. *Acknowledge* - Acknowledge what the other person is saying by reflecting their words back without any judgment. "So what I'm hearing you say is that you were upset this week because we did not get to hang out?"
2. *Agree* - State what you agree with from their statements, even if it is something small. "I can see that you value our friendship and social time a lot."
3. *Reframe* – Make sure your statements are positive, such as *can* or *yes*, instead of negative, like *cannot* or *are terrible*.
4. *Hedge* - Further reframe your statements with softer language such as perhaps, sometimes, or maybe.[210] "I can see that some people feel more loved when regularly contacted by their friends."

Approaching the conversation with curiosity is also helpful, so ask questions to show interest and create a better connection. For instance, "How does that work" or "Could you explain more about that?" This is especially important because a large percentage of disagreements result from words and concepts being defined differently between two parties.[249] People tend to assume that words are concrete, but we change their meaning based on our personal experiences. For instance, consider words like *love*, *freedom*, and *safety*. You need to give specific examples of what you mean by these things, or else you will not be heard right.

8.5 Supporting Others

By reading this book you might begin to understand just how common and widespread suffering is in the world. You can do a lot to lift up those around you. While most people won't actively seek help, there will be times that friends, family, or your partner will greatly appreciate support. Keep a close eye on loved ones after they have a difficult experience. Symptoms may not appear for several days or weeks. Your involvement largely depends on their openness to healing modalities. A willingness to heal may mean a person is trying but doing something you know is not the right direction - often however they have to learn what works and what does not on their own. As stated in Section 4.1, hitting rock bottom is quite motivating. Respect and trust their process, just like you respect and trust your own. That said, there is still a lot you can do to directly or indirectly assist a loved one, just be sure you are offering it as a gift rather than a demand:

1. **Listen** - Everyone loves being attentively listened to, and people going through hardship appreciate being able to vent their frustrations. Especially effective is *active listening* in which you make small statements like, "Yeah" or "That sucks" and paraphrase back what you're hearing like, "So you're feeling upset because you felt disrespected by them?" Even more effective is having this conversation while doing an activity together like walking, doodling, or kicking a ball.[132T]
2. **Show empathy** - Empathetically mirror emotions or mention how hard or how angry that thing would make you feel. It is generally not a good idea to argue with a person about what they should be feeling. Remember that all feelings are real and need to be released at an emotional rather than cognitive level. Instead of blaming a person for their feelings, ask them what happened or how you can support them. Be careful about sharing your own similar experience unless you explicitly ask if it is okay. Doing so may be perceived as rude by putting the focus on yourself instead of the person seeking support.
3. **Offer compassion** - Beyond empathy, compassion provides another level of emotional connection by offering your support - "That sounds really sad, what can I do to support you?" This offers help without being condescending while letting a loved one know that you care about them and respect their ability to take care of themselves. Unsolicited advice may come off as not really understanding a person's situation and can be emotionally insensitive. That said, you may have to offer suggestions like, "I could give you a hug, buy you a meal, or just listen to whatever you need to vent." Don't take what they say or do personally - this isn't about you, it is a mood caused by a combination of external and internal circumstances.
4. **Provide positivity** - Help the person remove themselves from their

thoughts with a positive experience. They may automatically turn you down in anxiety or disbelief unless you're more direct and offer specific suggestions, or reiterate that you really mean it. Introduce them to new pro-social activities and get them away from unhealthy coping mechanisms like alcohol. You could even go to a support group with them or learn co-counseling together.

5. ***Ask open-ended questions to help a person make healthier decisions*** - Rather than providing unsolicited advice, asking questions that help a person self-reflect allows them to come to conclusions themselves. However, you should not probe or try to force them to tell you uncomfortable things.
6. ***Help release trapped emotions*** - Many people do not allow their emotions to be released in healthy ways. See if you can assist a person in having an emotional release. You can help this pent-up energy move by offering to do an activity together, or by mirroring or naming their emotional state.
7. ***Stay in regular contact*** - Send a text, call, ask to hang out, share a funny meme, invite them out to eat, say nice things about them, and so on. People need people.
8. ***Correct self-destructive, abusive, and distorted thinking*** - If you catch a person making false statements about themselves or those around them, call it out using your personal experience as a reference. If a person says "I'm no good" you might share "Hey, I hear that you're having a really hard time right now and just want to make sure you know that I really enjoy our time together." If a person keeps reiterating the same story, you can make a boundary that you have already heard that and do not want to hear it again. Remind them that each time they share those words they are re-experiencing the painful event. Ask what they can do about their situation.
9. ***Ask before giving advice*** - Empowering a person to make changes on their own will lead to far more beneficial results than you attempting to give unsolicited advice. Sometimes people in difficult situations do not have the capacity to do a whole lot about their predicament, let alone openly listen. True healing is likely not possible unless a person wants to change with their own mental energy. This requires first that their nervous system is regulated, so be sure to help them do that first. You can provide tools and support, but the person you are caring for must find their own pathway to healing.
10. ***Give without expectation*** - If you do have a specific resource you

want to offer a person, do not expect them to follow through. Perhaps you give them a book or offer to go with them to a support group that helped you. While you can kindly suggest these things, do not try to force them. Ideally, you ask their permission first as well so they feel empowered about the decision. Books are especially nice because they will be there when a person is ready.
11. ***Self-care*** - Make sure you are taking care of yourself in the process of helping another person, it is easy to burn out by absorbing too much suffering from another person's problems.
12. ***Learning support skills*** - Many of these skills can be learned through co-counseling courses, nonviolent communication, and de-escalation training. You can read guides online or take an in-person class.

If you believe that someone close to you is considering killing themselves, there are things you can do to help prevent it. While some people commit suicide with no warnings, those who are open about their feelings are seeking help. Here are some actions you can take:

- Ask them directly if they are thinking of committing suicide and have a conversation about it. If they want it, help connect them with professional mental health support. A person depressed enough to commit suicide may not have the energy to seek help themselves.
- Express empathy for their feelings. Tell them that the feelings they are experiencing will pass with time.
- Call 1-800-273-8255 or text 988 for someone to talk to through the National Suicide Hotline. They can offer confidential guidance, support, and help connect you with local resources.
- Even if your loved one asks for secrecy, and even if it is uncomfortable, tell people who are legally responsible for their well-being, such as their parents or a partner. A person with suicidal ideations needs support, not silence.
- Remember, there is always help and hope, and every day is a new day with new possibilities.
- Do not allow a person to manipulate you into believing that you are the only reason why they are alive. Seek mental health support yourself to help navigate the emotional difficulties of a friend's suicidal ideations or attempts.
- For a more thorough guide on preventing suicide, see online resources

like the *Suicide Prevention Resource Center*.

Remember that your healing is not contingent upon the healing of your parents or anyone else. You can try by giving others resources or asserting boundaries and needs with nonviolent communication, but there are many other ways that you can improve your situation. Consider how long of a process healing has been for you; no one is going to change overnight. Go slow, but know that you are not responsible for healing the suffering in others, especially if they are not trying to heal. You are also in no way obligated to maintain a relationship that turns toxic because of a person's unaddressed suffering. You are free to pursue a better life. Never sacrifice your joy for the sake of an abusive individual. Sometimes the best thing you can do for people who are suffering, especially abusive fight types, is to leave them.

8.6 Repairing Relationships With Clarification And Imago

Keeping in mind the statements in the previous section, it is possible to transform damaged or unhealthy relationships. This includes with lovers, exes, friends, housemates, co-workers, and family. The contents of Chapters 5, 13, and 14 will also provide valuable insights for doing this work. However, some people with trapped emotions will have to heal themselves before they can heal their relationships. This is because their needs and boundaries may be quite unhealthy for a proper relationship to survive. That said, it may still be possible with the right techniques. Harville Hendrix and Helen Hunt, founders of *Imago Relationship Therapy*, suggest a basic framework for working through conflicts:

1. Have only one person sharing their feelings at a time until they feel heard and understood.[251]
2. Once the speaker has said their part, the listener reflects back what they heard in summary without judgment. What is the person expressing they like or dislike? What is this person's intention? This may be different than what that person initially states it is, or what you believe it to be. Sometimes it can be helpful to put this in the bigger context of their life, so consider if they are going through something difficult. "So you're feeling upset because.."
3. The speaker corrects these reflections until they are accurate. This may take several reflections going back and forth. The listener may finish by saying, "Did I get that right?"

4. The listener shows empathy by saying "I can see how being spoken to in that way would make you feel upset." They do not necessarily take the blame for the incident or agree with the situation, but just acknowledge the other person's feelings.
5. After the speaker responds to this show of empathy, the listener might ensure the topic is complete by saying, "Is there anything else?" Then this process will repeat until the speaker feels fully heard.
6. Once the speaker feels complete, then the roles can switch and the listener can have a chance to share their feelings or needs. For instance, "I felt hurt when you suddenly walked away from me without saying anything, but I understand that you're having a hard day. How can I support you right now and when is a good time to resume our conversation?"

During this process or after each person feels heard, agreements can be made about how to move forward. For instance, by using nonviolent communication and making specific requests, or reaching a middle ground. This said, having a person feel understood and heard can be more important than them getting what they want. Emotions are not about the objective reality, so get curious about the other person's experience.[209]

When conflict arises, it may be important to ask several clarifying questions about what a person meant by their words or actions. So often detrimental conflict occurs when we hear someone differently than they intended for us to, especially through written communication. We might also interpret the use of certain words different, or culturally have been raised to communicate in particular ways that are prone to conflict.

You might clarify by asking, "Are you anxious because you need a quieter space?" or, "Does this incident bring up some feelings from the past?" Even if you get this wrong, they will likely reveal what they are feeling after your inquiry. A person's words do not always match the reality they are experiencing, so it can be important to read their body language and facial expressions as well. Over several months or years, you might also note a recurring pattern in a person's behaviors and get curious about why those behaviors happen. Otherwise, some more general relationship repair advice includes:

1. **Taking initiative** - Stop expecting people to change on their own. If you want change you have to step up to the task and dedicate the required time and energy. When you are responsible for hurt feelings in another person, often the fastest way to repair is overcoming your

pride and telling that person what they want to hear. It is rarely important to be right when the goal is trying to happily reconnect. What a person needs doesn't even have to make sense to you.

2. **Finding empathy** – Zooming out to see the bigger picture may be important for reminding yourself that good times are possible. Recall a time that you enjoyed with each other, as well as times that you successfully repaired your connection.

3. **Finding a mediator or couples counselor** - Getting another person to provide insights, suggest exercises, translate confusing or aggressive language, and ensure each person gets time to speak is great for relationship repair. This is nothing to be ashamed of and should be normalized as a regular part of healthy bonding, especially as it shows that you and those you feel in conflict with care for the success of the connection.

4. **Talking about the past** - Open up with vulnerability and talk about what happened and how it impacted you. Ideally, use nonviolent communication with no judgments against the other person. Relationship repair will be greatly assisted when both parties understand their trapped emotions and tendencies developed through childhood. In this way, feelings of empathy are bolstered by giving context to emotions and behaviors.

5. **Accepting some discomfort** - What do you want to change about a person the most? Is it okay if only some of those things change? Can you find empathy and acceptance that a person's words might be ingrained in their familial and cultural background? Is it okay if they do not have the emotional or physical resources to leave a toxic relationship? Can you agree to disagree with some boundaries around what that looks like?

6. **Changing your expectations** - Accept that everyone is different and will never be the unique individual that you are. Stop focusing on what is not working and find alternatives. For instance, stop trying to control a person's interests or behaviors, and instead find common ground you can both at least somewhat enjoy. A person who is having fun and enjoying their time will feel much more compelled to change other behaviors as well. Consider organizing a special activity rather than relying on disappointing holidays and birthdays for bonding moments. You do not have to celebrate things that make you agitated, but you can also change how those celebrations are run. What bothers you? To avoid a big controversy, say, "This year I'd like to try

something a little different that I think will be fun." Alternatively, open up about your discomfort and work with everyone to create a better time. Review the elements of a healthy relationship in Chapter 14, what is missing in just being friends? Remember that you are not entitled to anything, it has to first be desired by both people.
7. **Firmly communicating your needs and boundaries** - See the contents of this chapter and Section 5.8.
8. **Identifying and apologizing for your role in the conflict** - See Section 8.3.
9. **Forgiving the other person** - See Section 13.13.
10. **Not giving up** - Tactics for healing relationships may have to be done slowly over weeks, months, or years. This may involve opening up and exploring a topic more and more, hitting a low point with the relationship, or repeating the same information several times until it sinks in.
11. **Read resources together** - For a romantic relationship, read a book together so you have a shared language to work through problems. For instance, check out *Your Brain On Love*, *Polysecure*, or *Fierce Intimacy*.
12. **Taking space and time apart** - Some people need the reality of separation to realize their devastating impact. This can create a "rock bottom" moment that is quite motivating for creating change. It can also force a person to find ways of occupying their time besides relying on you. For me, this has been most effective with at least 3 months, but a year is ideal depending on the situation. Sometimes maintaining social media ties can be helpful too by creating little windows of connection.

Please know that not all relationships are repairable, and that is okay. It is also not healthy or safe to attempt to repair certain relationships, especially those which involve physically or verbally abusive people. Abuse is always the fault of the abuser, never let them argue that you need to change something about yourself so they stop acting out. In these cases, letting go is the most compassionate thing that you can do for yourself, and for the other person too.

8.7 Effective Communication

Language is highly nuanced, so while simply following nonviolent communication, conversational receptiveness, or Imago Relationship Therapy frameworks can do a lot, here are additional suggestions for using communication effectively.

8.7.1 Regulate Your Nervous System

- Even if you're feeling triggered, it is often best to postpone a conversation until after you've rested or calmed yourself down a little bit – it's okay to come back to a conversation in the morning or ask for some space before responding
- Release some of your pent-up emotions before approaching a person with an intense conversation
- Have empathy by keeping in mind cultural diversity, brain wirings such as ADHD, and the trapped emotions inside people
- Remember that you are releasing trapped emotions as you communicate, so your perspectives and emotions may drastically shift as you speak - as such, try not to immediately make any drastic decisions, or at least try to stay open to possibilities
- Create new positive or neutral memories as quickly as possible after a conflict has been resolved to prevent the mind from ruminating on the past - do something fun together
- Speak in person rather than through texting or over the phone - this allows for eye contact, body language, and natural silences
- Walking and talking may sometimes be beneficial as a somatic release at certain points in a conversation, but it is best to face each other with eye contact
- Seek out the help of a therapist, mediator, or couples counselor

8.7.2 Leading With Positivity

- Ask a person for consent before entering into an emotionally difficult conversation
- Ask people to "do" instead of "not do" - it is much easier for people to visualize the positive
- Ask, "Can you do this favor for me?"
- Give people a positive reality to live up to by complimenting specifically what behaviors or identity you want to see in the future like *thank you for your patience, it's too bad that something so annoying happened to a kind person like you*, or, *that was a really skillful way of handling that conversation*

- Ask, "What can I do to help you meet my needs?"
- Not everything needs to be worked out or said immediately, especially if you are making the dangerous decision of communicating serious matters through text or over the phone
- Feeling sad or stressed after communicating a decision does not make it the wrong decision
- Instead of complaining about what you are not getting, it is typically better to ask for what you do want, especially if that person has had no way of knowing
- Try to appreciate and accept the *intention* a person has to communicate in a healthy manner, especially to respect the ways that different cultures and more neurodivergent speakers may process through conflict, empathy, and apologizing
- Never assume why a person does something - you are allowed to ask
- Remind the person you are talking with that you love them and are trying to create a stronger relationship
- Think about what you are going to say before you say it, or even write it out beforehand to air out any judgments or other aggressive words
- Sometimes conflict arises from basic design problems, of which there are many simple solutions and technologies which allow for multiple divergent needs to be met, or for a need to be more easily complied with – a person may need an electronic reminder about cleaning or a hidden spare key when they keep locking themselves out of the house
- Practice basic body movement mirroring to help build trust as explored in Section 14.1.4
- Only speak from observable facts and clarify the truth by asking questions
- Never start by holding a relationship hostage - for instance, "I will break up with you if this happens again"
- Focus on fighting the conflict rather than each other
- Each person has their own needs that they are personally responsible for getting met, so instead of making it a demand, offer to find solutions together that feel equitable
- Communication can be messy, and that's okay, the most important thing is that you're trying

8.7.3 General Techniques

- Keep your sentences short and simple so it is easier for people to listen

- Information is great, but explaining things too much can hurt a conversation - not everything on your mind needs to be said, try to summarize it
- It is easier to assert what you are unwilling to do rather than demanding another person change their behavior - for example, "I won't hang out with you if you have been drinking alcohol" versus "I need you to stop drinking alcohol"
- Identify and name your core story that is influencing your feelings as discussed in Section 6.3.1
- Remember that every culture communicates somewhat differently, so you may need to improve your *cultural intelligence* as explored in Section 15.4 to be effective
- Effective communication requires being compassionate and present, so try to get your nervous system regulated before talking
- Dealing with people in positions of power may dictate how you have to communicate
- While it would be great if everyone used nonviolent communication, you usually cannot expect or demand that a person does - this is a technique for you to use, not to force upon others, especially not in the middle of a conflict
- Figuring out a solution together is sometimes beneficial, but it is often best not to enter into a conversation with a wishy-washy stance - it is okay to ask for more time to journal or talk to a trusted ally and clarify what you are specifically needing
- Trying to communicate too quickly, or too long after an incident may make it more difficult for a person to listen to you - just attempt to do so within a few days
- Give recurring conflicts a name, and try noticing the pattern leading to them earlier and earlier before they blow up again[31]

8.7.4 Practice

- Journal out a conversation
- Practice NVC techniques with a friend, in a workshop, with your partner, or in your imagination so you are ready to use them when necessary
- Go back to conversations that have not gone so well in the past and rewrite them using nonviolent communication
- Role-play a current conflict with a therapist or friend

8.8 Non-Judgmental Language

The most important aspect of healthy communication is the use of non-judgmental language. For instance, "You're so irresponsible with money" versus "When you spend money like this I get scared about being able to save anything for emergencies." Judgmental phrases and words are evaluations and opinionated interpretations of the other person. This includes words such as "attacked, cheated, manipulated, provoked, rejected, and unwanted."[145B] While you may feel these words correctly describe the actions or character of another person, they tend to hide your true feelings or make the other person defensive.

Judgmental language can be replaced with the objective reality and "I" statements surrounding the emotions being felt such as anger or sadness. Consider writing out a conversation you want to have first to vent out any judgmental language. It can also be a very revealing exercise to challenge yourself to not judge anyone for a full day. You can also try the complaining bracelet method mentioned in Section 8.13.

Part of using non-judgmental language also involves not jumping to conclusions and instead considering the many reasons for a person acting the way that they did, or trying to connect with a person by asking them about their needs. When asking these questions, it may help not to blame yourself by using "I" language. For instance, instead of saying, "When I yelled at you..." try using "When people yell at you..." This helps prevent a person from feeling re-triggered from your actions and instead focuses on their broader reality.

8.9 Knowing The Source Of Your Need

The real issue you are upset about may be hidden underneath trapped emotions. For instance, you might think that you are upset about how your partner does not clean up around the house, but that feeling is coming from how one of your parents harshly criticized you for the slightest messes while growing up. In this case, you are upset at that parent and projecting it upon your partner. This may or may not diminish your feelings around cleaning, but it is worthwhile to mention it to your partner to help them empathize with where you are coming from. More examples include:

- You punish your child for their bad grades, but the actual source is that you struggled while in school and were scared about your future
- You need more of a certain love language from your partner (touch, gifts, acts of service, affirmation, or quality time), but that was the thing that your parents did not provide you and made you feel

unloved
- A person is being too loud for you, which is attached to your parent's shouting matches

Understanding the source of your suffering does not invalidate your needs, so still communicate what would make your life easier. Your feelings matter. However, you may realize that you are trying to control a person and deny them their independence. You can still request certain boundaries, rules, or wishes, but understand that it may be more important to transform yourself or reach a middle ground. After all, it is often hard to change others, especially when they have their own set of needs, wants, and trapped emotions. That is why it is so essential to use "I" statements, this is your reality you are trying to explain to another person. Learning how to let go of and assert more control is covered in Section 13.3.

8.10 If Your Request Is Rejected

You have several options if a person decides to reject your request:

1. Especially if the rejection is done aggressively or in defense, calmly reiterating your feelings and request can be important. In this retelling, you can add extra details, such as a specific experience, or go deeper into where your feelings come from. Again, do not slander or judge the other person, and make sure that your request is reasonable.
2. You can get curious about why a person is rejecting a request, or ask what they would do in your shoes. Often this will help tone down their defensiveness and open up their ability to listen.
3. You can try meeting in the middle, inquiring about what they would be comfortable doing because something needs to change.
4. Make your request more worthwhile and desirable to the other person. For instance, stop doing the other person's laundry until they are forced to do it themselves, agree to a reward, or do something where both of your interests intersect.
5. If this request is really important to you or not having it met would cause too much emotional suffering, you can decide to take space or end the relationship altogether. Do not jump to this option immediately though, give it some time, say a few weeks or a month, and see if having a second conversation works. If your request is again rejected, you can introduce the possibility of parting ways.
6. Remember that you should never expect one person to meet all of

your needs. Instead of trying to get a person to become someone who they are not, get your needs met by other friends, social activities, and new acquaintances. It is easiest to change yourself.

I want to be careful about suggesting giving power to the person you are making a request from. Many people with trapped emotions either fall into the taking or giving category. Givers, those with fawn behaviors, will easily comply with the demands of others at the slightest hint of conflict, whereas takers will rarely meet in the middle or back down. It is okay to have needs, even if it makes a person somewhat uncomfortable or temporarily makes your relationship stressful during the transition. Just keep in mind that needs can be unreasonable or abusive, and a person's refusal to meet your needs can also be unreasonable or abusive.

8.11 Not Communicating

For some, not communicating will be the better option, especially for cutting out abusive individuals or not feeding into an argument. There is often a choice to walk away, or to create a boundary like "I need you to speak to me kindly or I cannot continue spending this amount of time around you." Not everything has to be said and you do not need to have the last word or get closure. Are you feeding into creating an argument? Are you perpetuating an abusive relationship? If someone comes back into your life, it does not mean you have to engage with them or that you have to respond.

For others, communication is excruciatingly difficult due to social anxiety or always being shamed whenever they tried to speak up for their needs as a child. Silence in this case is a defense mechanism. Maintaining silence can also be cultural, such as with the passive-aggressive tendencies seen on the West Coast of the United States. While this silence can be quite abusive in its own right, it is usually not the intention of a person to harm others with silence. Their empowered voice will only open up after removing some of their trapped emotions and taking the vulnerable first steps to asserting themselves. That's what I love about NVC, it gives an easy-to-copy format to memorize and practice. Just remember that not everyone is as comfortable as you are in speaking up, and it may be up to you to identify and raise issues. If you've been struggling to communicate something:

- Say, "I'm sorry I've been distant lately"
- Say, "Hey you have felt kind of distant recently, is there anything wrong?"

- Consider how much pain not communicating is causing you or the other person, and that nothing will get better unless you speak up
- Remember that your feelings matter and are important

If you end up not communicating at all, it is still important to release the stressful energies and try to stay away from getting into reiterating negative conversations in your mind. Anger tends to create more anger. Constantly having bad thoughts about another person is a good indication that you need to use some of the techniques in this book such as mindfulness, grieving, or removing yourself from stress. Another option is writing a letter to the person you have strife with, but never actually giving it to them. Include all of your feelings and needs as we have been discussing. Just like with journaling, this can be quite cathartic and help you understand the source of your suffering. You may even realize that you played a role in the conflict, that you have hidden parts of yourself that want to be understood, or that this is actually more about your parents.

Sometimes communicating can also hurt your relationships, especially if there has been too much drama or you are consistently insecure. In these cases, it may be best to get your needs met without talking about it. For instance, you may be upset with someone because they have not contacted you lately. Instead of talking to them about this, just reach out to make plans. If they happily agree, it may be enough to dispel whatever feelings you were experiencing.

8.12 Delaying Communication

If your conversation gets too intense or you start feeling triggered in such a way that it is preventing you from speaking or acting nonviolently, it is okay to take a break. In fact, if you are not ready to have a conflict, or have an important appointment elsewhere, it is fine to tell a person that you need to connect later. Just be sure to establish a specific time that you are going to reconnect to finish the conversation or at least check in. Use this extra time for emotional releasing and journaling. You might also use this time to figure out what you need and will request. If someone asks for a break themselves, be sure to respect it and stop talking except to establish a time you can continue.

Triggered people often cannot resolve conflicts because their strong emotions prevent rationalizing healthy dialogues, thus also triggering the other person into negative feedback loops. Zach Brittle, the host of *Marriage Therapy Radio*, says that to settle your emotional extremes, you need at least a twenty-minute break in which you are not thinking about the conflict.[13] That might involve any of the techniques covered in Chapters 4 and 5, but might also involve a distraction like listening to a podcast. Brittle also asserts that it is really important to return to the conversation within twenty-four hours.

8.13 Misdirected Communication And Complaining

In *The Dance Of Anger*, Harriet Lerner explores how people often redirect their conflicts onto a third party unrelated to the real issue. This *triangle*, as she calls it, is often created through gossiping or complaining about another person without them knowing. While this may provide temporary relief or help brainstorm solutions, it typically hides a person's true concerns and directs frustrations at an intermediate party. This is common in families and romantic relationships but changes nothing. Confront the people who are bothering you and figure out solutions. If you are the one being gossiped to, do not feed into it - tell them to communicate with the person in question. Of course, there are many reasonable fears you might have about a direct confrontation including breakups or losing a job. The question then becomes, if you feel unsafe communicating, then is it a connection worth maintaining? It is important that you preserve your sense of self in any relationship.

Harriet Lerner also shares how we may communicate a need we have, but continue to act in ways that reinforce the undesirable behavior in another person. For instance, we might ask a housemate to take over more of the cleaning responsibilities, but upon not seeing them change their behaviors, we continue to clean just as much as we had previously. When you communicate your needs, you have to stay true to what you want for yourself. This may require that you meet halfway, reward the behavior, or find acceptance with a messier space. It really depends on what you are prioritizing. Just keep in mind that everyone has different levels of cleanliness, timeliness, and ways of dealing with toilet paper.

Often people want confirmation that they are right, even if they are wrong, and so they complain.[206] According to psychologists Robin Kowalski and Mike Baer, a person complaining most often just increases negative feelings in themselves and towards the supposed offender rather than resolving the situation. This is because each time a bad experience is talked about, it is being re-experienced. Productive complaining must then actually seek solutions to whatever is being complained about, and this requires that the person complaining is open to feedback. If you do complain, make sure it is framed as getting help reframing the experience or learning how to speak to the offender.

For chronic complainers, author Will Bowen suggests wearing a bracelet for 21 days. If you openly complain about something, you switch the bracelet to your other hand and have to restart the 21 days. You can also tap into your curiosity when wanting to complain and instead ask yourself, "Why does my partner not clean up around the house" or "Why do I care so much about having a clean house?" This can help you connect with your empathy and needs.

8.14 Incompatibility
Some disagreements simply cannot be resolved, especially when it involves cultural disagreements or differences in relationship needs. Rather than making it about the other person being wrong or toxic, or taking it personally as not being good enough, you can simply find peace as an incompatible match. That is not to say there is no growth to be done, but often people can only change so much for someone else. You can respect others but you do not have to get along with everyone.

Each person has specific things that are important for them in a connection, although often they do not know it yet when initially engaging with a new person. This might involve religion, politics, a certain type of physical touch, or good texting abilities. Of course, it is also perfectly fine to agree to no longer engage around a particular activity or topic and continue on normally otherwise. As previously explored in Section 8.6, not all problems need to be solved, and repairing or continuing a relationship does not require that you feel like you won an argument.[13]

8.15 Unavailable People
Perhaps a person has passed away, is unsafe to speak with, or is otherwise no longer available to directly communicate with. While it may seem strange, this person is a part of you now, existing through your memories and emotions. As such, you can visualize, speak with, or write a letter to them. You can even roleplay a conversation with a friend acting as the person you want to communicate with. This is just the beginning of the fascinating world of inner selves that we will explore in Chapter 10.

8.16 More About Communication
Since learning how to communicate is such a vital aspect of the healing process, many more parts of this book are devoted to it. Chapters 10 and 13 explore healthy ways of speaking to yourself. Section 13.13 teaches about forgiveness. Chapter 14 illuminates how to engage in healthy relationships and

break up with a person. Chapter 16 teaches about how to persuade others and speak to people within the context of creating social and environmental change.

***
Chapter Reflections

1. Which unresolved conflicts are causing discomfort in your life right now?
2. Would your unresolved conflicts benefit from using nonviolent communication or conversational receptiveness?
3. How do you currently communicate through conflict?
4. What techniques could improve your communication in different situations?
5. What are some past conflicts that could have benefited from using nonviolent communication?
6. Who do you need to apologize to or make amends to?
7. What assumptions have you made about a person that should be clarified?
8. What information do you assume that people already know and are you expecting a person to read your mind?
9. How have you avoided using direct communication with someone to work through a conflict?

Chapter 9

EMDR (Eye Movement Desensitization And Reprocessing)

*9.1 EMDR With A Therapist, 9.2 Solo EMDR,
9.3 Accelerated Resolution Therapy*

EMDR has gained a huge amount of popularity in recent years as an effective treatment for a wide variety of conditions including PTSD, addiction, phobias, anxiety, and depression. While why it works is not entirely understood, some researchers have found that horizontal back-and-forth eye movement deactivates the fear and stress response while simultaneously increasing the brain's memory connections.[74,226] In REM sleep this function hypothetically allows us to face difficult images and memories more easily in our dreams, but we can use it in our waking life as well.

EMDR is most effective for simple trapped emotions. It can also be used for more complex difficulties like abuse or neglect, but may just take many more sessions to be effective or require other techniques infused into the method.[97M] EMDR seems to continue working even after sessions have finished, so further recovery is often reported days or months later as experiences are fully able to integrate.

The mechanisms of EMDR may even be activated when playing certain video games. One study found that recalling distressing memories within 24 hours of a difficult event and playing a few minutes of Tetris shortly afterward helped to decrease the frequency of intrusive and painful memories.[85] Tetris requires focus, cognitive processing, and eye movement. It also creates some positive feelings by activating a person's reward centers. Even though the memories are uncomfortable, Tetris provides a person with evidence that joy and safety can still be found right now. This may be another explanation for why EMDR works, as it distracts parts of the brain that are holding onto a memory and forces a person back into their rational and present mind.

Regardless of how it works, EMDR helps move a difficult experience from the center of your attention into a simple fact of the past. It may have been awful, but it no longer causes you suffering. It also combines several of the modalities we've already discussed including emotional releasing, mindfulness, visualization, and exposure therapy.

EMDR is great because you do not have to relive the full difficult experience; you're only bringing up parts of it, then moving on to other memory associations. Simultaneously, you are allowed to experience the emotions and physical sensations in a safe container. EMDR can be used on trapped emotions you buried in your memories, immediately after a difficult situation, or if you are obsessively thinking about a difficult experience. Unlike prolonged exposure therapy, EMDR can also be used for a few minutes at a time or longer periods.

EMDR can sometimes negatively impact a person, especially when they do not have the tools to handle a difficult memory, or their therapist is unskilled in supporting them back to a state of mental safety. Especially if you have intense trapped emotions from any kind of repeated abuse or violence, be sure you have created an adequately safe container for your session and your life. In these cases, other skills and healing processes may be better to use first such as neurofeedback, mindfulness, creating community, basic self-care, visualization, and reframing stories.

EMDR is typically paired with a *positive counter* to a distressing memory. This helps integrate healthy feelings and beliefs an individual was otherwise lacking. These can be real memories, made up, or a mixture of both. For instance, if you got into a car accident and now hold the belief that you are incompetent, the positive counter might involve driving differently to avoid the accident and integrating the phrase "I am capable of protecting myself from harm." Alternatively, the various visualization practices explored in Sections 4.6 and 6.4 can be used to change the outcome of the difficult experience. These renegotiated memories further help soften the intensity of a difficult experience by giving you an alternative to think about. There's nothing you can do about the past, but there are things you can do to trust your ability to handle a situation in the future.

EMDR is ideally done with a therapist but can be learned on your own for small troubles, difficult emotions, and integrating positive feelings. The creator of EMDR, Francine Shapiro, was first inspired to develop the technique after noticing how the shifting of her eyes seemed to help relieve distressing feelings.[130] However, therapists provide direct feedback, notice changes in emotions, and help empower the client out of difficult states. If you struggle with words or feel distracted by talking, EMDR can even work while just receiving instruction from your therapist; you do not have to speak.[97N] We will explore how to use both solo and therapist-guided EMDR in this chapter.

In general, EMDR involves establishing a safe space and then recalling the most difficult part of an experience while switching between activating the right and left sides of the brain. This alternating rhythm is known as *bilateral stimulation*. Depending on your preference, bilateral stimulation might involve moving the eyes back and forth to a therapist's finger or visual display, having your knees alternatively tapped, wearing headphones with binaural tones switching between your ears, holding vibrating pads buzzing back and forth between your hands, rhythmic drumming, or a combination of these.[226] Different techniques will allow you to focus more easily, so don't be afraid to try several.

9.1 EMDR With A Therapist

To give therapists and people interested in exploring EMDR a good overview of the technique, I have summarized the steps. This information is derived from both my personal experiences with EMDR and Laurel Parnell's *A Therapist's Guide to EMDR: Tools and Techniques for Successful Treatment*. Parnell highlights many best practices for successfully implementing EMDR in therapy practices, even when working on attachment wounding and CPTSD. She also calls out EMDR therapists for frequently not establishing enough of a safe space or cutting sessions short for fear of their client's extreme emotional reactions.[130] These extreme emotions are to be expected, and the client, with a proper safe space and therapeutic resources, should be able to notify the therapist of what is too much. I highly suggest the book to any EMDR therapists wishing to make their practice even more effective.

An EMDR therapist will initially screen you. Clients who are suicidal, unable to connect with their feelings, dissociate, or cannot visualize a safe space may be first instructed to work with a doctor to start taking an antidepressant, alter their medication regimen, or start neurofeedback sessions mentioned in Section 5.2. Certain types of antidepressants can inhibit a person's ability to feel, and EMDR, like many techniques for releasing trapped emotions, requires a client to be able to feel strong emotions. On the other hand, medications can help a person cope with overwhelming and dangerous feelings. Hopefully a balance can be created, but a client may require developing alternative coping mechanisms to medications before being able to confront their difficult emotions with EMDR.

Following the screening the therapist will spend a few sessions establishing a trusting relationship with the client and teaching coping skills like developing a safe space and mindfulness. EMDR sessions can now begin, preferably in 90-minute sessions, but 50 minutes may work as well.[130] EMDR can typically release simple forms of trapped emotions within 1 to 5 sessions but may require dozens for longstanding problems that started in childhood. Initially bringing up parts of these difficult memories may be very emotionally draining, so be sure to take extra good care of yourself and regulate your nervous system as needed with the self-care tools explored in Chapter 4. You may need to take a decent break between EMDR sessions, or you may wish to have multiple sessions in quick succession. It is best to have your schedule open for self-care and connecting with loved ones following EMDR though. EMDR with a therapist typically goes something like this:

1. Visualize a positive anchor to ground yourself in, such as a good memory or safe space. As previously covered this can include real or fictional guardians and support figures as well as barriers and walls to keep unwanted energies out. Attach a word and feeling to this image and experience it while applying bilateral stimulation for about 10 iterations or 30 seconds.[130]
2. Bring up a recent or past difficult memory and consider if any similar instance (being abandoned, injured, ignored, etc.) was more extreme, or connect to the first time you experienced something like it. Identify the worst moment of that memory. You may be instructed at some point to write down all of the versions of this experience throughout your life to work on them individually. However, working through the first or most intense version is sometimes adequate. Also, identify an overarching goal that you are striving towards so you know when the EMDR is working such as being more open to physical touch or being able to establish boundaries.
3. Name the emotion you're feeling and note where it is in your body.
4. Attach a phrase to the memory describing what you believe about yourself in it such as "I feel weak" or "I'm an unreasonable person."
5. Optional: Rate how difficult this emotion is on a 1 to 10 scale.
6. Optional: Create a positive counter phrase such as "I feel strong" or "I feel happy" and rate it. At some point, the therapist may have you apply bilateral stimulation to this phrase. In this example, if you have a memory of feeling strong or happy, you can use that, but otherwise, you may be instructed to recall a time you witnessed a real or fictional

person being strong or feeling happy.
7. Combine the difficult memory, emotion, and phrase together and visualize it.
8. Use a bilateral stimulation such as eye movement while allowing your thoughts to freely associate and experiencing emotions as they arise. You might talk about what is happening or stay silent until the therapist inquires. More layers of the difficult experience could come up, or you might find yourself correcting a self-limiting belief that you had about yourself.
9. After a set amount of time or as the therapist notices emotional changes in your body, you will be asked "What is coming up for you now?" As you bring up other parts of the memory or other emotional difficulties, the therapist will direct you to apply bilateral stimulation to that visualization or memory. If you seem dissociated or have gone too far away from the original memory, the therapist may have you revisit it from the beginning.
10. Re-rate the difficult emotion and the opposing positive one. Is the difficult emotion lower? The therapist may have you continue until it stops going down, or when the positive emotion stops going up. If the positive emotion is particularly strong, you may be directed to use bilateral stimulation after holding the sensation in your awareness to help integrate the feeling.
11. If you become stuck or are looping over the same memory without your ratings changing, the therapist may interject, inquiring with "Who can help you," "What would you do differently now," "Are you safe now," or "What do you believe about yourself now?" They may also challenge any self-limiting beliefs. This can help create a positive counter-image you can pair with your positive phrase.
12. If the difficult emotion is too strong, signal this to your therapist. Go to your positive anchor and visualize it while using bilateral stimulation and breathe deeply. Continue only if you feel resourced, but know that experiencing strong emotions is an essential part of this process.
13. The goal is to reduce the current activated feelings about your difficult experience to a rating of zero and to increase the positive counter to a rating of at least a six. If this is accomplished, the positive counter is integrated with bilateral stimulation. If the difficult experience is at one or above, the therapist will ask "What is keeping it from being a zero?" You may then start working through that aspect of the experi-

ence.

14. Finish the session by going to your positive anchor and visualizing it while using bilateral stimulation. Talk about neutral things or what you're excited about for the week. If the issue brought up is unresolved, visualize storing the difficult memories in a safe box or creating a protective field around yourself that will keep you safe until the next session. Integration may continue between sessions in thoughts, dreams, conversations, and subconscious workings. You may find that while the memory was still charged when you left your session, it has successfully subsided by your next appointment.

Several of these steps may need to be omitted depending on the client, such as the rating scales or creating an opposing positive phrase. These may be distracting or demeaning to an especially triggered client. Clients don't even need a specific memory or image for these techniques to work, although it helps direct the session.

9.2 Solo EMDR

Something similar to the EMDR protocol just described can be self-administered, but it is better to only confront strong emotions that just arose and possibly small difficult memories or nightmares. This said, it is possible to take on some deeper trapped emotions, but it is essential that you feel relatively okay entering into the work, have a well-established safe space, and are capable of removing yourself from dangerous states. When I worked with an EMDR therapist I found them distracting and not someone I could open up around, so I found much better results practicing on my own.

Alongside not needing a therapist, the greatest benefit to solo EMDR is the ability to practice anytime and in a space that you fully control. This means that you can do sessions as frequently or infrequently as you want to and only when you feel the most focused and resourced. This is a technique I adapted from EMDR after hearing that therapists occasionally do this privately as well. It works for me but I guarantee nothing for others as there are no efficacy studies to my knowledge for doing solo EMDR. There are phone apps and online communities that support this practice though.

Even if you feel okay after a self-administered session, you may want to give yourself a week or so before confronting another difficult memory. The integration is still working after your sessions, and strong feelings can arise after several days. Teaching a compassionate and loving friend to guide you is not very difficult either. This may provide you with a stronger resource than being alone. You don't even need to talk during the session, just have them say lines periodically to keep you focused on your topic and switch the bilateral stimulation on and off.

You can also use solo EMDR to help integrate positive feelings and behaviors. This is especially helpful for people who lacked healthy role models as children and is much safer than digging up bad memories. Integrating positive experiences can help a person understand what love, empathy, compassion, and strength look like. Knowing these states will simultaneously help a person understand what abuse looks like in their relationships.

As previously described in the therapy-assisted model of EMDR, you can draw from emotions you've witnessed in real or fictional people. For example, you may have watched a movie in which you saw a loving family dynamic between parent and child, or there might be a public figure you correlate with strength. Embody this feeling while visualizing the person or scene with a descriptive phrase. You can also integrate times when you're feeling really good, especially when it is not associated with consuming an addictive substance or using an unhealthy coping mechanism. Similarly, you can apply solo EMDR to integrate visualizations of yourself being successful in the future. Essentially you are planting good seeds that will increase your resilience to stress and make your core beliefs more positive.

There are many free bilateral resources online, just search for "self-administered EMDR." For eye movement videos, make sure you are watching them on something larger than a phone screen so your eyes can trace back and forth far enough. Even a laptop might be too small but just look a little further off the screen's sides. While practicing on my own, I found it easiest to move my eyes back and forth without a video, but a target is helpful to pace and guide you. That said, without a video, you become free to use this technique almost anywhere you feel comfortable. Tapping either side of your head or knees may also work, or binaural tones. Otherwise, when using solo EMDR, you can mostly repeat the same steps previously detailed with a therapist:

1. Visualize a positive anchor to ground yourself in, such as a good memory or safe room. Attach a word and feeling to this image and experience it with bilateral stimulation for 30 seconds.
2. Bring up a recent or past difficult memory. Identify the most emotional moment of that memory. You can also consider if this is attached to a first or more difficult version of the experience.
3. Name the emotion you're feeling and note where it is in your body.

4. Attach a phrase to the memory summarizing what this experience makes you believe about yourself such as "I am incompetent" or "I am boring."
5. Combine the memory, emotion, and phrase together and visualize it.
6. Apply bilateral stimulation for 30 seconds or however long feels appropriate while allowing your thoughts to freely associate around the difficult memory.
7. Break away from the bilateral stimulation and check in with yourself. Is there a new charged memory associated with the original? Apply bilateral stimulation to that. If you have become distracted or find yourself in a different difficult experience, return to the original memory. If the difficult emotion is too strong, go to your positive anchor and visualize it while using bilateral stimulation for another 30 seconds.
8. Check in with how difficult the original memory is now.
9. Repeat this process from Step 5 until you can rate the charged feelings as a zero. If the feelings are intensifying instead of decreasing, you may need to take a break or seek support from your inner child, future self, or safe-place guardians as explored in Chapter 10. Ask yourself, "Who can help me? What would I do differently now? Am I currently safe in my physical body? What do I believe about myself now?" Identify any self-limiting beliefs as covered in Chapter 6.
10. Finish the session by going to your positive anchor and visualizing it while using bilateral stimulation and deep breathing. Think about what you are going to do for the rest of the day and week ahead.

Another option is simply combining bilateral eye movement with mindfully experiencing your emotions. I have had success with this following a stressful incident, especially when I do not have time to go through the full EMDR process. You may also want to explore self-administering the Tetris method mentioned earlier in this chapter. Lastly, I've found that EMDR can be combined with the journaling exercise discussed in Section 7.11. This may be especially useful for people who struggle to explore their thoughts and imagination or find themselves getting easily distracted.

9.3 Accelerated Resolution Therapy

Accelerated Resolution Therapy (ART) is similar to EMDR but promises to be a simpler, quicker, and less triggering therapy technique.[145] Essentially it works by combining eye movement with identifying a distressing memory and visualizing what you wish had happened instead. Maybe you stop a dog from attacking you or lock your abuser away in prison. Readers may want to experiment by combining the visualization techniques covered previously in Section 6.4 with a bilateral stimulation such as eye movement.

***

Chapter Reflections

1. Which of your trapped emotions might benefit from EMDR?
2. Are there EMDR therapists available in your area?
3. What is your preferred form of bilateral stimulation?
4. How could Tetris, Accelerated Resolution Therapy, or EMDR fit into your healing practice?
5. What kinds of positive thoughts, memories, mindsets, and feelings do you want to integrate into your core story using bilateral stimulation?

Chapter 10

Inner Family

10.1 Externalizing The Inner Family With Sandbox Therapy, 10.2 Parental, Adult, Child, Future, Ancestral, and Cultural Selves, 10.3 Right And Left Brains, 10.4 Initiating Contact With Your Inner Selves, 10.5 Inner Child And Playfulness, 10.6 Inner Loving Parents And Reparenting To Ideal Guardians, 10.7 Future Self, 10.8 Ancestral Self, 10.9 Cultural Self, 10.10 Birth And Death, 10.11 Creating Inner Selves

Building upon what we learned in Section 7.4 about "imaginary" friends, each experience and emotion of our past, present, and even future can be visualized as a unique individual to learn from, support, and speak with. This can include people like your 3-year-old, teenage, critical, fulfilled, older, addicted, and fearful selves. Each of these selves have their own personalities, fears, and hopes that are acting out in your current life. For instance, your adult self might get along well with your parents, but your child self might be scared and avoid them from something that happened in the past.

These parts of ourselves can be spoken with, hugged, and offended. We can inquire into which of these selves is acting out or needing support when we are struggling. When a part is acting out, we can say "This part in me believes ____." In this way, we separate what is a part and what is our true self. We can also work on these parts when we feel good and nourished. Most often when people talk about this work, they refer to *inner child work*, *parts work*, or *Inner Family Systems (IFS) therapy*.

Working with the inner selves is also helpful because it puts a little extra distance between you and a difficult experience. As Luise Reddermann, author of *Who You Were Before Trauma*, explains, retelling a triggering story is much easier when it is done through the third person.[142] In this way, you are acknowledging that who you were and your current self are separate individuals. It helps your body know what happened in the past is no longer a threat and that the present moment is safe. For really difficult memories, an individual may place extra space between themselves and their difficult experience by becoming an observer wherein all conversations and remembering happen in the third person. The observer witnesses your adult self speaking to your child self, or your child self speaking to your parents. For instance, you could have a pet you had growing up relate the experience.

10.1 Externalizing The Inner Family With Sandbox Therapy

Normally the inner family is visualized, or written with by hand, but you can also depict them visually. For instance, you can draw them individually, or create a family portrait of how you all relate to one another. You can also exhibit them with physical objects such as furniture and fruit, positioning them wherever you feel they exist in your emotional world.[970] This is similar to a technique called *sandbox therapy*, but that specifically incorporates a sandbox with lots of toy figurines.

You can do this at your home. Pick an object in the room that represents yourself, and then objects that represent the other characters in your visualization based on their comparative size, color, or other relatable characteristics. An angry father might be represented by a red ball, and a domineering mother by a big couch. What stands out to you? Is there anything you need to do to this configuration to make yourself feel safer? You can speak to these characters, reposition them, or bring in an ally to protect you from them. As explored with *Role-Playing And Theater* in Section 7.6, ideal versions of these characters can also be introduced who better depict healthy and loving individuals who would have cared for you better.

10.2 Parental, Adult, Child, Future, Ancestral, and Cultural Selves

In *Internal Family Systems* and *inner child work*, some of the inner parts to connect with include:

1. ***Adult*** - This is you, the decision-maker capable of changing your fate for the better or worse.
2. ***Child*** - Childhood is when many trapped emotions and interests first develop. Interacting with this state is known as "inner child work." This can also involve speaking to any version of you in the past including you as a teenager, young adult, or even a fetus in your mother's womb. People with trapped emotions are frequently controlled by their various inner children (age is such a fickle thing).

3. ***Parent*** - We learned many of our basic behaviors from our parents, and even though these may not have been healthy, we still adopted them without knowing a better alternative. Within each person, there is a critical parent and a loving parent. The critical parent is where the inner and outer critic explored in Section 5.9 exists. Healing the inner child often requires developing the loving parent and learning to manage the critical one. Depending on your experiences, it is also possible to "reparent" your inner child to parents you see as more ideal, compassionate, caring, or safe. You might be on good terms with your parents now, but it may still be necessary to work on the version of your parents that you grew up with.
4. ***True self*** – The true self is the version of you who has integrated all of the healthy versions of your parts. For instance, an inner child that feels safe and plays, an actively engaged loving parent that practices good self-care, and a critical parent who offers cautionary advice but does not control your every feeling and behavior.
5. ***Future adult*** - What you imagine or wish your future self to be. Your future self can speak to you and give you guidance, or you can ask them questions. Your future self may change over time as your current adult transforms.
6. ***Ancestors*** - Knowing your family history can grant you great insights into trapped emotions you might be predisposed to genetically. Your adult self can work with your ancestors to heal their own unresolved trapped emotions from war, abuse, or inequality.
7. ***Cultural*** - The cultural self includes the traditions and customs that you grew up around. This is separate from your innate biological instincts.
8. ***Birth and death*** - The beginning and end of our lives are especially significant. While we lack control over both of these states, they each contain significant emotional qualities that may need to be negotiated with.

All of the selves listed above also have different parts such as loving, critical, violent, and productive. As Richard C. Schwartz explores in his Internal Family Systems (IFS) book *Greater Than The Sum Of Our Parts*, each part can interact with other parts, has a unique personality, and may initially distrust you.[151] Pixar's animated film, *Inside Out*, does a great job of depicting this inner world. People wishing to learn about IFS professionally can read the *Internal Family Systems Skills Training Manual* or take professional courses through the *IFS Institute*. These courses are available to all regardless of educational background.

Schwartz has shown that compassionately speaking with, listening to, and befriending your parts is often necessary for changing behaviors and dealing with trapped emotions. No part needs to be destroyed or dismissed, but rather listened to, reasoned with, and given alternatives. For example, the critical parent might be reiterating how much they dislike someone, with each pass growing in slander toward that individual. The loving parent might then come in and ask the critical parent what is making them feel unsafe and explore the evidence that the individual is dangerous. Then the loving parent might tell the critical parent that after a thorough analysis, the person is just a little uncomfortable, but not dangerous. If any danger does arise, the loving parent promises they know how to handle it in a way that will maintain everyone's safety. The loving parent might also reassure the inner child, who is likely reacting to this person as a threat they experienced from their caregivers or some other difficult experience.

As protective parts learn that they are safe, they may go from having a reactionary role to an advisory one, mentioning their opinion instead of forcing you to comply. This is the goal, speaking for your parts instead of having your words controlled by them. For instance, you can talk about having insecurities rather than yelling. Then the "true self" can come forth. While many therapy modalities give up on clients who were unable to develop certain positive characteristics as children, Schwartz believes that this "true self" is inherently capable of love, kindness, and empathy in anyone.

Rather than letting one inner self dominate, you might hear them each out and then make an informed decision. Alternatively, a fearful part of yourself that normally would have run away can be spoken with. Consider inviting the parts of yourself that need to be heard to a visualized dinner to discuss their concerns and needs. What is a critical or angry part of you protecting? What would happen if they stepped back? What can you say or do to take on the leadership that these parts need to feel safe? What words can you express to let them know that something they feel upset about will never happen again? Nonviolent communication is a great tool to use for speaking with these parts as explored in Chapter 8.

All of your behaviors and trapped emotions connect to these selves, though the parent-child relationship is generally the most common. For instance, if you are having trouble in a romantic relationship, your inner child is often reacting to your parental upbringing. That is to say, how you react to your partner's behaviors might have nothing to do with them and everything to do with how your parents treated you as a child. Within this context, time itself is almost meaningless. Our brains are operating under different childhood states and memories that we experienced growing up.

10.3 Right And Left Brains

The parts of your brain can also be thought of as inner selves. Especially since people with severe trapped emotions have parts of their brain deactivated or underdeveloped, getting in touch with these parts can be important to healing. Dr. Jill Bolte-Taylor, famous for her TED Talk and book, *My Stroke of Insight*, says that the right and left sides of the brain control different aspects of our personalities.[239] Most notably, the left contains your identity and the right side contains the connection to your environment and others. Both of these sides have an emotional and a thinking part, thus giving rise to four distinct aspects of the personality:

- *Left thinking*: Logical and mathematical, compares and competes, the organizer of relationships between you and others, triggers the stress response
- *Left emotional*: Remembers the pains of the past and compares them to what you are witnessing now, may seek out addictions to comfort itself
- *Right thinking*: Feels peace, love, openness, and gratitude for life
- *Right emotional*: Experiences the present moment without judgment, playful, feels awe, creative

Jill suggests identifying and naming these different parts of yourself to start conversing with them and getting them to work together. As the title of her 2021 book suggests, she advocates for *Whole Brain Living*. For instance, you can utilize meditation, prayer, or psychedelics to shut off the left hemisphere's egoic judgments and experience more of the present moment and spiritual connectedness of the right. Or, maybe you need to work through a problem, so you turn on the left-thinking side of your brain. When you are reacting emotionally, you may know that just one part of your brain is activated, but you can seek the counsel of everyone else to check in about how important that thing is. There are some criticisms with this format of the brain as seen in the book's reviewers, but I think it can still be a helpful tool for considering different aspects of yourself. To learn more, read the book, check out <www.drjilltaylor.com>, or listen to episode 195 of the *Therapist Uncensored* podcast.

10.4 Initiating Contact With Your Inner Selves

When first connecting with one of your inner selves, do so slowly. Introduce yourself and be patient. Do not force them to do anything. These are individuals that may have felt neglected for a very long time, so be curious and empathetic. It may be important to first develop your skills as a loving parent to these inner selves. Healthy love and responsibly raising a child are covered in the next section, plus Sections 3.1 and 15.10. Using techniques like NVC presented in Chapter 8 may also be helpful.

There are several ways to speak to your inner selves. You may not be able to visualize their faces, but just their general thoughts, habits, or emotions. In her book, *Recovery of Your Inner Child*, Lucia Capacchione explores ways to access the inner child, but the techniques are appropriate for speaking to any of the inner selves. Some of these techniques can also be found in the Adult Children of Alcoholics and Dysfunctional Families workbook titled *The Loving Parent Guidebook*.

One of the primary methods suggested to initiate conversation is using your dominant hand to communicate as an adult, and your non-dominant hand to communicate as the inner child.[19A] Done back and forth through writing and drawing pictures, you come to understand your inner child's unmet needs and what kind of support they want to conquer the suffering they continue to experience at the hands of their parents, bullies, injuries, or loneliness. Set a timer for five minutes and try it out. Some people suggest writing in the third person, but I tend to do it in the first person when speaking as the adult self. Try not to judge what arises through your inner child. This includes drawing with stick figures, incomplete sentences, and wobbly handwriting. I've also had success writing with my dominant hand, but many people are pleasantly surprised by what happens when connecting with a less controlled version of themselves. You might become aware of feeling sad or overwhelmed and then initiate a conversation:

- *Adult*: Hey, I can see that you're feeling upset today, what's the matter?
- *Inner child*: All you do is work, when are we going to do something fun?
- *Adult*: I'm sorry, I really have been going non-stop haven't I?
- *Inner child*: Yeah.
- *Adult*: I have a big deadline coming up, but that doesn't excuse me for ignoring you. I'm sorry. Let's do something fun tonight.

What would you like to do?
- **Inner child**: Yay okay let's play a game with our friends!

I also share an example in Section 17.17 about talking to the inner child about overwhelming sounds. Some people may be able to have these kinds of conversations in their imagination. Using the imagination is especially useful as it allows you to check in with your inner selves in real time, knowing when a self needs comfort or has something important to say. For instance, your inner child may protest being around your parents, or the inner critic may be making your head full of self-limiting beliefs. Knowing the source of these feelings and thoughts gives you much greater power to calm them down or comply with their requests and prevent a full-blown anxiety attack or depressive episode from occurring.

10.5 Inner Child And Playfulness

You may have to observe children to understand what your inner child naturally needs and wants, but most people will innately know this when connected with their emotions and positive memories. Children are playful, like to feel safe, want consensual touch, want to feel protected by their parents, enjoy spending time with other children, have an innate curiosity about the world, and do not judge themselves or their creations. Most importantly, children are nourished by an empathetic parent who acknowledges and understands their emotions.[49] Often when we are triggered into a flashback, the inner child is reliving an experience where they wanted one of these things to be provided. You now have the unique opportunity to provide that to your inner child as their loving parent. Of course, different ages correspond to different behaviors. For instance, your inner teenager may be more rebellious, angry, introverted, or creative.

When first speaking to your inner child, or directly after experiencing some hardship, you may simply want to shower the child with love, kindness, and apology. Reassure your inner child that you are here to protect them now. That you love them. That you will never again let them be hurt by the things that destroyed their sense of safety growing up. That you are now their friend, ally, and guardian. That you understand their frustration with you when putting them in danger. Beyond these times, it is good to communicate with your inner child at least weekly to check in with them. Are they being nourished? Do they feel safe? Have you been ignoring their desire to play and enjoy life? Just spending a few minutes together is enough. Here are some examples of how you might talk to your inner child as a loving parent:

1. I know that you're scared about going to this party, but I will protect you. I'll make sure no one is there to make fun of you. And if anything too scary happens, we can leave.
2. What do you want to do today?
3. Hey buddy, is something the matter? You seem really upset about something right now.
4. Why are you feeling lonely? Is there anything you need from me?

You can also give your inner child affirmations. Pete Walker has a great list of these in his book, *Complex PTSD*.[184D] It includes things like:

- I love you
- That was really cool what you just showed me
- I will always be here to protect you
- I accept you just the way you are
- I am so happy you exist
- I will always support your curiosity
- You are allowed to make mistakes
- You are wonderful

A healthy adult regularly accesses their inner child in acts of playfulness and being emotionally vulnerable. Developing these two traits will also help heal your inner child. Connecting with your child self can include laughing with friends, dressing up in costumes, painting an image no one else will see, playing games, writing an imaginative story, expressing emotions, and sharing how you're feeling.

What brought you joy as a child? How did you perform those activities without judgment on yourself? Generally foods and activities you loved as a child will be quite nourishing to you as an adult, even if you have labeled them as childish or unhealthy. That's not to say you should eat bags and bags of candy and spend all day playing video games, but within reason, these are very fulfilling experiences when done out of enjoyment rather than escapism. You may also need to find healthier versions of play or versions that keep you accountable to regular play. Activities like rock climbing, acting in theater, tennis, kickball, stand-up comedy, disc golf, or playing music with others are good areas to consider. What sounds good to your inner child? Seeking out a therapist who specializes in play may also be beneficial.

10.6 Inner Loving Parents And Reparenting To Ideal Guardians

Your inner parents are reflected by the guardian figures you grew up with. These include personas like the mother, father, critical parent, protective parent, loving parent, and so on. In high school, my classmate casually said "I'm going to hang out with my mom later." I imagined turning in disbelief and responding with, "You're going to hang out with your what?" I said nothing, but the idea that people would happily spend time with their parents was completely foreign to me. Just like myself, it is difficult for children to know what else is possible when they have witnessed the same thing their entire lives. There are, in fact, healthy, compassionate, and loving parents in the world, and you can cultivate them within your inner family.

Knowing if your legal guardians were unhealthy can be difficult. For instance, they may have been toxic to you as a child, but the people they are now you actually like and appreciate. You may also have idealized one parent but will come to realize that they were complacent in or bolstered your difficulties. Even if you do know that your guardian figures were toxic, many people mistakenly believe that healing is only possible by first healing their mother or father. This is false and often prevents healing for yourself and your guardian figures. Speaking to the inner selves can also help people who were raised without one or more parents. Remember, the goal is to heal *your* nervous system. You do not have to repair your relationship with your parents to do that, but you might have to repair your relationship with your inner family and put yourself around healthy people.

Healing from abusive or emotionally unavailable parents involves developing your *inner loving parent*. This may involve things like paying attention to your inner child, empathetically speaking to them, giving them words of encouragement you wish your parents had given you, treating them with love and affection, teaching them skills, allowing them playtime, explaining why you need to return to work, or holding them. The inner loving parent sets reasonable limits to certain activities like media activities and balances that time with exercise, eating well, or getting outside. What can you say to yourself to feel loved? Try visualizing your adult self cradling the baby version of you while saying words of affirmation to them.

Your healing also relies on quieting the voices of the *inner critical parent* through internal dialogues with them. When you feel you are being self-critical, open a conversation with that voice using nonviolent communication. Hear what they have to say, then ask if they would be willing to step aside to allow your inner loving parent to speak. This was explored in Section 5.9.

People sometimes refer to this process as *reparenting*.[184C] This is the act of treating your inner child like you wish you had been treated growing up. You may have a mother figure, father figure, or multiple guardian figures care for the inner child. These parents may exhibit energies that are nurturing, loving, assertive, self-protective, or empowering to the ability to say no.

The inner child may also benefit from being reparented into a family of ideal guardian figures who can protect and nourish them while you, the adult, are away. This gives your inner child more opportunities to heal old wounds and develop vital skills they may have missed out on in difficult home environments. Reparenting your inner child is another visualization practice. Often reparenting is first done when relating a difficult experience of the inner child. When the inner child is in danger or is feeling especially hurt by their parents, a therapist might ask, "What is your inner child needing right now?" If that need involves anything with loving and compassionate parents or safety from guardian figures, it may be an ideal time to reparent.

In the book *Who You Were Before Trauma*, Luise Reddermann generally suggests that you not be reparented to humans, but instead "compassionate beings" that exemplify qualities that your guardian figures lacked.[142] Most importantly they should exude a sense of safety and could take the form of cats, birds, elves, dwarves, and so on. You can also reparent to the idealized versions of your mom and dad, the loving parent you yourself have become, or a higher power that you established in Section 4.12. Visualize introducing your inner child to these compassionate beings, making sure that the child feels good about the decision, or if they're needing anything else to feel loved and protected.

You can then start reimagining your entire life, year by year, with these healthy guardian figures. This will allow your inner child to know, perhaps for the first time, what it is like to be loved, cherished, and treated with respect. Dr. Daniel Brown believes that this practice is especially powerful when these guardian figures showcase healthy aspects of attachment and parenting.[227] These include making you feel safe and protected, being attuned to your needs, soothing you when you're upset, expressing delight about your life and existence, as well as supporting your exploration, creativity, and curiosity. What does it feel like to be lovingly held, or to be spoken to with a soft and kind voice? Try doing this practice once a week to foster a healthy inner world. Laurel Parnell also suggests combining this technique with bilateral stimulation to help integrate these positive experiences into your psyche as explored in Chapter 9.[226]

In the *Adult Children of Alcoholics and Dysfunctional Families* support group, people are encouraged to see a higher power of their choosing as their true family. This is because a family does not have to be biologically connected, and can instead be chosen. After the ritual I described in Section 7.3, nature became one of my higher powers and a family figure for me. No longer bound to the unhealthy cultural demands of tolerating abusive family dynamics, I was able to take a healthy amount of space and heal in safety.

If your family of origin is triggering to your inner child, remember that as an adult you are never required to put up with perpetually stressful, toxic, or abusive behaviors. You are never required to support your parent's emotional immaturity. Instead, you are always allowed to establish boundaries and take space as needed. This is especially true when your parents refuse to do emotional work, avoid communication, disrespect your boundaries, or cannot self-reflect about their stressful behaviors. Give them an ultimatum, tell them you're going to be out of touch for a while on vacation, or explain that you're trying to find more happiness in life and cannot handle their stressful behaviors right now. You can include some resources in this message for them to seek support. If necessary, block their phone number and social media presence or move houses as soon as you have the resources to do so.

Once you have space, you can start asking your inner child about what would have helped them feel safe while growing up. What would they make your parents do to create that safety? You can visualize these things, like giving your parents a timeout, making them move out of the house, or having your idealized parents come to denounce their behaviors. Similar to taking on the inner and outer critics, this empowers your self-compassion and ability to stand up for yourself, especially when confronted by danger.

10.7 Future Self

Visualizing your future self can reveal a lot, putting into perspective where your current actions are leading you or what might need to change to feel awesome. This future self of course has infinite versions. One might be your ideal self, another the self you become if you change nothing, another self you become by going back to school. When speaking to your future self, it is important to recognize that it is impossible to rationalize emotions. That is to say, you should consider going to that party because you have no idea how a state of being will feel until you experience it. Nonetheless, the future self can be a strong guidepost.

Contacting this future self is especially great at revealing how much control we have over the future, and simultaneously, how much our current self is preventing that ideal future. It reminds us that every relationship and feeling we have now may still exist for many decades. How then do you want to treat your friends, your family, your abusers, and yourself? Start building a grand future now.

Exercise: Just like the other selves, you can draw, write with, or imagine the connection between you and your future self. However, try using your non-dominant hand to speak as your current self, and your dominant hand to speak as your future self. Do not hold onto this future self too closely, but consider, who is that person in a year, five years, or ten years? What steps did your current form take to get there? What inspirational advice does this future self have for you? What are their regrets? What stressful relationships had they wanted to end sooner? What people had they wished they had communicated better with? What red flags were popping up? Do they have empathy for a struggle you're experiencing now?

10.8 Ancestral Self

Who you are today has been influenced by your ancestors stretching back hundreds of thousands of years. Much of this has become intrinsic to your genetics and takes form in your appearance, diet, and basic biology and psychology. Beyond this, your recent ancestors influence you the most. They directly impacted your parents and grandparents, who directly influenced you with genes, your upbringing, culture, and ancestral trapped emotions.

You may need to speak to your parents or grandparents, or do other research through an ancestry website to understand who your ancestors were. Having an object of the ancestor you are communicating with may help, but the process is otherwise similar to speaking to your inner parent. However, the focus will be the difficulties your ancestors experienced and passed on to your inner parents, and then on to you or your inner child. In your exploration of these individuals, be on the lookout for war, religious upbringing, alcoholism, death of loved ones, economic standing, discrimination, and disease. This kind of perspective allows you to have empathy for the behaviors of your parents and grandparents, finally allowing for the healing that they most dearly desired. You might even visualize going back in time as your adult self to assist your ancestors in facing whatever caused them such suffering.

10.9 Cultural Self

Identifying the cultural self can be tricky if a person lacks diversity growing up, but proper self-reflection, research, and travel can help reveal it. For instance, people who have traveled between the East and West Coasts of the USA will notice a direct abrasiveness in some East Coasters, and a passive aggressiveness in some West Coasters. Neither is necessarily bad, but many people struggle when interacting with the other. I for one wish that East Coasters were sometimes nicer and that West Coasters could speak up about their thoughts and feelings.

Especially difficult is acknowledging when the cultural self is problematic. If your parents, friends, classmates, and other community members all believe in or act a certain way, how could it be wrong or cause you suffering? Perhaps most famously problematic is slavery, but until recently, many people upheld this as a normal part of life. There are smaller examples too like who you find attractive, how you define success, and alcohol consumption. Cultural ideologies include both what your adult self believes and does not believe. Some cultural ideologies hurt you and others, while some are quite nourishing and promote healing. We will cover transforming culture later in Part III, but for now know that culture is another one of your selves you can speak with, challenge, and renegotiate.

10.10 Birth And Death

Often birth and death are seen as separate from ourselves, but are another part of our existence. These states can be spoken with, listened to, and befriended. While birth is typically celebrated and death becomes feared, many more possibilities exist. People may regret being born, and they may find peace with the coming of death. I list these together because they are closely connected and it can be useful to speak to both when coming to terms with one's birth or death or seeking wisdom from these parts at the beginning and end of your journey. Many people connect with these states while on psychedelics, as we will explore in Chapter 11.

10.11 Creating Inner Selves

In Section 7.4 we started exploring how people create inner selves as imaginary friends that help empower the psyche. These entities gain more sway over your mindset and emotions the more you believe in them. This is easiest when a community, culture, or environment already believes in their existence and their ability to manifest within you, but you can also integrate them on your own. For instance, you can ritualistically summon spirits, visualize asking for and receiving some of Earth's power, pray to gods to give you strength, embody the emotional qualities of a fictional character, or imagine having a personality characteristic of someone you respect. Create space in your life to honor these selves. Maybe you have an altar dedicated to them, practice speaking to them weekly, re-read the novel that describes them, listen to music that connects you to them, paint pictures of them, visit natural places that act as conduits into their essence, or attend a worship group to honor them. Who do you want on your team?

***

Chapter Reflections

1. Who is included in your inner family?
2. How does your inner child, inner teen, or critical parent take over and act for you?
3. What does being a loving parent mean to you?
4. How could you be more like a loving parent to yourself?
5. Who is your ideal family and what would life have been like growing up with them? How do they treat your inner child?
6. Who are your future, ancestral, and cultural selves?
7. How is your critical parent trying to protect you?
8. How does your inner child like to play?
9. What are your inner selves trying to tell you right now?
10. How does your future self feel about your current decisions and life? How is it impacting them?
11. What affirmations can you tell to your inner child?
12. What are some healthy inner selves you can integrate into your psyche?

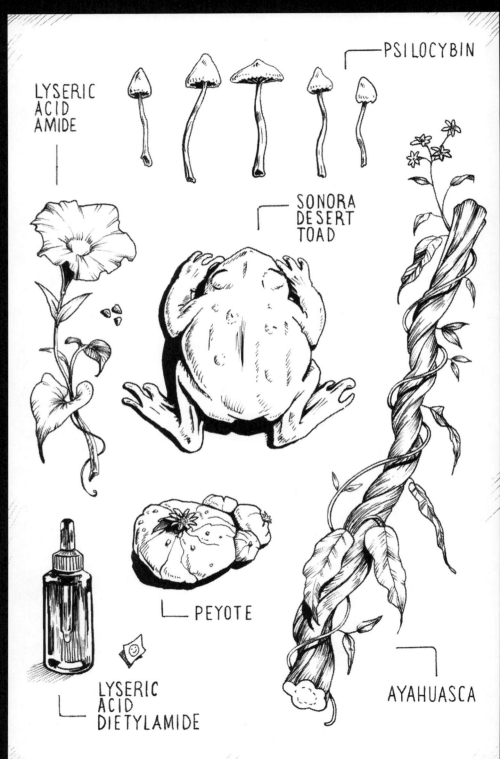

Chapter 11

Psychedelic Therapy And Integration

11.1 Legality, 11.2 Risks, 11.3 Possible Effects, 11.4 Tripping With Others, 11.5 My Trips, 11.6 LSD, 11.7 Psilocybin Mushrooms, 11.8 MDMA, 11.9 Preparing For And Going On A Safe Psychedelic Journey, 11.10 Navigating A Bad Trip, 11.11 Trip Sitting And Guiding, 11.12 Integration, 11.13 Microdosing

Psychedelic-assisted therapy has been shown to have incredible results with addiction, depression, trapped emotions, creativity, problem-solving, healing relationships, acceptance of death, and more.[37] It does so by creating an expedited pathway into many of the healing modalities we have already discussed - mindfulness, lessening hyperfocus, broadening perspective, considering different possibilities to stuck stories, and breaking self-limiting beliefs. Larger doses allow the brain to rewire itself and create a new reality. While recent science is illuminating the amazing powers of psychedelic therapy in releasing trapped emotions, humans have been using mind-altering substances for thousands of years for personal growth, spiritual connection, and creative insights.

Psychedelic-assisted therapy is very different from doing mushrooms or MDMA alone or at a festival. A therapist not only filters out people who might react poorly to the treatment, but also mentally prepares a client, is present throughout the entire trip, and follows up with at least one integration session in the week following the trip. For the sake of ease, I will be including MDMA as a psychedelic even though it works quite differently than substances like LSD, psilocybin mushrooms, DMT, peyote, and ayahuasca. There is also ketamine that I mentioned briefly in Section 4.13, but do not cover here, since using it therapeutically for pain, depression, anxiety, or PTSD requires fairly controlled amounts that are best administered with professional help.[215] Listen to Tim Ferris's podcast interview with Dr. John Krystal to learn more. This chapter includes many of my own experiences and research discoveries on psychedelics, but for a greater collection of resources, I suggest <www.erowid.org> and the Multidisciplinary Association for Psychedelic Studies (MAPS) <www.maps.org>.

Psychedelics as a therapeutic tool work by temporarily deactivating the ego and dramatically increasing the free association between conscious and subconscious parts of the mind.[134] In this way, the brain can move past reiterating the same thoughts and consider new and unique approaches. Disabling the ego additionally connects users to the idea that the world is greater than themselves, sometimes in the form of nature, the universe, friends, family, or god(s). This is a childlike state in which the ability to learn, be creative, and find genuine awe in the surrounding world are bolstered. A similar state is also reached by practitioners of mindfulness meditation.[134A] With trapped emotions often carried by a sense of stuckness, psychedelics melt away those barriers built by obsessive thinking.

While there are hundreds of psychedelic substances and compounds, this chapter focuses on three of the most common and safe ones - MDMA, LSD, and psilocybin mushrooms. If you feel that these substances are not right for you, psychedelic experiences can also come about through certain types of meditation and holotropic breathwork, but those go beyond the scope of this book. First I want to introduce a few terms used in this chapter:

- *Psychedelic/psychoactive*: A substance that alters human perception and consciousness
- *Tripper/voyager/psychonaut*: A person who uses a psychedelic
- *Trip*: The psychedelic experience
- *Tripping*: Being on psychedelics
- *Trip sitting*: Someone who takes care of people who are tripping, but does not guide them
- *Trip guide*: Someone who takes care of people tripping and helps guide the experience with sounds, images, and conversations

11.1 Legality

Unfortunately, psychedelics are considered illegal in many parts of the world, though that is changing. In 2020 Oregon passed legislation for psychedelic-assisted therapy clinics to be created, and decriminalized possession of small quantities of all drugs (though they are still illegal to possess or sell as an individual). If you want an in-depth history of the scientific discovery, impressive research studies, and banning of the substances in the United States, I highly suggest Michael Pollan's *How To Change Your Mind* and James Fadiman's *The Psychedelic Explorer's Guide*.

In brief, starting in the 1950s, there were about ten years of rigorous scientific studies into psilocybin and LSD with overwhelmingly positive psychiatric applications. However, in the 1960s psychedelics became criticized for being used extensively by the public in unsafe settings and by researchers with questionable scientific methodologies. Psychedelics inherently broke many of the rules that the research and medical communities had followed for decades. It was quite different from an antidepressant, and researchers found the greatest benefit came when users had a strong mystical experience.[134B] As therapists began combining spirituality and religion with science to push people into this mystical state, it upset many researchers, government agents, and concerned citizens.

While still relatively safe, the stories of people falling victim to manic episodes and the occasional death brought about a huge outcry from the media. It did not help that people like Timothy Leary and Richard Alpert (later known as Ram Dass) used their Harvard University positions to dose thousands of people without following good safety protocols. Thus soon began over fifty years of psychedelics being made illegal and labeled Schedule I substances with no medical benefits and with a high potential for abuse.

While using psychedelics recreationally can be therapeutic and transformative, I am not advocating for using psychedelics in this way nor am I suggesting you do anything illegal. Psychedelics can be dangerous and are not for everyone. Certain oppressed communities may also be especially hesitant to consider these options as they have been unfairly treated in relation to drug possession compared to White people. That said, as people take drugs and medicines regardless of legality or safety, I will be offering some personal insights and stories, as well as recent research and best-use practices. Many cultures have also historically used these substances, and in some parts of the world they are legal. For instance, within the USA, the Native American Church currently has the right to use peyote.

This is by no means a comprehensive guide and other resources should be consulted before partaking in any psychoactive substance. Users should also be careful not to take any psychedelic that comes from an endangered natural source such as peyote, especially when it is central to an Indigenous group's spiritual beliefs. Some people also note the importance of acknowledging which community a substance was originally derived from as it often led to that group being harmed in some way when it was forcibly taken or otherwise shared with the world.

11.2 Risks

When using psychedelics or within the weeks following, people genetically predisposed to schizophrenia or bipolar may have a psychotic or manic episode that permanently alters their life. While this can also occur through using medications, too much stress, cannabis consumption, sleep deprivation, and several illegal substances, many people associate their first major episode with psychedelics. With the proper support, people usually come out of this episode after a few days or weeks and find ways to manage their symptoms, but it is generally advised to avoid psychoactive substances if any of your family has been diagnosed with schizophrenia or bipolar. As previously mentioned, bipolar is also often misdiagnosed as depression and should be another factor that people consider.

Improper settings can lead to overwhelming and regrettably bad trips, leaving emotional scars, physical injury, or even death. An acquaintance of mine having a bad trip tragically ran from a party, fell into a ravine, and died. Do not take these substances lightly. MDMA and similar compounds can be deadly for people too - these include, but are not limited to, people with heart issues or who are taking MAO inhibitors.[119] You can learn more at <https://dancesafe.org>. Dance Safe has test kits to ensure the purity of your substances as people sometimes sell things diluted with dangerous compounds like *fentanyl* that can kill you.

Psychedelic trips can also dig up traumatic memories that a person has forgotten and is unprepared to deal with. People having severe depressive episodes or fresh memories of a difficult experience are in danger of a bad trip and worsening their symptoms. Granted, a trained guide may be able to help move a person to a positive outcome. Using psychedelics can furthermore drastically change a person's life perspectives and pathway, potentially hurting loved ones, or making that person struggle to function in society. Granted, this is not necessarily a bad thing, especially if a person has not been genuine in their passions or has been putting up with abusive behaviors.

The most widely used psychedelics are quite safe relative to drugs like meth, heroin, and alcohol. Humans and other mammals have been ingesting psychedelic substances for hundreds of thousands of years, and it seems to have potentially helped in our survival by increasing hunting abilities and problem-solving insights.[121] Substances like psilocybin mushrooms and LSD are not addictive and are almost impossible to overdose on.[37] Dosage also greatly alters the experience. Microdoses (a tenth or less of a normal dose) can be used as an antidepressant or antianxiety medicine effective within a few days. Medium doses can provide great insights into everyday life, and large doses are gateways into profound spiritual experiences. While difficult or impossible to overdose on, large doses can be overwhelming and increase the previously stated risks.

Without the dosage or environment in mind, certain substances are easier for individuals to trip on than others. If a person has a bad trip on one substance, they may swear it off, though I've heard of people being guided through a trip to heal their relationship with that substance. MDMA and similar compounds typically are the easiest trips, though the hangover can be brutal if handled wrong. This is followed by LSD, psilocybin mushrooms, and then ayahuasca.

LSD lasts a long time but usually does not cause the nausea that natural psychedelics often do. Psilocybin lasts a relatively short time but can be nauseating. Even small dosages of it also make it difficult for me to be around other people. Ayahuasca is almost always done guided and in high doses, lending to intense and life-shattering trips. It is generally not suggested to start with ayahuasca and I personally never intend to try it myself but also know people who have benefited from it. That said, ayahuasca is becoming endangered and some believe that natural sources of it should be exclusively reserved for use by Indigenous practitioners. As such, I do not include details on the usage of ayahuasca in this book.

11.3 Possible Effects

Psychedelics like psilocybin mushrooms and LSD have a range of effects. Some of these are terrifying or very uncomfortable and is part of why having a trip guide is very beneficial. A guide can provide reminders that these feelings are temporary and will pass. Trippers may experience:

- Ego death in which their individual dissolves and they become one with the universe
- An inflated ego with more confidence or overconfidence about their ideas
- Sexual desires, in which case it is very important that individuals accompanying them do not have sex, but merely talk about the feelings arising
- Feelings of insanity and fear of permanently losing one's mind in the middle of a trip (you probably will not lose your mind)
- Time slowing down, a lot can happen in a minute

- Lack of hunger, desiring very specific flavors, and things tasting weird
- Creating a whole world out of the current vantage point - simply changing the viewing angle, soundscape, or other stimuli can completely transform a trip
- Feeling unsafe or exposed until the correct environment is selected, such as under a blanket or away from the public's eyes
- Visual and auditory hallucinations
- Nausea and potential vomiting, especially on natural psychedelics such as mushrooms
- Deep insights that are quickly forgotten, which is why I like to journal or tell a trip guide things to jot down
- Forgiveness for people
- Suddenly recognizing new needs and boundaries
- An utterly confusing series of events that do not make sense and no meaning can be derived from
- People and a person's reflection looking very strange or terrifying - I tend to avoid mirrors, but this varies between trippers
- That whatever substance is taken is sentient and speaks
- The lack of desire to move (some psychedelics can even cause temporary paralysis)
- Moving through a story (which is why people say they're tripping or going on a trip)
- Having an immense amount of energy and difficulty sleeping; it is good to do psychedelics earlier in the day
- Exhaustion and mental fuzziness the following day; it is important to take care of oneself before, during, and after a trip
- Short flashbacks in which moments of a trip return weeks, months, and even years later
- Mystical, religious, and spiritual experiences

The first times I smoked cannabis and tried mushrooms, I experienced nothing. It wasn't until the second or third time that I regularly felt the desired effects. For people taking psychedelics for the first time, it is possible they will not react. This may be because of the substances being improperly stored in hot, humid, airy, or bright environments. For storage of more than a few days, psychoactive substances are best kept in the refrigerator or freezer in an airtight container. Alternatively, some people who haven't tripped before seem to require a certain amount in their system before the brain agrees to let go of control.

Drugs such as certain SSRI antidepressants also inhibit the brain's ability to experience psychedelics. While not suggested, I have known some people to stop taking their antidepressants for a day or several days leading up to a trip, though weeks may be required for a full experience. A person taking inhibitory drugs may just need to take more of the psychedelic, but that is of course risky as there is no way to determine how much. You can search online for "antidepressant and psychedelic drug interactions" for more specifics. There are also many myths surrounding the use of vitamin C and consuming citrus to intensify trips. What does seem true is that substances such as grapefruit and lemon juice will strengthen a psilocybin mushroom experience, but not necessarily others.[190]

11.4 Tripping With Others

Tripping with a friend or as a group can be a great time, but it can also add unexpected variables that distract from the medicinal nature of trips or create uncomfortable or nightmarish situations. It is best to keep groups small and to be intentional about the experience. If willing, someone should be designated as a "trip sitter" to help anyone struggling with a particular experience or needing something. More about trip sitting and guiding will be covered later in this chapter. Unless you feel really secure and content in a relationship, it's generally unadvised to take psychedelics with a romantic partner or a crush. In the right context, such as with a trip guide, this could be very therapeutic and healing, but detrimental if things go awry.

All substances have a standard experiential arc to them. People who do substances together at the same time tend to form a bond as if they are adventuring on a long journey together. This being the case, if you are late to the party and try to catch up with everyone, you may end up feeling left out and dampen your trip experience. Perhaps if done within an hour you'll be able to still partake on a similar level, but if you are dosing late it would be better to mentally prepare yourself for more of a solo trip.

11.5 My Trips

Millions of people have safely taken psychedelic substances outside of ideal conditions, with many first being introduced to tripping in chaotic music festivals and raves. This is true for me as well, so I want to take this opportunity to share my own experiences with psychoactive substances. Before that, I do want to note that it is impossible to fully articulate what being on a psychoactive substance is like. It defies the logic that language is derived from, plunging the user deep into a vivid subconscious landscape of the mind. I wish I could properly describe to you the amazing beauty I have seen. Writers like Michael Pollan and Aldous Huxley achieve some semblance of the truth, but one can only describe so much of the thousands of complex images and thoughts that arise. It is therefore better to talk less about the specifics and more about the long-term effects. In any case, this is what we're most concerned about, and what separates psychedelics from being just another party drug.

11.6 LSD

In my early college days, I had my first psychedelic experience on LSD. No one told me anything about the intricacies of the substance, but I felt relatively comfortable during the Winter break when many of the housing cooperative's members were away. The old brick mansion was special to me with colorfully painted walls and a spiraling tower straight out of a magical fantasy novel.

LSD can take up to an hour to start feeling anything, and I wasn't sure what to expect other than being told the dose was probably too low to have any visual effects. I had never even drunk alcohol, so I'm unsure what compelled me to try a psychedelic right then. Maybe it is just what college students do.

My roommate had recently wheatpasted a giant outline of a whale onto the wall outside our room and offered my friend and me paints to fill it in with. After doing that for a while and still not feeling anything, we wandered next door where more people were hanging out. A dog started barking though and I became anxious, uncomfortably anxious.

I returned to my room and hid under my blankets like a scared child. I guess I had started feeling it. Psychedelics increase sensitivity to stimuli and many people, similar to me, find themselves reverting to a partially childlike mentality. I didn't want to be in my room though, and after calming down I ascended the stairs to watch the city from the rooftop four stories up. That was too cold though, and I found myself in the attic wishing I were simultaneously warm, near people, but not interacting with them. I had an "aha!" moment and descended to the first-story living room. Here my housemates had lovingly built a fort out of our many couches. I climbed in and spent the next several hours journaling, occasionally entertaining a visitor checking in on me. This journaling session was significant. While many people cannot write while tripping, I find it often important for me to remember what thoughts and realizations transpired during the trip.

Growing up I had been deeply antagonistic to relationships, probably from seeing my parent's messy marriage and how friends who dated always seemed to become badly hurt. In my journal, I humorously identified with the couch fort, seeing that we shared many of the same characteristics. Something was missing though, and I wrote, "I am a couch fort, and I need a couch fort lover." I had decided then and there that I wanted a girlfriend, that experiencing love was worth it, and that relationships involved more than just suffering.

LSD and other psychedelics help loosen the stories that we hold onto, allowing for quick insight and transformation unparalleled by any other method. While my interest in dating may have arisen anyways, who knows how long that could have been? Future LSD trips were not nearly so groundbreaking, but consistently reminded me of my self-worth, my desire to spend more time with friends and loved ones, and the meaning of my work. I generally felt better about myself and my relationships after tripping.

LSD most frequently appears on blotter paper, gelatins, and diluted liquid drops. Just one drop, gelatin, or blotter square is a standard dosage amount but I have heard it can vary widely between 50 to 150 micrograms. Sub-perceptible or microdoses (covered later in this chapter) range from 5 to 20 micrograms, and heavy doses exceed 400 micrograms.[196] The dosage amount and purity of the LSD changes the trip substantially, and it is difficult to gauge just how strong "a hit" of LSD received from friends or benevolent strangers will be, especially as everyone reacts to it a little differently. LSD lasts for eight to ten hours, with several unique phases including:

1. Waiting to start feeling something followed by the visual focus becoming intensified
2. Small hallucinations and noticeably creative thoughts, with fine motor skills becoming more difficult
3. Intensifying hallucinations and finding more acceptance with the trip
4. Peaking with strong visuals and rapid thoughts possibly including seeing fractals and having spiritual experiences
5. Comedown with visuals and thoughts softening and regaining some fine motor skill
6. Only small distortions remain and are possibly accompanied by feelings of happiness and peace
7. Fully sober, often accompanied by tired contentment and possibly hunger, but may still feel quite energized

Especially with the experience of time slowing down, a trip can feel like an uncomfortably long time. While LSD typically creates less nausea than natural psychedelics do, I have experienced some batches of LSD causing uncomfortable sensations. This has included nausea and having the inability to focus on a single stream of thought as a constant barrage of short images and half-thoughts appear for hours of the trip. It was once explained to me that this might be caused by slight variations in the LSD's purity, but it might also just be how I personally reacted. There are also some substances sold as LSD that closely mimic it, so I may have been having something else.

11.7 Psilocybin Mushrooms

Months after my first LSD trip, I consumed a large dose (3.5 grams) of psilocybin mushrooms brewed in tea. The heat thankfully decreases nausea and hides the flavor that my taste buds find difficult to stomach. Two friends accompanied me in the forest, and I couldn't even stand up. The whole world was moving and all the plants appeared sentient, moving as if in dance and kindly wandering across my body. This time I couldn't write, and I found myself in a trance-like state with my eyes closed. I breathed heavily and rocked back and forth in rhythm with the feelings of sickness, which seemed to help calm my stomach. In my mind, I was floating in an enormous cylindrical tube whose walls were ornately decorated with precious gems. My two friends were floating there with me, taking on playful animal forms and giving me instructions on what to do. Unfortunately, unable to accomplish some of these feats, I felt their disappointment.

While this trip was much more intense and uncomfortable than the first, I still came out of it with a deeper comfort in my body, physically and sexually. I also felt embarrassed. I really believed that my friends were there in my head and heard everything. I never discussed the events that had transpired though, and it took me quite a while to believe that they hadn't somehow been projecting their energies into my body, that it was all just my imagination working.

In future trips with mushrooms, I discovered that I was much more sensitive to external stimuli than to other substances. Unlike the LSD high in which I could wander around a festival or socialize with a group of people, the slightest amount of mushrooms causes me to become highly introverted. Everyone reacts differently though, and many people are quite extroverted on mushrooms as well.

Dosing with raw mushrooms is not an exact science as even the same mushroom species can greatly range in their psychedelic compounds available per weight. For dried psilocybe cubensis however the dosing scale generally follows that 0.1 - 0.5 grams is a microdose, 1 gram is a low dose, 1.75 grams is a medium dose, 3.5 grams is a large dose, and 5 grams is a "heroic dose."[166] Just keep in mind that more is not necessarily better, though it may be powerfully transformative for some individuals.

Psilocybin mushrooms last for much less time than LSD does, just four to six hours. Many people report that mushroom trips feel more natural, but it is hard to separate our experience from the beliefs we enter into the trip with. As with all psychedelics you have control over the world being created. If you don't like the trip, you can change it with your own mental efforts or simply by changing your sensual stimuli like what you're looking at, your movements, or the music being played. Whatever you expect to happen will become your reality, so it is dangerous for people to trip who believe it will make them mentally unstable or are actively questioning their self-worth due to a recent breakup. That said, a professional guide can help you navigate through these rougher waters.

Inspired by these two experiences with psychedelics, I soon found myself in my first intimate relationship. While short-lived, it still opened me up to connecting with people on a more meaningful level and experiencing a celebrated part of human existence.

11.8 MDMA

My first time on MDMA was at Burning Man with some acquaintances and several people I had just recently met in our camp. I was impatiently waiting on the group of eight to bicycle over to watch *The Crystal Method* perform, an electronic act that I grew up enjoying (though can't say I have the same interest in these days). Eventually, we started on our way, each freshly dosed with a gross-tasting white powder I believed was MDMA (you can't always believe what people say without a drug test kit, and similar substances like MDA also exist).

Just like my first times on LSD and mushrooms, I knew very little of what I was about to experience. All I knew was that MDMA was quite different from the trippy substances I had previously taken. Call me naive, but I trusted these relative strangers I had been mingling with the past few days in Burning Man's harsh sun, immense art, and booming music. So about halfway to our destination, it's not surprising that one member of our group asked to stop for a minute. I was annoyed, but complied, not wanting to lose everyone as the sun was quickly setting and tens of thousands of people darted around on their lit-up bicycles. We sat down in a circle and began chatting with each other. Soon we started taking turns praising each other's strengths and speaking openly about our insecurities. I found my previous impatience reprehensible, reconnecting with the importance of community and cherishing these people. I loved each one of them, these were my friends, my allies, and I wanted to support them through thick and thin. I was happy, and we eventually headed back to camp to continue chatting into the night.

Later I was given a tablet of 5-HTP, a precursor to serotonin. I was instructed to take it in the morning to counterbalance the depressive side effects that many people experience in the following hours or days. People have mixed experiences with 5-HTP, but it does seem to help some prevent a lasting depressive episode, especially if taken for the three days before the MDMA roll. There are also many other regimens to follow before and after taking MDMA. You can find good ones at <www.erowid.org> and <www.reddit.com/r/MDMA>.

Without using a recovery regimen, the hangover can often be brutal, even pushing people into suicidal ideations or causing breakups. This may be even worse if your doses are mixed with anything you were not expecting. Take extra care of yourself the following few days and continuously remember what caused this difficult episode – hopefully, a beautiful few hours that were marked by how truly amazing life is. Even without any extra supplementation though, your serotonin levels should return to normal within a week. RollSafe suggests never taking more than 120 mg of MDMA per session.[144] They note that the vast majority of substances sold as MDMA are not actually MDMA, or have other substances in them. Getting a test kit is important for your safety. Check out their MDMA dosing guide at RollSafe.org.

MDMA lasts about four hours. It works by flooding the body with serotonin, causing things like lights, sounds, and touch to feel especially amazing. The immense joy is perhaps why people refer to people as "rolling" while on the substance. It can create compassion and empathy in a group of strangers, forgiveness between partners, and self-love if taken alone. A place like Burning Man becomes immensely beautiful when provided with a safe and nourishing environment.

In one study MDMA assisted therapy sessions for PTSD were two to three times more effective than the leading medications in reducing PTSD and depressive symptoms.[38] Participants were given up to three, eight-hour sessions of MDMA-assisted therapy over three months, and up to twelve integrative sessions surrounding them. This may be in part due to MDMA's ability to reopen early developmental periods in the brain that are otherwise fairly difficult to change.[203] Studies like these are why MDMA was given breakthrough medical status and in 2022 are passing Phase 3 clinical trials in the United States.

Unfortunately, MDMA by itself may not solve a person's problems outside of a therapeutic environment and can cause immense emotional pain when you realize that your recent experience is not reflected in everyday life. For myself, taking MDMA in a stressful relationship convinced me that I wanted it to work out, even though I had already identified that we were essentially incompatible. It is hard not to allow such an extraordinarily beautiful experience to color your vision. My emotions that I had been distancing from came back in full force, wanting to shower my partner with love and affection. As a result, the inevitable breakup two months later was extra levels of horrible and haunted me for quite a long time.

While you might feel more secure and happy about a relationship for a month or so, these effects will dissipate unless you work out your fundamental problems. You need to integrate the lessons you learn. This is true for all psychoactive substances and is why using these substances assisted with therapy and reflective integration sessions is so beneficial - they break down the stories we tell ourselves while also examining the underlying patterns and beliefs we hold onto. While some people have some amazing healing experiences with loved ones tripping together, it's generally better not to casually trip with someone you have too many unresolved struggles or unknowns with.

11.9 Preparing For And Going On A Safe Psychedelic Journey

The worth of any psychedelic experience will often benefit by following some general guidelines:

1. ***Setup*** - Ideally get the next two days following the trip off. Starting at least one day before the trip, take good care of yourself. Eat a little lighter with nourishing meals. Get plenty of sleep and stay away from screens, heavy meals, or caffeine later in the day. Journal about life and identify some questions or problems you want assistance with. Create a playlist of non-vocal, emotionally neutral, instrumental music - classical, lo-fi electronic, or worldly tunes do well. Depending on the substance you are taking, four to eight hours of music is ideal.
2. ***Ensuring quality*** - While hopefully you are sourcing your substances from a trusted individual who has already tested them, substances sold on the black market leave a lot of room for ill-intentioned dealings. There are test kits available to ensure what you're consuming is pure, or at least not deadly. At festivals, you may find groups

like *The Bunk Police* or *Dance Safe* that sell these kits or provide free testing. Perhaps due to how cheap it is to synthesize, LSD is rarely adulterated, but MDMA is commonly mixed with other substances that may cause undesirable effects. As for psilocybin mushrooms, there are many deadly look-alikes out in the wild. Most mushrooms you buy though will be grown from lab-collected spores, eliminating the chance for improper identification.

3. **Choose a guide or trip sitter** - While someone professionally trained in psychedelic-assisted therapy is ideal, almost anyone you trust who is empathetic and kind can make a great trip sitter. Trip guiding and sitting will be covered later in this chapter.

4. **Set and setting** - Choose a safe, calm, and cozy environment that minimizes outside distractions. If you're not in nature, make at least one corner of the space aesthetically pleasing. This could be an altar, pictures of loved ones, or art. Even in nature, it is good to have an object that grounds you in positive feelings such as a photo, book, flower, or crystal. Interestingly, when being treated with psychedelic-assisted therapy for things like depression, fear of dying, or addictions, participants who have a stronger mystical experience during the trip are more likely to benefit from the treatment.[134B] This is believed to work because it constantly reminds a person otherwise trapped in their ego and hyperfocusing on their problems that their difficulties are small and they are not alone. Therefore, many trip guides include religious or spiritual items in the space.

5. **Before dosing** - It is generally best to eat light before dosing and little to nothing during the trip, but users need to listen to their bodies and stay hydrated. Put your phone into airplane mode (if that feels safe) and keep water, a journal, and music controls nearby. It may be wise to leave any important items such as your keys, wallet, or ID in a secure location.

6. **Do not** - During or soon after a trip absolutely never drive. Even if you feel relatively normal again it may surprise you how difficult certain activities are. Have someone else drive you if necessary, but ideally, you can sleep wherever you tripped. It is also generally better not to engage in sexual activities, especially not with someone who is acting as a guide. Do not trip if you are suicidal or in a dark place. Never trip with a romantic partner you are struggling with outside of a therapeutic setting. Do not make any major life changes within two weeks of tripping unless they involve removing yourself from an abusive or

otherwise dangerous situation.
7. **Dosing** - Review your journal notes and consider why you wish to go on a psychedelic trip. Say a prayer or set intentions, either with yourself or a group of companions, then take a dose that you feel comfortable with.
8. **Tripping** - How you trip is largely up to you. Much of the research involves participants blindfolded, possibly with headphones playing non-lyrical classical or world music, but I prefer a mixture of journaling, closing my eyes, and staying present with my surroundings. You can talk to your trip guide, tell them to take notes, or seek out your safe objects for reassurance. Most trip guides suggest going *through* dark and scary experiences rather than avoiding them, but if you're alone I suggest only doing this if you feel adequately prepared (which can be difficult to understand while tripping). Confronting the dark spaces of a trip can be quite difficult and uncomfortable, but is also often where deeper healing may happen. You can always inquire about the uncomfortable energies, "What are you doing in my mind and what do you have to teach me?" Stand your ground, this is your body and mind you are interacting with. In terms of hallucinations, these can be neat and bring a lot of appreciation for the beauty in the world, but some people consider them distractions from the true therapeutic parts that a trip can create.
9. **Booster** - After 2 hours or so after initially dosing you can take a booster dose if you aren't as high as you would like to be.
10. **Coming down** - As you come down from the trip, revisit the problems and relationships you wanted to explore. Consider each deeply and see if you have any special insights.
11. **Post-trip** - After the trip, eat some food if you feel hungry. It may be difficult to sleep for several hours depending on how high of a dose you took. Talk to friends if you feel up for it, or journal about the experience if you didn't get the chance to while tripping.
12. **The following days** - Nourish yourself and take it easy. In some cases, you may feel depressed but know that these feelings should alleviate within a few days when your chemicals balance out. People who take MDMA should look online at pre and post-loading regimens that will help lessen the comedown. Journal. How can you integrate what you learned? Don't make any drastic changes unless they are for your safety, but make a plan for improving your life, relationships, and self. If the desire to create drastic changes still exists in two weeks,

go for it.

11.10 Navigating A Bad Trip

Bad trips happen. Sometimes these can be uncomfortable, terrifying, or just annoying. If you are with a guide or sitter tell them what is coming up. If you are at a festival, a medical team such as *Zendo* should be able to help. These trained volunteers de-escalate your intense experience, providing a calming space for you to recuperate in. The general advice is to go through the experience rather than avoiding it, but that might not always be possible or may simply be too difficult. If you are alone, orient yourself toward whatever kind of positive environment or anchor you have created. The *Fireside Project* is also a non-profit that provides psychedelic peer support by calling or texting 62-FIRESIDE. You can learn more at <https://firesideproject.org>.

I have found that on a normal dose of a psychedelic, it's still possible to access my standard state of being. This is especially easier with your eyes open and periodically switching between where you focus your attention. Many psychedelic effects are stronger when your focus is placed on a single area. Some people also use substances like alcohol to dilute the intensity of a trip, but this can be dangerous. Especially with how little has been eaten, alcohol increases the risk of vomiting or overdosing. Just remember, uncomfortable psychedelic mind states are temporary - you are not losing your mind, and your normal state of consciousness will return. You will be fine again soon.

11.11 Trip Sitting And Guiding

Many people find great pleasure in serving psychedelic voyagers by acting as a sitter or guide. These individuals are sober while attending to others, but it is generally suggested that they have previously had their own psychedelic experiences. A *sitter* can be just about anyone capable of maintaining compassion, empathy, and attentiveness. They ensure that tripping individuals stay safe from physical harm and provide any needs that arise such as water, food, music, jotting down important details, helping change the scenery, or driving people home. The sitters can also listen empathetically but are in no way directing the course of a trip.

If emergencies arise sitters can also call for professional help, but it is beneficial for sitters to know some de-escalation techniques. Sitters must understand that psychedelic trips can elicit strong but healthy emotions. Seeing your friend crying or having other releases might prompt you to step in and interrupt what would otherwise be a cathartic experience. Interrupting a person moving through a dark place can prevent them from recovering on the other side of the trip. It is suggested to read through James Fadiman's *The Psychedelic Explorer's Guide* before trip sitting or guiding.

Trip guides are capable of maximizing the therapeutic benefits of a psychedelic experience. These individuals have formal training with other guides and follow specific protocols largely established by the first generation of psychedelic researchers and therapists in the United States. Sitters and guides alike will benefit from reading resources like *The Zendo Project Training Manual*, *The Manual of Psychedelic Support*, *The Secret Chief Revealed*, and the works of Stanislav Grof. The easiest way to get involved in this work is by volunteering with a festival medical team like *Zendo* to assist people through psychedelic crises. Although some criticize it for being too lenient, Oregon's 2020 psilocybin-assisted therapy bill also allows for anyone with a high school diploma to become formally trained as a guide. More states are sure to follow.

Just like a therapist, every guide is different and it is important to feel safe and trust them. Interview them and make sure you feel comfortable. The day before a trip may be spent establishing this relationship through a variety of means. A general explanation of what you may soon experience will also be given, hopefully airing out any concerns about not returning to your normal state of consciousness. During a trip the guide may set the music, periodically ask how or where you are, or instruct you in various activities. The following day will be spent integrating the experience.

11.12 Integration

Psychedelics may give you profound mental shifts during the trip itself and the days following, but often the realizations you make require action. While you may feel deeply motivated about your new insights, it is easy to slip back into old patterns unless you constructively apply that energy. This is known as *integration*:

1. Don't rush back into living your normal life, do your best to slow down and give space to this profound experience you just had. Journal, create art, meditate, and spend time in nature.
2. Explore the deeper meanings of your trip. Research the symbology that arose, share your experience with trusted individuals, and interview family members about your history. You can also connect with other psychedelic explorers at conferences, festivals, integration meetups, online, and generally anywhere that new age or spiritually minded people congregate.
3. Identify the changes you want to make.

4. Create a reasonable plan for integrating those changes. Habits are best formed one at a time. See Chapter 12.
5. Create a schedule, start practicing, sign up for classes, seek help, communicate with people, read a book about the subject, and so on.
6. Become the new you.

Integration can be challenging. Your psychedelic experience may have brought up difficult memories and insights or profoundly confusing and seemingly nonsensical content. For some, the images will quickly fade as an interesting experiment. For others, the integration process may strongly disrupt your life or entirely remove you from everything you once believed to be true. This could create hurt feelings among friends, family, co-workers, or partners. It may also put your health or financial stability at risk. Remember, it is best to wait a couple of weeks before making major changes as a psychedelic can temporarily make you ignore everything else other than your personal discoveries. Only you can make this decision though. Just be careful, and know it is okay to slow down and implement these realizations over time.

Sharing your psychedelic trip with a loved one or therapist can be insightful. However, depending on your comfort level and sense of trust with this individual, you may choose to withhold parts of your story. If they have never had their own psychedelic experience, it may be wise to omit that you used psychedelics altogether and simply share newly arising thoughts and feelings. Remember that many people, even therapists, maintain inaccurate stigmas about the use of psychedelics. While you may have had an extraordinary experience, traditional therapy and psychedelic therapy are considerably different. At the very least, the individual you share with must believe that your experience was true and valuable. They must also be more inclined toward curiosity about your personal journey than pushing their own agenda.

While you may not have another psychedelic trip for quite some time, if ever again, many people recognize that joyous and present states similar to a psychedelic high can be maintained through more traditional means. These include meditation, holotropic breathwork, spirituality, yoga, time in nature, and the arts. Each of these allows for a deeper connection to the sensual and introspective aspects of life, and may be a worthy addition to your integrative goals.

A list of psychedelic integration therapists can be found at <https://integration.maps.org> and <https://psychedelic.support/network>. You can also ask your therapist if they know anyone, or if they are at all familiar with psychedelics and psychedelic therapy. Many supportive communities also exist online at places like Reddit and Facebook.

11.13 Microdosing

Sub-perceptual or small doses of certain psychedelics, also known as microdoses, are capable of alleviating depressive symptoms and increasing motivation and creativity.[37] This amount can still carry the previously mentioned risks so do not take it lightly, but it does tend to be safer. Again, this is not medical advice and you should talk to a doctor or wait for more solid studies to come out before experimenting.

After hearing glowing praises of microdosing from some friends I decided to try it for myself. This was near the end of 2019, one of the most stressful years of my life. Between working with a difficult publisher, trying to save a floundering relationship, and living with a triggering housemate, I found myself miserable and unmotivated. In desperation, I dissolved a hit of LSD into a tincture bottle filled with ten dropperfuls of water. After it dissolved and I gave the concoction an extra shake, I took one dropperful. This turned out to be a bit more than sub-perceptible, but I could still function just fine. In fact, it made me feel better. Not like a drug high, but like a normal human being who wasn't sensitive to every small difficulty that arose. I continued dosing every few days at a fifth of a dropperful, which gave me enough of a boost to continue working and try sorting through things with my army of woe.

There's only so much medicine can do for a person's mood, and my misery didn't really end until I broke up with my girlfriend, moved out of my house, and finished writing my book, but I believe microdosing helped give me the strength to do these things. I continued consuming my tincture for the next few months until I ran out, experiencing a fairly positive mood throughout.

The following 6 weeks I was doing well, but the arrival of COVID, renewed difficulties with my ex, and experimenting with drinking small amounts of alcohol after three months of sobriety threw me into a severe bout of depression. I was beginning to consider ending my life until I remembered about microdosing. Within a short while I was able to create a new tincture of LSD. After one day of medicating, my mood improved and I started feeling normal again. I told my ex I needed space, and I found ways of creating community through the difficult conditions of COVID's first year.

People most often microdose with LSD or psilocybin mushrooms taking two days off after a dose, though I've sometimes dosed multiple days in a row or stopped for a week. Researchers do not believe that the body forms an addiction to psychedelics so there is no withdrawal.[37] The idea is that just like with a normal trip, the body needs time to integrate the experience though. Generally 1/10th of a hit is suggested, but as previously explained it can be difficult to know the exact strength of any given substance. I personally do 1/20th to 1/30th of a normal dosage, making a $5 tincture last anywhere from three months to several years. Experiment with what's right for you.

The dosage should be nearly sub-perceptual, but you will still likely notice some changes if you're in tune with your body. Most people can go about their daily life the same, but I have some caveats for myself. Even at the low doses I've taken I sometimes hesitate to drive because I become more focused on small distractions. The days I dose can be more anxiety-ridden and I'm more sensitive to external stimuli. It's especially important to listen to my bodily needs if I'm feeling overwhelmed. Sleeping can also be more difficult with a heightened amount of energy, so I dose early and keep in mind that I may not be able to nap. These sensations may last as long as a normal dosage of a substance - eight hours for LSD and four hours for psilocybin.

In terms of benefits, the day I dose I often experience having more energy, more motivation, extra levels of playfulness, and heightened positivity. I typically can work on projects longer and when struggling with a problem often have an insight or new way of looking at it by the evening. The day after dosing I usually feel quite balanced and level-headed, possibly with some continued positivity. The day after that is fairly normal.

There are currently no properly controlled studies to support or negate my claims about microdosing. Some research points to microdosing benefits being a placebo, while a plethora of self-experimenting individuals and other research report beneficial results.

***

Chapter Reflections

1. What are your beliefs and reservations about psychedelic therapy?
2. Do you or your family have a history of any conditions that may cause concern about using psychoactive substances?
3. If you have used psychedelics, have you spent the time to use them intentionally and with space to integrate the experience?
4. What have you yet to integrate from your psychedelic trips?
5. What resources exist in your community to legalize psychedelic therapy and stop the war on drugs?

PART III

BEHAVIORS, MINDSET, RELATIONSHIPS, AND ENVIRONMENT

Chapter 12

Habits And Addictions

12.1 Habits, 12.2 Addictions, 12.3 The Big No List

Now that you have some tools for releasing your trapped emotions, we need to discuss the maladaptive behaviors you may have formed and the skills you never learned. While it is great if you can reconcile with your past suffering, that may mean nothing if you keep putting yourself into emotionally tumultuous situations, practice unhealthy behaviors, or continue to have self-limiting beliefs. These patterns may have arisen from your culture, family, or self-protective defenses. They may also exist because things like childhood neglect or abuse prevent the development of certain brain areas, and extreme difficulties can also shut off parts of the brain. Thus, changing certain behaviors may coincide with releasing some of your trapped emotions or healing your attachment wounds. The latter is explored in Section 14.2 and 17.6.

While changing aspects of your life may initially feel awkward and unnatural, you eventually go from practicing something to integrating it into your identity. You can reinvent yourself. This chapter deals primarily with techniques for transforming unhealthy behaviors, while the following ones involve changing your mindset, relationships, and surrounding environment.

12.1 Habits

Habits are unconsciously performed actions or things we regularly do without thinking about them. You can have a habit of brushing your teeth or panicking when you see someone. According to James Clear, author of *Atomic Habits*, a habit has four parts to it: the "habit cue", the craving for the habit, the habit itself, and a reward for performing the habit.[208] An example would be the sight of cookies (the habit cue) leading you to desire cookies (the craving), which prompts you to purchase and eat cookies (the habit), which in turn triggers your taste receptors and happy chemicals (the reward). Habit cues include anything from sights and sounds to smells and feelings. They can even manifest in the memories of these things. Once the habit has been initiated, the brain automates the process and is free to think about other thoughts and actions.

Everyone forms habits at a different rate, though three to six weeks of daily practice has become a popularized number for people to strive for when attempting to embed a new habit.[100,64] If you perform an action regularly enough, it should stay permanently wired within your neural makeup after this amount of time.[32] This is great for healthy habits, but also makes breaking an unhealthy habit exceptionally difficult. Even if you do break a habit, being around old habit cues can quickly make the habit reform.[53] This is especially challenging as the rewards for an unhealthy behavior are often more immediate than the rewards for a healthy behavior. So how can you transform these? Tips for forming habits include:

1. ***Repeat*** - Repeat the behavior often, at regular intervals. Daily repetition helps, but so long as you practice consistently, you can do it on specific days of the week instead. Even if you sometimes practice a skill wrong, remember that failure is an opportunity to learn from your mistakes and that the most successful people fail a lot.
2. ***Start small*** - Form one habit at a time. It does not matter how much time you perform the habit for, just doing it is helping your brain create new neural pathways. That means doing a 1-minute meditation or a 5-minute workout is still beneficial. You can incrementally increase this number as you become more engaged in the activity.
3. ***Focus on small goals*** - At a physiological level, proximity to your goal completion significantly increases motivation and the ease to get there, so make smaller goals within your larger objective.[71,69] For instance, even though you might be trying to do twenty push-ups, making goal increments of five will give you four reward pay-offs throughout the journey there. Hyperfocus on the short-term and what is immediately in front of you. Celebrate the small victories.
4. ***Create a growth mindset*** - Instead of focusing on the reward of accomplishing your goal, make the journey itself a reward.[69] As we will explore in Section 13.4, this is important because relying on spikes of dopamine in an activity actually makes you enjoy that activity less, especially after you get the reward. You can create a *growth mindset* by noticing your incremental improvements and successes, and acknowledging the positive difference you are creating through the healthy stress you are enduring. For instance, "I know this run is

improving my health", or, "I'm proud of myself for taking care of my well-being." You can also celebrate your losses as educational moments and say "I'm not losing, I'm learning." Again, successful people fail a lot and learn from their mistakes.

5. *Schedule* - Schedule the habit with specifics of when and for how long. For instance, for 30 minutes on Mondays, Wednesdays, and Fridays at 9:00 AM, I will _____. If your work or life schedule shifts around, make a time reference to accommodate it, such as "when I get off work" or "after breakfast." I've found right after I wake up to be the only reliable time that I can start a new habit.

6. *Make it visible* - Make the habit or reward for the habit more visible. Put supplements next to your bed, healthy foods on the kitchen counter, or a book you should read in your bag. Keep a daily log of how you feel from performing the habit, or treat yourself to something nice for accomplishing the behavior. Make a bet with others and if you do not accomplish your goals you lose money. You can also research the science of why something is healthy for you.

7. *Keep the reward random* - Intermittent random rewards do better at building a behavior than getting consistent rewards do.[69] For instance, if you complete your habit, you could roll a six-sided die and get a treat if you roll a certain number.

8. *Visualize your desired outcome* - When you visualize your desire, it makes it much easier to see healthy alternatives as an option.[9] For instance, imagining yourself as an elderly person can help you understand why investing in your retirement is important to start now. That said, visualizing the entire process of success can decrease your motivation by prematurely giving an imagined mental reward, decreasing your drive to pursue that reward in reality.[71]

9. *Visualize and practice for the obstacles* - Becoming aware of and preparing for likely obstacles along your way will help you overcome them as they arise.[182] When ___ happens, I will ___.

10. *Gamify* - Make a game out of the activity, either competing against yourself or other people. Games greatly increase motivation. For instance, how many push-ups can you do, or how long can you meditate for? Compare with your previous best scores and reward yourself for hitting certain milestones. There are many different habit-tracking apps to make this easier. You can also read the book *SuperBetter* by Jane McGonigal for a deep dive into gamifying your life.

11. *Work together* - Team up by forming the habit with someone else,

such as an exercise buddy. This way you will both feel obligated to not skip your exercise schedule. You can also seek help through classes, life coaches, therapists, support groups, and pets who need walks.

12. **Positive pairing** - Take an activity you have positive associations with and pair it with a habit you are trying to form. For instance, listen to music you really like while working out or use a stationary bike while watching TV. This works best if you only allow yourself to engage in the positive activity when you are practicing the habit you are trying to form.
13. **Rethink** - If you are not motivated to do a healthy activity, try thinking of it in a more interesting way. For instance, *to love my whole body, to document beauty and magic, to get away from those silly humans, to get artistic inspiration*, or *to see my tree friends.* You can also make an excuse for it. To travel and speak to people more easily, you can have the mission of taking specific photographs, obtaining new recipes, meeting your extended family, or foraging for the tastiest mushrooms.
14. **Force yourself** - It may be uncomfortable, but really, you're never going to want to do something you don't feel motivated to do or have yet to create a habit for. As Amy Cuddy says, "Fake it till you make it." After a few days to weeks, you may suddenly enjoy something you never thought you had an interest in. Give it a chance. The first time I danced in daylight sober I had a panic attack, and then it got easier and really fun. Having an initial negative reaction does not mean that you will always find an activity unpleasant.
15. **Create space** – Abstain from activities or addictions that are distracting you from what you really want. Try 30 days without media, alcohol, porn, junk food, or whatever else might be holding you back.

On the opposite end, here are some tips for deforming habits:

1. **Recognize the habit cues and rewards** - This will give you some power over the habit, understanding how it is initiated and where it is coming from.
2. **Rules** - Make reasonable rules for regulating your behaviors. For instance, I will only watch media in the evening or with friends, or I can only eat out if I exercise first. This makes it much easier to alter your behaviors than outright saying you cannot ever do a thing. You

might also remind yourself of a label you identify with or have the intention of embodying such as sober, vegetarian, physically strong, artist, or a person who supports those in need. Lastly, you can make rules which slow down your consumption of the substance. For instance, being part of a book club or requiring yourself to reflect on and integrate what you learned from a movie.

3. ***Decrease stress*** - Food, drugs, alcohol, and other addictions are often the result of stress, so to deform these types of habits, you may have to first create a more stable and calm life for yourself.[158] More about addictions is covered in the next section.

4. ***Parallel habits*** - If a habit cue such as stress or seeing junk food causes you to perform an unhealthy habit, train yourself to perform a healthy habit when you receive those habit cues instead. For instance, if you smell cookies, instead of going to pursue cookies, do push-ups or breathe deeply. This is called a *parallel habit*.

5. ***Remove unhealthy habit cues from your life*** - Even if it means ending a friendship or changing your living space, it will help you transform your habits if you get away from the habit cues.

6. ***Change your environment*** - The easiest way to change a habit is by doing so on vacation or after you move away because you are removed from the habit cues of your normal environment.[53]

7. ***Distance yourself*** - Put the habit just a little further out of reach so you think twice before initiating it. For instance, connect with people who do not perform that habit, temporarily block websites with a blocking program, place an addictive food out of sight, or use a time-lock safe to secure a device or food from yourself for a set time.

8. ***Become aware of marketing*** - To prevent businesses from making you eat certain foods or compulsively buy their goods, understand how colors, smells, language, and advertisements are used to manipulate your purchasing decisions, news consumption, and social media scrolling. Also learning about nutrition, malnourishment, and preventable diseases will give you further reason to make healthier choices. This education can be especially influential in children and teenagers if done properly - shaming people for their decisions may have the opposite of your intended effect.

9. ***Remind yourself of the negative*** - Write brief statements over and over again about your rationale for ending a habit and how that habit negatively impacts you. Read this list periodically or whenever you fall back into a habit you want to change. It might look something

like my own list I once made: *Eating sweets makes me feel awful the next day, I love my body so I do not eat sweets, I do not sleep well when I eat sweets, I do not like getting cavities so do not need to eat sweets, I feel healthier on the days I do not consume sweets, I do not like the way that I break out in acne when I eat sweets*, and so on. Try to fill out at least half to a full page with statements like these. When confronted with the habit cue, this gives your brain enough pause to make a rational decision before automatically taking an action.
10. **Create a negative association** - Associate the habit with something negative after performing it. For instance, look at something very disgusting after doing it.

You need positive habits to replace negative ones. For instance, you will likely relapse into your old behaviors unless you have a routine and community reinforcing your healing. Change comes through practice. You can only learn so much simply by reading, so you have to apply what you learn as well. Groups will give you structure, practical solutions, space to vent, peers who understand your struggles, and educational resources. This assistance can be found in groups specific to correcting a behavior such as an addiction or codependency support group, or in other communities such as religious, spiritual, meditation, or yoga groups. While I try my best to cover important guidelines throughout this book, only you can take the leap of committing to a routine.

Another thing that helps with transforming habits is developing a higher tolerance to distress.[233] According to psychologist Todd Kashdan, having more distress tolerance equates to being much better at keeping commitments you make to yourself and others. This is because you can decrease the overwhelm experienced going through hard things. Many of the activities throughout this book help build distress tolerance. These include a good self-care regimen, being in accepting environments, knowing coping skills like deep breathing, approaching situations with curiosity, and having a healthy social network.[235] Even just talking about your failures and how you learned from them builds resiliency.[234] Challenging yourself and successfully doing hard things also helps, including with physical distress.[233] For instance, cold showers, big hikes, learning a new skill, or long travel trips. A certain amount of stress is essential for us to thrive in life, so be sure to periodically embrace the healthy forms of it.

Forming and deforming habits can be very uncomfortable. However, if you expect this, you can ignore the excuses you may create. These could include things like it's not fun or it's too hard. Whatever you commit to, stick with it and know that it may take a month or more to start feeling joy and ease in a transformation. It often helps me to understand the science behind why something is good or bad too, like if a food will help prevent disease or inflammation, I'll put up with the flavor better. To learn more about habits, read *Atomic Habits* by James Clear, or, *The Power of Habit* by Charles Duhig. There are also smartphone and computer applications available for helping you form and deform habits. Now let's talk about another form of habit, an addiction.

12.2 Addictions

Addictions are typically used to self-soothe or create community and relationships (as empty as they may be). Typically addictions make the experience of trapped emotions much worse after the high has worn off. Not all substances considered addictive are problematic to consume, but people who believe they "healthily" consume addictive substances may still have problems arising they are unaware of. This is the great difficulty with addictions, users are often in denial about having a problem. The goal is to form a healthy relationship with your behaviors - whether that means cutting it back or cutting it out altogether.

Is a substance preventing you from meaningful relationships? Is it causing you to feel sick, depressed, or unhealthy? Is it preventing you from achieving your goals? Are people upset with you about your consumption patterns? Are you ignoring other obligations or things you once found enjoyable? You may instinctively respond "no" to each of these questions without really being aware of the answer.

Even if you overcome an addiction, you still have to repair the maladaptive behaviors that were picked up along the way. For instance, you may have missed out on how to socialize, take care of your body, or be interested in healthy forms of play. How do you want to develop as a person and what's getting in your way? Just like with a garden, you may have to clear the field to have space for new growth.

12.2.1 The Causes Of Addiction

Be mindful and think about the time, money, and other resources you pour into your addictive hobby. Remember that certain addictions can be trapped emotions playing out and feel entirely natural, but only you can decide to create change in your life. Genetic factors can play a role in how easily a person becomes addicted to a substance, especially people with conditions like

ADHD.[219,220] However, addictions are not diseases. People with these genetic traits are still able to quit because addictions are caused by four specific things that can be dealt with. These include the addictiveness of a substance, the culture supporting the addiction, inaccurate beliefs about a substance, and stress.

1. ***Stress*** - The primary cause of addictions is stress. Addictions are used to escape one's life, feel less anxious at social gatherings, numb intense feelings and memories, and have brief moments of feeling good in an otherwise depressed state. Unfortunately, addictions tend to make the stress worse and even prevent healing by numbing our ability to be mindful of and experience our feelings and needs.
2. ***The addictiveness of a substance*** - Some substances are more chemically addicting for the brain than others. This typically involves the release of feel-good chemicals like dopamine or allowing the mind to dissociate from something stressful. Over time, a tolerance is built and greater quantities of the substance are needed to experience the same effect. The negative side effects are usually delayed, making it harder to directly associate the substance with something bad. This is further complicated by the brain easily letting go of negative experiences and only remembering the chemical high it had.
3. ***The culture supporting the addiction*** - Many addictive substances and behaviors are celebrated in societies worldwide. For instance, alcohol is reinforced with having it associated as cool, fun, a party essential, delicious, healthy, and an adult thing to do. However, most of these points are not true. Instead, they are simply things we have convinced ourselves of due to the peer pressure, media marketing, and normality that surrounds alcohol and alcoholism.
4. ***Inaccurate beliefs about a substance*** - People often assert that an addictive substance makes them feel good, is healthy, helps them relax, is the only way they can enjoy themselves, gives them courage, tastes good, is not addictive for them, or is how they maintain friendships. Again, these are subjective points that tend to ignore the truth. For instance, it actually makes them depressed, their friendships are shallow, it makes them forget the evening's good times and embarrassing things they do while intoxicated, or they use it to avoid themselves.

12.2.2 Overcoming Addictions
There are many ways to overcome addictions. Just be warned that cutting

them out too quickly can be dangerous for people who, for instance, drink heavily every single day. People like this should seek medical assistance or at least cut back their usage slowly. Otherwise, treating an addiction typically goes something like this:

1. Establish the desire to quit.
2. De-stress your life through self-care, healthy friendships, finding a positive work environment, better eating, cutting out stressful people, and releasing trapped emotions. Understand that you are consuming addictive things because you are stressed and have other options that will likely help you much more. Another way of thinking about it is that you are replacing your addiction with one which is much healthier and provides a more stable form of joy in your life.
3. Establish a connection to something greater than yourself such as nature, community, an activist cause, the universe, or a higher power. Whereas depressed and stressed states cause you to hyperfocus on yourself, devotion to something greater acts as a constant reminder that you are not alone and your problems are manageable.
4. Learn about the negative impacts of addiction, especially chronic diseases, changes in sleep, time and money expenditures, destruction of meaningful social connections, and so on.
5. Practice mindfulness on how a substance tastes and makes you feel. Over time you will form a negative association with the substance. This may involve taking a final dose on the less enjoyable spectrum of your addiction like hard alcohol to simply see how foul the substance actually is. The more quickly and strongly a substance negatively impacts you, the easier it is to cast into a negative light. You can manipulate this by making an experience as unenjoyable as possible. This is something that Allen Carr suggests in his books on quitting addictions and has personally worked for me.[21]
6. Become aware of the inaccurate cultural norms you are being influenced by.
7. Find friends and communities that do not consume the addictive substance or push you to consume it. Generally, put the addictive substance slightly further away from yourself or out of sight.
8. When you get a craving, do something else. Go to a free Twelve Step meeting, pen pal online, clean your room, text several friends and make plans to hang out, breathe deeply and return to the present moment, exercise, attend an online meditation, identify the source of

your suffering with HALT (Hungry, Angry, Lonely, Tired) and address it appropriately, go somewhere else like to a cafe or walk around the neighborhood, look through your photos, journal, or share something humorous with a friend.
9. Understand how dopamine works in the body as explored in Section 13.4.
10. Establish specific goals and focus on these incremental victories rather than immediately aiming for complete abstinence. As discussed later in this chapter, it is possible to have success while using a substance. This is a practice and learning process, and you may need to try several different methods or de-stress your life before being able to alter your relationship to an addiction.
11. Rejoice in all the positive benefits of not consuming the substance, or, of consuming it in a more regulated way that does not interrupt your goals.
12. Understand that any feelings of withdrawal will pass with time, especially as you keep busy with healthier coping strategies and a supportive community.

Willpower alone typically is not enough to quit an addiction, because your amount of willpower fluctuates greatly hour to hour and day to day, but you can use it to help you along some of these steps. Generally, you are trying to create a life you don't want to escape from. Done successfully, you either succeed in the goals you established for yourself or no longer are consuming the addictive substance.

12.2.3 Support Groups And Professional Help For Addictions
There are a lot of programs that can help support your addiction recovery. EMDR and psychedelic-assisted therapies are quite effective, as well as certain medications a doctor can suggest. As discussed in Section 4.7, different people will benefit from Twelve Step programs or therapy. People who specifically want help quitting alcohol without AA can seek support through *The Luckiest Club*, the Buddhist program *Refuge Recovery*, or books like *The Easy Way to Control Alcohol* by Allen Carr and *Quit Like A Woman* by Holly Whitaker. Holly Whitaker's book builds on Allen Carr's work and provides some further insights into addiction, especially discussing marginalized communities and the many problems of AA. However, Allen Carr's book is a much more practical guide for quitting. For more options, check out the *American Addiction Centers* website or search online for *alternatives to Twelve Step Pro-*

grams.

12.2.4 Harm Reduction

For substance addictions, a support group or therapist that incorporates a *harm reduction* approach may be more suitable for people seeking relief. A harm reduction model meets a person where they're at in their drug usage and establishes healthy goals that do not necessarily equate to abstinence. For instance, a person might reflect on how a certain amount of substance usage is interrupting their ability to a healthy outcome like working or being successful in school. They then reduce their consumption to an amount that allows them to better meet their goals and aspirations. Adapted from the <https://harmreduction.org> *Principles of Harm Reduction*, harm reduction incorporates ideas such as:

- Drug use should not be condemned, but the potential for harm should be reduced
- Drug use is complicated and there are ways of teaching people safer methods of using drugs
- A person or community may still be healthy or successful even if they use drugs
- A person using drugs should not be judged or coerced
- People seeking help should have a voice in creating the program serving them
- Users of drugs should be empowered in their ability to heal and create positive outcomes, especially with the support of others who have had similar struggles
- Poverty, class, race, isolation, trauma, and gender can all impact a person's ability to deal with addiction
- Drugs can have a harmful or dangerous impact on a person's life

In this way it, is possible to heal your relationship to certain addictive substances rather than totally cutting them out. You can manage your consumption and step back if it becomes unhealthy. When confronted by something I have had an addictive streak to, I ask myself things like: *Is this something that my inner child wants to joyfully play with or is this my wounded self trying to hide? Is this going to make me feel better or worse tomorrow? Does this benefit my future or the people that I love? How can I make this into a reward for my successes rather than a constant habit?*

Gaining control over addictions may still require a period of abstinence for some people. This is because consuming just a little bit reactivates old habitual pathways. In the case of alcohol, it inhibits your reasoning and dehydrates you as well, increasing the chance of not just having one drink, but many.[194] For me, complete abstinence is often a lot easier to handle so that I don't become tempted to create looser and looser rules for myself. However, a harm reduction approach can go a long way toward establishing a life in which you prioritize other goals first before partaking in your chosen treats. I have also picked up a few tactics while dealing with my own addictions. I primarily struggled with the consumption of food and media, but my journey of controlling these addictions is applicable to other substances as well.

12.2.5 Food Addictions

Food is a basic human need, so broad abstinence is not an option. It is also the first comforting substance we experience, creating a strong positive correlation. *Food deserts* make whole foods unavailable to certain populations, and nutrition may be ignored for affordability. While some people become obsessed with "health" foods, there is no shame in eating the things you like. You are allowed to define what healthy means for yourself. That said, certain dietary choices are detrimental to one's mental and physical health, the environment, and the healthcare system, so ideally people find a balanced diet. Many of us also experience food addictions that do not serve our well-being.

Ever since my teenage years certain foods have caused me to break out in acne or cysts. I hated my appearance and tried everything. Without health insurance or financial resources, speaking to a doctor or getting an allergen test wasn't an option, so I just stopped eating most foods. I became vegetarian, then vegan, and for a time primarily subsisted on rice. While this helped my face, it eventually caused me to become malnourished and likely pushed me deeper into my depressive states. Fortunately, I started to understand nutrition and decided to find a more balanced, omnivorous diet. Sort of.

In college, while volunteering for food organizations and living in community settings, I became surrounded by an unlimited supply of free food, especially bread and sweets. As addicts do, I rationalized overeating in ways like "I'd like to gain some weight" or "If I don't eat this, it's going to go to waste!" The food didn't even taste good, and I'd have too much energy or feel too sick to sleep well. Potlucks were especially hard. After a few alcoholic beverages, I would just hover around the food taking small bites of everything over and over again. One day I ate two loaves of bread. I felt awful, and once again reminded myself that it would have done me much better to donate or compost that food.

My life felt like it was falling apart in more ways than one, and I decided to move back to my hometown to clear my head. I knew my food consumption was causing me to suffer, and I decided to try being more proactive about it. I sat down and wrote over and over again how awful bread and sugar made me feel, how it made me break out, how I didn't want to feel or look that way, and how it was ruining my teeth. After filling a page with statements like these I started telling people I was allergic to gluten and concentrated sweeteners, which was not so far from the truth and helped ease the naysayers. Even alternative-minded folks though would question it with joking statements like, "But you're so skinny, why would you eat less?" They had no idea how much food I was consuming or how sick I had been making myself feel for the past few years - I just had a high metabolism, one that didn't let me gain weight.

In the end, this strategy worked. I did not touch or crave bread and sweets for years, and now have a healthy relationship with occasionally eating them. I moved the negativity I experienced by consuming them to the front of my attention. Instead of allowing my habitual responses to take over, I remembered the full shittiness I went through when eating bread and sugar. In some ways, I am lucky that my negative reactions happen so quickly. Things like weight gain or heart disease are slow to appear and might not have raised the "this is a big problem" alarm bell. I still do sometimes overeat, but it tends to be with healthier things and specifically when I'm going through a stressful time. I know that if I de-stress, drink a lot of water, and get back on my normal eating regimen, I'll feel better.

There are a few other practices I've employed that help too. I stay away from the sight of food, the kitchen, and food smells unless I am about to eat. I also find it helpful to stay away from those things while eating and for a period afterward. I eat most of my food earlier in the day and only light carbs at night. I also keep my eating schedule pretty consistent and know what I am going to eat ahead of time. I try not to take the whole bag of food like tortilla chips, but instead, portion out a little bit and eat that, putting the rest away. I wait until I'm hungry before I eat, and try to make sure I am not dehydrated. It's been really helpful that most foods people offer me I am slightly allergic to as well, so I have excuses prepared that people won't question or tease me about. I also ask myself what type of hunger I am experiencing. Is it dehydration, habitual hunger, stress hunger, or real hunger?

12.2.6 Media Addictions And Digital Detoxing
Too much media can distort your entire sense of reality, including your

notion of success, interest in your friends, what body types you're attracted to, how you respond to conflict, and general excitement about life. What is the media you consume training you to believe? I grew up consuming a lot of media, especially video games. It was a pastime that I didn't question. I was an ace student and I didn't want to be around my parents, so I spent those extra hours slaying demons and saving the world. In college, however, I felt called to bigger things. I noticed I was spending all of my free time in fictional worlds instead of creating art or making meaningful connections.

One day I decided I wasn't going to consume any media for five months. No music, no movies, no fictional books, and no video games. However, I had one exception. If I was with other people I would participate in their media consumption, but that was rare as at the time I lived in the country. I also still allowed myself to read informational works and news. My *digital detox* was a good experience. I felt more connected to the world around me and I created a lot of art. I also could appreciate the media I was consuming quite a lot more afterward, recognizing that it was only in the past few hundred years that humans have been able to consume art alone at all hours of the day. For the most part, I could now regulate my video game playing to a healthy level. Usually.

I would still use video games if I had a panic attack or was generally stressed out, allowing my mind to be fully consumed by the interactive media. This sometimes led back into addictive playing patterns, but I also developed some strategies to break away again. For instance, if I was going to play through a whole video game, I wanted there to be an engaging storyline or to feel like it was working my brain. I wanted it to be art rather than purely an addiction. If I felt like I was wasting away, I'd play hours and hours in, and then delete my save file. For whatever reason, this seemed easier to do late at night. I get bored of doing the same things over again, so I typically didn't start a new game.

One time I uninstalled the game, reinstalled it, uninstalled it and destroyed the install disc, then downloaded the game online and reinstalled it. What finally allowed me to break this cycle was starting to play a new game. While I may have gotten hooked on it, I only played an hour in and it didn't entice me in the same way yet. Now with two choices, whenever I thought about playing my previous game, I had the decision to play another. This gave me enough of a pause to stop playing games altogether.

I've also utilized programs that allow the blocking of websites and apps. For websites I had login information for, I changed my password to something random, or deleted my account. While I could totally abstain from playing video games, I still enjoy them as an interactive art medium and a form of play that my inner child enjoys. Knowing this, I made it a reward I could engage with on weekends or with friends. This helped prevent it from getting in the way of my weekday work while making it into something exciting to look forward to. Simultaneously I know that there are things in the world that make me much happier and bring me more meaning. Sometimes I even recognize that the video games I play are not a hobby I can talk about with most others and so push myself to read a popular book or watch a show instead.

12.2.7 Start Now
As you can see, I used several techniques to break free from my addictions. I pushed how they were negatively impacting my life to the front of my awareness. I set specific boundaries that still allowed me to consume the addictive substance but within reason. I reminded myself of what was actually important to me in life. If you feel ready to do so, I invite you to take the first step in interrupting your addictions. What is that first step for you?

12.3 The Big No List
In her book, *Quit Like A Woman,* Holly Whitaker suggests listing out the various things that you have control over, but destroy your mood or damage your healing process. As you do your healing work, you will begin identifying the people, words, activities, and other things that consistently trigger you. Some triggers you can healthfully regulate and stop as they become a problem, but others send you down into a horrible spiral of flashbacks or addictive behaviors. Making these into a list and acknowledging what you are giving a big no to will greatly help in your healing. These might include certain addictive substances, exes, types of games, genres of stories, violence in movies, and so on. While these might eventually find their way into the healthy regulating category, adhering to your boundaries even under social pressure will help you feel so much better.

My big no list includes alcohol if I'm feeling stressed at all, scary or violent movies, living with housemates I can't be friends with, living with loud people, buying sweets for myself, eating large meals at night, media without a meaningful story, several ex-girlfriends, and spending all day alone. What's your big no list? Take some time to write it out.

***
Chapter Reflections

1. What are some habits you would like to form and deform?
2. What is a small step you can take toward changing your habits?
3. What are your addictions and in what ways are they holding you back from living your ideal life?
4. What are your addictions helping you avoid?
5. What are the stories you tell yourself that reinforce your use of an addictive substance?
6. What are some ways that you can start decreasing your usage of an addiction?
7. What is your *big no list*?

Chapter 13

Reforming Mental States

13.1 Healthy And Regulated Nervous System, 13.2 Ego, Awe, And Developing Or Diminishing The Self, 13.3 Control, 13.4 Confidence Through Intelligence, Hormones, And Dopamine, 13.5 Guilt, Shame, And Resentment, 13.6 Blame And Identifying How You Reinforce Your Suffering, 13.7 Developing Compassion And Empathy, 13.8 Self-Compassion, 13.9 Self-Love, 13.10 Positive Self-Talk And Affirmations, 13.11 Positive Energy And Creating Defining Moments, 13.12 Happiness, 13.13 Forgiving Yourself And Others

In Chapter 6 you learned several techniques for overcoming self-limiting beliefs. In this chapter, we explore this in more detail by covering things like letting go of control, developing self-love, and forgiving yourself and others.

13.1 Healthy And Regulated Nervous System

Let's first learn what a healthy and regulated nervous system looks like. As explored in Chapter 3, people with these systems can:

- Use a *flock response* to first read the emotions and cues of others in a potentially dangerous situation before responding with fight, flight, freeze, or fawning behaviors[132P]
- Feel empathy or compassion for others' hardships
- Forgive others (within reason) or move on from difficulty without too much rumination
- Cut out toxic or non-mutual relationships
- Communicate about feelings, needs, stress, and conflict without resorting to physical or verbal violence
- React to and protect oneself from physical or verbal violence
- Regulate one's intake of food, drugs, media, and adrenaline-boosting activities
- Identify and avoid relationships with red flags

- Express emotions such as crying, laughter, frustration, etc.
- Handle quick shifts in energy like a loud sound or plans changing

Further traits include:

- Frequent feelings of happiness or contentment
- Close, mutually supportive, and long-lasting friendships and romantic relationships
- Experiencing feelings of love for yourself and others
- Playfulness (while alone, with pets, and around others)
- Trusting the integrity of your relationships
- Believing that people are trying their best and generally are not intentionally trying to harm you

Please note that stress, pain, and suffering are also healthy parts of life. This list is not meant to stigmatize your immediate difficulties or judge your self-worth, but rather give you the ability to see patterns and areas in which you can grow. As an exercise you can score yourself for each trait from 1-10, 1 being an area you're unfamiliar with or need improvement, and 10 being an area you feel confident in. It's okay if every area is a 1, I was once there too. All traits are good to work on and almost everyone can improve each in some way. Perhaps you begin working on one that is more pertinent to the trapped emotions you are dealing with, or perhaps it is easiest to start with something unrelated to increase your resilience. You may not understand what several of the listed items mean or have inaccurate notions of them. However, as you do this work and you explore the intricacies of a healthy nervous system, the meanings will become clearer.

The types of dysregulation you have adopted are largely dependent upon what difficulty you experienced. Even though you may not remember your past, figuring out your behavior patterns can be discovered through mindful self-reflection and journaling. Compare your behaviors to friends, or to actors that you think portray these characteristics in movies. Consider how you feel in different situations, around people, alone, or when stressed out. Perhaps someone has commented about how you act out in certain ways, or there is a pattern in how people treat you that point to certain possibilities. There is also the option of asking a trusted ally directly.

13.2 Ego, Awe, And Developing Or Diminishing The Self

The ego is your sense of self. Think of it as your inner voice that helps protect you and holds together your identity. This ego is helpful in many ways but can become unhealthy when it loses touch with the external world. This is what marks depression, addiction, narcissism, anxiety, and many other conditions of hyperfocus on the internal self.[134] American culture promotes strong independence and bolsters the ego, but this is quite harmful, separating oneself from the bigger picture of community, nature, and spiritual connection. For some people, shrinking the ego can have numerous benefits and is one key to increasing happiness, making your problems smaller, changing self-limiting beliefs, and gaining more power over your trapped emotions. There are several ways to do this:

1. ***Devote yourself to something greater than yourself*** - This shouldn't be just another individual, but something like a community, an activist cause, volunteering, or a spiritual or religious pathway. If that feels overwhelming, you can start with a pet or some house plants. The goal of Buddhism and the indirect effect of many other spiritual traditions is to shrink the ego. Going on hikes and spending time in nature is another option.
2. ***Experience awe*** - Visit the ocean, old-growth forests, or other epic types of nature. The longer you spend in these spaces, the better - a day will relax you, and a week might change your life. See a band that makes you feel emotional. Spend time traveling to other countries or seeing beautiful displays of architecture. Learn about the wonders of the world through science or reading history. Look at photos taken by the *James Webb Space Telescope*. Reflect on the incredible feats of life and technology while talking to your inner child. Psychologist Dacher Keltner says that even just staring at the leaves of a tree can inspire awe.[248] He shares that awe can also be grown by going on regular *awe walks* in which you note all the amazing things you see.
3. ***Have a spiritual or mystical experience*** - While this may sound outlandish for people who do not believe in a god or feel distant from their spiritual faith, there are still methods. Twelve Step programs are modeled to help people reach a spiritual breakthrough. Meditation and nature are great. Some art can also help us reconnect to the spiritual.
4. ***Mindfulness and meditation practices*** - Fully experiencing the present moment without thoughts of the past or future doesn't allow any room for the ego to take control. Mindfulness deactivates the part of the brain that the ego resides in.

5. ***Psychedelics*** - When done properly psychedelics help a person experience several of the above items. Unfortunately as previously covered, psychedelics are still illegal in most parts of the world and can be dangerous to use. See Chapter 11.

Alternatively, some people actually might need to increase their ego and sense of self. This is especially true for oppressed people or people who have difficulty speaking up for themselves.

1. ***Establish your purpose*** - Find a way to believe that you were created for a reason, that you have a purpose in the world. What makes you angry? What fills you with joy? What can you offer your friends, nature, society, or social justice causes?
2. ***Build your identity*** - Develop your personality and find some hobbies to enjoy and friends to enjoy them with.
3. ***Go inward*** - Speak to the inner parts of yourself as covered in Chapter 10, or connect to your dream world as covered in Section 7.5. You can also journal or develop a deep internal bond to become your own best friend.
4. ***Stop comparing yourself to others*** – You are a unique individual with unique abilities, interests, and needs. As explored in Sections 3.6 and 13.4, you cannot necessarily use the same tactics to reach success as someone else. Instead of angrily obsessing over wishing you were different, ask yourself "What unique gifts can I offer the world?"
5. ***Speak up*** - Establish healthy boundaries, flex your ability to say no, and take time to do the things you want to. Check in with what you need and listen to your body when feeling overwhelmed or tired. See *Healthy Angering* in Section 5.8 and guidelines for nonviolent communication in Chapter 8. Find opportunities to practice by checking in with yourself before giving an answer. Use mindfulness to observe what your "no" feels like and understand when that sensation is arising. Acknowledge when you are people-pleasing. Identify when you have denied yourself saying yes or no and ask yourself why.
6. ***Consume empowering media*** - Find stories that feature your gender, race, or culture in a heroic, empowering, or successful way. Seeing yourself in the characters can impart some of their self-confidence onto you. For instance, check out the *Women of Impact* podcast. These people do not need to be perfect but can help you reflect on how the hard work of healing pays off.

7. **Limit who you give power to** - Some people will believe anything anyone says and allow it to deeply hurt them. Instead of listening to internet trolls, random strangers, or abusive voices, choose a core circle of people you love or regard highly and only listen to their opinions about you and your work.
8. **Stop trying to read minds** - Unless people directly tell you otherwise, start believing that things are okay. So much suffering is caused by reading into a person's tone of voice, facial expressions, and actions. This is especially common in sensitive individuals. Clarify by asking what these cues mean instead of assuming the worst and feeling hurt. More often than not, a person is just having a bad day or has a resting evil face like me.
9. **Psychedelics** - These can also help bolster a deflated ego. Again, they're illegal and can be dangerous if used improperly. See Chapter 11.
10. **Affirmations** - See the *Positive Self-Talk* section later in this chapter.
11. **Small Victories** - Set small goals and projects you can succeed at as explored in Section 4.2.

13.3 Control

Having a big ego and needing to be in control are often related, but they are different. A common attribute of people with trapped emotions is the need to control their environment, or on the opposite end, the inability to speak up about their needs. For controlling people, unless the sounds, people, communication, and activities are just a certain way, unless you get exactly what you want, then the situation becomes unsafe or a complete catastrophe. This all-or-nothing thinking is very hard on relationships as people are often expected to meet unreasonable standards, read your mind, or not get their own needs met. Your need for control is an attempt at protecting yourself from past times you were hurt, but controlling behaviors prevent many activities from being fun or emotionally connecting. In other words, control limits your ability to make friends, love, and enjoy life. This type of hypervigilance not only drives people away, it also prevents you from appreciating the myriad of cultures and personalities in the world.

On the other hand, people who lack the assertiveness to demand their needs be met often live in the shadows of controlling and abusive people. These are the fawn-type personalities or overly empathetic people that put others before themselves. Perhaps this is done to maintain personal safety when belonging to an oppressed community, but often it is something ingrained from culture, especially in women.

Most people will be more dominant in either controlling behaviors or lacking assertiveness, but both can be present depending on the situation. Perhaps you always clean up after your partner because they never do so themselves (lack of control), but you also become easily annoyed with traffic (controlling). Alternatively, you might always do things alone and be staunchly independent (controlling), but also struggle to ask your friend to slow down while driving dangerously (lack of control). Both are important to correct.

Look for opportunities to let go of control, or look for opportunities to assert your needs. This does not mean that control dynamics are always involved. Independence can certainly be very empowering, or you may have different standards for things like cleanliness. Having control over your environment and having reliable people who meet certain standards can also be important in healing by creating a stable and safe space. Just be aware that the dynamic of control can be unhealthy and negatively affect your interpersonal relationships. In general, but with some exceptions, keep in mind:

- You cannot control your immediate thoughts, but you can control which thoughts you believe, how you react to them, and which ones you decide to focus on instead
- You cannot control your feelings, but you can control how you interpret, express, and release your feelings
- You cannot control the past, but you can control the work you do to heal unresolved stresses and trapped emotions
- You cannot control the future, but you can control how you prepare for the future in the present moment
- You cannot control what others do, but you can control how you communicate your needs, boundaries, and expectations
- You cannot control the feelings, boundaries, and needs of others, but you can control how you respond to the feelings, boundaries, and needs of others
- You cannot control if others forgive you, but you can control who you forgive and if you apologize for your actions
- You cannot control the body you were born with, but you can control what you believe about your body and how you decorate it
- You cannot control how unhealthy certain people and activities are, but you can control your hobbies, interests, and who you spend your time with

Look for opportunities to let go of control:

- Allow for spontaneous adventures and play
- Be okay with imperfection and speaking with people who slightly annoy you, one moment doesn't have to ruin your day
- Consider if you can or will do something about a situation - if not, move on
- Collaborate with someone or ask for help
- Identify what is not your responsibility or what you cannot actually control
- Still go to a party even if there's someone there who makes you a little uncomfortable
- Acknowledge how you can only control yourself and that the diversity of ways of being in the world is beautiful
- Listen or breathe deeply instead of speaking up immediately
- Notice all-or-nothing thinking and try to accept that a middle ground exists
- Practice consent and be happy that your love interests are advocating for their needs, even if that means receiving a "no"
- Get curious and empathetic, why is this important to them?
- Slow down, breathe deeply, or use some coping mechanisms to calm yourself
- Try a new hobby or restaurant instead of going to the same one all the time
- Ask what another person wants
- Know that it is okay to make mistakes, no one is perfect
- Stop expecting things from others, especially constant regularity - take each experience as a unique gift
- Remember that it is impossible to rationalize your future emotions, you have no idea how you'll feel on that vacation or playing that game
- Accept that the world around you just is - there is no need to judge that sound, that person, that color, the traffic, or anything, because you cannot control them, they simply are being
- Accept that other people are not the same as you and never will be
- Accept that you are human and have basic needs to feel mentally well
- Accept the body you were born into

Find opportunities to assert your needs:

- Get clear on your needs and wants and make space for them in your life
- If it is safe to do so tell the blunt truth and be the first person to speak up about an issue
- Create and enforce healthy boundaries in your relationships
- Use nonviolent communication to advocate for your needs (see Section 5.8 and Chapter 8)
- Practice and teach people consent
- Stop drinking alcohol, which inherently makes you give up your power and ability to assert your needs
- Stop helping everyone at the expense of your individuality
- Practice owning your actions and stop apologizing for everything
- Practice having boundaries with the time, energy, and emotional labor you are willing to give others
- Practice saying "no" and putting yourself first
- Spend some time alone and practicing self-care
- Get away from people who don't respect your boundaries
- Believe that you matter

Balance is key, and healthy relationships will allow all parties some control. Abusive behaviors should always be countered with an attempt to control them though - if it is safe you can create a boundary, and if it is unsafe you can silently cut a person out. In general, the people surrounding you should care about your feelings. Open up about how something is making you feel. For instance, "I'm having a lot of stress coming up about this vacation and leaving work behind, but I know it'll be good for the family," or "I'm scared that you won't like me anymore if I ask for what I want." If your trusted allies cannot support you through these feelings, they probably aren't that healthy for you or need to be spoken with about empathy and good communication. That said, asserting your needs and feelings too much can be destructive by limiting the amount of control you allow others. Keep the balance in mind, but know that you matter.

13.4 Confidence Through Intelligence, Hormones, And Dopamine

It does not matter how introverted or old you are, what your IQ or gender is, or how well you did in school, you are capable of so much in this life. You can be a leader, an artist, a scientist, or just happy. Unfortunately, your gifts may not have been celebrated or cultivated in a way that allowed them to grow. Perhaps you had a teacher who did not teach in a way conducive to your learning style, your family told you to get a more traditional career, or you never had the opportunity to explore what you felt passionate about because of the lack of programs in your school. Simply being believed in and told you will succeed does a lot in terms of personal success. As a result, you may have to renegotiate some of the voices who previously talked down to you.

13.4.1 Intelligence
In the USA, logical and mathematical intelligence tends to be the most revered and focused on, but there are many types of intelligence that people excel in. According to Howard Gardener, these include:

- ***Logical-mathematical*** - excels in problem-solving and abstract ideas
- ***Linguistic*** - good with words, speaking, writing, and memorizing
- ***Naturalist*** - proficient in botany and has an enjoyment of being in nature
- ***Visual-spatial*** - design-focused and easily sees patterns
- ***Bodily-kinesthetic*** - intelligent with experiential, hands-on, and movement activities such as sports and dance
- ***Musical*** - attuned to sound, rhythm, and making music
- ***Interpersonal*** - socially skilled and engages easily with others
- ***Intrapersonal*** - emotionally skilled with empathy, self-reflection, and self-awareness

While not included in Gardner's list, *cultural intelligence* also dictates a person's ability to respectfully navigate the nuances of different cultures locally and abroad. We'll talk more about it in Section 15.4. The difference between people who excel in a particular intelligence in educational environments is at least fifty percent determined by inherited genes.[154] These various genes control several learning skills such as having the ability to focus or be empathetic. You can be proficient in any of these intelligences though, it may just be easier for some people, or require certain technologies, medications, or techniques to assist you.

While sheer willpower and training can help boost an intelligence to a certain extent, it may be that you have to learn something in a unique way to succeed. Unfortunately, education systems tend not to be so flexible. Reclaiming your dreams from youth can be quite empowering though. Consider taking classes, learning online, or teaching yourself based on how you like to personally learn. Remember that the most successful people fail a lot, so start reframing your attitude toward making mistakes as learning experiences on the pathway to victory. On the other hand, you may find great relief in knowing that some things come easier to you than others, and it is perfectly fine being content with what you feel naturally good at.

13.4.2 Estrogen, Testosterone, And Confidence
Understanding the chemical side of confidence can also help. Katty Kay explores the impact of estrogen and testosterone in her book, *The Confidence Code*. Depending on what hormones you have, you may be more or less confident than others. This is especially apparent when comparing the average male hormone levels, which are typically higher in testosterone and lower in estrogen, to the average female hormone levels, which often have relatively less testosterone and more estrogen.

In one study, even though female participants tended to perform just as well or better than the male participants in a number of areas, the female ones often underestimated their ability.[92] On the other hand, the male participants typically overestimated their ability. While this is likely in part due to social influences, some amount of it is because of how much estrogen or testosterone a person has in their body.[159] Testosterone boosts confidence, while estrogen increases risk avoidance.

Having lower testosterone and higher estrogen decreases confidence, but also helps a person plan, make more thoughtful decisions, and pay attention to details. Becoming aware of how lower confidence does not translate into lower ability may help you find the belief that you are potentially more capable and qualified than you think. Try applying for your dream job or ask that person you have a crush on out. On the other hand, people with relatively higher testosterone and less estrogen may want to practice forms of slowing down by journaling, talking with a trusted ally, or using mindfulness practices before acting on a decision.

There is of course a lot of variability in how much testosterone or estrogen any individual person has. As having too much or too little of a hormone may cause problems or greatly impact your mental health, you may want to get your hormones tested and talk to a doctor about adjusting them. For an overview of the science, risks, and medications for altering hormones, listen to episode 85 of the Huberman Lab Podcast, titled *Dr. Peter Attia: Exercise, Nutrition, Hormones for Vitality & Longevity*.

13.4.3 Dopamine And Motivation

Dopamine also impacts motivation and is explored in Episodes 39 and 80 of the Huberman Lab Podcast.[77,69] Everyone has a different baseline level of dopamine.[257] According to Dr. Andrew Huberman, dopamine is produced by any mental reward like task completion, sex, delicious foods, and several illicit drugs. The only problem is that instead of returning to a baseline, most dopamine peaks result in dopamine lows which may be felt as a disinterest in activities, depression, or an addictive obsession with getting the high again. Even something like texting people or listening to music while working out can create dopamine peaks in that activity that then make it boring unless you have that texting or music every time.

In one study, children who enjoyed drawing started being given a sticker for each drawing they completed, but then lost interest in drawing when the reward stopped being given. The goal then is to not rely on bursts of dopamine, but instead to moderate a sustainable level of dopamine and to increase your baseline levels of it. Check in with your doctor before ingesting anything, but there are a few ways you can regulate your dopamine levels:

- Creating a *growth mindset* as explored in Chapter 12.1 with forming habits - that is, focusing on the benefit and pleasure of the journey itself instead of the reward for completing it
- Having close social connections with friends, family, and lovers
- Sharing touch
- Giving and receiving gratitude
- Being in a community that respects and shares your beliefs, or just having your beliefs affirmed
- Keeping your dopamine peaks random instead of regular or forced with substances
- Getting fifteen minutes or more of sun exposure on as much of your body as possible within an hour of waking up, or at least getting outside within the first three hours of the day for your eyes to be exposed to natural light
- Cutting screen use and making sure your room is as dark as possible between the hours of 10 PM and 4 AM
- Doing *non-sleep deep rest* (NSDR) or *yoga nidra* for 10 to 30 minutes to restore dopamine levels - guided practices can be found online[75]
- Using intentional cold exposure as explored in Section 4.15 - this creates one of the longest-sustaining dopamine highs without a low
- Consuming one to two cups of a caffeinated beverage, especially

yerba mate, which helps increase the body's ability to absorb dopamine
- Ensuring you are getting adequate levels of vitamin B6
- Not spiking dopamine before or after an activity
- Not relying on external sources of dopamine to make an activity fun such as podcasts, music, your phone, pornography, or alcohol - stay present and find joy in the activity itself
- Not using melatonin to help you sleep
- Resetting your dopamine cravings by abstaining from an activity - for instance, turning off your phone, intermittent fasting, or removing sugar for a period of time can make your phone or food a lot more exciting when you return to them
- Recovering from dopamine lows will happen much faster if you do an activity that you do not want to do, something that requires effort and some discomfort like jumping in cold water, cleaning, or a task you have been putting off[256]

That's not to say that dopamine highs are bad, but your motivation for more mundane things will improve if you can cut back from relying on dopamine. On the other hand, pumping yourself up with music, an empowering speech, or a workout might be just the thing you need to accomplish your goals. Just be aware of how different spikes in dopamine are healthier than others, and that abstaining from your typical boosts can do a lot toward making experiences even more pleasurable in the future. If you're feeling burnt out or bored from an activity, or you simply do not want to start something, it may be because of how you're relying on dopamine too much. You can read *Dopamine Nation* by Dr. Anna Lembke to learn more.

13.4.4 General Methods For Increasing Confidence
If your confidence is low, consider boosting it with:

1. The techniques previously outlined in Section 13.4.
2. Journaling about your good qualities, or asking a friend to share them with you.
3. Practicing so much that you know a previous obstacle will be easy to overcome.
4. Dedicating to a higher purpose such as protecting something or spreading an idea.
5. Reading about, watching, or listening to the victories accomplished

by people you identify with. I have found a lot of inspiration listening to interviews with successful creatives on *The Chase Jarvis Live Show*.
6. Becoming aware of the influences from your family or culture which have dictated who you are. Consider who you really want to be. Redefine what success means outside of owning a home, having a child, going to college, or being partnered. Many people find themselves miserable in the pursuit of these things, and there can be considerable joy without them.
7. Remembering that it's never too late to start achieving your dreams. Even if you're 80 years old, there's still the option of falling in love, finding fulfillment, traveling the world, or becoming a professional artist. Success does not know age.

13.5 Guilt, Shame, And Resentment

Guilt is the painful feeling of having done something wrong to another. This can be healthy or unhealthy depending on your actual level of responsibility. Ideally, guilt acts as a healthy form of trapped emotions, an understanding to never make that mistake again because you don't want to cause harm. Healthy guilt might arise when running a stop sign and hitting another car, or making a joke that hurts someone's feelings. In the future, you will be more careful about stop signs and making harmful jokes. However, if you are sensitive or anxious, you may blow out of proportion how bad the thing was.

Examples of unhealthy guilt include taking responsibility for your parent's behaviors or monetary hardships and feeling self-hatred from a friend not responding to your last text message. These things were not your responsibility and there is nothing you can change in yourself to fix them. Sometimes it is important to identify the system that caused something to happen and connect with your healthy anger to agitate for change (see Section 5.8 and Chapters 15 and 16). For instance, you may blame yourself for a friend's suicide, but in actuality, that suicide was most likely caused by cultural norms and a failure of the mental health industry.

Shame and resentment also sit close to guilt. Shame is the inherent feeling that you are a bad or worthless person. It often arises in conjunction with guilt, but does not inspire change or acknowledge that you may have harmed others. It is a state of helpless resignation and may entirely ignore the healthy guilt that you should be feeling instead. It is therefore important to identify shame and unhealthy guilt. You must either turn them into healthy guilt or understand that you are creating a fabricated story that has no place in your healing. Emotional release techniques will assist in this transformation. You can learn more about guilt and shame through Brené Brown's books and talks.

Lastly, resentment is the angry belief that you were treated unfairly or were forced to do something that you did not want to. Typically you have a choice of whether you do something that you will resent. In her book, *Quit Like A Woman*, Holly Whitaker suggests always choosing feeling guilty over feeling resentful.[194A] This may involve knowing your limits and asking another person to take on some extra responsibility or work. While a person may feel somewhat hurt by a last-minute cancellation or other change of plans, do your best to explain your feelings and needs with nonviolent communication and reschedule.

13.6 Blame And Identifying How You Reinforce Your Suffering

While there have been many external factors to create your suffering, it is important to identify how you perpetuate it yourself. You might have a whole host of excuses for why you're lonely, need certain addictive substances, or cannot stay in a romantic relationship. Often people blame others for their suffering, but you need to acknowledge that blame hardly ever changes anything. It sucks and is not fair, but often only you can transform your life for the better.

Be proactive about your healing, and stop expecting the people around you to suddenly give you what you so desperately want. That may mean having zero tolerance for abusive behaviors in your core circle of friends, family, housemates, and co-workers. If your parents, friends, or lovers do not change their behaviors after being asked to, it is likely that they never will. When we remove those things which cause us suffering, healing will begin immediately and we will have immensely more energy to create change.

Understanding this greatly helped me in appreciating my family of origin for the ways they did show up. While my biological parents are responsible for much of my suffering, I try not to blame them because I know they were caught up in a larger system of suffering caused by society and their own unresolved trapped emotions and attachment wounds. While it would be nice if they could make up for the events that transpired, or transform their behaviors, this is unlikely to happen. That is all to say that they cannot fix me, only I can fix myself and break the cycle of suffering which began generations ago. I can uphold my boundaries, assert needs, suggest resources for them to read, and communicate feelings, but expecting change or blaming them only ends in me feeling worse.

13.7 Developing Compassion And Empathy

People with trapped emotions and attachment wounds may have an over or under developed feeling of compassion or empathy. Knowing how to access these states and when to switch them off is important for being a good friend, lover, employee, ally, and leader. Empathy is the ability to understand, accept, and feel what another person is feeling.[252,253] Compassion is a feeling of concern or sympathy for another that evokes a desire to help. Empathy often precedes compassion and is an automatic response. On the other hand, compassion is a deliberate choice.

According to Richard Schwartz, founder of *Internal Family Systems* therapy, compassion and empathy can be developed even if a child did not have these growing up.[151] By speaking with and healing the different parts of yourself, you can become acquainted with these innate and essential social skills. Having someone role-play as an ideal, loving, and empathetic version of one of your parents may also help. See Section 7.6 about roleplaying techniques and Section 17.6 on healing attachment wounds.

Having securely attached relationships as explored in Section 14.2 also increase compassion and empathy, although are not easy for everyone to acquire.[204] As a starting point, getting some potted plants, adopting a kitten, or entering into an animal therapy program will act as a safe way to establish trust and mutuality, educating on how to respond accordingly when these lifeforms become distressed.[970] While it might not be an immediate transformation, the love and affection granted by a cat or dog can melt away some of the protective layers a person had to develop when confronted by deep suffering. A therapist will also be beneficial in showcasing healthy attachment.

People do tend to have more empathy for those they identify with, so when interacting with someone, it is important to find common ground you can speak from.[204] This is often easiest for marginalized communities and people who have faced some difficulty in life, but everyone shares something in common such as enjoying certain foods and activities. Your awareness of what you share can be greatly improved by increasing your *cultural intelligence* and learning about history as explored in Section 15.4. Thinking that someone is not personally responsible for the pain they experience also helps.[204] Thus, connecting societal issues such as racism, capitalism, greed, poor medical services, bad parenting, religious abuse, and so on, to a person's struggles may help you see them in another light. Reading fiction regularly helps build empathy as well by exposing you to different cultures, ideas, and the humanity behind them.[244] The more you like a fiction book with characters different than you, the more empathetic it will help make you feel toward those characters. Psychologist Dacher Keltner also says that staring at the leaves of a tree or being in nature can increase empathy and decrease greed.[248]

Compassion and empathy can also be practiced until they become habitually natural because simply making the effort to care is enough. You might not like a person much but know that showing compassion is the right thing to do. This is especially important for people who have higher levels of testosterone as it decreases access to empathetic states.[205] It also may require doing work to diminish the power of the outer critic's judgmental thoughts as explored in Section 5.9.

If you notice someone is distressed, ask how they are or verbally reflect the emotional state they seem to be in. If they open up to you, you can say "That sounds really hard," or, "I'm here for you, let me know how I can support you." Active listening and checking in on people are also great. Unsolicited advice, teasing people, or ignoring a person's emotions will not help. Consider reading Marshall Rosenberg's book *Nonviolent Communication* or seek out other training for nonviolent communication as explored in Chapter 8 as a practical way to infuse empathy and compassion into your conversations. Brené Brown has a lot of great information on this topic as well if you want to dive deeper into it. Just keep in mind that providing explanations for a person's suffering is never empathetic or compassionate and typically comes off as rude. This includes jargon like "Mercury is in retrograde." Ask consent before giving advice or acting all-knowing. Empathy and compassion should be approached with curiosity.

This all said, empathy and compassion aren't always good things. People who are too empathetic might ignore their personal needs or struggle in leadership positions. Elizabeth Segal, author of *Social Empathy*, points out that empathy can hinder efficiency, innovation, and free thinking.[204] Overly empathetic people might also never turn their difficult feelings into compassionate action which addresses the root of the problem. This is why social and environmental news reports can be quite overwhelming with a constant barrage of society's problems without any way of taking action on all of them.

You need to be able to both enter into and exit states of empathy and compassion. As Jack Kornfield says, "If your compassion does not include yourself, then it is incomplete." Deeply empathetic and less empathetic individuals are both valuable in society, but it may be greatly beneficial to develop the ability to switch between empathy and more assertive, big-picture, or self-compassionate states. My general rule is to focus on the areas I know I am going to support and only put myself around sources of distress that I have the capacity in time and energy for. Check in with yourself before committing to fixing someone else's problems. Are you taken care of? Can you shrink the scope of what you're willing to do for a person so that your needs can still be met? Having a healthy self-care routine will greatly bolster your ability to show up for others and prevent burnout.

13.8 Self-Compassion

Having self-compassion is an extremely powerful tool in loosening the grip of shame and self-hatred that often arise when dealing with trapped emotions. Developing compassion for yourself is a practice, but these steps can also be used when you enter into a flashback or triggered space:

1. Know that your emotions are real and important. You have the right to feel and express them. If you're feeling tired, that's okay! If you're feeling sad, that's okay! These are part of life and are information for you to use to heal, de-stress, and grow. Acknowledge your feelings, and if you can, respond to them accordingly. For instance, take a nap or cry. Of course, if you're feeling angry, it is best to find the root of that experience in stress or grief. Self-compassion also means developing enough emotional mastery so that your releases do not harm yourself or others.
2. What difficulties did you go through in your past to make you feel this way? Those things may have been very difficult. Acknowledge how painful they were and understand anyone would struggle having experienced something like that. Know that this is not a sign of weakness, but rather a sign of strength that you survived such pain. This type of self-compassion is sometimes unlocked by first hearing others talking about how similar incidents impacted them. You can also create a *life history* as explored in Section 7.2.
3. What is going right in your life? Write out all the things that are supporting your well-being, even small things. This might include things like the tree being alive outside, your job, the air, or a text a friend sent you. Often we are hyperfocused on the negative when triggered but there is always gratitude just behind that darkness.

13.9 Self-Love

One of your greatest resources will be developing a sense of love for yourself. That is, accepting your imperfections, knowing you are worthy of happiness, learning to take care of your physical, mental, and spiritual bodies, and having compassion for the struggles you have weathered. For me, I sometimes hate myself, my body, my decisions, and how I speak. Some things make me feel completely inadequate and question my life. To get out of that spiral it has helped me to practice forms of self-love covered throughout this book such as:

- Showing love to my inner child as covered in Chapter 10
- Forgiving myself
- Using healthy angering, creating personal boundaries, and saying no
- Writing out a list of my accomplishments and what I'm good at
- Developing self-compassion for the hard times or when I make mistakes
- Practicing self-care and putting it first before other obligations when possible
- Creating a life I do not wish to escape from
- Focusing on the positive aspects of myself rather than what I cannot or do not want to be
- Accepting myself regardless of what society thinks a normal body, brain, or life is supposed to be
- Asking for my needs to be met
- Accepting myself for basic mental needs like introverting, taking a day for self-care, skipping a party, or sometimes being a little awkward

Like many of the principles throughout this book, self-love is a practice. Give time to it each day. Find ways to say *I love myself, I love my body, I love my mind, I love the life I have built for myself, I love the people I have surrounded myself with, I love how I decorate my room, I love the adventures I go on, I love my alone time, I love my imagination, I love my creativity, I love my time with friends, I love my willingness to create the life I deserve*. It is okay if some of these are hard, or if you do not believe them yet. Finding a place of neutral acceptance in which you do not feel stressed out by these various factors can be equally beneficial. It can also be quite powerful acknowledging the things you need to change for these statements to be true.

13.10 Positive Self-Talk And Affirmations

Quieting self-limiting beliefs and feelings of shame may also involve bolstering yourself with positive self-talk. This may involve highlighting your positive aspects, congratulating yourself on a job well done, expressing gratitude for the day's events, or using affirmations. The only requirement is that you have to believe the things that you tell yourself - you typically can't lie yourself into believing something. Therefore you may have to start small, and it may be a very quiet belief initially. However, maintained practice will increase your sense of self-love, appreciation for life, and ability to see the positive aspects of existence. Try taping affirmations up in your mirror to read anytime you use the bathroom, listen to them online, or include them as part of your journaling routine. Consider things like:

- I'm proud of myself for improving my previous test score
- I am grateful that my friend contacted me today, that makes me feel cared for and loved
- This food is amazing!
- I can continue growing as a person, *and* I am already enough
- I'm glad I know what I need right now and can listen to my body
- I'm not losing, I'm learning
- "My body is not an apology" - *Sonya Renee Taylor*
- I am breathing, therefore I am successful
- I am not my thoughts, my emotions, or my past, but I am this present experience
- "Anything worth doing is worth doing badly" - *G.K. Chesterton*
- I am allowed to make mistakes, I do not need to be perfect
- I cannot change my past, but I can work in the present toward a fulfilling future
- I have the opportunity to succeed if I try
- Today may be hard, but that does not dictate the rest of my life
- I am doing a good job considering all the difficult things I have experienced
- I know that this person is having a hard day and that their frustrations are not about me
- I know that I am safe
- Stress is not the same as danger
- I know that I have taken every reasonable precaution to keep my inner child safe
- Failure is not indicative of my future ability; I can learn, improve, and try again
- The world is abundant and there is always more love, more connection, and more goodness available

Affirmations can be especially powerful when combined with a meditation or self-hypnosis practice as covered in Chapter 5 and Section 7.7. Try deep breathing for a minute or two before launching into positive self-talk. By calming the mind, you allow new ideas to flow into it more easily. As you continue repeating an affirmation over time, you can also try getting more and more specific with the flavors, actions, and textures in that affirmation. Make it become a visual process that you can experience.

Some therapists like Pete Walker suggest creating a personal "Human Bill of Rights" that you use to list things that you believe you deserve just for being alive. These include things such as respect, the ability to leave abusive people, and having your basic needs met. You can see Pete Walker's book *Complex PTSD* or website <www.pete-walker.com> for a more complete list. Try reading your list daily as a morning or evening ritual. For specific struggles, you can also journal about what is true or what you know to be positive. Each time you find yourself caught ruminating on negative thoughts, go to this journal entry. The contents on *Self-Limiting Beliefs And Stories* in Section 6.3 may be helpful in this process as well.

I have also found it joyful to practice a positive external focus. As I walk or bicycle, I give a silent compliment to each object I pass - "Wow your color is amazing," or "That tree is really beautiful." This helps me keep away from negative thoughts and stay mindfully aware of the present moment. Try spending a day documenting beauty and seeking out magic. While developing positivity is a great asset, be careful about toxic positivity. You do not want to ignore your feelings of grief or anger that arise. You also must avoid telling others to just smile or get over it - this is unhelpful and insensitive.

13.11 Positive Energy And Creating Defining Moments

It is impossible to describe to you how immensely beautiful life can be, but what I can say is that whatever you have experienced, and whatever you are feeling right now, there are ever-deepening states of contentment, joy, and love that anyone can reach under the proper conditions. Some of these are sustainable states of contentment and joy that are the primary focus of this book, while others are defining moments that instill positive energy into your psyche.

Positive energy is often harder to obtain for people who have trapped emotions pushing them down because it becomes easy to disregard the positive through anxiety or a stressful point of focus. Sometimes it is important to de-stress enough to experience the goodness a moment offers. That said, regularly experiencing positive moments in our lives can provide a sustained source of vibrancy, inspiration, and healing. Just one defining moment is enough to make an entire experience, day, or trip worthwhile. Even if difficult things also happen, in the long-term, it is the defining moments that stand out years into the future. You may think that these moments are entirely random, but as Chip and Dan Heath point out in their book *The Power Of Moments*, defining moments can be intentionally created.[58]

Defining moments are often fun, novel, or surprising. They typically require vulnerability such as interacting with others, traveling, or doing something out of the ordinary. They may involve:

- Specific people who create a special moment for you
- A sensory surprise that you are expecting but cannot appreciate until actually sensed such as food, beautiful nature, or artwork
- Exploring a curiosity you have had or doing something you have always wanted to do
- Completing something arduous such as a college degree, sports competition, or creative project
- Sensory-enhancing substances such as MDMA or LSD - see Chapter 11 on general legality and risks
- Having the opposite experience of your norm such as deep relaxation, time with a distant friend, or not working
- Being understood or having kind words spoken to you by a loved one
- Doing something that previously created a defining moment but you haven't done in a long time
- De-stressing enough to appreciate a moment with techniques outlined in Chapters 4 and 5 - CBD and other calming agents may help, but alcohol is generally not suggested as it dulls the senses, increases depression, and generally dilutes the chance of a moment being memorable
- Making a normal experience more epic such as watching a movie the day it comes out on the big screen or reading a book together in a group
- Reaching out to an artist you appreciate and telling them a story about how you or your friends interacted with their work
- Frequently celebrating the way you want to and having zero tolerance for stressful baggage in your celebrations - for instance, feel empowered to ask people to leave who weren't invited or who are annoying

Defining moments like these automatically instill positive energy into your body. You can deepen this experience by recording the memories through photos, journaling, or even a box that you collect notes and pictures of your defining moments in. This said, attachment to what was, or wishing life was always like that can be unhealthy. Defining moments might also turn sour when you break up with a lover or discover the friends you were spending time with are toxic. You will still have benefited from these times in the moment, but while mourning the loss, you should create new defining moments. This will help initiate yourself into a new version of you by finding joy in the changes you have created. Simultaneously, holding onto these moments you shared with someone can help quite a lot when trying to find the desire to forgive them. If you only hold onto the bad times, it is unlikely you'll be able to move past a conflict.

13.12 Happiness

Pursuing happiness tends not to work well for most people as it typically relies on seeking out quick shots of pleasure from the external world. This builds a tolerance to the hits of dopamine that people sometimes wrongly associate with happiness and often leads to addictive behaviors. As they constantly seek out more pleasure, they also avoid vulnerability or dealing with their issues. Generally, avoiding your negative emotions or expecting certain outcomes decreases happiness.[236] While a certain amount of happiness is caused by genetic factors, sustainable happiness comes from practicing certain behaviors and creating a stable foundation of happiness in your life.[94]

According to psychologist Ed Diener, author of the book *Happiness*, happy feelings can be improved with:

1. Having better social bonds, especially with reciprocal and supportive connections.[23] A decades-long Harvard study found that relationship satisfaction was the number one indicator of well-being and happiness.[122] People who are part of a religious or spiritual community tend to be happier primarily because of this.[109] In a similar way, people who give to others tend to derive a longer-lasting burst of happiness than if they give to themselves.[34] That is, so long as they already have their basic needs met. This might involve donating money or time to a person or cause. The effect increases the more a person cares about whatever they are giving to.[8]
2. Having more money, but only if earning that money does not replace enjoying life.[23]
3. Living in a happier country, with the U.S. ranking pretty high, but behind several European countries. Countries with war or poverty tend to rank lower. Having happy friends close by, as well as consum-

ing happier media also seem to improve happiness according to Dr. Andrew Weil.[39] This is because we mirror the people around us we like.[64]

4. Focusing more on what is positive and beautiful about a thing than what is negative, including the past, present, and future. As explored earlier, this can be increased through practice such as mindfulness, keeping a gratitude journal, building curiosity, or reframing the stories you tell yourself.[113] Dan Gilbert, author of *Stumbling on Happiness*, shows that having fewer choices and not being able to take back your decisions actually makes you happier with what you choose.[47] I speculate that this helps bolster the happiness in religious and spiritual minds too by having a specific system to abide by. Gilbert also shares that after 90 days to a year, a person who had a good experience and a person who has a bad experience will usually be equally happy. This is in part because most difficulties dissipate naturally within 90 days, but also because people are capable of reframing a bad experience into something that was beneficial and positive.[125,47]

To this list, I would also add removing yourself from perpetually stressful situations, dealing with your trapped emotions, and the seven most important self-care techniques presented in Section 4.9 with the MENDSSS acronym. Dr. Rangan Chatterjee further explores happiness in his book *Happy Mind, Happy Life*.[86] He shows that happiness is created not through success or having a perfect life, but by building three characteristics:

1. ***Alignment*** - Is the life that you're living aligned with your values and beliefs?
2. ***Contentment*** - Are you content with what you are doing with your life?
3. ***Control*** - Are you able to do the things that you want to do when you want?

13.13 Forgiving Yourself And Others

Holding onto hatred or revenge fantasies can be quite painful and prevent us from releasing trapped emotions. When we associate a person with a bad experience, we can choose to forgive or not forgive that person. Depending on what the other person did, you must decide whether or not forgiving them is the better option. Would it cause you relief or result in more suffering?

As Pete Walker says in his book, *The Tao of Fully Feeling*, it's not healthy to forgive someone before you have properly grieved out the difficult emotions you are feeling from their actions.[185] Furthermore, it is simply not healthy to forgive certain acts. It can be really empowering to decide that you will not forgive someone. Of course, you do not want to continue obsessing over how a person harmed you, but maybe you feel safely resolved after establishing a boundary and having that boundary respected. You may also oscillate between forgiveness and needing to release more painful emotions as different memories arise surrounding a person. That, or you may see warning signs that an incident is about to repeat itself and then act accordingly. Forgiveness does not mean you become defenseless to past harm.

You may or may not announce that you are formally forgiving a person, but forgiveness is always a personal choice. It may be impossible or unsafe to communicate with a person, but these people can still be forgiven if you want to. When forgiveness is not an option, you can simply let go and move on from the situation, but that may mean ending the connection or moving away. It also still requires emotional release and renegotiating the events that transpired. In these cases it can be good to practice empathy or compassion, understanding the life that led this person to do hurtful things.

In *The Tao Of Fully Feeling* Pete Walker describes creating a family history in which he grieves and angers at his parents, but then considers all the events that caused his parents to become abusive as well. This included his parents' parents and grandparents, the industrial revolution, Christianity, and an abusive and all-powerful God. While it is good to identify the roots of suffering in the world and understand that abuse is typically perpetuated by other abuse, releasing your emotions surrounding the closest sources of your pain is essential. You eventually might be able to forgive or partly forgive the transgressions of another, but don't brush them off as a simple victim of the world. Remember, even if a person dies, the pain they caused you will not go away – your trapped emotions need to be released. See Section 7.2 about creating a family history.

13.13.1 Forgiving Someone Else
If you want to forgive someone, you must do three things:

1. Desire to both forgive and continue creating new memories with the person in question, or at least focus on the positive aspects and memories.
2. Release any intense feelings you have about what a person did which are making you feel unsafe or insecure. For some situations, this

release is best handled alone, but for people who respect you, communicating directly to them may be helpful.
3. Stop thinking about what that person did or did not do. Consider all the good things about that person and get curious about how you are focusing on only the bad aspects of them. Use healthy angering to stop compulsive negative thoughts, or reframe and correct stories you may be telling yourself (see Chapters 5 and 6). That does not mean that you put yourself in a dangerous situation again. Instead, you stop thinking about it because you have learned from the situation and either feel sure it is not going to happen again or know how to handle it in the future. One way to stop thinking about the past is to create new positive memories with the person you are forgiving.

The easiest method of forgiving someone is to first communicate, preferably in person, whatever is frustrating you and what the other party could do to make it better. Ideally this is done using nonviolent communication as covered in Chapter 8. If they value the connection, typically loved ones will listen and heed your desires, re-establishing a sense of safety and respect in the relationship.

When communicating your frustration, avoid using judgments and instead keep with observable facts and feelings from your perspective. For instance: "When I learned my vase was broken I felt really upset. I know you were playing but I am having trouble trusting you around my possessions. Do you have any ideas for how we can prevent this in the future?" That will help a person feel much more open to communicating rather than saying something like, "You're a careless asshole." If a person does not heed your desires or continues an undesirable behavior, you may have to accept a part of this person that you dislike, let them go entirely, or change your personal behaviors.

Forgiveness can also be partial or based on certain criteria being met. For instance, with certain friends or parents, you may acknowledge only feeling safe for an hour at a time, or while around other people. If a person breaks a boundary that you establish with them, you may no longer forgive them. It is okay to see someone as dangerous or unhealthy. It is also okay to cut people out of your life or take space for undesignated amounts of time. This applies to anyone, regardless of their biological connection to you or what they have given you in the past. You do not owe abusive people anything.

13.13.2 Forgiving Yourself
While in many instances we need to forgive others, in some we need to forgive

ourselves to relieve the self-criticism that emotionally weighs on us. Follow these steps:

1. Desire to forgive yourself.
2. Understand why what you did in the specific instance caused yourself or others suffering. Be willing to avoid recreating that series of events again. It may help to look out for the habit cues or patterns that cause you to act in certain ways.
3. Offer apologies or reparations to those you hurt if appropriate. Forgiving yourself is a lot easier if you have done everything possible to repair the situation and have left your final words as positive, apologizing, and openly willing to fix things. See Chapter 8.
4. Release any intense emotions surrounding the incident, see Chapter 5.
5. Stop thinking about what you did or did not do. You may have to practice thought-stopping or thought replacement as explored in Section 5.9 and Chapter 6.
6. Continue with your life by participating in daily activities and spending time with people. It is most difficult to forgive yourself when you are isolated.

13.13.3 *Helpful Tips*
1. Try using the *loving-kindness meditation* explored in Section 4.6.
2. Take time away from your source of frustration and form new memories with other people. You may forget why you were angry at the person in question or at least cool down enough to want to give them another chance. If you were close enough, the good memories often overwhelm the bad ones.
3. Imagine the person you are in conflict with as a small child. Feel their pureness before being hurt and acting out that pain onto others.
4. Make a list comparing the pros and cons of forgiving a person versus holding onto the difficult feelings you have about them.
5. See a therapist and work through stressful experiences surrounding a difficult-to-forgive person.
6. Don't wait around for the other person to apologize. Sometimes finding, naming, and apologizing for your own role in a conflict can greatly help soften a difficult conversation.
7. Create a gratitude list by writing down everything that you have appreciated about a person – does one bad experience have to destroy

the connection you have? Read this many times over.
8. Forgive yourself and others as soon as possible. It may become more difficult to do so the longer you wait if you have reiterating negative thoughts and still have to see the person around.
9. Understand that behind all anger is stress and grief. Instead of focusing on the anger, find out why you are stressed or sad.
10. If you can, will yourself to dream or do visualization exercises about a person - working out emotions in your imagination can assist in the process of forgiveness.
11. Walk in their shoes and have empathy. Were they being intentionally hurtful? Did they have trauma from youth? What systems of oppression has that person experienced? What were their parents like? What brain wirings might be pushing them to be this way?
12. How many times do you forgive a person before you realize that they are not worth the pain? Is there a recurring pattern of events that you need to forgive others for? Why is that? Is there anything attached to your youth, previous relationships, or cultural heritage causing you to attract certain patterns or be hurt by them?
13. Just because something hurts you, you think that something is wrong, or something bothers you, doesn't mean that you're right. There are at times no good answers to proceed with, but it can still be beneficial to communicate your feelings, work on yourself, or practice forgiveness.
14. After forgiving someone, consider how they showed up in positive ways, how the incident made you stronger, or how it led you to something important in your life.

***

Chapter Reflections

1. How does your nervous system express regulation and dysregulation?
2. How has your big or small ego hurt others or yourself?
3. In what ways could you shrink or build your ego?
4. What helps you experience awe and connect to the bigger picture?
5. How are you currently trying to control a situation which you cannot control?
6. How can you let go of control of others and take more responsibility for your own life?

7. What events diminished your confidence in different types of activities?
8. What activities, job positions, or social connections are you holding yourself back from due to your confidence?
9. In what ways do you learn best?
10. What kinds of education or practice would help you become more confident?
11. Has the desire for spikes in dopamine made certain activities boring for you?
12. In what ways has your culture defined success for you?
13. In what ways could you redefine success to make yourself freer and happier?
14. What kinds of guilt, shame, and resentment currently exist in your life?
15. How can you improve the amount of compassion, empathy, and love that you experience toward others and yourself?
16. What kinds of words or phrases boost your mood?
17. What are some especially positive moments you have had in your life?
18. How can you create more profoundly positive moments in your life each month or year?
19. How can you incorporate more activities into your life that improve happiness?
20. How is not forgiving someone negatively impacting your mood?
21. Who do you want to forgive and what is holding you back?
22. What past events have you not yet forgiven yourself for and what is holding you back?
23. How do you perpetuate your own suffering?
24. Who do you blame for your suffering, what do you expect from them, and are those expectations going to fix anything?

Chapter 14

Healthy Relationships

14.1 Friendships, 14.2 Romantic Relationships And Secure Attachment, 14.3 Breaking Up With Someone, 14.4 Being Broken Up With, 14.5 Community And Individualism

In their book *What Happened To You*, Bruce Perry and Oprah Winfrey explore how a lot of healing from trauma can take place in the thousands of tiny social interactions we have with safe, consistent, and comforting friends, family, and other loved ones.[132M,132N] Perry explains that having access to a number of these connections creates better recovery outcomes than only having a therapist does.[132O] The emotional co-regulation that a trusted ally offers shortly after an incident greatly reduces the likelihood of it becoming a trapped emotion in the body.[245] As has been confirmed in many studies, Dr. Bessel Van Der Kolk states that having safe and reciprocal relationships is the most important factor for good mental health as well.[97H]

Relationships with calm or nourishing people or animals help regulate our nervous system when we begin to feel overwhelmed. They make us know the past is behind us and right now is okay. These relationships also greatly influence our personalities, interests, and behaviors, and so we may assist our healing by being surrounded with people living the type of life we desire.[17] Especially consider the five people you spend the most time with and their communities. How are these people influencing you, and do they represent who you want to become?

Humans are social creatures, but if you grew up with abusive parents or were indoctrinated by a culture that reinforces toxic relationships, you may either find yourself gravitating towards unhealthy connections or avoiding people altogether. Even if you're an introvert, having a network of allies will greatly help you enjoy life and gain access to important resources. This includes friendships and romantic partnerships, but also animals, therapists, support groups, co-workers, or dance partners. It can also just involve being among a group of people you feel safe around, have a little crush on, play games with, or treat you kindly. The closer and more secure you feel together though, the better. It is also generally more regulating to connect with people in-person rather than online or over the phone, so try to prioritize face-to-face contact. Social media, phone, and virtual spaces may initially feel safer, or help nourish a connection you only get to see periodically, but do your best to move towards in-person contact.

Since my childhood was so dysfunctional, I largely missed out on how to socialize, be playful, interact at parties, or date. For a lot of my life I've focused on more intellectual conversations and have found loud people difficult to be around unless with romantic partners or other really safe friends. This was likely made more complicated by being a sensitive extrovert. While I love being around people, I can become easily overwhelmed by certain personalities or the wrong group dynamic.

As much as I wanted friends and lovers, these factors contributed to my social life taking a long time to blossom. Over the years I even referred to myself as the most popular loner. Everyone knew me and seemed to generally like me, but no one would reach out to spend time together. The relationships I had were fleeting or felt distant. That has been changing in recent years as I have slowly learned what it takes to be a desirable friend and partner. There is power and healing in community, so I want to introduce some techniques for forming healthy platonic and romantic bonds. Generally, the goal is to remove people who make us feel unsafe or uncared for, and instead establish more nourishing and secure attachments.

I want to acknowledge that modern society does not make connection easy. I was raised on stories of best friends who are like a healthy and deeply reliable family, but it turns out that creating those connections is difficult for a lot of people. Individualism is rampant, neighborhood interactivity is low, people are constantly moving away for school or jobs, romantic love is prioritized over platonic love, people choose to ghost each other rather than communicate through differences, many social activities are expensive, and communal living options are limited. Discrimination, workaholism, social media, capitalism, globalization, and poverty all exacerbate these problems further. Whereas religion, spirituality, extended family, and relying on one another once maintained community life, many of us in industrialized societies have been expelled from these ways. However, there is a lot we can do to fight back and reclaim the stability that healthy relationships and community offer us.

Please note that depending on where you are in your healing journey, you may be addicted to instability in relationships and find healthy connections rather boring.[132U] This may be felt outright or a few months into a new relationship after you've experienced the chemical high of *new relationship energy* (NRE). The goal in this case is to identify abusive relationships as explored in Chapter 3, learn about your relationship behaviors, and find healthier activities, interests, and conversations that keep you invested in a relationship. The following sections cover many tools for establishing these traits and some of the psychology behind healthy connection.

Just remember that all relationships involve some amount of conflict and stress, and that these are not necessarily indicators of abuse or an unhealthy connection. Communication, creating boundaries, and asserting your needs are all part of connecting with others. If your ability to build healthy connections is especially damaged, consider rebuilding your socialization first with an animal companion, therapist, volunteer activity, sport, or choir group.[97CZ,97DZ] Even just visualizing holding a dog or cat that loves you can be beneficial.[243] I have also found that being in the woods can provide some relational energy, but this may require a specific mindset that acknowledges how these older plants support your well-being. Some people even benefit from playing cooperative online video games as a first step, but it is important that this activity eventually balances itself with or transitions into building socialization in-person rather than becoming an addiction.

Keep in mind that, while relationships are an essential aspect of regulating your nervous system, it is important not to expect those closest to you to meet all of your emotional needs. Once you have a friendly ally, use that stability to begin learning how to self-regulate, create more secure attachments, build community, and form a loving relationship with yourself.

Understanding your personality traits can also be important, especially for navigating conflict. For instance, are you introverted or extroverted? Are you a highly sensitive person as explored in Section 2.3? Do you tend toward a more avoidant, anxious, disorganized, or secure relating as explored in Section 3.4 and later in this chapter? Do you have ADHD or some type of neurodivergent mind? Speak up about your unique needs and let people know that it's not personal.

14.1 Friendships

Friendships typically form around mutual interests and activities. However, some hobbies are much easier to connect around than others. It's also important to note that in-person connections have the ability to be much more regulating to your mental health than online or long-distance ones do.[25] Eye contact, natural silences, and nonverbal communication are really important.

I suggest doing an inventory of how you spend your time. While it may require vulnerability, what activities can you add a social component to? Which ones could you replace or do less of in place of something that allows you to connect to others more easily? Are some of your current hobbies reinforcing unhealthy thinking or primarily introducing you to toxic people?

Making friends does often get harder the older you get. This is because many people, yourself included, may only have time for their work or family after finishing their school years. In school, you are constantly meeting new people and have a shared culture to engage around. After that you have to be especially intentional about connecting with others, so here are some ideas to help you along.

14.1.1 Social Activities

You never know where you'll meet a new friend, so try to say yes more. Challenge yourself into new activities and social engagements, even if you're feeling tired or anxious. There are hundreds of activities to choose from and great people to meet in each. However, some communities are more likely to contain safe people who are emotionally intelligent and capable of having meaningful conversations about life. These include personal growth seminars, yoga, meditation, ecstatic dance, support groups, community gardening, social causes, revolutionary spaces, and light martial arts groups. Some are also more friendly for socially anxious people to participate in if you find groups draining. Websites like Meetup, Facebook, and Craigslist can give you a plethora of daily options as well depending on where you are located. I do want to caution against finding all of your friends through personal growth circles though. While this is a great starting place, it can attract people who are solely geared toward talking about emotions rather than finding nourishment in activities and play. I urge you to try and find both as it will help you relate to a wider variety of people as you heal.

I love foreign animation, artsy story-based video games, and comics, but I noticed that I do not really get along with most of the people who consume these things. They generally don't assist in my ability to form meaningful relationships with people I meet naturally. The friends I've made who do share these hobbies enjoy them alongside more social activities like playing board games, hiking, and going to open mics, so I adopted those as well. Generally speaking, you may need to devote yourself to versions of fun and play which are compatible with the social group or friendships that you desire. To really get out of my comfort zone, I've also added in rock climbing, dancing, and cooking food for people. I could have started playing online video games, but these have never interested me much and I prefer meeting people in real life, probably in part for the potential of sharing touch and eye contact. Online pen-paling websites like <https://interpals.net> and social apps like *Clubhouse* can provide some great social engagement though from the safety of your own home.

Most relationships you form are on a moving spectrum. You start off distant, put in the energy to grow closer, and then become friends. Over the years that connection then naturally ebbs and flows. You may completely lose contact for several years before reconnecting at a chance visit, reach out after feeling nostalgic for the old times, or never see each other again. You may also grow much closer and form emotional or physical intimacy as lovers after not seeing each other for a span of time. That is to say that your relationships may last your whole life, but within that space, are unpredictable and unlikely to remain consistent. While it sometimes feels depressing to me, there is so much joy and possibility in each connection that we form. However, this does mean that it is often important to continue meeting new people throughout your life.

Basing your friendships in communities or activities can be really healthy and keep things stable and interesting. By that I mean relying on the community instead of any individual to consistently get your social needs met. That said, communities can also be insular. Even if you are socializing, you may be running into the same people who are not quite right for you or do not grow you in the right ways. That, or, the community is not conducive to actually making friendships. For instance, partner dance will create a lot more potential for connection than going to the gym. This may also be due to how you are engaging in the community.

More potential connections become available the more volunteer roles you take on, the more you show up, and the better you get at an activity. Being of service and giving to individuals or communities tends to make you very likable. Consider helping put the chairs away, bringing your special bean dip, or volunteering at an arts festival. You can also practice creating defining moments as explored in the previous chapter. Spend some time considering what kinds of people you do want to surround yourself with, and start engaging deeply in those interests and spaces. If you feel anxious about an activity, visualize what that experience might look like, watch a video of the activity, or initially participate only as much as feels comfortable for you.

14.1.2 Establishing A New Connection
Asking to start hanging out with a person can be a bit overwhelming. For this

reason, I enjoy having neutral things I can connect with a new person around. For instance I host a monthly open mic and a weekly artsy potluck. The invited are not necessarily coming to hang out with me but to experience the event, participate, and meet a community of people. I am pretty jealous of musicians for their ability to so easily connect with anyone else who plays music.

Just remember, humans want to socialize. So long as you're not creepy, you're fine. You're also sometimes going to make mistakes, people just won't be interested, or they won't have time. That's okay. There are a lot of people out there, and some of them are going to be excited about your friendship, it's just a matter of being vulnerable to possibility.

Part of creating connections is being seen. Perform at open mics, karaoke, and stand-up comedy. Host events or volunteer at local non-profits. Having a presence on social media can help remind people that you exist. Sharing high-quality content and seeing certain people interacting with it regularly might be a good opening for a closer friendship to start as well. You can also wear clothing that shares your personality and interests, or regularly engage in conversational topics that people find interesting or funny. For me, replacing the obscure media I consumed with educational, comedic, and popular genres that I still enjoyed helped facilitate more connection, conversation, and trained my brain to be more humorous out and about.

14.1.3 Mutuality
Relationships must be mutual. Both people need to get something out of it and respect each other's boundaries. As a result, it is important to not just have hobbies to share but to be conversationally adept as well. It's almost universal that people love humor, information, and being empathetically supported with kindness. Catch up on the local news, the latest science breakthroughs, or world history. Reading popular books or watching popular shows as they come out will also give you some great talking points, so long as that person is also into similar genres. Get into a hobby or sport that a person also likes, or ask them to show you how it's done. If you're a fairly serious person, try including a regular dosage of stand-up comedy, comic strips, and cute animal videos into your life. However, avoid repeating humor that involves slandering a group of people or teasing your friend, especially for new connections. If your friend is struggling, reach out to them, listen to their woes, and offer fun activities to do together. Offer compliments and surprise them with gifts or treats.

According to the Gottman Institute, developing healthy relationships requires positively acting on a high percentage of *bids for attention*.[16] Bids for attention from another person may include things like sending a meme, giving a gift, asking to play a game, or mentioning wanting to one day see a meteor shower. Your participation in these bids strengthens the connection, while ignoring them or not responding quickly enough may destroy the relationship. These are not always very apparent though, especially in romantic relationships, so it may be important to clarify. Knowing that, you can also work to make your own bids for attention more clear. For instance, ask for what you're wanting directly, create an event page, or establish a specific date and time.

14.1.4 Mirroring
Mirroring a person's emotions and movements can also be important for building a bond or quickly creating trust.[155] Children not raised with healthy mirroring may struggle to form secure relationships until they learn some of the social cues they missed out on.[97v] Mirroring should be done with subtlety and after you have gained some likability with a person - it may otherwise come off as weird or creepy. Exact mirroring is also generally not advised.

You can share in a person's delight by laughing, smiling, or getting excited with them. If they are feeling sad you might lower the volume of your voice, breathe at a similar rate, or shrink your body. If they get closer to you, you can lean in. When a person says or does something playful, you can mimic the motion, laugh, or build on the gesture by going along with whatever reality they've set you up with. These acts make a person feel comfortable and help align your neural circuitry. Mirroring exercises are often practiced in drama and dance classes, but you can also experiment with a friend in movement, facial gestures, and eye gazing.

14.1.5 Engaging Questions
People tend to find it easy to talk about themselves, so be engaged in what the other person is saying and ask meaningful questions about their life. You could even get a question card deck that people pull from, like the *Holstee Reflection Cards*. Instead of "How are you" or "What is the weather like these days," try to be engaging or more specific:

- How did your _____ go?
- What was the best part of your day?
- Did you have any dreams last night?
- Have you ever heard about _____?

- Have you ever read/watched/listened to _____?
- If you could be president, what would you change?
- If you had only one month left to live, how would you spend your time?
- What do you think about _____?

14.1.6 Beyond Hanging Out
Outside of just hanging out, there are a few ways to deepen your relationship with a person. You can ask someone to teach you a skill they know. Sharing music, news, humor, memes, and shows you enjoy can be a fun way to maintain contact while apart. Message or text people an image or link. Express gratitude and show interest in a friend's life. You can also give physical gifts, plan a trip together, or buy them a meal. Organizing a special event with a group of friends will also gain you a lot of appreciation. Consider campouts, hikes, laser tag parties, days at the beach, or visiting an art museum.

14.1.7 Types Of Friends
There are many different types of friendship. Some friends are available more than others, though all friends should try to make time for you and be communicative. Unfortunately, this seems difficult for many people in a world with so much going on and people focused primarily on trying to find meaningful romantic relationships or survive in capitalism. Many people also live with social anxiety and various levels of ADHD, but it's up to you whether or not you maintain these relationships. Close friends are typically consistent for at least a good period of time and make an effort to maintain contact. These are most common in housemates, coworkers, schoolmates, and people who participate in the same activities as you. In other words, deep friendships often require closer proximity or being part of larger communities and dedicated activities.

One-sided connections can still be nourishing so long as you have realistic expectations of a person. Perhaps you rarely see them or must be the person to initiate contact. Try not to blame yourself for the behaviors of others, and cut them out if the connection feels toxic. Although, if you notice a pattern in how your friends treat you avoidantly, you may want to consider why that is. Perhaps you are demanding too much emotional energy from them, are inconsistent, argumentative, or are not engaging in fun activities. You may also gravitate towards unstable and chaotic people due to unresolved trapped emotions.

14.1.8 Sharing Suffering

While friends may be great at cheering you up while you are down, remember that suffering tends to create more suffering. Repetitively complaining or venting about the same thing is draining to others and is generally not a constructive outlet for getting better. Venting too much can slow your healing process.[44] Remember that you are re-experiencing these events each time you talk about them. If you have a lot of thoughts to process, seeking the aid of a therapist or member of a support group may be better than expending the energies of a friend.

Unless your complaints are being used to work toward a healthy solution, consider transforming your social time used for venting into healthy outlets like exercising or cooking a nice meal. This is not to say that you should keep silent about your troubles, just be conscious that too much sharing of sadness, frustration, or anger, especially over the same thing, may be difficult for others. Also, just because you want to say something does not mean that it has to be said. Walk in another person's shoes and give yourself time to calm emotions and process thoughts rationally. Doing so will make your friends love you all the more. People tend to gravitate towards joy and good feelings. As Don Miguel Ruiz writes in *The Four Agreements*, "Be impeccable with your word."

14.1.9 Your "Authentic Self"

Please note that I have some issues with people that say to just be your "authentic self." Authenticity is great when you already have healthy ways of relating, but otherwise can prevent you from identifying yourself as the root of the problem. Ignoring healthy social and self-care techniques is a you problem. Of course, you also have a unique collection of interests, perspectives, passions, and stories that you can and should tap into along the way. By doing so, your authentic self becomes another inner self that you can seek advice from, but not necessarily allow to dictate your life as explored in Chapter 10.

What do you look like when you take away all of your anxiety, or you feel free to express yourself in any way that you want? What did you love while growing up? What have you always wanted to do? Infuse some of these into your life to really shine and get the attention of others.

14.2 Romantic Relationships And Secure Attachment

Romantic relationships may spring forth from strangers, acquaintances, friends, or even previous lovers. There are many types of romantic relationships such as monogamous, polyamorous, asexual, emotionally intimate friends, and cuddling. Being in a romantic relationship can bring a lot of joy and stability to life. That said, it is not required for happiness, and being single can provide a lot of nourishment. Single people tend to have better friendships and engage in more personal growth.[30] On the other hand, single people lack many of the privileges granted to partnered or married people and are often considered okay to discriminate against compared to couples.

For people with trapped emotions, relationships can be quite confusing and overwhelming, especially if any partner becomes triggered or issues need to be communicated through. However, creating healthier relationships is possible as you increase your understanding of yourself and the people you are attracted to. In this section, you'll learn about secure relating, how attraction works, what love is, communication techniques, relationship styles, love languages, and tactics for keeping a relationship exciting. In general, know that if you share physical intimacy with a person, you should talk about what that does and does not mean if it exists outside the context of something like dance or casual hugs. Intimacy is relational and typically creates emotions whether or not you want it to.

14.2.1 Attachment Styles
Anxious, avoidant, anxious-avoidant, and secure attachment styles were described in Section 3.4. Again, anxious attachments tend to have codependent tendencies and lack trust, avoidant attachments typically shy away from healthy levels of emotional or physical intimacy, and anxious-avoidant attachments switch between the two. Understanding your attachment style and working toward making it secure is essential to forming healthy relationships. Keep in mind that there is your personal attachment tendency, and then there is the attachment created in the relationship itself. Two insecurely attached people can create a secure relationship, whereas two securely attached people could create an insecurely attached relationship.

There are many ways to build a secure relationship explored throughout this section. However, you may need to treat your attachment wounding or complex PTSD before you can identify and foster healthy relationships. This topic is explored in Section 17.6 and combines a number of the techniques explored throughout the book such as visualization, inner child work, experiencing healthy connection, and building social awareness.

Even with healthy attachment, according to relationship specialist Jessica Fern, establishing a true secure relationship takes upwards of two years to accomplish.[41] However, in the meantime, a couple may develop many elements that this security involves such as co-regulation, mutual acceptance, emotional support, physical compatibility, and healthy autonomy. Both monogamous and polyamorous partners can develop securely attached relationships, but it often requires intentionally co-creating that bond. This can be done with dedicated practice, role-playing communication tactics, or reading together about the techniques throughout the following sections.

If you or your partner have anxious or avoidant tendencies, here are some strategies for working with them. Just remember that these steps may need to be taken slowly so the individual and relationship can adjust smoothly. Some of these suggestions are going to be uncomfortable, but you do them because you care about and cherish your partner.

For anxious, avoidant, and anxious-avoidant attachments:

- Try to ask for or work on one thing at a time
- Acknowledge your specific attachment tendencies and also that you are committed to working on them
- Remember that it is okay to compromise as necessary
- Anxious and avoidant behaviors primarily arise when triggered, so every attachment style must learn how to self-regulate and deal with their inner and outer critics with the techniques explored in Chapters 4, 5, and 10
- Understand that your partner triggering your attachment wounds always relates to an event in your past
- Learn how to empathize with and reflect back what your partner says
- If you can see that your partner is having an anxious or avoidant episode, help them regulate with supportive communication and checking in to see what they need – do this before trying to rationalize with them
- Understand and empathize with the needs of your own and your partner's attachment styles
- Get into a relationship with a securely attached person to help model healthy relating and to make it so that only one of you has to transition behaviors
- Find examples of and put yourself around securely attached people in your life – for many, this starts with a therapist or religious figure
- Seek out the help of a therapist or couple's counselor - even if you think nothing is wrong with the relationship, it is better to start early

For avoidant people:

- Let go of your ego as explored in Section 13.2
- Let go of your need for things to be perfect
- Let go of your need for control as explored in Section 13.3
- Let your partner know specific details about when you will be unavailable and for how long
- Find ways of complaining about and judging people less as explored in Sections 8.8 and 8.13
- Identify the ways in which you enjoy people
- Learn about interdependence and find ways of feeling your desire for it
- Learn how to identify emotions and speak about them
- If you feel overwhelmed by your partner's need for attention, find middle ground with activities that take off some of that pressure, like a collaborative project, game, movie, or puzzle
- Imagine if your partner suddenly disappeared or died, can you hold onto those feelings of connection and desire?
- Recall positive memories you have with your partner[228]
- Acknowledge your need to go slowly in relationships, but make sure this is paired with continuing to grow the connection
- Try intimacy-building practices that do not require much time or effort such as partner yoga, listening attentively to each other, or back-and-forth question games – try the *36 Questions For Increasing Closeness* through the Greater Good Magazine website or the *Holstee Reflection Cards*[228]

For anxious people:

- Bolster your ego as explored in Section 13.2
- Learn that you have the right to ask for your needs to be met and do have control over aspects of your life as explored in Section 13.3
- Fix your self-limiting beliefs as explored in Section 6.3
- Become aware of and develop boundaries to the things you do not want to be doing
- Ask your partner to express gratitude for you more often when it is genuinely felt[229]
- Stop assuming what your partner feels or believes and instead ask them directly to clarify – believe them and remind yourself of all the

ways you and your partner have built trust in the past
- When you are missing your partner, recall a good time with texts, images, voicemails, or your memory
- Learn nonviolent communication to clarify and ask for your needs to be met rather than lashing out
- Instead of constantly reaching out to your partner, put time into something special for them to share when you can reconnect in person like a meal or gift
- Write out all the ways in which your partner is showing up for you
- Learn about codependency and ways of empowering and enjoying your independence
- Respect your partner's need for alone time by developing more friendships and hobbies
- Get your needs met outside of your partner by creating new friendships and social ties
- Do not immediately rely on your partner to soothe you
- Develop healthy communication strategies as explored in Chapter 8 to bring up your feelings and needs

As someone dating a person who is anxious or avoidant, try your best to be supportive when your partner attempts more secure ways of relating. You may pick up on certain cues that something is needed and can help facilitate it. For instance, someone avoidant might want to talk about their feelings but not quite know it or need a little push. Just be careful about forcing things, someone avoidant might also need more time to process a feeling before knowing how to put it into words.

14.2.2 Love And Attraction
Love and intimacy do not require sex, and sex does not require love or intimacy. This is important to understand if your body is taken over by horny chemicals. Sexual attraction is often confused with love and closeness. They are very different things, but can nicely complement each other. Please see Chapter 3 to refresh your memory on what love is.

Keep in mind that friendships can be intimate and loving, and being attracted to a person does not mean you have to date them. Strong attraction often arises toward people who remind us of our family and caregivers - even if they were or are abusive. Be mindful of this if you are needing to end a cycle of dysfunctional or otherwise unhealthy relationships. Some people may need to reassess and transform what they find attractive in other people. Just because mutual feelings of attraction exist does not mean it is a compatible or healthy relationship. Be sure to have your friends and your rational mind thoroughly analyze a connection before diving in headfirst.

If you notice yourself having a pattern of unhealthy relationship dynamics, consider journaling about it to help break your cycle.[31] For instance, you might write out the negative characteristics your partners have shared or their attachment styles. You might also find characteristics that your parents or siblings share with these people, so recognize the traits you are unconsciously seeking out from childhood attachments. Some of these may be good, and some bad, but once you bring them to your conscious awareness, you can choose what you allow into your life. What are your green and red flags?

14.2.3 Four Destructive Forms Of Communication

Maintaining a healthy romantic relationship involves many of the same aspects of a secure friendship. There are some differences however due to how much time you might be spending together and the extra complications around physical affection, jealousy, money, and boundaries. Especially if your lives merge together in any capacity, things can get tricky. Know however that disagreements are normal and healthy, so long as there is good communication as explored in Chapter 8.

According to John Gottman, the four most destructive forms of communication in a relationship are criticism, contempt, defensiveness, and stonewalling[49]:

1. **Criticism** - Saying something bad about a person's character, such as "You never get me gifts, you're so selfish." Compare this to a complaint, which is a specific thing that a person did which upsets you and often includes your feelings. For instance, "You never get me gifts and that makes me feel sad and insecure about our relationship."
2. **Contempt** - Speaking to a person as if they are worthless and unworthy of respect or love. This often involves name-calling, ridicule, teasing, and abuse.
3. **Defensiveness** - Ignoring the merits of what a person says and instead arguing about how it isn't true or how your perspective is correct. For the most part, everyone's feelings are valid.
4. **Stonewalling** - Keeping silent around or leaving an emotionally charged conversation.

You should generally avoid doing these, or apologize if you catch yourself doing them. Ideally, you instead use nonviolent communication, or at the very least learn how to remove these four elements from your speech. Remember too that not everything needs to be said. It will help your relationship a lot if you mull over things and have emotional releases before putting it onto your partner. Don't use them as an emotional dumping ground.

14.2.4 Polyamory, Novogamy, And Radical Monogamy
Polyamory is a word describing a diverse style of relationship in which emotional or physical intimacy are not exclusive to a single individual. This could involve having multiple sexual partners, being married but with emotionally intimate and cuddly friends, having three or more partners living together, and so on. Polyamory may even involve being in a primary relationship with yourself, your higher power, or the Earth before anyone else. Polyamory leads with the assumption that you can rarely get all your needs met by just one person. Generally in polyamory, couples can co-create agreements that work uniquely for them rather than assuming what the relationship is supposed to be like as often happens in monogamy. Not all forms of polyamory work for everyone though, and that is fine. Just be sure that you describe specifically what polyamory means for you and your relationships. Simply saying you are polyamorous is very vague and tends to lead to hurt feelings.

In prairie voles who exhibit both monogamy and polyamory, the difference in the behavior is primarily explained by a chemical called vasopressin.[79] Genetic differences in the vasopressin receptor seem to impact human pair bonding as well.[188] Even though polyamory may not be for everyone at a chemical level, I do believe that the polyamorous ethos is important to adopt for being in relationship with yourself and making space for friendships alongside your partner. The rationale for adopting polyamory is also explored in books like *Opening Up* by Tristan Taormino.

While I cannot include a complete guide on creating healthy poly connections, I do highly suggest reading *Polysecure* by Jessica Fern. This book has been a great help for me in the times I have been in polyamorous relationships, and I consider it a useful read for even monogamous couples. This is especially true for understanding attachment theory from a trauma-informed lens and breaking away from monogamy as a default system.

There is a growing movement of *radical monogamy* in which people choose monogamy as an informed decision.[104] It can be very healthy for monogamous couples to understand how monogamy can hide personal insecurity, prevent communication, create boredom, promote codependency, stifle queer relationships, and destroy connections that are relatively healthy but cannot meet all the needs a person has. There is a reason why so many people cheat on or divorce their partners. Radical monogamy gives couples more freedom to create a relationship that works for them instead of copying their grandparents or the cisgender and hetereonormative relationships found in media. For instance, it is okay to live apart, have close friendships, alter gender roles, or not get married.

There is also the relatively new concept of *novogamy*, coined by Dr. Jorge Ferrer in his book, *Love & Freedom: Transcending Monogamy and Polyamory*. Novogamy involves choosing the relationship style that best suits you and your partner at a given time, rather than saying you are exclusively one thing or another.[171] It is essentially the same as the polyamorous style of *relationship anarchy* in which you uniquely define each relationship you engage in, but also includes monogamy as a valid option.

When considered fully, many people find that they are polyamorous or at least want to explore it as a possibility. Some important points Fern makes in *Polysecure* include:

- Polyamory can bring up attachment wounds formed in childhood or from previous relationships - these trapped emotions may prevent secure attachment from forming, rather than being the fault of polyamory itself
- Even in committed partnerships, polyamory is inherently less stable than monogamy due to changing dynamics with new partners and a need to maintain a healthy romantic connection rather than just relying on the system of monogamy
- Special considerations must be made for creating secure attachment in polyamorous connections - for instance, how do you know when you are saturated with too many partners, how can you give each of your partners quality time, and how can you feel happy about your partner's happiness?
- Polyamory requires extra communication compared to monogamy, especially as it pertains to time management, sexually transmitted diseases, and addressing the feelings of jealousy or insecurity that may arise
- Jealousy is natural and will come up, but can be worked through

In my personal experience, establishing each person's expectations and what they define as a healthy open relationship is an essential first step within the infinite configurations that polyamory can take on. Dr. Elizabeth Sheff suggests each partner write out and share a list of "something they absolutely must have in a relationship; something they would like, but are willing to flex on; and something they absolutely will not allow in a relationship."[12] This list may change over time as people become more secure and familiar with polyamory. Make sure that you consider the feelings and needs of everyone involved, and do not just ignore them for your primary partner or nesting partner. This includes your more casual partners. If you are trying to create secure attachment with your partners, everyone's voices matter.

It is also important not to ask your partner or partners to do too much emotional labor. Know that your insecurity may be helped by communicating specific things that you need to feel okay, but that insecurity is often rooted in your attachment wounds and is not necessarily your partner's fault. Try your best to do the work you can on your own while reflecting on how your partner is showing up for you. Of course, seek reassurance as needed.

One of the most important aspects of creating a healthy polyamorous relationship is developing a concept known as *compersion*. This is the opposite of jealousy and involves being happy for another person's happiness. Finding joy in your partner or partners connecting with others and getting their needs met is a great way to cut through insecurity. That said, compersion and jealousy can simultaneously exist on a moving spectrum.[29] Sexual and relational satisfaction, feeling secure, and being committed to the values and ideas of polyamory all help a person develop compersion.[172] Dealing with insecurity and jealousy is further explored in Section 17.15.

Basic routines, relationships agreements, regular check-ins, boundaries about how much is shared about other partners, or a temporary pause on dating any new people can go a long way to bolstering the security of a polyamorous relationship. Polyamory typically gets easier as you witness your partner or partners continuing to show up for you with love, affection, and a willingness to communicate through difficult feelings - but of course, it is a different story if these things are not happening or you have attachment wounds and trapped emotions.

Polyamory *rationally* makes sense to a lot of people, but it often ends up initially being much more emotionally difficult than people predict. Some people are also just bad at secure polyamory, or use polyamory as an excuse for aloofness and poor communication - but these traits are pretty common in monogamy as well. Be mindful of dynamics in which your partner refuses to observe their own shortcomings or will not do the hard work that relationships require. Polyamory does seem to be easiest when a couple both have other partners to connect with, but it is the unfortunate reality that finding new people to date is exponentially harder for some people than others. That said, it is fine if you just have one person while your partner seeks out more connections, so long as communication and healthy intimacy are still happening.

Polyamory is a completely different world and mindset from monogamy, so it can be very helpful to consume books and other media from polyamorous voices. I especially like the Multiamory podcast and Jessica Fern's book, *Polysecure*. There is also a Better Humans article that I found insightful by Silvia Bastos titled *How to Master Communication in Open, Polyamorous and Other Relationships*.[12]

14.2.5 Entering Into A Romantic Relationship

The steps to getting into a romantic relationship vary a lot between different people and cultures - and it is constantly changing. You'll need to learn what a particular person is most likely needing to be receptive. Perhaps it is going out with them on a date, first forming a friendship and then waiting for the right moment to ask for intimacy, dressing in a certain way and having a certain body type, making enough bad jokes, having the right photos online, sharing a particular interest, following a specific relationship style, earning a certain amount of money, being interested in having children, reading particular books, having a passion, or doing something for the world beyond your personal survival – there are a lot of possibilities for what people find attractive.

Gender norms aside, when flirting with a stranger there are a few nearly universal tactics that many people appreciate you use:

1. **Being safe and respectful** - For instance, don't corner them, make sexual comments about their body, sexually touch them, or say bad things about them if they turn you down or aren't interested.
2. **Ensuring that they aren't stuck with you** - Say that you've only got a few minutes, or you hadn't connected with them yet but were hoping to if it's alright with them.
3. **Seek consent** - To be safe with someone you do not have existing touch agreements with, verbal consent should be sought for touch including hugs, kisses, and anything sexual. Consent should be sought for any increasing amount of touch, and consent should be sought again for the same action even if you got it on a different day. Verbal consent tends to go better when a person knows that a "no" will be happily respected, so be sure to make it clear that "no" or "we don't have to" are entirely acceptable answers.[28] Do not sexually

engage with someone who has been drinking alcohol unless you have consent before their first drink. Do not try to persuade a person away from their "no." Remember that "no" is not a rejection of you, just the thing that you are asking for. Handling rejection is covered in Section 17.14.

4. **Check in nonverbally** - Are they laughing? Are they getting closer to you? Do they maintain eye contact and is that contact bright and cheerful? These things indicate that they're probably interested.

5. **Fun, humor, and positivity** - Humor is one of the most important skills for successful relationships. People love to laugh, so make some jokes and be playful, but don't be mean about it. Even more importantly, people love having their jokes laughed at.[200] Play can include things like dance, sports, role-playing, or games. Generally, complaining, being depressed, or showing uncertainty early on in a connection will not help. Find people other than your romantic interest to share these feelings with.

6. **Show off your altruism** - According to several studies conducted on heterosexual men and women, women were most likely to select men as long-term partners who showed altruistic personalities.[56] Altruistic men also seemed to have more sex. Altruism includes actions like helping with tasks, giving to charities, volunteering at nonprofits, offering compliments, and saying nice things about others.

7. **Peacocking** - Wear something interesting or get a tattoo that gives a person an easy way to ask you a question or compliment you. Certain interests and job positions are also quite attractive to some people.

8. **Confidence** - Be confident, but without expectations. Stammering or not knowing what to say next tends not to work well with flirting, although some people find it cute.

9. **Mirroring** - Subtle mirroring, especially in movement and emotional tone, helps a person trust you.[43] This can also be quite powerful in dance.

10. **Good questions and meaningful conversation** - People love talking about themselves as well as the things they are passionate about. If the other person doesn't respond with questions of their own though, they might not be that interested in talking. It's useful to have a wide breadth of knowledge for connecting with a person so you can relate your own experiences such as "I also lived there last year!" or "I love that book series, how do you think it will end?" If you're not great at

back-and-forth banter, consider memorizing some topics of interest and questions, especially for when silences arise.
11. **Solidify the connection** - Depending on how the first interaction goes you can ask your new acquaintance for their contact info, invite them to do an activity you enjoy (typically best if it's public), or keep hanging out through the night (remember consent and ask for permission).

With already established acquaintances and friends, social proximity is important to successful flirting. In other words, put yourself around the person you're interested in by engaging in the same activities, attending events they invite you to, asking to hang out, or striking up conversations through text, phone, and social media conversations. Sending funny memes is a tactic a lot of people use in the modern era to stay in touch. Don't be rude or obsessive, but do note if they are being receptive and enjoy having you around. A potential romantic interest will often only give you so much time to make a move before they either think you only want friendship or they find someone else, so make a decision.

Sometimes this social contact naturally flows into a romantic place with people getting physically and emotionally closer, but other times you need to announce it to your crush in different ways or leave little intimate suggestions that they can pursue if interested. You can also remove some of the awkwardness by just saying that you'd like to buy them dinner or take them to some other one-on-one activity, but this isn't as straightforward and could still be seen as simply a friendly gesture. To be clear, you might use a more direct method, such as:

1. Formally ask them, "Can I take you out on a date?"
2. Be honest and tell them. "Hey, I have a crush on you and was wondering how you felt about me?"
3. In intimate situations, let them know, "I really like you, find you attractive, and would love to make out with you right now." Or just, "Can we cuddle?"
4. Many people casually or indirectly talk about their relationship needs by telling a crush about previous relationships, general criteria they are looking for, or interest in having children. This method, though not direct, allows you both to learn more about each other and makes it clear you are both seeking a relationship.
5. Show your interest in being intimate by throwing it into a list. For

instance "I realized the other week that five things keep me happy: music, good conversations with friends, cuddling, nature, and movies." It gives your crush an opportunity to make their own list or reciprocate by saying that they love similar things, like cuddling. You could also say that you're like a cat or a dog, and mention how much you like touch along with the personality traits you associate with those creatures.

You do have to be forward with people about your desires or interest in them, or even lack of interest. Some people get a lot of attention whether they want it or not, while others have to make forward advances, which often leads to a lot of desperate advances and unwanted attention. This is a common and unhealthy dynamic, especially based on how attractive a culture deems a person's body type and fashion choices. Unfortunately, you will likely have to work with this dynamic, at least until dating and gender cultures change more.

Even though I hate it and they reinforce many toxic aspects of society, gender norms play a huge role in dating. Some people benefit from these norms, while others are deeply hurt by them. I talk about the pitfalls of gender in Section 15.9, but depending on who you're interested in, you can become aware of these norms and leverage them to your advantage when necessary. For instance, as a heterosexual man, I have to accept that I am expected by most women to initiate romantic interest and that rejection is a normal part of dating that will happen **a lot**. Instead of being devastated, I can understand that this is just part of the game. This expectation to be forward may also be true for LGBTQ+ folk or heterosexual women who do not fit into the mainstream notion of attractiveness.

14.2.6 Love Languages

While establishing and once in a relationship, it can be useful to note your own and your partner's love languages. A love language is a person's preferred way of being shown affection and helps build trust and affection. It is beneficial if a couple shares the same love language, or at least is open to providing the ones that their partner enjoys. It can also be important to note if you or your partner has a dislike of certain love languages. For me, I eventually realized that I need people who are great at cuddling and value quality one-on-one time. This has saved me a lot of time realizing that I'm incompatible with women who are not that into touch or are constantly busy with work and socializing. According to Gary Chapman, there are five love languages:

1. ***Receiving gifts*** - What physical items does your partner enjoy? These include things like flowers or being taken out to dinner.
2. ***Spending quality time together*** - Some activities create stronger bonds than others. Consider emotional conversations, supporting each other, or just having a one-on-one activity that creates a happy memory. Quality time varies from person to person, and it is important for you to learn what this means for yourself and your partner.
3. ***Words of affirmation*** - Say nice things about your partner like "You're such a great partner," "I'm here for you because I love you," or, "I appreciate how I feel when I'm around you."
4. ***Acts of service*** - Help your partner with studying or running errands.
5. ***Physical touch*** - This may involve specific forms of touch, such as tight cuddling or good sex in which both partners are getting off and having their kinks explored. Communicate and ask.

14.2.7 Sex And Porn

Sexuality has many healthy flavors spanning from people entirely disinterested in sex to those who want to get it on daily with an infinite number of genders and body types. For those wanting a sexual life, know that there are people who want to have sex with you so long as your personality is attractive. As previously said, this means that you can focus on developing the things that you can change, like your personality and fashion, instead of those that you often cannot, such as the body you were born with.

Sex can be fun, cathartic, healing, affirming, and connecting, but can also harm others or be scary to engage in for some people. This is especially true for people that experienced any kind of abuse, had their gender identity shamed as a child, were raised under religious guilt, or have a body deemed as less desirable by the fashion and health industries. Beyond the previous suggestions for rebuilding trust in touch and your appearance, there are a lot of great resources on sexually empowering yourself.

Books on finding your sexual freedom include *My Body Is Not An Apology* by Sonya Renee Taylor, *Pleasure Activism* by Adrienne Maree Brown, *Mating In Captivity* by Esther Perel, and *Come As You Are* by Emily Nagoski. Learning about consensual non-monogamy or polyamory by reading books like Jessica Fern's *Polysecure* may also help, especially if you have a history of cheating on your partners, having a high sex drive, or struggle to stay in relationships for long. Another option is exploring your body, identity, and sexuality in a safer space by connecting with the queer, feminist, LGBTQ+, kink, or tantric communities. Some forms of partner dance can also be quite titillating. Healing trapped emotions associated with touch is also covered in Section 17.21.

According to relationship therapist Esther Perel, sex and love are cultivated in differently.[259] In her book, *Mating In Captivity*, she explains that a stable and committed relationship helps bolster feelings of love and safety, but often dampens a couple's sex life. Sex requires excitement, curiosity, and desire. Things like moving in together, forming predictable patterns, or constantly sharing affection can actually erode sexual desire. If the sexual spark has left a couple, Perel suggests spending less time together, limiting nonsexual affection, creating more novelty in your hangouts, relying on your partner less for your emotional needs, and introducing the possibility of other sexual partners.

Interest in sex can also be increased or decreased depending on certain substances. These include birth control, antidepressants, and a number of other drugs and herbs. Consumption of 1.5 grams to 3 grams of *maca root powder* taken daily for 8 to 12 weeks can increase sexual desire without altering estrogen or testosterone.[79] It even seems capable of offsetting sexual disinterest caused by taking SSRI antidepressants. *Phenylethylamine* (PEA) found in chocolate has similar effects. Indonesian *tongkat ali*, also known as *longjack*, can also increase libido but increases testosterone as well. Talk to your doctor and read safety warnings before trying any of these.

Of course, just being interested in and having sex does not mean you are good at it. This is especially true considering that most depictions of sex in media are fictitious, not consensual, unsafe, or based on only getting men off. There are a lot of ways to have sex, and they do not even have to involve orgasm or penetration at all. Improving your sexual game can start by reading some of the previously mentioned books to deepen your understanding of foreplay, the sensual centers of the body, and how people orgasm. In general though, the most important thing is learning what your partner likes and sharing what gets you off as well.

Although sex is generally a good thing, it can also be dangerous or mentally unhealthy for you. People with trapped emotions may become addicted to sex and use it as an escape that ends up hurting themselves and other people. It is important to communicate what you are looking for, use consent, get STD testing, and understand which methods of contraception work and which do not. Introducing sex into a relationship almost always amps up the intensity of feelings between people. While some of this is positive, the likelihood of jealousy and depression increases. If you find yourself constantly getting into casual relationships, getting hurt, or hurting others, it is important to examine your relationship with sex. Remember that intimacy does not require sex and that being single can be really stabilizing.

Masturbation is another avenue to orgasmic pleasure and is disease-free, pregnancy-free, and people-free. This can be a great addition to loving yourself, especially for those who experience anxiety about sex or struggle with relationships. Masturbation is generally seen as having a positive impact on mood and self-esteem, but it can increase feelings of loneliness and depression in some people.[22] This is likely due to holding cultural ideas that masturbation is bad, which then causes feelings of shame and guilt to arise. However, people may also experience a dopamine high that then crashes below their baseline as explored in Section 13.4. That, or a person may feel self-criticism needing to get off alone rather than with a partner, especially when using pornography. If these feelings arise for you, consider exploring ways of removing the cultural stigmas you grew up with surrounding sex, or changing how you relate to those you desire. For instance, not sexually objectifying them when you interact. You can also try masturbating less or without pornography.

There is a major concern with the use of pornography as a masturbatory tool. Pornography can be part of a healthy masturbatory experience, but it can also be damaging to one's psyche. Mainstream porn tends to promote unrealistic gender, relationship, and sexual roles, and rarely represents how real sexual encounters occur. This corresponds closely to most other media, but pornography changes how we relate to others much faster due to its high chemical rewards. Dependency on porn can interfere with daily tasks, cause social anxiety, make it more difficult to enjoy sex with a partner, create unrealistic expectations about dating, and induce unhealthy thinking about yourself or others. It can also decrease the desire for real sexual partners, which may then limit motivation for reflecting on personal behaviors and changing for the better.[70]

Fortunately, in pornography, there is much more choice with what you consume than in other media as it is unattached from the mental demands of pop culture. For instance, any type of body can be found online, "feminist porn" promotes healthier views on sex and the people involved, erotic fiction and smut can turn you on with words alone, and those with a vivid imagination can have quite exciting times in their thoughts. In the end, it is up to you to decide if sex or porn has become problematic in your life. You can find help by reading Section 12.2 about addictions, seeking therapy, downloading porn-blocking software, or joining a support group like *Sex Addicts Anonymous*.

14.2.8 Creating A Long-Term Relationship

The first few weeks of flirting and starting to date often have to be handled perfectly. There is very little room for drama as people usually expect to have a lot of fun to solidify the connection. Beyond this point, there are a lot of ways to maintain a long-term relationship. In Chapter 8 of *Polysecure*, Jessica Fern shares some with the acronym HEARTS:

1. ***Here*** - Being present while sharing space, making it known when you are available, and not being on your phone while spending time together.
2. ***Expressed delight*** - Making a person know you feel they are special with touch, gaze, gifts, and words. This is also accomplished by showing excitement for and celebrating their accomplishments.
3. ***Attunement*** - Asking specific questions, empathizing by putting yourself in the shoes of your partner, and paraphrasing or mirroring what they said. Not multitasking or ignoring.
4. ***Rituals*** - Creating reliable and regular times of connection, establishing labels of what your relationship is, attending certain events, and giving special attention to how you greet each other or part ways.
5. ***Turning towards after conflict*** - Relationship ruptures happen, what matters is how you go about repairing them and reconnecting to the desire to be in a relationship together. Admit what you were responsible for. Being genuine is more important than being perfect. Needing to be right or needing to prove your partner wrong hurts repair. Pauses are okay if you need to take time to think or collect yourself! Relationship repair was covered in Section 8.6.
6. ***Secure attachment with self*** - You cannot rely on others all the time to regulate your emotions, especially as your allies become unavailable through traveling, a breakup, or death. They may help you create a secure attachment within yourself, but you also need to do work to create that security as explored previously in this chapter. Techniques to do this are also covered in Chapters 4 and 13. Fern shares that the previous aspects of the HEARTS acronym can be used in the relationship with yourself as well.

These techniques can be further supported with a number of techniques. Consider to:

- Establish a monthly relationship check-in day to air out anything that

needs to be said rather than letting things build-up
- Write a gratitude list about your partner
- Explore each other sexually and learn what the other enjoys - several resources for developing your sexuality and relationship to touch are explored in Chapter 17
- Communicate about how you communicate, understand your tendencies with handling conflict, and establish some preferences in dealing with emotional conversations
- Make sure you are getting enough sleep, which has been shown to increase empathy, healthy hormone levels, conflict resolution, and interest in sex[72]
- Take more time being alone or take regular solo vacations if you spend all your time together
- Conversely, spend more quality and novel time together if your relationship has become mundane or repetitive
- Do something together you've never done before
- Reassert your independence and balance it with healthy dependency - maintain your interests, friendships, and personality when in relationships
- Become engaged in something your partner cares about deeply, or find a new activity to participate in together
- Stop watching porn so you can feel more excited about your partner's body
- Communicate your needs and start getting them met by your partner, yourself, and other people
- Ask for reassurance if you experience jealousy or doubt
- Learn about attachment theory
- See a couple's counselor
- Read books together like *Nonviolent Communication*, *All About Love*, *Your Brain On Love*, *Polysecure*, *Sex At Dawn*, *Mating In Captivity*, and *The Dance Of Anger*
- Remember that all relationships have conflict, all relationships take work, and no one is perfect

After establishing a relationship, be wary of spending all your time with a partner. This is one sign of codependency. Doing so may make the relationship unhealthy and will make the end of a relationship much harder. Continue to seek out new friends and spend time with old ones, even if a lover is also your "best" or "only true" friend. One useful technique for maintaining stability is to get into a relationship with yourself. Love yourself. Go out with yourself. Do things that make you feel fulfilled and good. Acknowledge when you aren't spending enough time with yourself, and make it known!

Relationships are much more likely to succeed if a couple is stoked about each other from the beginning. It is easy to become caught up in the initial excitement of a new person, but if there are any red flags or you're saying "I like them but..." it may be better to hold off for a better match. That said, relationships will always require some sacrifices on your part and your partner's to make everything work out. It may take several months of learning about each other and trying different things before you successfully mesh together and learn that it's your perfect relationship. The number one factor for making it work out is communicating. Figure out ways to meet each other's needs, or what needs must be found outside of the relationship. Remember that all relationships have conflict, and working through those disagreements rather than avoiding them makes the connection stronger.

As you date more people, you will gain a better idea of who your ideal match is and what factors you need to personally work on to obtain such a person. Get clear about what you are and what you are not willing to give up in a relationship. What are your red and green flags? No one is perfect, including you. Maybe there is a theme in your relationships ending, such as being told you need to dress or behave a little nicer, or you can't find compatible people with your current set of hobbies or the place you're living. You will only learn through the vulnerable act of making yourself available to date.

If a partner is physically or verbally abusive, manipulative, does not respect boundaries, does not communicate well, makes it so that you have to give up your interests, or needs more than you can give, it is not a healthy relationship and should be changed or ended. Even if breakups are difficult, there are many other people to fall in love with, and being your own stable person can be really joyful.

14.3 Breaking Up With Someone

If you need to communicate a breakup with someone, take account of the negative aspects of the relationship that are holding you back from happiness and fulfillment. Connect with your healthy anger and the life you would rather be living. Remember that there are always other options out there and that singlehood can be quite nourishing. Try to use nonviolent communication. For partners who are safe, be kind but hold your ground. It is easy to want to comfort and bend to the will of someone you have loved, but that is unlikely to serve you or them in the long term.

Not everything needs to be said, but it is nice to give specifics as to why you feel incompatible with this person now. Just remember that communicating through conflict is a healthy part of all relationships. Before you end the relationship, you may be able to repair it. Or, even if you do end it, perhaps it can become a platonic friendship in the future. Repairing relationships was covered in Section 8.6, and learning how to handle being broken up with is covered in the next section.

After ending a relationship, take account of any patterns you have been repeating between partners. Become aware of your tendencies through your attachment style, love languages, and the personality traits you seek out. Beware of red flags such as disliking a person's friends, aggression, or lack of emotional intelligence. Try dating someone who breaks the cycle of "your type" if that type has traditionally become toxic or unhealthy.

If you have been living with your partner, a breakup may mean having to continue sharing space for a while until one of you can relocate. For the weeks or months in this new dynamic:

- Create and communicate boundaries about how you will continue living together with chores, finances, conversations, and using common spaces
- Make a specific plan for one person or another moving out
- Stop sharing the same room
- Even if you are being attacked, try staying neutral and return to non-violent communication as much as possible
- Do not invite new romantic interests over to the house
- Do not drink alcohol, especially not together
- Start decoupling your possessions and finances
- Spend time outside of the house as much as possible to create a new life for yourself
- Explore options for traveling or staying with friends and family

14.4 Being Broken Up With

There's no getting around it, breakups with a friend, lover, or parent are hard. You have formed many familiar patterns with this person that are suddenly gone. This includes all of the happy brain chemicals and the time in your schedule that they occupied. In this way your connections with others act somewhat like addictions. A breakup is not a failure, but rather a learning experience. There are whole books devoted to healthy decoupling and divorce, but I've found ten things that will help:

1. ***End it on a positive note*** - Even though you may be heartbroken, making your last statement positive, or at least neutral, makes healing so much easier for all parties involved. This is because it gives you a different point to focus on than all the difficult things that happened. Especially if you know you did hurtful things, you can apologize, say you really appreciated your time together, or wish them well in life. You can even say you are always open to communicating or reconnecting as friends in the months to follow, but this should not be an expectation. State that you understand if the connection never rekindles. Do not try to somehow prove them wrong or win them back. This communication may have to happen through some kind of written form, especially if you are already starting to take space.
2. ***Grieve*** - This person was close to you, it's important to adequately grieve the loss. Take however long you need to release your sadness and other feelings.
3. ***Take space*** - Some people you will never again be able to communicate with, while with others you can resume a healthy relationship after a small break. People often flail in figuring out which is appropriate and how much time together is healthy. Do you still feel jealous about their new relationships, sensitive to their mannerisms, or obligated to caretake for them? You probably need more time apart. That said, sometimes exposure to these things will quickly create a new norm you can handle. Generally for shorter relationships a month is adequate, but longer relationships need at least 3 to 6 months if not years to settle emotions. Even if certain things still bother you when reconnecting, remember that you're only going to hang out with them in a limited capacity and with plenty of boundaries. Totally removing a person may be difficult in shared friend groups and small towns, but do your best, and use emotional releases as needed. I've even found that logging out of social media or turning off my phone can be helpful so that the hope of someone contacting me is minimized.
4. ***Erase any traces*** - During your time apart, I suggest removing any trace of your ex's existence from your life including photos, social media connections, and gifts. You don't have to destroy things, just put them in a box and tuck it away under your bed or have a friend keep it safe. For social media connections, healing can happen by staying friends, but it's good to unfollow or temporarily block their content. Even briefly seeing an ex on social media after a breakup has

been shown to increase negative feelings and slow down recovery time.[27] On the other hand, a ritualistic burning of your memories can feel amazing.
5. ***Establish boundaries*** - If you need to communicate, what is the appropriate channel to do so through? How long are you taking a break for? Of course, in relationships you are strictly cutting out, there's no need to communicate much of this information, just get away and start your new life. Boundaries can be renegotiated as needed, but however much you excruciatingly miss the smell of their shampoo, try to maintain those boundaries. This said, you cannot always control the behaviors of someone else, and you may have to transform your own behaviors to create safety.
6. ***Do stuff*** - Instead of going full despair bear on the world, allow your hobbies and friends to fill in your schedule. Take on volunteer work, make art, and start meeting new people. If you start feeling jealousy, then you can have emotional releases and remember the need to meet more people and do more things with your life.
7. ***Reflect*** - While you should start building a new life, too many distractions can slow down your recovery.[27] These could include things like drinking alcohol and media consumption. It is important to spend time reflecting on the relationship and feeling your emotions through journaling, art, and movement. What can you learn about yourself? Why did you break up? What does this mean for who you want to pursue in the future? Did you fall into a dysfunctional pattern again or use poor communication? While not true for all relationships, a powerful moment for me when navigating a breakup was realizing that neither of us had to be at fault for anything, we could just be incompatible personalities. The reflection process could also involve celebrating your broken heart for all the things you have learned and can apply for a better match in the future.
8. ***Create new emotional connections or be single*** - My favorite get-over-super-sad-breakups technique is finding a new crush. I've also heard the wise advice that making out with two people who you like and trust does wonders, although doing this with random people you don't care about probably isn't a good idea. Of course, being single for a while can be healthy for growing into a better partner and learning about your relationship needs. Be your own crush! Revel in the wonders of singlehood such as getting good sleep for the first time in years, stacking partially read books onto your bed, and adopting a

fluffy creature. I also highly recommend reading *Your Brain On Love* by Stan Tatkin, and *Polysecure* by Jessica Fern.

9. **Remember the negative** - Withdrawal from a breakup can act similar to any addiction. Like the advice previously given for getting off substances in Section 12.2, as you become tempted to reconnect with an ex, remind yourself of the reasons why things didn't work out. Write out a list of why you are incompatible, and push that to the front of your attention. The number of rekindled relationships I've seen succeed within a year of people breaking up is slim to none. Maybe you'll be the lucky one who somehow beats those odds, but I would put my energy elsewhere. Remember that the world is abundant and that there are always healthier, happier, and more compatible matches out there for you. That's not to say that you or the other person is perfect - either of you may need to significantly change before you are good enough for your ideal match, but that transformation takes time. Even if you get back together, you're going to be triggered by the same things unless you both are willing to do the work through therapy or support groups. Ex-lovers can be great friends or successfully get back together years later after making significant changes, but generally it is good to give it some time and space.

10. **Remember your self-worth** - What do you find beautiful, attractive, or good about yourself? Why do people like you? What made you happy before the relationship? What hobbies and interests did you enjoy? What kind of self-care practice did you engage with? What friends did you spend time with?

Remember that true closure as spoken about in some self-help circles and breakup guides may not actually be possible.[175] Pauline Boss explores this topic in her book, *The Myth of Closure*. Do not expect your ex to say something that will suddenly make everything better. Closure must often come from within. Seeking out emotional reassurance may delay your healing process and act as a way of avoiding the reality of the situation. Breakups hurt, but as we have explored, that suffering can be transformed over time into new insights and a pathway toward healthier relationships.

14.5 Community And Individualism

As previously mentioned, basing your social time in communities can be really healthy. This is because communities tend to be much more stable than any friend or partner ever will be. It also gives your relationships more substance when supported by a community, especially when that involves a fun activity like dance, rock climbing, chess, or sharing songs. Communities are great places to meet new people, or, it can make it a lot easier to invite a person to hang out by telling them about the community. These include activity-based communities, spiritual communities, housing communities, gaming communities, support group communities, volunteer communities, or communities you make from a friend group or neighborhood.

Building a community simply requires a shared goal and regular attendance, it does not necessitate people to be friends. Try committing to at least one community you participate in once a week or more though. The more you participate, the more benefits you will get from the community. Think of it as a relationship you have to cultivate, just like with a friend or lover. Fully immersing yourself in a housing community can also be deeply gratifying. Check out the *Foundation For Intentional Communities* website <www.ic.org>, or, college students can visit the *North American Students of Cooperation* (NASCO) website <www.nasco.coop>.

Some communities do require more vulnerability than others. Individualistic people are often seeking perfection - they are avoiding things like conflict, stress, trying out new things, looking at their own behaviors, and dealing with the mannerisms of others. However, this avoidance comes at a price. The benefits of community, just like any other relationship, require some personal sacrifices. It won't necessarily be comfortable at first, but what springs forth from joining together with others is truly amazing.

I can speak to this personally from living in housing cooperatives. While sharing a space with over thirty people was stressful at times, it also brought me some of my most cherished moments. I also benefited greatly from almost daily online meetings of *Adult Children of Alcoholics and Dysfunctional Families*, even though it sometimes required I skipped other events going on. Lots of communities already exist, but to create your own:

- Host a potluck, open mic, or make dinner with friends
- Tear down your fence and share a yard with a neighbor
- Hold an activity at your house such as playing board games, a movie night, yoga, or meditation
- Live together with friends
- Tell people about a support group, concert, or activity you're excited about
- At any type of gathering, direct people to talk to at least one stranger,

or create randomized groupings for activities
- Host a "speed friending" event or part of the event where everyone gets to meet one-on-one for a brief questionnaire
- Create a text group with your favorite people to easily invite them to things
- Start a sports team or introduce a new game like juggle fighting
- Introduce yourself to everyone that lives on your city block
- Share your tools and books
- Teach people a skill
- Co-parent your children with another family
- Host a neighborhood garage sale
- Have a neighborhood "house to house" party, or in your own house, a "room to room" party
- Let neighbors know the skills and resources you have to share
- Create a neighborhood tool share
- Ask the community to pitch in for a collective fund to pay for things in this list or public needs like fixing a road
- Advertise neighborhood councils to gather and pressure the city to do something you want to see happen
- Create a business that people commonly express interest in
- Put up art around your neighborhood
- Put a community message board in your front yard so people can advertise their events
- Volunteer for an organization or at a festival
- Put up a poetry or tiny art sharing board
- Share bills such as internet and garbage collection with your neighbors
- Colorfully paint fire hydrants, utility boxes, and city blocks
- Plant fruit trees for the public
- Ask stores or bars to host your event, or just show up and do it
- Create and maintain community spaces such as grange halls and parks
- Collectively rent a building
- Petition for low-cost and cooperative housing
- Ask your city to fund art projects
- Start a group that plays kickball or catch at the park

Humans are communal creatures. You rely on billions of other organisms and tens of thousands of humans to sustain your life. This includes your food, technology, water, and comforts. You are not alone. For instance, your breath is shared with creatures of all sizes and was created from a diverse array of plant life. Individualism is a problem that disconnects us from caring for the natural world and each other. It reflects a sick society, so why have so many people become individualistic? Even though people are more connected than ever before, they have fewer meaningful social interactions. In some ways this is because of a natural limit to how large of a group the brain can handle. The *Dunbar Number* theorizes that human communities max out at about 150 members before people start taking advantage of or ignoring each other. At a cultural level though there are many more reasons for our lack of deep connections:

- Individualism is glorified and being independent and living alone is even a benchmark of success in many circles
- Technology allows us to complete amazing feats alone
- Digital communication creates less capacity for closeness than connecting in-person does
- The stress of modern society makes addictions such as media, workaholism, and alcoholism more desirable to use for drowning out the nagging sense that something is wrong
- Globalization makes invisible both the process in which goods are created and the working conditions people are subjected to
- Discrimination pushes people apart
- People are disconnected from the complicated web of life in nature
- People lack the communication skills to handle conflict in a healthy way
- Big businesses prevent employees from unionizing
- Public areas are developed into storefronts and suburbs
- Housing and land laws prevent groups of people from living together
- Competition promotes division instead of cooperation and mutual support
- People don't have time to gather because they work too many hours
- Children are convinced to move away from their communities to attend college for better jobs
- In the name of saving money, houses are built as if designed by failed architecture students

Creating community may require that you understand how individualism has crept into the lives of so many people, including your own. Many items in the following list are not purely bad, especially for more introverted people. However, when a culture or a person's life becomes too full of them, they push us away from community. This isn't meant to shame your need for more alone time. Taking space to be by yourself can be really regulating because you can control the environment. Just be aware that coming out of isolation is an important aspect of healing for many people. So what does individualism look like?

- Living, working, or driving alone
- Ignoring the interests of another person and just talking about yourself
- Not asking for help, sharing, knowing your neighbors, or communicating through conflicts
- Thinking you are better than those around you or that you have nothing worthwhile to offer
- Abandoning or neglecting your friendships for a romantic partner
- Accumulating wealth and material goods
- Various forms of solo media consumption
- The nuclear family
- Competition instead of cooperation
- Cities and nations without public transit
- Believing humans are superior to other forms of life
- Destruction of the environment
- Discrimination
- Believing that humans are alone in the universe
- Money, hierarchy, and capitalism
- Addictions to things like drugs and media
- Having set beliefs about how reality works
- Law enforcement

Take some time to consider how these forces impact yourself, your community, or your culture. What steps can you take to begin removing yourself and your culture from solitude? Use the information in this chapter to start creating healthier connections and community. This one act is essential for not only your healing but the healing of society as well.

***
Chapter Reflections

1. Who are your friends and allies?

2. How can you be a better friend?
3. Which of your hobbies or self-limiting beliefs are holding you back from creating meaningful social connections?
4. Do you use mirroring while socializing?
5. In what ways do you incorporate play into your social time?
6. What aspects of your social time could be better directed at a therapist, support group, or health professional?
7. What is your attachment style and how can you move towards more secure relating?
8. How do you address conflicts in romantic relationships?
9. What are your love languages?
10. What behaviors could you change that would help create more long-term relationships in your life?
11. How can you become more secure with yourself while in a relationship?
12. How do you break your dating patterns? What are your red flags and green flags when considering the health of a relationship?
13. How do you stay present while with your friends or partner?
14. At what point do you know that it is time to change or end a relationship?
15. What communities would you like to start engaging with, and which ones do you already engage with?
16. In what ways do you perpetuate individuality?
17. What would help you, your neighbors, or your city become more community oriented?
18. What is your ideal community and what would you have to do to create it? What aspects of it could you start fostering now?

Chapter 15

Changing Your Environment

15.1 Personal Environment, 15.2 Businesses And Community Groups, 15.3 Creating A Less Stressful Culture And Society, 15.4 Discrimination, 15.5 Stopping Discrimination In Yourself, 15.6 Law Enforcement And Restorative Justice, 15.7 Media, 15.8 Capitalism And Mutual Aid, 15.9 Gender, 15.10 Good Parenting, 15.11 Healing The Natural World, 15.12 Culture

Changing your behaviors, mindset, and relationships is all easier in the right environment. It can assist in your feeling safe, regulating your emotions, having resources to heal from trapped emotions, finding healthy people, and generally enjoying life. Your environment includes the surrounding cultures, biodiversity, access to nature, businesses, support services, arts, community activities, architecture, laws, and political climate. Some ideas for healthier environments were introduced in Chapters 4 and 14, but then what are some methods for you to actualize these changes?

15.1 Personal Environment

Changing your immediate environment is fairly straight forward and can be accomplished with many of the tools already discussed throughout the book. You buy some potted plants, decorate your space, get a nice sound system, clean, apply for a new job, hang artwork, communicate through strife, or move to a new location. Temporarily changing your environment can also have benefits. For instance, you could hike weekly, do computer work at a cafe, wear headphones, or go out of town once a month. What would nourish your life? What would give you greater access to healthy relationships and space which feels safe and relaxing?

15.2 Businesses And Community Groups

At the next level, you may have identified something that your neighborhood or city needs, or that you're interested in, but it does not exist yet. Maybe it's a public service, a business, something fun, or a celebration of the arts. As discussed in Sections 4.11, 14.5, and 15.2, you can seek help or gauge interest from a small business development center and then start putting the word out through social media, fliers, and newspapers. Specific business plans and methods of starting casual groups may be found online. You can also ask a chat AI to build one for you. In general:

- Decide what your activity or business will entail
- Create a plan of action
- Decide a name
- Seek out help
- Collect funding if funding is necessary
- Establish a location for your activity such as your house or church
- File any relevant paperwork
- Purchase the necessary equipment
- Advertise your group
- Begin operations, but do not expect success or big attendance within the first year
- Give it time to build momentum while advertising, making your offerings better, and listening to any feedback

15.3 Creating A Less Stressful Culture And Society

Beyond your immediate surroundings, we need to talk about forces in the world that create suffering and make healing harder for everyone. Most trapped emotions are entirely preventable, but many cultures and societies are not focused on personal wellness. While people may perpetuate trapped emotions between each other, there are larger systems in place that maintain this toxic spread. Since suffering creates suffering, these problems hurt both underprivileged and privileged people. Not only that, but it also destroys the biodiversity surrounding everyone. This means that a part of healing involves connecting with the world outside of your immediate focus and being of service to humanity and nature. These things are not the easiest to address, but larger systems can be dismantled as has been shown through more and more rights being won by various groups of people and laws being created to protect biodiversity.

While you may be unable to offer much until after you have a sufficiently stable base to work from, a lot of healing can happen when giving to others. Being of service improves social connections and feelings of happiness and fulfillment. Any act of giving may be helpful so long as it does not hurt another person, or yourself. However, some specific actions are more impactful than others. Your personal healing is part of this though and a beautiful gift to your community, so take care of yourself as necessary.

15.4 Discrimination
Information about coping with discrimination and the limitations of what information is covered in this book were introduced in Section 4.10. Discrimination especially impacts people who are Black, indigenous, of color, living with disabilities, women, poor, non-binary, homosexual, transgender, or deemed unattractive by social norms. While less talked about, many others also face discrimination such as people who are introverted, elderly, highly sensitive, polyamorous, neurodivergent, or single.

Privileges are benefits a person receives without any effort on their own part. However, privileges inherently harm those who do not have that privilege. The most privileged people are White, cisgender, able-bodied, heterosexual, and rich men. Discrimination is partly upheld because it maintains the power that White people and religious organizations have traditionally used to control the masses. This largely plays out subconsciously - that is, White people, and especially White heterosexual men, do not realize how their culture, language, and behaviors oppress others. However, to give power to other groups is to decrease the power of the White heterosexual man, which in turn makes those men react defensively.

Often discrimination and oppression involve a group with more privilege or power acting out on a group with less privilege or power. However, any oppressed group may also perpetuate discriminatory beliefs against others and themselves.[89] For instance, people of mixed races may be rejected from joining a cultural group, colorism in Black communities is common in which lighter skin is deemed better, and women may vote for or date the men taking away their rights. White women may discriminate against people of color, Black men may discriminate against women, and homosexual people may discriminate against transgender people.

Sources of discrimination are complicated and tend to play on many interwoven parts that self-perpetuate. For example, Black drivers are 20% more likely than White drivers to be stopped by police when visible during the day, and once stopped, are up to twice as likely to have their cars searched, even though they are less likely to be carrying drugs or weapons as compared to White people.[133] Black people are much more likely to be persecuted for drug possession, even though White and Black people use drugs at similar rates.[153] They are also given longer sentences for the same crimes that White people commit. Racial biases like these have caused Black people to make up about a third of prisoners in the United States, even though they only constitute about 12% of the adult population.[50] Having a parent go to prison then increases a family's risk of poverty or staying in poverty.

Poverty in the Black community is also perpetuated by other factors. Black people have never been given reparations after being "freed" from colonial slavery or after segregation was made illegal, thus often making their starting point poverty. In general, it is difficult to climb out of poverty in the United States, especially as it tends to be more expensive being poor.[164] This is further compounded by things like schools in Black neighborhoods tending to be less funded than schools in White neighborhoods, and that Black people are less likely to be hired for a job than White people even if they have the same credentials.[45]

Things like losing a parent and living in poverty increase a child's risk of acting out in violence or committing crime.[141] As schools do not often teach about Black history and racism, there are few White people that can be considered true allies – including therapists. As most therapists are White, are unfamiliar with Black culture and history, or are simply seen as a "White person thing", Black people may be less likely to seek support.[186] Altogether these factors perpetuate many struggles within the Black community. Many forms of discrimination like racism are also integrated into almost every aspect of American society, making it especially difficult to find safety.

While some of these factors are unique to the Black community, each oppressed group shares a list like this that harms them and perpetuates that harm over generations. How then do we stop discrimination on a broad scale? The solution needs to come from the individual, community, business, and government levels. Oppression is upheld through things like group beliefs, lack of cultural intelligence, lack of education on historical discrimination, government policies, laws, police, media, privilege, and capitalism creating poverty. We'll explore many of these factors in this section and throughout the chapter.

15.4.1 Implicit Bias
Implicit biases are subconscious thoughts and actions that show a preference for one group over another. They can form very early in childhood.[246] According to implicit bias researcher Mahzarin Banaji, personally having implicit bias does not mean you will perform discriminatory acts, but it does increase the likelihood that you will. Thus, communities, cities, and states with higher rates of implicit bias lead to things like women getting lower test

scores in the sciences, and more violence being acted out toward Black people.

Banaji says that the best way to change implicit biases is to change the environment and laws that help uphold these subconscious belief structures. For instance, affirmative action campaigns. However, doing this is easier when people are informed about why the changes are important. How will a group benefit and in what ways are they currently being discriminated against? Things improve as people become educated, laws are changed, and emotional appeals create empathy for certain populations. For instance, implicit bias has greatly decreased with gay and Black populations over the past twenty years. On the other hand, things have not gotten much better for those who are elderly, overweight, or disabled, in part because people are not talking about the discrimination these groups face as much. You can take the online *Implicit Association Test* through Harvard at <https://implicit.harvard.edu>.

15.4.2 Lack Of Education
Discriminatory misconceptions need to be corrected. Statistical facts, infographics, and awareness campaigns will be useful for dismantling them. Schools and businesses need to integrate anti-oppression practices and education into their programs. Cafés, libraries, and retirement homes can host open discussions about these topics. Multi-racial healing circles may allow for creating safety and regulating nervous systems around bodies that have trapped emotions to each other.

Using information that actually highlights discrimination is important. For instance, there may be many reasons why more Black people go to prison than White people do, but that alone does not show a clear racial prejudice. On the other hand, studies showing that Black people tend to go to prison longer for the same crime that White people commit shows racial bias.

15.4.3 Cultural Intelligence
Teaching *cultural intelligence* is also important. Too often when educating about discrimination, an oppressed group is reduced to just that - an oppressed group without all the other aspects that make being human great. Education needs to highlight the positive, negative, and neutral aspects of cross-cultural interactions.

Cultural intelligence is different from cultural awareness. It includes not only your understanding of a culture but also how to respectfully interact with it. As language is so important when introducing the subject of discrimination to audiences, I believe that adopting a framework of cultural intelligence would greatly increase interest in these subjects. This is because the term cultural intelligence incorporates:

- Cultural history
- How a culture might be triggered by your actions
- Cultural customs such as celebrating, eating, and worshiping
- Important language nuances in verbal and non-verbal speech
- Understanding sensitive subjects like racism, sexism, gender identity, and how they intersect
- Positive benefits to yourself and the culture you are interacting with
- Understanding how harmful ignorance can be
- Understanding that you are not abandoning your own beliefs, you are learning to respect others
- Discernment between ignorance and intentional harm
- Awareness that while some generalities can be made within a culture, there is a lot of diversity within a culture that must also be respected
- Awareness of the ways in which a society discriminates against certain groups
- Understanding that we live in a globalized world and the United States is a cross-cultural hub that should be a leader in cultural intelligence and diversity

More generally, increasing a person's cultural intelligence increases their ability to see how flexible and contrasting cultures can be, with no one group being right, but every group deserving empathy and respect. Whereas terms like racism, sexism, or transphobia are primarily focused on shame and how an individual changing their behaviors will benefit others, cultural intelligence infers benefits to both groups. Unfortunately, some people do not have much empathy and need a personal incentive to engage in anti-oppression work. Specifically, it has been found that having higher cultural intelligence increases a person's ability to creatively solve problems, succeed in business, maintain a feeling of safety when confronted by cultural surprises, create meaningful connections, and navigate aspects of a culture that otherwise creates discomfort for outsiders.[111]

This concept of cultural intelligence can be used very broadly beyond people who live in different countries than you. For instance, what are the nuances that you should know about when interacting with an introvert, trans person, lesbian, police officer, Muslim, or corporate CEO? How about someone living with ADHD, anxiety, bipolar, or autism? While it does not detail these more specific areas, David Livermore's book, *Leading With Cultural Intelligence* gives many examples of how different cultures operate and the benefits of cultural intelligence. He suggests that you can increase your cultural intelligence by traveling, reading memoirs, watching films, studying history, learning foreign customs and languages, and interacting with people online through pen-paling or other conversational mediums.

15.4.4 Youth Exposure
The communal identity of "us" is developed at a young age, and so children exposed to more diversity will have a greater capacity to accept differences in individuals, to a point. Our cultures, schools, parents, peers, and media consumption frequently instill beliefs about others that are discriminatory. These sources may reinforce stereotypes against specific body types, skin colors, levels of income, sexualities, professions, or many other attributes, identities, and behaviors. The result creates trapped emotions and fear responses to certain groups of people, even if you have grown up around them.

Therefore, children must be exposed to diversity with a historical lens of oppression. Why is that body type portrayed as the villain or joked about so often? Why are some people impoverished? Why do you not say certain words or wear certain things? What kinds of atrocities have been acted out against Native Americans, Black people, women, and transgender people? While positive exposure to diversity is also important, informing youth like this gives them the tools to empathize with those who have been deeply hurt by oppression as well as identify misinformation and oppressive attitudes as they arise.

15.4.5 Adult Exposure
Creating positive interactions between diverse groups will help root out negative emotions and instill good memories instead. Food, games, and partner dances are always effective ways to gather people together. These events need structure to help break the awkwardness and force cross-cultural connections and emotional bonds to form. Consider introductions, a list of questions, or working on a project together. Another option is having mothers and their toddlers from diverse backgrounds gather together to play and connect. This may have a huge impact on developing inclusiveness in the toddlers and healing any discrimination rooted in ancestral trapped emotions the newborns or mothers have.[105]

While events that specifically shame or call out traditionally discriminatory groups may attract a handful of people to be educated, wider change will happen best through celebration, fun, and nonviolent communication. This is because when you educate through shaming others, you trigger and reinforce their trapped emotions. There are healthy and constructive ways to communicate, and there are communication methods that unfortunately strengthen the powers that you are fighting against. Aggressive anger must be openly expressed sometimes to create safety, but otherwise can you release that pent-up energy in communal grieving or somatic exercises before confronting an offender? Refresh yourself on healthy angering in Section 5.8 and Chapter 8, and educate yourself about nonviolent action in Kazu Haga's book, *Healing Resistance*.

On the flip side, traditionally privileged folks need to understand the pain and suffering that their ignorance, intolerance, privileges, misconceptions, and discriminatory acts have caused others. Be empathetic and give space for the anger expressed. Marginalized groups have every right to be openly angry, even if it might make you uncomfortable or sometimes hurts their causes. When you patiently hear these voices and respond with compassion, it can greatly help nourish a person's healing process.

15.4.6 Performative Allyship

One misconception perpetuated largely by liberals is that doing anything is helpful for oppressed communities. This is far from the truth and often results in something known as *performative allyship* - that is, doing the bare minimum to make it seem like you care about a group of people, but your actions just serve to make yourself feel better. These include things like reposting articles, wearing a safety pin, displaying a *Black Lives Matter* sign, or arguing that you are not racist because you voted for some politician or have a friend who is Black. While often well-meaning, these individuals need to wake up to the reality of what actually helps marginalized communities. Ask yourself, "What harm can I do by taking this action? Is this helpful? How will it help exactly?" Better yet, ask the people that you want to help what you can do. Many ideas are covered throughout this part of the book, but see the list at the end of this section for some specifics.

15.4.7 Politics

Marginalized communities overwhelmingly vote for left-leaning candidates, giving right-wing voters and politicians a strong incentive to withhold power from underprivileged people.[5] Conservative bodies do this through a variety of means including discriminatory laws, redrawing voter districts to tilt votes in their favor (known as gerrymandering), the Electoral College ignoring huge portions of the population, corporate influence buying elections, fear tactics, preventing the implementation of vote-by-mail options, and not voting for marginalized people. Of course, liberal politicians also use some of these same tactics for their benefit, although typically not as well as their opposition. Left-leaning politicians also often act in performative allyship while ignoring the true needs of oppressed communities. The end of this section offers some solutions.

15.4.8 Group Dynamics
Many groups such as churches, businesses, sports teams, and volunteer organizations have oppressive ideologies ingrained within their ethos. Sometimes these are based in ignorance, and sometimes they are meant to discriminate with hatred. It is important to either promote and create groups that practice anti-oppression, or that you personally work to root out oppressive ideologies from existing groups. As previously stated, Kaitlin B. Curtice discusses how to do anti-oppressive work within churches in her book, *Native*. Information in Section 4.10, and Chapters 15 and 16 may also be useful.

In general, question how a group is allowing for stereotypes or negative attitudes to perpetuate and how you can create a more inclusive space. Why isn't there diversity within your group? Educate yourself and ask what could make your group more inviting to oppressed communities.

In the book, *Mutual Aid*, Dean Spade argues that using *consensus* as a philosophy and voting dynamic creates the most anti-oppressive groups.[161] Consensus means that everyone in a group has equal decision-making power and must all agree before something is passed. That said, consensus can be slow and potentially erase an anti-oppressive motion with a single blocking vote. Consensus is typically best with smaller groups and only when there is a shared goal.

In any group dynamics, be sure to lift up the voices of oppressed communities. For instance, call on people who have been keeping silent or trying to speak and not being given the space to do so. Vocally reiterate and agree with what has been said by someone who might not have as much power to be listened to as you do. Do not take their ideas as your own or speak for them. Another option is to have ways to write out opinions, possibly with anonymity, to give a safer way to express ideas.

Some discriminatory beliefs are central to a community identity and may need to be abolished or otherwise silenced altogether. This includes certain ideas around religion, gender, genes, skin color, love, and health. I discuss more about specific tactics for dismantling ideologies in the next chapter.

Consider helping to end groups like White nationalists or churches that promote sexist or homophobic ideologies. In the USA, discriminatory beliefs are primarily perpetuated by White men who have historically benefited by taking power away from others. However, as previously mentioned, they can also be perpetuated within marginalized communities.[120]

Within your community, it is important to detach a person's race, skin color, or gender from the hobbies and beliefs they are expected to have. This includes making it acceptable to engage in activities that are traditionally seen as something only White people, cisgender men, or cisgender women enjoy. Doing so will allow marginalized communities much greater access to healing resources and to become their authentic selves. Starting this trend may be difficult if your gender, race, or religion is not represented within an activity, but consider creating a new group that specifically represents your race or gender. Or if there are enough allies present, become the first one who then makes it easier for future participants to join knowing they have at least one person who is sensitive to their lived experiences.

As an oppressed person, pursue the interests you are curious about and challenge the naysayers. For instance, the Black outdoors and birding community started a campaign using social media to post pictures of themselves out in nature.[170] This normalized being outdoors as not just a White person thing and also helped other Black people feel some community when they may have thought they were the only ones exploring nature.

Changing group dynamics may also involve creating laws, collective shaming, or asserting something as problematic. This said, leftist activists must be careful about using *cancel* or *call-out culture* in their work as an immediate first step when dealing with these forces. Too often this strategy ignores correcting misconceptions of well-meaning people and more often creates new opposition or further aggravates the existing opposition. Cancel culture is explored more in Section 16.5.

15.4.9 Inviting Diversity
Diversity does not just happen magically, it requires that the spaces are inviting and create safety for oppressed communities. This might mean that individuals attending who face oppression are given a voice in how things are structured, financial resources are provided for them to attend or share their perspective, or the more privileged attendees are already educated in the history of oppression and know how to interact with other cultures respectfully. It may also mean that the people who normally attend that group accept however a person from a different culture or class of privilege shows up. For

instance, a person may not have the money to afford a suit or the brand clothing for yoga, but this does not mean they should be treated differently.

One more misconception that primarily circulates within activist communities is that people of color and other marginalized groups are immune from the many "isms" of society like sexism, colorism, and ableism. This can be very harmful as it may promote diversity but then reinforce positions of power that are dominated by heteronormative men. For instance, heterosexual and cisgender Black men getting better representation still leaves out women, trans, and queer folk. Just remember that we need racial and ethnic diversity, but we also need diverse voices within that diversity.

15.4.10 Lifting Up Everyone With Equitable Solutions
In the end, lifting up everyone is essential to overcoming trapped emotions. This will require making up for the hundreds of years certain people have been oppressed and continue to be discriminated against today. Equality is therefore not enough, we need equitable solutions that level the playing field. These include:

- Mandating diversity in schools, workplaces, and neighborhoods - this may require affirmative action laws and making housing affordable in more White, affluent neighborhoods
- Educating children with diverse materials that discuss the less glamorous parts of history such as genocides and slavery
- Providing money and informational resources for starting new businesses, paying rent, and buying homes - these resources need to not just be offered, but also be made accessible to marginalized communities as reparations for past harms - rather than sending a "White hero" to "save" a group, be sure to let the community decide how to use the money
- Giving discounts to historically oppressed communities at your business, or having the government create a program like Food Stamps that provides a set amount of money each month as reparations
- Empowering marginalized communities by supporting their endeavors in their creativity, career focus, or education
- Giving land back to Indigenous groups and renaming landmarks to Indigenous names
- Creating rent control, building more affordable and communal housing, establishing laws that slow down forced evictions, making companies like Airbnb illegal, and ending property buying as an invest-

ment practice
- Mandating *Ranked Choice Voting*, or even better, *Score Then Automatic Runoff* (STAR) voting - both of these systems fix numerous problems within the political system and give third-party candidates a chance at winning - see <www.starvoting.us>
- Making voting more accessible by mandating vote-by-mail options and striking down any voter identification laws
- Electing politicians who represent the needs of marginalized communities
- Getting marginalized voices into politics and places of power - just racial diversity is not enough, we also need gender, age, economic, and ability diversity within that racial diversity to break away from privileged people dominating the political sphere
- Increasing accessibility around cities with building, street, sidewalk, bike lane, public transit, and park improvements
- Increasing accessibility to and from rural areas including bus lines into the city and bike lanes
- Being gender inclusive in workplaces, bathrooms, health insurance, hospitals, and so on
- Creating community centers for marginalized people
- Standing up directly against racist acts and starting uncomfortable conversations
- Volunteering and asking how you can be of service instead of making assumptions
- As explored in the next sections, creating new standards for law enforcement, media, capitalism, and gender

As you can see, discrimination reaches into almost every facet of society. There are many solutions, but a great place to start is dismantling it within yourself.

15.5 Stopping Discrimination In Yourself

Discrimination can be quite subtle and often happens at a subconscious level, such as with who you find attractive, select as a work partner, speak with, or sell a house to. You may also subconsciously single out or ignore a person of color. This is sometimes known as a *microaggression*, although this is not a good word to describe what is actually happening.[108] Microaggressions are harmful, but rather than aggression, they more likely are happening from a place of anxiety, habit, choosing familiarity, or unawareness.

While blatant discriminatory actions can be fairly easy to identify in yourself, microaggressions require a deeper inquiry into things like your gender, interests, cultural framework, communication styles, internalized biases, relational behaviors, and trapped emotions. Explore the reasons why most of your friends and co-workers are White, why few upper job positions are held by women, or why you are only attracted to certain types of bodies. Discrimination is so normalized that an underprivileged person may also be unaware of how they shift their personality while around a more privileged group. For instance, a person of color may have a *fawn response* while interacting with a White person, changing their normal behaviors and becoming apologetic to decrease the risk of harm they have historically experienced.

Anti-oppression work and learning about how you have perpetuated harmful behaviors against others can bring up a lot of emotions. This may trigger trapped emotions, insecurity, guilt, or shame, either from a resistance to observing how your personal privileges cause harm to others or from how social justice writers often portray more privileged people. In Chapter 16, we'll explore how the language used and attitudes held in anti-oppression circles often hold people back from wanting to do this work. Witnessing the deep anger and sadness expressed by certain communities as well as the atrocities acted out against them can also create deep discomfort or even create trapped emotions in your own body.

I implore you to be gentle with yourself while learning about and rooting out discriminatory attitudes. Use self-care and regulate your nervous system as necessary. Shame may arise in which you feel that you are a bad person, but try to see the objective reality, that you are part of an oppressive society that was intentionally established by people a long time ago to benefit certain groups of people. Even though you may not be aware of your impact on others, you were born into a system that causes harm and is perpetuated by things like family, culture, media, peer pressure, language, school, capitalism, and government. While you may feel uncomfortable or guilty, you can use that energy to create positive change in the world. The question is then, why should you do this work even through the strife it may cause you?

1. White supremacy and privilege hurt everyone, including the people who seemingly benefit from them. For instance, racism causes White people to vote against social welfare programs, even though White people utilize them the most.[199] White supremacy hides environmental destruction by pushing unsustainable and toxic processes into other nations and poor or Black neighborhoods. Racism decreases the

ability of White people to make meaningful friendships and learn from other cultures. White supremacy disconnects White people from their history, ancestral spirituality, and the land their people once inhabited.
2. Privileged people and their loved ones can become underprivileged at any time through injury, disease, addiction, disaster, aging, or losing a job.
3. As previously mentioned in Chapter 13, helping others feels good and increases your happiness.
4. You can directly decrease the amount of depression, hopelessness, suicide, poverty, addiction, and crime in the world. As mentioned in Section 4.10, creating a safe place where a person facing oppression feels respected, supported, and understood greatly increases their health outcomes.
5. You will personally feel safer and less stressed out while around different types of people and bodies.
6. Having a diverse team while working on a project improves the final results.[48]
7. Having *cultural intelligence* helps increase success in business and relationships, especially as it relates to understanding people and how to mediate with them.[83]
8. In his book *Patriarchy Blues*, Frederick Joseph makes the case that people have a moral obligation to support anyone with less privilege than they themselves have in any given category. White people should be proactive in supporting and defending people of color, cisgender people should support transgender people, and men should dismantle the sexism waged against women. Humanity is healthiest when it strives to create supportive communities.
9. Authors like Resmaa Menakem believe that the fight against racial discrimination must be led by White people as they originally established racist ideologies and now hold the most power to change them. Even though White people are not at fault for what their ancestors did, and they may lack many privileges as an individual, White people can much more safely petition for change and challenge oppressive ideologies than many other groups. Even if done in ignorance, White people are also the most likely to engage in activities that perpetuate racism in society or trigger non-White people.

Whatever privileges you hold, the work of creating a safer society for everyone starts with identifying and working through the discriminatory attitudes you hold. At the individual level, discrimination is most often perpetuated by misinformation, ignorance, trapped emotions, and group beliefs. There are also larger cultural and institutional structures that automate the continuation of discriminatory practices in yourself covered previously:

1. **Misinformation** - Misinformation most often arises from untrue generalizations or stereotypes that get passed around. However, this deprives a person of their unique humanity.
2. **Ignorance** - Some areas of the USA have worked to hide homelessness, poverty, the colonization and genocide of Native Americans, and the history and continuation of slavery in prisons. If you are unaware of the lived experiences and histories of others, you cannot be culturally sensitive to their struggles or triggers. You also cannot be aware of the discriminatory attitudes you have developed through what your parents told you or the subtle messaging you consume daily through media, friends, and school.
3. **Perceived differences** - People tend to treat others better who they perceive as sharing similar cultures, beliefs, or interests. The keyword here is perceive. A person's skin color, sexuality, gender, religion, fashion, or body size do not tell you how well you will get along with that person. Your brain is using stereotypes it has created instead of giving people a decent chance. In the book, *So You Want to Talk about Race*, Ijeoma Oluo shares an example describing a group of educated and middle-class Black people hesitating when another group of Black people, perceived as lower-class, ask to join in their festivities.[128] In the book, *Trans Like Me*, CN Lester mentions how trans people are often considered only for their transness rather than the rest of their humanity.[103]
4. **Group beliefs** - Many groups perpetuate discriminatory beliefs. Some of these beliefs are inherent to the group, and others come from misinformation or ignorance. For instance, many religious and spiritual groups use ancient literature, typically written by men, to preach sexism, homophobia, and transphobia. Schools often only teach in a style accessible to one type of intelligence or do not account for trapped emotions in children, thus limiting who can succeed. White people tend to believe that it is okay to culturally appropriate anyone's beliefs, music, clothing, or style and make it their own, even though this often hurts oppressed communities by triggering trapped

emotions and taking money and intellectual property away from that culture.
5. **Trapped emotions** - Misinformation, ignorance, and group beliefs may all play into you developing a trigger response around certain groups of people. You may become stressed out, angry, overwhelmed, or act out any number of other emotions and behaviors. Humans also often discriminate against people and things which they are either unfamiliar with or were taught as being undesirable. One study showed that even just separating people into different groups created increased feelings of negativity between those groups.[181] As previously mentioned, some believe that this fear response can also be genetically inherited through the trauma experienced by your ancestors.[120] In *My Grandmother's Hands*, Resmaa Menakem explores how this phenomenon reinforces racial tensions and fear responses in both White folk and people of color. Healing ancestral trapped emotions is explored in Section 17.19.

Based on these five facets, you can start dismantling discrimination by:

1. **Becoming educated** - Read about the history and lived experiences of oppressed peoples. Understand how being White, a man, heterosexual, cisgender, or financially stable gives you privileges that many people do not have. The truth is that almost anyone who is not a White, cisgender, heterosexual, and able-bodied man earning at least a middle-class income will face oppression that negatively impacts their life. This extends to their mental health, physical health, job options, education options, housing options, police interactions, income, and so much more.[195,103,24] Understand how your typical behaviors and words might be considered dangerous or offensive to a marginalized group.
2. **Reading** - See the *Gender, Race, and Social Justice* section in the Works Referenced which includes books like *The New Jim Crow* by Michelle Alexander, *Trans Like Me* by CN Lester, *The People's History of the United States of America* by Howard Zinn, *Everything You Wanted To Know About Indians But Were Afraid To Ask* by Anton Treuer, *So You Want to Talk about Race* by Ijeoma Oluo, *Black Fatigue* by Mary-Frances Winters, and *My Body Is Not An Apology* by Sonya Renee Taylor. There's also the *Revisioning History* book series, which tells the histories of queer people, people living with disabili-

ties, Indigenous people, African American people, Latinx people, and Black women in the United States. Resources like these will both educate you and make your body feel safer around cultures and appearances that you are less familiar with. In *My Grandmother's Hands*, Resmaa Menakem suggests using visualization to imagine yourself experiencing what certain groups have had to such as slavery, concentration camps, genocide, or prison.[120]

3. ***Identifying your stereotypes*** - Know when you are judging a person as unworthy of your attention because of characteristics like their physical appearance or sexuality. Greet each person as a unique human being. Try to find common ground rather than focusing on the characteristics which you do not understand or feel incompatible with. Get curious and excited about your differences. Who is this person and what can you learn from them? A person can still become a very good friend, lover, ally, or teacher even if you do not immediately see commonality. In this process, identify where your oppressive ideologies came from. What biases have you been trained to believe? Common ones include that women are weak, Black people are aggressive, and only thin body types can be successful or have love. Understand that everyone is capable of a version of success if given the support and tools to do so.

4. ***Identify your privileges and support those they impact*** - In general, it is important to understand your privileges and use them to help support those who are underprivileged. For instance, men can support people of other genders, and White people can support Black people, Native Americans, and people of color. It is important though that this support is helpful and desired by a group.

5. ***Finding inclusive people, media, and groups*** - Take note of the lack of diversity you consume through fashion, science, spirituality, fiction, news, and comedy. Cut out the people, media, and groups who create misinformation or reinforce negative stereotypes. Connect with a more accepting church, school, or workplace. Watch news that reports on the experiences of oppressed communities such as Democracy Now.

6. ***Experiencing people*** - Start putting yourself around a more diverse group of people. You can begin by following people on social media from demographics other than your own. Go to their art performances, speeches, and businesses. You can also visualize being around certain bodies or minds and treating them with respect and kindness.

Traveling will impart a great amount of cultural intelligence, especially to places where you do not speak the language. The more places you visit, the more you will come to understand and respect the many unique differences between people. Menakem and Peter Levine say that a lot of healing starts to happen when people have positive experiences across cultural divides.[105,120] This may involve identifying what you have in common with someone you see as different from you. It may also involve working together with diverse groups of people. Earlier I mentioned that splitting people up into different groups creates negative feelings toward the other group, but being part of the same group improves feelings. If you are called out or otherwise trigger someone, apologize, even if you don't quite understand why your actions were problematic. Simply knowing that you harmed someone is enough, so be empathetic. If possible, avoid having an underprivileged group explain to you why something is problematic. Do your own research or ask a more informed friend. See each person you meet as a teacher with valuable lessons.

7. **Dealing with trapped emotions** - Becoming informed, increasing your exposure to diversity, stepping away from discriminatory voices, and visualizing having positive experiences with people different than you will do a lot toward renegotiating any stories you might be telling yourself about a group of people. However, uprooting trapped emotions causing oppressive behaviors may also require emotional releases and regulating your nervous system before interacting with a group you find triggering. If you have an emotional response toward a marginalized or oppressed group, pause and investigate that feeling. Try to tune in with your body and ask yourself, "Is this feeling rational? Is there any evidence that I am in danger? How am I perpetuating discrimination, oppression, or stereotypes right now? Am I listening or am I trying to be right?" Perform emotional releases away from the people or cultures that trigger you as necessary (see Chapter 5). Speak to your inner selves about how a person's difference in appearance, habits, or language does not make them dangerous (see Chapter 10). Try using EMDR to integrate positive experiences and visualizations interacting with diversity. Consider creating or joining a group that supports you through this process, such as a men's group for detangling toxic masculinity and oppression against women.

8. **Regulating your energy** - Being around strangers, unfamiliar cultural practices, people you share very little with, or things that trigger

trapped emotions all can consume energy. As you may fear messing up or not knowing how to interact, you must mindfully focus and cannot be habitual with your words and actions. While initially doing this work putting yourself around more diverse populations, you may need to be aware of your energy and stress levels. This will allow you to have a neutral or good experience instead of one in which you become triggered into overwhelm or anger. While the goal is to eventually not feel drained or triggered while around certain types of bodies and personalities, it may be a gradual process getting there. As you learn the histories of different cultures and how to respectfully interact with them, the energy it takes to be around them will decrease. Consider reframing the words your inner critical parent says. For instance, instead of focusing on your incompatibilities, say to yourself, "I have something to learn here."

9. ***Practicing anti-oppression*** - Since the default culture in places like the United States of America is oppression, some writers like Ibram X. Kendi believe that you must be actively fighting for a better future in order for anyone to consider you anti-oppressive or anti-racist.[93] Practicing anti-oppression, inclusiveness, and making amends to oppressed people will especially help heal your own trapped emotions, shame, and guilt. In general, you can identify your privileges and speak up for or support people who lack the power and influence you have. For instance, men can support people of other genders, and White people can support Black people, Native Americans, and people of color. It is important though that this support is helpful and desired by a group. More ways of practicing anti-oppression are covered in Chapter 16.

You are going to make mistakes and sometimes be uncomfortable, and that is okay - you are making the world a more inclusive and equitable space. Know that you will never fully understand the suffering of a group less privileged than you experiences, but you can be an ally and use your privileges to make people feel more comfortable, respected, and supported toward an equitable future. However, recognize that even while you may have good intentions, your actions can still have harmful consequences for others. It is generally good to ask people what kind of support they would like, if any at all.

To become a safer person for oppressed communities, interactions with others **must always consider the trapped emotions that oppressed** groups have to certain actions, the history of oppression different groups have faced, and how to lift up oppressed populations with equitable solutions. The following are some general guidelines for interacting with traditionally underprivileged groups in the United States, but there are many more groups not covered here. However, this should act as a decent blueprint. These guidelines were developed through what I have read and heard explained how different groups want to be treated, but should not be considered absolute fact. Keep in mind that there is a lot of diversity within each group, so if someone asks to be treated differently, go with that instead!

1. ***General guidelines*** - Most of all, always listen to oppressed folks and believe them when they tell you about their feelings and experiences. Make room for their voices to be heard and feelings to be expressed. Hold back your reactivity and strong emotions until you can release and process away from oppressed communities. Talk to a person about things other than their race, gender, or oppression. Remember that experiencing power differentials can be triggering for some, so do what you can to ensure oppressed communities have decision-making and leadership power.[132Q] Anything that can help alleviate the financial strain historically experienced by many oppressed people is also good such as direct monetary donations, giving a discount, allowing free entrance to events, or buying from their businesses. Always respect their bodies, language, accents, and personal space. Understand that the rules you abide by may be inherently oppressive or impossible for certain people to follow, so try not being too angry when an oppressed group "breaks" your notion of right and wrong.
2. ***Black, Indigenous, people of color (BIPOC)*** - Learn about current and historical aggressions acted out against specific groups. In the United States, this includes but is not limited to, Black, Indigenous, Latinx, Arabian, and Asian people. Approach people who are from a different race or culture with an open heart and respectful friendliness. Never joke about their language, accent, name, culture, or times in which they were oppressed. Raise awareness about when the media inaccurately depicts these groups. Check in before using images, ideas, words, fashions, or sounds derived from their cultures. If you do, openly note which group of people those things are from. If you are selling goods that use aspects of a culture you do not belong to, you should stop and give money to that culture you are appropriating

from. Support affirmative action initiatives that help diversify spaces and make up for the institutionalized oppression that groups face. If you are a White person or from a historically oppressive group, be careful asking people of color, especially Black people, to do things for free - this can be quite triggering when White people have stolen so much from oppressed groups.
3. **_Indigenous peoples_** - Do not make art with designs and symbols belonging to Indigenous peoples. Do not wear culturally sensitive or spiritual items such as Native American headdresses. Know who originally inhabited the land you are currently residing on and how they were displaced. Include Indigenous peoples in conversations surrounding land use and conservation. Support their autonomy, land ownership, and past legal agreements which have been ignored or held up in court.
4. **_Women_** - Don't assume what women can or can't do physically or emotionally. Treating women like unfeeling objects by catcalling or staring at them is absolutely not okay. Do not assume that women want your attention just because you find them attractive. Ask for consent when seeking women to do emotional labor for you or to share space with you, especially if you are a man. Emotional labor involves listening to a person's emotions and difficulties, usually while holding back their own emotions. Ask for consent when initiating any kind of intimacy, and at any increased level of intimacy. If you do not know a woman well, do not comment on her body, and only compliment things that you know she intentionally controls like clothing and personality. Do not tell a woman to smile or be happy. Do not force women to be the ones responsible for contraception. Be empathetic and understanding around the emotional and physical changes that result from symptoms of PMS and periods. Support maternity leave and empower women to pursue careers traditionally dominated by men.
5. **_LGBTQ+_** - Respect their gender and sexual choices. Just because a person is not heterosexual does not mean they want to date you. Even if you have a different cultural understanding of gender, use a person's preferred pronouns. Ask for a person's preferred gender pronouns before assuming. Do not joke about a person's appearance or choice of clothing. Support people in pursuing their dreams, expressing emotions, or asserting themselves regardless of their chosen gender. Understand that a person can be born intersex, or both partially

male and female, and that the gender binary is a fairly recent invention.[103] Understand that many trans people know by the age of eight that they are trans and need space and support to explore it. Focus less on a person's gender or sex and more on their interests and personality. More about gender is covered in Section 15.9.
6. **Elderly people and people living with a disability** - Focus on what a person is capable of (a lot) rather than what they are not capable of. An important distinction is that people live with disabilities, but as a whole, they are not disabled. This empowers people in the many ways they are capable rather than being labeled as somehow broken or less than others. Do not assume a person wants help, and always ask before providing any kind of support. Try to host your events in spaces that have accessibility options for people with different physical needs.
7. **People you perceive as overweight** - Don't assume that a person's weight is simply determined based on what they eat or how much they exercise. Don't call people fat, overweight, or obese. Some people are working to reclaim fat as a neutral descriptor though. Food addiction is a thing but it is not your place to change a person's behaviors, especially as it is often based upon trapped emotions. Do not assume a person is unhealthy based on their weight.

Recognizing your own learned biases and lifting up everyone is essential to overcoming trapped emotions in society. You can make an effort to understand others' struggles, be compassionate to their hardships, purchase from marginalized business owners, be inviting, apologize when you say something offensive, and do your best to correct misconceptions and discriminatory language that you hear used by others. I'll discuss tactics to do so in Chapter 16. We all carry discriminatory beliefs about others, but remember that you are not your thoughts - you are your actions. Even if some of these actions might feel wrong to you, even if you feel triggered around certain types of bodies, you can still perform actions to correct the suffering in the world.

There are some gray areas in what is and is not considered discrimination. Similar to abuse, there is intentional and unintentional discrimination. There are also cultural differences such as what defines gender (I've counted four major parties in gender). Cultural beliefs are especially tricky because no one is technically wrong, although when those different beliefs interact, someone may be discriminated against and harmed. Even if your intent is well-meaning, it can still negatively impact a person and is not an excuse for ignoring the harm caused. In general, everyone is worthy of their basic human needs being met including sustenance, safety, love, empathy, rest, community, creativity, freedom, and purpose. While you don't have to believe what another culture does, you can do your best to respect them, especially if they are a traditionally underprivileged group.

15.6 Law Enforcement And Restorative Justice

Law enforcement in the United States is woefully problematic and ineffective. Rather than protecting people, the police have been largely responsible for protecting corporate interests by striking down labor movements and perpetuating the oppression of marginalized communities.[102] For a breakdown of many of the historical problems with policing, check out Kazu Haga's article titled, *Policing Isn't Working For Cops Either*. Resmaa Menakem discusses how to help heal the over-stressed and racist police forces of America in his book, *My Grandmother's Hands*. Resmaa provides several suggestions for law enforcement groups including self-care, community interaction, increased training, and transforming the police force altogether:

1. ***Self-care*** – Police should start the day with calming practices like meditation or yoga. Trauma therapy resources must be made available. The department should pay for regular massages for officers. Officers should be able to identify when they are becoming overwhelmed after particularly stressful encounters and take the rest of the day off or at least take a break.
2. ***Community interaction*** - Police should be interacting with members of the public as friendly allies rather than suspicious agitators. Mandatory interactive community meetups like those mentioned in the previous two sections will help law enforcement release some of the fear responses they have regarding diverse communities.
3. ***Increased training*** - Police in the USA are some of the least trained public officers in the world. Training must be increased to reflect the difficulty the duties of law enforcement encompass. Especially important to include would be self-care, mediation, and de-escalation tactics.
4. ***Transforming and defunding law enforcement*** - Abolishing the police and creating a new system of law enforcement is another option gaining momentum today. This is because the majority of policing activities are entirely meaningless as police do not prevent crime, they merely punish people who have been unfairly treated by

society. Study after study shows that providing basic social needs is far more effective at preventing crime than police are. Things like basic housing, food, and mental health services are much cheaper than increasing a police budget or keeping someone in prison. Police often argue they need more funding because of how dangerous criminals are, but funding social services would make violent crime much less likely and help protect the lives of police. Law enforcement should be protecting citizens and supporting the health of a community rather than attempting to change behaviors through ineffective punishments. Officers need to be held accountable for unjust acts, and laws that allow *qualified immunity* must be abolished. Qualified immunity allows government workers, including the police, to commit many crimes without punishment.

There are many activities that the police should not handle at all. For instance, those experiencing mental health crises and homelessness did not choose to be that way and typically do not need force or guns involved. Programs like White Bird's trained crisis support team, CAHOOTS, in Eugene, Oregon, offer an excellent alternative. People can call the unarmed CAHOOTS directly, or 911 will dispatch CAHOOTS, for mental health crises and conflicts related to people experiencing homelessness instead of the police.

Restorative justice and *transformative justice* solutions are needed to replace the current justice system that seeks to simply punish. Restorative justice works at the individual and communal levels to help heal both the victim of the crime and its perpetrator. This can greatly assist in healing trapped emotions. Transformative justice focuses on also fixing larger societal issues in which one group perpetuates harm against another. It takes into account living in a reality of poverty, the oppression of marginalized communities, lack of access to medical care, and various mental health struggles. Restorative and transformative justice may include things like:

- Publicly funded mental health asylums that treat patients with compassion
- Giving prisoners therapists
- Teaching prisoners skills to help them become functioning members of society rather than repeat offenders
- Having the victim of the crime and its perpetrator understand why the incident happened and caused harm, and mutually consent to a

method of resolving difficult feelings between parties, such as by making direct amends through volunteering, apologizing, or monetary reimbursement
- Ending the ineffective war on drugs and creating education and rehab programs for healthy substance use - the war on drugs was likely invented to criminalize Black people and anti-war leftists[135A]
- Abolishing private profit-driven prisons and solitary confinement
- Rewriting the 13th Amendment, which currently allows for the perpetuation of slavery in the form of prisons
- Unarmed security forces that handle things like speeding tickets and school disturbances
- Communities coming together to deal with crime in constructive ways like increasing access to nature, after-school activities, neighborhood watches, cleaning up trash, meal programs, housing for the homeless, and more art
- *Community defense programs* that allow community members to play a direct role in fighting oppression and supporting healthier ways of being
- Independent auditing of police departments that removes officers with problematic records
- Better wages and jobs for people to escape from poverty, one of the biggest factors that cause violent crime[167]
- More diversity in the field of law by giving financial aid to people of color for college[190]

15.7 Media

The majority of popular media is made by privileged people. News, fiction, and movies overwhelmingly lack diversity or discriminate against it. While we cannot necessarily expect people to represent cultures they are not a part of in their works, or to consume media which they do not relate to, we do need more diversity positively represented in media. This diversity helps normalize the different appearances, beliefs, and cultures. It is important that this media isn't just preaching about the woes of society or acting as social justice propaganda, we also need purely fun and engaging media - this will greatly increase the audience. We need:

- Writers and directors to cast diverse characters in their stories
- Writers and directors to be of a diverse background
- Having characters other than just White men who are smart and able

to save themselves
- Publishers of media to accept content from marginalized communities
- A variety of genders that are depicted as strong, intelligent, and capable while simultaneously not being sexually objectified
- To support marginalized communities in having the time and resources to create powerful works of art and to share their stories
- Characters who are played by people who actually represent the role in real life - Native Americans as Native Americans, trans people as trans people, and so on
- Healthy humor that avoids using teasing, sarcasm, or making fun of characters for their so-called defects or status as a marginalized character
- News that shares uplifting stories as well as unbiased accounts of current happenings - outlets like Democracy Now, Associated Press, BBC, New York Times, and NPR are decent at providing quality news but could probably do better too
- Media which highlights the accomplishments of oppressed communities throughout history, especially those accomplishments which are wrongly associated with White people.

Even if you release your trapped emotions toward certain groups, discriminatory energies may quickly return unless you get away from the voices that carry them. For instance, TV shows and movies often depict Black people as dangerous villains or support characters for the hero. Fashion magazines, pornography, and actors show primarily one body type. Gender norms are reinforced, and certain abilities are revered while others are demoralized. Individuals should become informed about how the media is impacting their beliefs and consider healthier alternatives. While it would be impossible to cut out all discriminatory media, there should be a balance. This helps expose the mind to a diversity of fellow community members and humanizes their existence. While it is best to remove these voices altogether, even just becoming aware of discriminatory forces will allow a person to not fall victim to subtle messaging.

Performing a *digital detox* like the one I described in Section 12.2 can also be quite powerful. Consider leaving your phone off, logging out of your social media accounts, or putting a pause on consuming media for a set period of time. I have found that steps like these make me immediately feel less isolated, be more mindful, and redirect those hours to healthier pursuits. Try it out for an hour a day to start, and then work your way up to checking in with the digital world just two or three times a day.

It can also be amazingly transformative when you exchange toxic media with work that uplifts and educates.[39,64] Consider consuming the media of people being grateful, positive, feminist, inclusive, diverse, communal, spiritually connected, and healthy. This will help rewire your brain to pursue these states as well.

15.8 Capitalism And Mutual Aid

Money is a useful tool backed by our belief in it – it eases the work of making transactions efficiently for any material object or service - just imagine a car dealership having to barter for every car it sold! However, almost any economy based on competitive material exchanges, rather than on the sharing of wealth, creates uneven distributions of power and harms the environment. This is especially true of capitalism.

The economic system and wealth of the United States were founded on slavery, stolen land, and the destruction of the environment. These practices continue today in prison labor (which is a form of slavery), wars to colonize foreign lands, the policing of labor movements to prevent common people from earning decent wages, as well as deadly environmental policies. Capitalism is based on the notion of infinite growth in a finite world. It is therefore impossible to maintain forever. As a competitive system, it guarantees that a certain percentage of the population will always be without jobs, food, and money, even as it demands more people have more jobs, more resources, more food, more robots, more houses, more attractiveness, more everything.

Since capitalism is purely profit-driven without ethical or moral standards, it especially exploits the labor of marginalized and impoverished communities. As can be seen in political lobbying efforts, one aspect of this exploitation is that businesses externalize as many costs as possible to the public, mostly to impoverished groups in the form of taxes and pollution. According to a worldwide study conducted by Oxfam in 2018, the 42 richest people control as much wealth as the 3.7 billion poorest. This is an obvious indication of a broken system that has been manipulated to strongly favor the rich. Poverty is created, it is typically not your fault and has little to do with how hardworking you are.

Perhaps a capitalist monetary system could work well under certain conditions, but as it stands, it is primarily a destructive force. The existence of franchises, corporations, the global market, certain laws and taxes, banks, and different skills being more monetarily valued than others causes money to be hoarded by a select few rather than used. Since money is a unit of exchange for almost any material good, hoarding money cuts down on the availability of everything people need to survive, including food, shelter, medical support, general well-being, and so on. This wouldn't be a big problem if working full-time for minimum wage (another form of exploitation) was enough to survive on, but that isn't the case in most cities, especially with a family.[3]

Since people have to work so much to survive, they do not have time to care about the world around them, including the environment or social justice causes. They also don't have money to afford ethical alternatives or take time off work to protest their situation, they're just trying to survive in the game. So what needs to happen?

- Creating a culture of sharing, gifting, and mutual support
- Establishing a living wage and ending things like tipping culture and devaluing certain jobs as less skilled
- Establishing more communal living, multiple families living together, and extended family living with a nuclear family
- Creating stronger union protections
- Promoting play and relaxation as a sign of success rather than working all the time
- Building more cooperative housing and businesses
- Creating and enforcing laws that limit the price of rent and prevent landlords from randomly evicting tenants
- Teaching children how to grow food and making it okay to have a garden instead of a lawn
- Turning housing into a public asset and ending the private housing market
- Increasing taxes on big businesses and corporations
- Ending the myriad of tax loopholes for high-earning individuals and businesses - it is contradictingly more expensive to survive when you are poor, and many laws exist to punish the poor
- Establishing limits on what a CEO and administration can earn compared to its employees
- Creating *right to repair* laws that force companies to make devices repairable by the buyer
- Increasing social welfare programs for food, education, and medical care
- Creating a *universal basic income*, especially as robots take over more jobs

- Providing better education in public schools and universities by teaching practical skills such as creativity, business, money management, and effective communication

Out of all of these, the easiest option is to create more community as explored in Chapter 14. However, many people are too independent to have community, live together, and share resources to drive down costs. There are also lots of laws that hold back communities from forming, such as limiting the number of people who can occupy a building or the number of buildings that can be built on a property. The culture and enforcement of independence may then be the greatest force to overcome in fixing many of society's problems, including income inequality.

Another option for disrupting capitalism is to focus on *mutual aid* projects. In the book *Mutual Aid*, Dean Spade explores how these projects create an alternative to the failing system of capitalism and create community-led change. They can take on many forms, like legal advocacy, handing out free food, supporting protesters, sex and race education, filling in potholes, and disaster preparation.[161] However, unlike many non-profit, charity, and social services, mutual aid programs are free and do not bar entry to anyone. They are based on solidarity, inclusion, anti-oppression, harm reduction, consensus, and meeting people where they are at. As a result, they can act much faster and more effectively than many government programs.

Often mutual aid is led by people who need or benefit from the services, instead of administrators who are creating policies without truly understanding the problems being dealt with. Mutual aid shows what a society led by its citizens could look like. Effective groups are sometimes used as models for government programs, but these programs usually limit the inclusiveness found in true mutual aid spaces. Explore ways in which the local, state, or federal government is failing your community, and how people can come together to make it better. You can further explore this topic in the podcast *It Could Happen Here* with Robert Evans.

15.9 Gender

Gender has several definitions and varies quite a lot depending on which culture you are interacting with. In the mainstream it is a concept that rules how a person is supposed to dress and act based on their perceived biological sex. This is harmful on multiple levels. For men, mainstream gender norms may dictate that:

- Grieving and crying are signs of weakness
- Addressing disagreement with anger or violence is okay
- Individuality and workaholism are signs of success
- You must maintain an outward perception of strength and dominance
- Certain jobs are more masculine than others, especially physical labor, science, and politics
- You should earn more and have a higher position than your partner
- You should be able to do things alone
- You can be loud and talk over people freely
- It is okay to blame others and ignore responsibility in a disagreement
- You are expected to initiate conversation and romance with women
- Touch between men is inappropriate unless you are gay
- Intimacy can only be sexual
- It is okay to objectify women as sexual items without a will of their own
- You find submissiveness attractive
- You find smart, independent, opinionated, and empowered women unattractive
- Confidence equates to being right

Women have made huge strides in the past century to change what mainstream gender norms expect of them. Some of these are still common however and include:

- You should be caring, submissive, small, pleasant, and quiet
- You are supposed to do emotional labor for others
- Being partnered and having children are signs of success
- Certain jobs are more feminine than others, especially caregiving and many support roles
- You are considered too emotional to be professional or authoritative in positions of power
- You are expected to be uneducated or incapable of understanding certain things
- You should be weak and require help
- You should not express anger, strong opinions, or basic needs
- You should not do work or have interests considered masculine, but only be a housewife or do service work
- You should take responsibility for the errors of others

- You are supposed to earn less in a relationship
- You are supposed to dress in a way that may involve very uncomfortable clothing or completely contradicting characteristics
- You should be fit, thin, and curvy
- You are supposed to survive in a world where many technologies and medical treatments are only tested on men - read *Invisible Women* by Caroline Criado Perez
- You are expected to pleasure others without necessarily getting pleasure in return
- You find forwardness, strength, and dominance attractive
- You find emotionally intelligent and more feminine men unattractive

Mainstream gender norms are slowly opening up more for trans, intersex, and nonbinary people, but these groups continue to face immense discrimination, derogatory language, and violence. These norms dictate that:

- You conform to a gender within the gender binary
- You conform to the gender that most closely matches your perceived biological sex through physical appearance, voice, or clothing
- You conform to your sex or gender assigned at birth
- You have reproductive parts or only have one type of reproductive part
- You comply with what others consider your "correct" gender
- You not use public bathrooms, changing rooms, lockers, or other gendered facilities
- You not attend gendered events such as a women's book club even if you identify as a woman
- You explicitly state your gender to people who are uncertain
- The medical community does not have to learn how to address your needs
- You are not allowed gender-affirming support through insurance
- You accept the various ways that people discriminate against you
- People can discuss or share your sexual or gender identity without your consent

Trans, non-binary, and intersex individuals are expected to comply with these standards mentally and physically, making it nearly impossible to find acceptance in public, at the workplace, in family, or when seeking medical assistance. Gender binary norms also put unrealistic standards on people who cannot or do not want to adhere to the gender binary. For instance, many women cannot change their physical appearance except through very expensive surgeries or unhealthy diets. Women also are taught not to express anger so may have trouble protesting against unjust acts, blaming perpetrators, or releasing trapped emotions. Similarly, since men are not supposed to grieve or communicate nonviolently, they end up trapping more and more emotions that later erupt in unhealthy ways. This perpetuates violence and rape culture. The idea that people must be in a relationship or marry to be successful and happy also hurts everyone.

Gender binary norms create terrible confusion, reinforce abusive behaviors, and increase dissatisfaction. If you grew up not knowing an alternative, the stress created by being forced into a gender may be invisible to you, but understand that gender norms negatively impact everyone, especially nonbinary and trans people. That said, people also benefit from these roles, primarily men and to a lesser extent stereotypically attractive women. As these groups often utilize their privileges to perpetuate the gender binary and succeed more easily in life, the gender binary continues. That said, even people who do not benefit from gender norms may still consciously or unconsciously reinforce them including women, nonbinary, and trans people. Among other things, these norms are reinforced in parenting, media, toys, schools, bathrooms, fashion, workplaces, relationships, and forcing surgeries on intersex children.[103]

There are an infinite number of ways to disrupt gender norms, but there are five main tactics making headway:

1. Expanding what gender looks like and increasing the number of genders available to choose from. Children should be empowered to decide rather than be forced to comply with particular toys, clothing, hobbies, colors, names, bathrooms, or genders.
2. Abolishing gender, or at least compulsory gender, and simply accepting a person, whatever they look or behave like - so long as it is respectful. This may also involve defining relationship dynamics that are co-created between partners rather than relying on standards established by default monogamy as explored in Section 14.2.
3. Increasing the rights, protections, medical understanding, employment options, and political representation of women, trans, and nonbinary people.
4. Empowering people other than cisgender men to speak up for their needs, say no, and take on jobs or positions of power traditionally

reserved for cisgender men. This of course has to be balanced with the dangers that women, trans, intersex, and nonbinary people sometimes face when expressing their authentic selves. The feelings of love, acceptance, and safety should not be contingent on having to say yes to emotional labor, relationships, or sex.
5. Educating men about toxic masculinity and teaching them healthier and happier ways of being a man, such as asking for consent, being vulnerable, and crying. It especially helps to teach men about how "being a man" actually forces them to give up a lot of power in terms of living in fear of what they are allowed or not allowed to do. As being a cisgender man comes with the most privilege within these issues, cisgender men should try to be proactive in educating themselves and creating space and safety for others.

15.10 Good Parenting

According to Dr. Bessel Van Der Kolk, not a child's IQ, neurotype, personality at birth, nor mom's personality predict serious behavioral problems in adulthood.[97AZ] The only predictor is how the parents interacted with their child. Destructive parenting is pervasive in society and many cultural norms create trapped emotions in children. These include things like the nuclear family system, verbal and physical abuse being normalized, and parents who are often unavailable in dissociative substances or work. Your child will reflect what they experience in their environment, especially from your actions.

Look at yourself before you blame the child for how they are acting. According to John Gottman in his book, *Raising An Emotionally Intelligent Child*, the most important factor in raising a healthy child is empathetically acknowledging a child's emotions while simultaneously correcting bad or dangerous behaviors and instilling healthy lessons on how to navigate the world. This does not mean you always give your child what they want, but rather you acknowledge their emotions as valid and explain why it has to be another way. Besides that, children need several specific things to grow up mentally healthy:

1. Having lots of safe and consensual touch. While touch should never be forced, more touch from trusted people is typically good for children.
2. Having plenty of physical play time with others and less screen time.
3. Having a good school environment with lots of recess time, small class sizes, and creative outlets. This is especially important for neuro-

divergent children who may need special resources to succeed and have their strengths celebrated. If your child is not liking school, they are probably not getting the right encouragement or support. Consider homeschooling networks, Waldorf schools, outdoor schools, and alternative schools. Teachers should be able to identify symptoms of trapped emotions in their students so as to work with them instead of punishing them.

4. Experiencing vibrant environments with lots of art, creative supplies, and educational toys.
5. Having opinions respected and the ability to say no. Try making decisions together.
6. Being treated as intelligent and capable. Avoid overparenting or controlling behaviors and let children figure things out on their own. Balance safety with independent exploration. Children are really smart, especially if you treat them like it from a young age. Hold back from reacting to your anxiety, children will let you know when they need help.
7. Having a caregiver that mirrors their joy and delight.
8. Never being lied to. Give children the specific reasons and consequences of certain actions like not brushing their teeth or having unprotected sex. Be honest with your feelings, but also do not require them to be adults or take on parental roles for you.
9. Witnessing healthy behaviors and stable relationships to mirror from their caregiver.
10. Being taught how to identify emotions and how to talk about them.
11. Being given small tasks to help out, no matter how slow it makes your life.
12. Having an environment free from alcohol or people getting drunk. Alcohol can be quite damaging by making parents inconsistent with their personalities.
13. Being provided with more positive reinforcement than negative reinforcement. Studies have shown that children given lots of positive reinforcement and the resources to succeed perform better in all areas of life.[178]
14. Having lots of quality time with their caregiver. Address your addictions to substances like alcohol, work, or media that replaces this quality time or makes you dissociate away from your child. Ideally, children have at least one parent or co-parent around at all times in the first few years of their life. This makes having paternity leave

really important at your job.
15. Having a curious parent. Inquire about what is going on with your child, do not just react harshly or tell them what you believe.
16. Having consistency with their environments, social times, and friends. Moving is really hard on children.
17. Having playmates and interaction with strangers.
18. Having the ability to explore curiosities and have questions respectfully answered.
19. Having healthy, consistent, and reasonable rules such as around addictive substances, safety from physical danger, and how to treat others.
20. Having caregivers that explain their reasoning, especially when not allowing certain behaviors. Nonviolent communication (NVC) as covered in Chapter 8 is a great tool.
21. Having interactions that exhibit patience, forgiveness, apology, and empathy.
22. Being instilled with a sense of awe and spiritual connectedness, especially through exploration of nature, science, and the power of possibility. Outdoor, alternative, and Waldorf Schools are good at teaching these qualities.
23. Learning delayed gratification.
24. Learning nonviolence and being rewarded by practicing it at home and school. Provide a special treat to the child at the end of the semester if there are no physical confrontations during that time.[55]
25. Having as many secure attachments as possible, most likely in extended family.
26. Learning healthy angering and crying. The world is not always fair, and we do not always get what we want, and that is okay. Let your child release their frustrations.
27. Having transitions celebrated. Create a ritual or party to help smooth big changes such as sleeping in their very own room or entering into a new school.
28. Having parents that regularly nourish themselves and release pent-up emotions in healthy ways. Tell your child if you are having a hard day, do not take it out on them.
29. Having a safe home environment. Even if divorce is also hard on children, leaving verbal or physical abuse is generally better for the child.[132H]
30. Having a consistent home environment. Be very careful when dating

and introducing a new partner to a child, especially when that partner takes your attention away from the child.[132G]

This all said, we don't live in an ideal world. Capitalism and modern society often force us to neglect those we care about the most. You may be dealing with a lot of trapped emotions from your past, or are a single parent who can't be around much. Children can survive through a lot though. They are resilient, smart, and capable. Do your best, and communicate what's going on for you. They'll be okay, but if your situation changes, you might be able to undo some of the pain your children have experienced. Understand that this will take time though. The contents of this book are not meant for treating the trapped emotions in children, but consider reading *Trauma-Proofing Your Kids* by Maggie Kline and Peter Levine or *What Happened to You?* by Dr. Bruce D. Perry and Oprah Winfrey to help address their suffering.

Several societal changes would also make children much healthier. These include requiring businesses to offer at least several months of paid time off for parents, establishing a living wage that allows just one parent to work, improving health insurance, reducing the number of hours people work, relying on medications less, increasing access to after-school programs, increasing children's access to school therapists, making all forms of physical punishment illegal, reducing or eliminating homework, making contraception universally available for everyone, federally legalizing abortion, and increasing the amount of time that is spent engaging in creativity and play at school. Transforming society also starts with raising children with healthier ways of being. I hope that in the coming years, more and more schools will implement programs discussing self-care, consent, communication, healthy relationships, and dealing with trapped emotions.

15.11 Healing The Natural World

Part of healing humanity requires that we also heal the natural world because, without it, we are not going to last long. Having access to nature also has numerous benefits for your health, especially your mental health. While some advances in technology could help make things better, these are mostly distractions from the solutions that we already have. For instance:

- Ending consumerist culture
- Making technologies more easily repairable and creating "right-to-repair laws"
- Making things more easily recyclable and compostable

- Creating better access to recycling and composting programs
- Making products more durable
- Localizing industries and buying local
- Requiring corporations and big businesses to put a portion of their funds into ecological restoration and community development
- Banning lawns and supporting gardens with biodiversity
- Teaching children the importance of healthy biodiversity and their part in natural systems that take place on Earth
- Funding more public transit, especially busses
- Making cities more bikeable and walkable
- Utilizing remote work and video conferencing more
- Building houses and apartments so that they are naturally heated and cooled
- Decreasing the population with better access to birth control and contraception for all sexes
- Reducing the amount of meat and dairy which is consumed and replacing it with more fruits, nuts, vegetables, and insects
- Creating stricter laws for logging old-growth or around riparian areas

For the most part, I believe that bigger change is necessary to avoid a climate crisis. It is generally not healthy or productive to blame individuals for society's problems. Rather, governments, businesses, and cultures are responsible for creating new systems to fix ecological damage. More than anything we need people advocating for change at every level of society, especially toward those with power to do so.

15.12 Culture

Culture is a complicated topic to address. On one hand, culture is beautiful, delicious, and interesting. It provides us with so many insights seeing the cultures of others, and team diversity has been shown to improve the quality of projects.[48] However, culture has also become this untouchable element of personality. "It is just my culture", or "This is the way we do things around here," do not allow for personal accountability. It masks the elements of a culture that cause division, hatred, and trapped emotions to proliferate in everyday life. Things like abusive masculinity, alcoholism, workaholism, discrimination, and aggression are all supported by cultures. Children are then expected to follow a culture without question, and people are shamed for exploring activities or beliefs that fall outside the group identity, thus perpetuating any problematic aspects of the culture.

This is further complicated when two or more cultures interact or mix together, bringing into question the ethics, beliefs, and intellectual property of each group. There are many strong opinions on how to handle this mixing, and I personally do not have any kind of solid answers other than those that help move towards a more equitable, kind, and free world. In the next chapter, I will discuss how to create change within different cultures, but in the meantime, some healthy cultural characteristics to adopt include:

- Supporting local businesses
- Creating community
- Allowing for radical self-expression and exploring new ideas and activities
- Being touch positive and practicing consent
- Normalizing platonic touch like hugging and cuddling with friends and family
- Understanding that the placebo effect impacts whole cultures and that you can lift people up with empowering language in what it means to be a nation, race, gender, and so on
- Turning your property into a *land trust* and designating rent and housing sales limits
- Using healthy communication to assert boundaries, express feelings, and ask for your needs to be met
- Allowing people to express their cultural styles like hair and clothing anywhere, including professional settings
- Protecting people with less privilege than you
- Creating mixed-age communities and including elderly people in activities more
- Smiling at and saying hello to strangers
- Exposing and celebrating the contributions to society made by various oppressed communities rather than allowing White people and men to erase or take credit for those actions
- Supporting a person from any background to explore an activity like camping or enjoying a musical genre, so long as that activity does not disrespect, take money away from, or otherwise harm an oppressed community
- Practicing harm reduction with drug usage – see Section 12.2 and <https://harmreduction.org/>
- Being a healthy role model for children and teaching them about basic self-care

- Practicing the principles of *permaculture* and *solar punk* which both create powerful options for a sustainable and positive future - check them out online
- Sharing your resources and practicing *mutual aid*
- Working through your trapped emotions
- Deconstructing unhealthy gender norms that you practice or expect of others
- Empowering traditionally marginalized voices
- Paying reparations to communities for culturally appropriated or stolen intellectual property like music, clothing, fine art, and medicine
- Raising up the voices of marginalized groups to give them more political power
- Creating more spaces with nature and greenery

You might be asking yourself, but how do we implement all these changes in society? For the majority of people, at least some of their suffering is institutionalized by culture and the government. So long as systems are in place that proliferate things like racism, ableism, income inequality, and gender norms, victims will feel unsafe and be unable to fully release their trapped emotions. This is why many find themselves, in one way or another, becoming changemakers as explored in Chapter 16.

***

Chapter Reflections

1. How does discrimination show up in your community?
2. How do people perpetuate discrimination in your peer group, workplace, city, and state?
3. What can you do to support oppressed individuals or communities in your area?
4. What is the history of discriminatory practices in your family, city, state, and nation?
5. In what ways do you discriminate against others?
6. What are your privileges?
7. What support groups, focus groups, or book clubs could you join or create to help dismantle the oppression you practice?
8. In what ways would supporting anti-oppression causes also benefit you?

9. How can you start being more inclusive?
10. What do you find frightening about unfamiliar things?
11. In what ways have you practiced performative allyship?
12. How can you help your community group, workplace, or church practice anti-oppression and become more diverse?
13. In which ways do you associate a person's appearance with their personality and interests?
14. Which appearances have you established as those which you will not get along with and what led you to this belief?
15. How can you create better representation and safety for your culture, race, or gender within an activity such as hiking, rock climbing, yoga, or meditation?
16. How can you share your culture through celebration?
17. What are some interests you have avoided developing because of how it is seen as a White person thing or attached to a specific gender?
18. How can you help improve your personal and your community's cultural intelligence?
19. What social services would help mitigate the need for law enforcement in your city?
20. Does your police force do any activities to help them have positive experiences around diverse populations or the community that they are serving?
21. Does your police force integrate any activities into their work that helps regulate their nervous systems and stay calm?
22. Which city counselors are giving money to law enforcement instead of social services?
23. What harmful narratives or stereotypes are told in the media you consume?
24. What harmful narratives do you perpetuate and which groups do you exclude in the media that you create?
25. In what ways can you localize, rely on community and cooperation more, and make money less important in your life?
26. In what ways is your local, state, or federal government failing, and could a mutual aid project help fix their failings?
27. In what ways do you perpetuate gender stereotypes?
28. What activities or personality traits have you developed or avoided due to your gender or sex assigned at birth?
29. In what ways can you help support more expressions of gender?
30. In what ways has your parenting or caregiving been harmful to chil-

dren?
31. In what ways can you practice better parenting and caregiving to children?
32. How does your culture perpetuate discrimination?
33. What are healthier things that your culture could stand for?

Chapter 16

Becoming A Changemaker

16.1 Effective Change In Grassroots And Mass Movements, 16.2 Reminders For Activists, 16.3 Communication For Activists, 16.4 Persuasion, 16.5 Beyond Blame, Victimhood, And Cancel Culture

Changing your environment for the better may require creating, destroying, or reimagining certain cultures, laws, economic systems, corporations, or governments. I don't care if you're five or a hundred years old, you can impact the world for the better. Chapter 15 introduced many aspects of a healthier society, but then what are strategies for demanding and implementing those changes?

Changemakers can take on many forms including volunteers, voters, or rebels against cultural norms. These are examples of *activists* and can provide a lot of meaning and community in life. The following sections introduce many reminders for creating effective change with language and psychology. This is an introductory guide and other books will give more specifics to activist tactics such as *Healing Resistance* by Kazu Haga, *Emergent Strategy* by Adrienne Maree Brown, *My Grandmother's Hands* by Resmaa Menakem, *The Body Is Not An Apology* by Sonya Renee Taylor, and *Coming Back To Life* by Joanna Macy and Molly Young Brown.

It is important to acknowledge that many marginalized and oppressed people feel forced into activism, especially if they are one of the few people belonging to a particular demographic in an area. Even though this can create strong feelings of anger and unfairness, living a normal life may feel impossible or, at least, unethical. However, it should be known that self-care and being your authentic self is also a radical form of activism.

You might be surprised how taking care of yourself can uplift others and make you more effective in creating change. Knowing when you are overwhelmed, taking on too much, or just needing a break is powerful. Systemic forms of discrimination and environmental destruction are huge problems to tackle that will take many years and many hands to solve. You do not always need to speak up, take on leadership roles, or represent marginalized groups. You have the right to rest, have fun, take care of your family, and improve your personal life. When you let go of trying to control the state of the world, you can give yourself space to create safety and heal. This rest is still resistance because when you heal, it helps those around you heal as well.

Now I want to be careful here, while some people feel forced into activism, many others simply feel unfamiliar or uncomfortable with it. As previously explored in Chapter 15, being of service to society and the natural world are an essential part of healing, especially as it involves devotion to something greater than your personal problems and connecting with a community of passionate minds. Even more importantly, it connects you to the world which you are intricately a part of. The pain of others and the destruction of the natural world are impacting you, your friends, and your descendants. If you do not recognize the impact these things have had on your life, please see Chapter 15 about what is possible.

This does not mean you have to devote your entire life to activism or deprive yourself of the things that you love in life. While we do need people working at changing every level of society, very small shifts in action can have benefits that ripple out in profound ways. For instance, choosing in yourself to end a pattern of addiction or abuse your family has perpetuated for generations. Even just smiling at and saying hello to strangers can be powerful.

Some people do have more power to support the greater good than others and help those with less privilege. Again, focusing on your self-care can be a radical form of activism, so know where you are at in your healing journey. Especially if you have extra needs with your physical or mental health, or safety concerns from being part of an oppressed community, it is okay to advocate for others to do the work.

16.1 Effective Change In Grassroots And Mass Movements

Some forms of activism can be split into actions that feel good at an ethical or spiritual level, and actions that work to create broader change. Many potential changemakers feel they are being effective by only doing things that personally feel good. For instance, recycling or eating organic food. These are not necessarily creating real change when you realize that most plastic is not recyclable, organic food is not necessarily sustainable, and many people cannot afford "ethical" alternatives. Learn about some of the false information you have been fed, and direct your anger at the real source of social woes. You have to consider that the people in power will do almost anything to secure more power to dictate the lives of you, your loved ones, and oppressed communities. Can you become inspired by the pure desire to uplift people or save life on Earth? What are you willing to do?

Activists who are only willing to take actions that feel good or pursue instant gratification are limited in their ability to create broad change. Taken to an extreme, you could live separated from civilization on your off-grid farm and argue that you are living in harmony with nature, but your ability to influence people, politics, and businesses will be extremely limited. In other words, you could be 100% ethical and sustainable in isolation, or you could help a city full of people be 1% better in these areas.

You need to be practical with the dollars you are spending and the activities you are bringing into or cutting out of your life. Is not owning a car going to destroy the automotive industry in the United States where there is very bad public transit, or is it just going to slow down your ability to take action? Think bigger. Direct your activism at what is effective and allows you to do more. How can you create direct and large-scale change? What do people need? Remember that you are a culture trying to spread your beliefs by transforming or destroying other cultures. Don't try to sugarcoat it, how can you do this effectively?

No one is perfect, and in today's globalized world, almost anything you do will be hurtful to someone or something. Depriving yourself of everything that causes suffering in the world will prevent you from working effectively or having as great of a reach. What can you do to achieve real success? Consider healing your emotional wounds, starting a corporation, organizing a protest, creating a new community, learning how to use the tools your opposition uses, or volunteering with existing activist groups. Just be sure you are taking care of yourself and still having fun - you are human after all.

What is actually useful? Is talking badly about the police creating change? Or would collecting funding to create an alternative to the police like White Bird's *CAHOOTS* be better? Many social problems are actually design problems. That is, the ease of changing behaviors drastically increases when the correct technique or technology is applied. These techniques and technologies may already exist, need to be implemented in unique ways, or must be newly created. What are you personally willing to do to create a happier and more beautiful world? Here are some ideas:

1. Make sure that your movement is actually creating change by implementing randomized controlled trials to test the impact you are hav-

ing. Methods for doing so are highlighted by the 2019 Nobel Prize winners in economics, who have shown which methods of fighting poverty are effective and which are not.[230]
2. Instead of using technical terminology from the social justice lexicon, state what is actually going on such as an unmet need or trapped emotion being triggered.
3. Take on a leadership position, even if you feel too shy or have been told your entire life that you can only support others. Many oppressed communities are often made to believe that they are powerless, but are actually quite capable and have a long history of leading others in creating change.
4. Connect online. Talk about your story on social media, and share viable and proven alternatives to people promoting oppressive ideologies. Normalize your existence as a human being with feelings, needs, and fun hobbies. Create hashtag movements that connect people together around an activity, such as the previously mentioned Black folks birding and enjoying nature. Find common ground with people in the arts and sciences by talking about music or interesting discoveries.
5. Read Kazu Haga's book, *Healing Resistance* for a great introduction to nonviolent action as taught by Martin Luther King Jr. You need to learn how to communicate with people you disagree with as covered in Section 16.3 and previously in Chapter 8.
6. Understand your opposition, listen to their news, and be able to determine how those ideas came to be. Identify what basic needs are lacking, which ideas are rooted in misunderstandings, and which ideas have some reason to them. What kinds of trapped emotions are perpetuating their behaviors? Parental upbringing, media consumption, religious beliefs, and political affiliation are some of the most prominent reasons to explain behaviors. These behaviors typically appear as basic needs that people are missing or fear missing, especially community and safety. They may also involve fears around lacking more basic things like food. How can you assure people that their basic needs will be met? Are you addressing the correct problem?
7. Expose cultures to more diversity and create positive associations with that diversity.
8. Educate younger audiences by speaking at schools.
9. Petition for protective laws or work as a canvasser collecting signa-

tures for reforms.
10. Build community among neighbors and marginalized communities.
11. Since communal dialogues are often reinforced online, laws need to be created that call out misinformation and hate speech. Even more, algorithms need to be changed to prevent a person's biases from being reflected in their social media feeds and search queries.
12. Build mutual aid projects that support your community or city at a grassroots level. Provide the care, services, and goods you need through each other such as food and education. Create your ideal world within the ten city blocks immediately surrounding you. This can deeply inspire other people to create similar changes within their neighborhoods, or for a city or state to adopt your model.
13. Vote at the local, state, and national levels.
14. Implement voting reform, especially with *Score Then Automatic Runoff* (STAR) voting. See <www.starvoting.us>.
15. I've noticed a trend in leftist activism focusing almost exclusively at the local, micro, or grassroots levels. While this is important and feels good, we also need people who are willing to be politicians, start big businesses, and grow grassroot models into mass movements across the nation. Sometimes the effort to create change is less comfortable or requires more professional skills than one might like it to. However, you can do a lot when gaining positions of power at a monetary, business, or political level. Consider reading about the stories behind the *Patagonia* clothing company, *Ocean Cleanup*, or *Optimism Brewing Company*.
16. Teach workshops in schools or convince a school to adopt principles like nonviolence and reward that behavior.[55]
17. Demand money be redirected from the police force to social services.
18. Donate a percentage of your income to activist causes.
19. Use positivity, humor, facts, and empathy to help people question the status quo. In other words, whenever possible, be likable, avoid expressing anger, and never act like you're better than another person.
20. Identify the stories held by a neighborhood, culture, community, state, or nation, especially the ones about themselves. Work on transforming those stories into something more empowering. For instance, turn oppressors into people who support those in need, or a dangerous neighborhood into one that supports creativity and the arts.
21. Make it fun with community, food, art, and music. Joy is resistance.

22. Use the principle of cost, care, and convenience. Does it save them money? Do they care about it at a moral, ethical, or emotional level? Does it make their life easier or save them money? Solutions that meet at least two of these three factors will have a much greater chance of success. This is why actions like striking are so effective.
23. Connect your mission directly to how it impacts the individual(s) you are attempting to change – such as with the cost, care, and convenience just mentioned.
24. Organize a strike, the bigger the better. This is one of the most effective tactics as money is the most important thing to businesses and the government. Support people striking with food, money, childcare, and other basic needs.
25. Vote with your dollars by buying from ethical or local sources, or by creating an awareness campaign for people to stop purchasing a specific product.
26. Use direct action tactics such as protesting, blockades, and sit-ins to create awareness, gather support, and make time for legal processes to create institutional changes. Be sure you are prepared for repercussions though - actions like these often lead to exposing police brutality and governmental corruption bought by corporate dollars.
27. Become a lawyer to support activist causes or join a firm that specializes in protecting activists. Check out the *Civil Liberties Defense Center* at <https://cldc.org/>.

Some of these tactics are easier than others. Success in navigating the complex obstacles that may arise could require specific training or practice.[55] Most activists never take the time to learn basic human psychology, communication tactics, or marketing. These topics will immensely help your causes. It is much easier to react appropriately when techniques become habitual or you have roleplayed how to overcome obstacles. The next sections share some of these tools.

16.2 Reminders For Activists

I want to make several things clear:

1. All cultures are made up of traditions and opinions. There is no absolute right and wrong or good and evil, only the subjective idea of what you personally believe to be true. This creates your reality, and everyone's reality is true for them. As an activist, you are working to

create new cultural possibilities, destroy other cultures whose reality contradicts your own reality, or at least force disagreeable cultures to respect your own culture.
2. Everything you attempt to change involves people with trapped emotions. This is most often seen in people becoming defensive. As soon as a person becomes defensive, you often have either reinforced their problematic beliefs or shut them off from being reasoned with.
3. People often don't give a hoot about you or your morals, they care about their basic needs being met and their culture and community being respected.
4. No one has the exact same privileges, mental health, and physical ability as you do. Do not force too much work on others, and check in with how your comrades are doing.
5. Avoid strategizing as if your opposition has the same neurotype, ability, or intelligence as you do. For instance, some people genetically are more fearful of unfamiliar things, or cannot experience empathy as easily as others. You have to meet people where they are right now.
6. Changing ideologies takes time, so try not to take it personally. A common assumption activists make is that their strong emotions toward a cause will be shared by everyone else. They believe this to the extent that they think yelling or aggressively attacking others will win allies. What these activists forget is that it took themselves a very long time to arrive at their current set of beliefs. Perhaps it was growing up in a certain environment such as the forest or city. Perhaps it was being the black sheep within a family. Perhaps it was facing oppression growing up. Whatever it was, realize that convincing people that your movement is worthwhile is an involved task and takes time.
7. Power structures still exist within activist communities and oppressed groups. Make sure you are leaving space for people with less privilege to speak, lead, and make decisions. For instance, if you are part of a Black mutual aid group and are a Black cisgender man, help raise up the voices of women, trans people, and non-binary people.
8. Voting and city governance works, more or less, but you also cannot rely on the government to implement certain changes. A healthy world will only come about by working inside and outside of existing systems. Without some form of external pressure, you cannot expect the government to create the changes that society needs, nor society to create the changes that individuals need. Mass movements and

grassroot campaigns are necessary to create a healthier world, and must mutually support each other. Grassroot campaigns have a lot of power to create change but often suffer from never spreading their ideas beyond a small area. Leaders and volunteers need to think about the big and small picture of a movement. For instance, a new social service could team up with a university to track how their services impact the city.

16.3 Communication For Activists

When enough people speak out aggressively against an action, or laws are made to protect marginalized groups, it may silence offenders, but it often does not change their inherent beliefs or trapped emotions. Sometimes this is the best that can be done, and is especially useful for emerging marginalized groups as they establish their existence and ability to fight back. However, it is not ideal, because it reinforces the trapped emotions in the opposition. That is, they will still pass along beliefs to their children and community, and continue to vote the same. Therefore, creating healthy dialogues and communicating through conflict is necessary.

Most everyone is just trying to get by. Everyone has the same basic needs, no matter what their upbringing, politics, or race are. Relating your vision of the world to those basic needs is one of the most powerful ways of speaking to any culture or personality type. Challenge yourself to have empathy and think about what unmet needs you and the person you are communicating with have before speaking. What do you have in common? Most of all, avoid creating stereotypes for groups. It only alienates people from one another and reinforces those behaviors.

Responding with violent communication may sometimes be beneficial when you are attacked by someone. While violent communication is not ideal, remaining silent to injustices creates no change. Responding violently may be your only option when there is little time between standing up for yourself and never seeing a person again. A verbally violent rebuttal more than anything gives your ego a boost (though can also make you feel worse), and may also make a definitive awareness that an action or phrase was problematic. However, this is very dependent upon how the perpetrator communicates and thinks. While violence may sometimes create change, it can never build or repair relationships.[55]

That is why I highly suggest learning nonviolent communication because it tries to create openness and dialogues to reach understanding between people. It also forces you to slow down and think about how you are speaking before possibly making a violent situation even more violent. See Chapter 8. Beyond what was previously mentioned in the basics, here are some general suggestions for communicating as an activist:

1. Regulate your nervous system before speaking. This is especially important as too often people act out their triggers within activist spaces through infighting, disagreements, cancel culture, and anger. Regulating your nervous system therefore is not just for you, it helps your cause succeed by staying together, focusing on solutions, and preventing members from burning out or developing trapped emotions to activism. Even if you haven't fully dealt with your trapped emotions, it is essential that you understand how your behaviors are potentially triggering others and making a situation worse.
2. Similarly, regulate the nervous system of your opposition before arguing your side. You must calm your opponent down and establish a neutral or safe-feeling relationship with them before they can listen to you.[132R] Saying something mean or defensive only acts to further push them away from processing rationally or being able to connect with their rationality and narrative memory.
3. Be willing to meet in the middle. While assimilation is easy for younger people, sometimes the best you can do for older audiences is to agree that you're not going to talk about it. Small transformations are still big victories and may be the start of larger changes over time. Remember that you do not need to prove a person wrong to reach a place of healthy repair or respect.
4. Call people in instead of out. Start a conversation and express curiosity about a person's ideas. Ask questions and listen. Use nonviolent communication. Express your own ideas only once you've shown respect to the person's intelligence and emotions. "I'm curious where you learned that from since I've heard otherwise from a few sources." Yelling, seeking revenge, or speaking with hatred, rarely, if ever, convinces a person that they are wrong. These forms of violent communication tend to worsen the mood of both parties and breed thoughts of revenge and feelings of anger.
5. Avoid using technical or judgmental terminology that is difficult to explain or insults a person until later on in a conversation. These include words like 'racist' or 'sexist'. Instead speak from your personal needs, feelings, and experiences. You can introduce technical language to someone later on in a conflict, but doing so immediately is

likely to raise their defensiveness or cause confusion. You're trying to build a relationship instead of an enemy. Technical language is important for spreading cultural ideas, but remember that many words like racism, gender, anarchism, feminism, and so forth have entire books written on them with a variety of different perspectives. Expecting non-allies to understand the meaning of these terms can be very hurtful to your cause.

6. Conflict within groups is inevitable, so learn how to mediate conflicts with the tools shared in Chapter 8. This said, all groups should have membership termination policies that kick out toxic people who drag everyone down. It is almost always better to remove people who hurt the emotional well-being of a group than to put up with their behaviors. Not everyone works well together, and that is okay.

7. Disagreeing actually makes a person feel emotionally stronger, likely because affirming one's own beliefs creates a surge in dopamine.[182,69] Therefore, we often ignore others even if it's good advice. A person who enters into an argument with you or makes statements with anger or violence often must first be calmed down and mediated with to listen to your side.

8. The acceptance of information from others will greatly increase if you are respecting their culture and speaking their language. This language includes all aspects of a person, including their tone of voice, word choice, fashion, gender, body motions, weight, skin color, culture, job, place of dwelling, and beliefs. That means it might be useful having a person of privilege, someone religious, or a farmer making statements on behalf of a marginalized group if you are trying to reach particular people. Always start a conversation by finding common ground by asking questions with genuine curiosity.[182] What do you agree on? Show interest in their perspectives. You want to avoid raising a person's defenses, and a basic way to do this is by being friendly and making a person like you or associate you with positive emotions first.

9. Have empathy, remembering that everyone has basic needs to fulfill, troubles to take care of, and a past you know nothing or very little about.

10. Use positive reinforcement. Positive reinforcement is more effective than negative reinforcement, such as yelling or saying *don't do that*. This is because rewarding a person for good behavior gives them a reason to exhibit a new behavior, whereas punishing someone for

bad behavior does nothing toward showing them an alternative. It's also just harder to imagine what a negative looks like in practice.
11. Those who ignore or mock your desire for change may not be willing to alter their behaviors. It may be best to not waste your time on these individuals.
12. It is imperative that when you are badmouthing one system, you have an alternative to replace it with. This alternative must have some data supporting how it is better for individuals or society. If it does not exist yet, focus on creating that alternative first, even on a small scale. Your goal should be to build workable systems, not more arguments.
13. Meaningful conversations rely on a person having *psychological safety*, or the knowledge that if something incorrect is said, that their character will not be attacked.[182] Check yourself, make sure you are talking about the topic rather than the person.

People often learn best when their personal intelligence is empowered, so try not to treat them like an idiot or lecture at them. One way to get around this is by giving a person an experience or a book. Just like habits, beliefs are deeply rooted in the psyche. One of the best ways to loosen belief structures is when a person experiences new things, gets into a relationship, goes traveling, or is empowered to learn on their own terms.

It is important to note that a person's culture is usually reinforced by a community such as a church, political group, news outlet, or social media. It may therefore be essential to focus on the people and communities you already have relationships with because change often has to come from within. Family and romantic ties are typically the easiest way to be an insider and have a certain level of respect listened to. This is partly why the gay rights movement was so successful because a significant percentage of people identify as homosexual and many families chose the love of their child over religious views and other peer pressures. In general, people who embrace a community idea are easiest to change when:

- They are approached by someone else belonging to that community
- They can see that their basic needs are not being met
- A law forces them to change
- They lose access to their community, such as certain news outlets getting shut down or blocked by a computer-savvy teenager

16.4 Persuasion

Psychologist Robert Cialdini believes that there are seven primary methods of persuading others.[221] These include:

1. **Reciprocity** - By giving to others, even very small things, a person will be much more likely to give back or feel indebted to you. This can also work by accepting a person's gifts and invitations.
2. **Scarcity** - When a product has a limited supply, people want it more and are willing to do or give more to obtain it. This can also work by informing people what they will miss out on by not believing or possessing something.
3. **Authority** - The more influence, power, or education a person has, the more likely they are to be listened to. For instance, police, politicians, doctors, and professors are listened to more readily than people without those positions, especially if their credentials are outwardly displayed in dress or certificates.
4. **Consistency** - People want to stay consistent with their values and how they have responded in the past. If people agree to a small ask, they are much more likely to agree to a bigger ask down the road so long as it is similar to the first thing. Cialdini uses an example of a small yard sign later being upgraded to a larger one.
5. **Liking** - People are more willing to be persuaded by those that they like. According to Cialdini, we like people more who are similar to us, say nice things about us, give us things, or actively support our goals and interests.[222]
6. **Social proof** - A person is more likely to change behaviors if they are shown that a large number of other people are also acting a certain way. People want to fit in. This is especially effective when you link a behavior to similar people, such as neighbors, church members, or households in the same income bracket.
7. **Unity** - Similar to the fifth principle of *liking* above, the final persuasive technique Cialdini shares is the idea that people are more willing to change for those sharing similar qualities to themselves such as a sports team, culture, or religion.

These tactics are often exploited by marketing strategists but can be adopted by activists as well. More about these can be learned in Cialdini's books *Influence* and *Pre-suasion*. You can also find more information online or on the Hidden Brain podcast episodes *Persuasion: Part 1* and *Persuasion:*

Part 2.

16.5 Beyond Blame, Victimhood, And Cancel Culture

Activists frequently carry a lot of blame toward themselves and others. They try to live a perfect life while simultaneously being martyrs for their cause. This is often rooted in trapped emotions, especially surrounding workaholism and fawning behaviors. You are not the cause of the world's problems, nor is your neighbor, nor is your friend, nor is any one individual. As an activist, it is important to stop blaming yourself and the victims of larger systems of oppression. Hold people accountable, but don't blame them. It's not helping. In fact, it's distracting from the real problem and ends up wasting your life away drowning in meaningless conflict and guilt.

Everyone has to start somewhere. You are not perfect and you are going to mess up and offend people sometimes. What matters is that you care and are willing to learn through your own research and by being empathetic to the words of others. In fact, no matter how you go about it, partaking in industrialized civilization directly or indirectly oppresses a human being or other living entity. Even so, working within systems of oppression generally allows you to create much more positive change than if you separated yourself from civilization and were "completely" anti-oppressive.

Both privileged and underprivileged people may experience guilt for the real and perceived privileges they were born with. It is fine to be privileged, so long as you are not using those privileges to intentionally support the continued oppression of others. You can transform your guilt into gratitude, using your privileges to constructively fight for a better world within the limits of your personal wellness. It is okay to take care of yourself and indulge in your privileges and the wonders that mainstream society has to offer. Oppression is fought much better with a positive mindset.

Sometimes your actions may hurt certain communities, but you can react by correcting your behaviors or calling out a system that unfairly gave you an opportunity when it did not provide that same opportunity to others. For instance, as a White person, you might question your boss about why you got a promotion, but your colored or female colleague who has been there longer than you, did not. You can also use your privilege to support others, such as by standing between a Black person and an outwardly racist individual at a protest.

Some people may fall into self-righteous victimhood in which they excuse their toxic behaviors by arguing they are more oppressed than others. In some activist circles, these people create hierarchies of who is "most right" based on who has the least privilege. However, just because you were oppressed does not mean your suffering or ideas are more important than another's. Black athlete and actor Terry Crews tackles this subject in his book *Tough*. His podcast interview on Episode 587 of *The Tim Ferriss Show* powerfully summarizes some of the key points and makes a case against the "oppression Olympics."

Watch out for working with people who use toxic language or always have a negative mindset. Just because someone says something is "bad" does not necessarily mean it is, so do your research. Become informed and do not jump on bandwagons of new ideas. Many activist, volunteer, and advocacy groups practice forms of *groupthink* and do not fully consider what they are sharing and spreading.

Cancel culture has become quite popular in leftist circles as well. This method calls out a person's actions as bad and then boycotts their art, social media, and business. Any future association with that canceled person then pins you as a bad person. This method is sometimes important when there is limited time to address an issue or there is a great disparity in roles of power, especially when facing up against corporate or political powers. However, it is too often used outside of this power disparity, which turns up being problematic for several reasons:

1. It conflates ignorance with intentional acts, which is classist and requires people to be able to read your mind or already know everything about your culture.
2. It demands that people be perfect (you are not perfect).
3. It does not educate a person or allow them to correct their behaviors.
4. Much like the police, it uses punishment instead of methods of restorative or transformative justice.
5. It wastes many activists' time and energy constantly patrolling for slight infractions instead of focusing on creating real change.
6. It dismisses all the good things a person has done and created, sometimes over a single sentence.
7. It perpetuates the cancellation of a person for years, even if the conflict has been settled by the original parties.
8. It makes potential allies terrified to interact with you or your cause and prevents discussions. One study titled, *The ironic impact of activists: Negative stereotypes reduce social change influence*, found that people did not support environmentalist and feminist causes specifically due to what they saw as "eccentric and militant" behavior.[10]

Read more about the perils of cancel culture in *We Will Not Cancel Us: And Other Dreams of Transformative Justice* by Adrienne Maree Brown and *Canceling Comedians While The World Burns* by Ben Burgis. In general, we need to understand that cultural and language differences exist. We need to understand the source of the problems we are fighting against. We need to use our time and emotional energy wisely. We need allies who are diverse and do not necessarily believe the things that we do. We need to assume that everyone is trying their best. Cancel culture prevents conversations that might otherwise heal and transform a person into an ally.

16.6 Creating A Mass Movement

Mass movements are essential to changing deeply rooted systems oppressing and destroying life on Earth. All mass movements start with an individual strongly believing in something and becoming a leader, but it is only with their followers that they have power – and you need a lot of power to take on the ideas and people in control.

Most mass movements have appealed to a large population, have scientific or moral backing, find support from rich and powerful people, can secure a large amount of funding, effectively use news and social media outlets to spread information, improve a group's access to their basic needs, and generally make the world a more equitable place. Successful movements will employ effective propaganda and make their followers excited to participate. In nations with powerful law enforcement bodies, nonviolent movements tend to be more effective.

Often artists will be the first to introduce a movement to a mainstream population such as through books, fictional stories, songs, poems, paintings, workshops, and theater. Mass movements can gain great sway if depicted in mainstream television productions or spoken about by famous musicians. This is often more effective by showing instead of telling an audience about a cause. For instance, running a sitcom with homosexual characters or including a diversity of races in a commercial. The goal is to normalize an idea to the extent that people start coming out in their community in support of the cause. Using subtlety and slowly introducing a concept helps prevent an audience from outright blocking an idea from becoming part of their reality. That said, shock value and fear can also work if an audience already cares about a cause but is simply unaware of it – this is typically the case when it relates broadly to the viewers' basic needs, for instance in the case of environmental concerns or war.

Changing society is a very difficult task with political and business leaders maintaining power over the masses. What is needed is a tactic that connects people together in such a way that it takes power away from the ruling class. Some methods of accomplishing this feat are by sharing more, buying less, building communities, localizing economies, giving more power to workers with democratic or consensus-based processes, decentralizing resources, and healing the trapped emotions that divide people. The more self-sufficient areas are and the more citizens work together, the better.

For instance, at a national scale, a volunteer-based people's cooperative could distribute food and other essential goods for the amount it cost to produce – perhaps based on a membership subscription fee that would save members money but also require them to participate in running the program. Goods could be sourced from ethical growers and distributors, or even from volunteer-run farms and processing facilities. This idea could be taken further to create other products as well such as sustainable technologies and health insurance. Simultaneously member meetups, parties, and other local events would deepen bonds and reinforce healthy behaviors in participants. Property could even be purchased and managed in land trusts. Altogether, such a cooperative would build a stronger and stronger community that undermines many of the destructive forces political and corporate leaders use to control populations.

Regardless of whether or not this idea ever becomes a reality, it highlights the most essential aspect of unifying people together – creating a very desirable incentive that transcends a person's beliefs. Being nourished, having fun, making friends, and saving money are things that all people want dearly. What does the society you want to live in look like? What tactics can you weave together to save the environment? The people? The world? What would make your neighborhood just a little bit more beautiful? These past two chapters have highlighted some possibilities. You as an individual have so much power to make your vision come true, especially when you call upon your community to help you get there.

***

Chapter Reflections

1. In what ways can you balance taking care of your mental health with starting to challenge the toxic aspects of your culture and society?
2. How have you traditionally acted in conflicts with people you have opposing beliefs with?
3. What tactics does your opposition use that you could learn from?

How are you making your life harder or activism less effective by not using those things?
4. How could you apply nonviolent communication to listen and respond more constructively to people you disagree with?
5. In what ways have you dehumanized or villainized the people you are trying to change?
6. What do you share in common with the people who you would like to change?
7. What are the trapped emotions you have to the people you want to change, and what trapped emotions do they have to you?
8. What ideas do you hold that have emerged from groupthink? How are those ideas hurting your movement?
9. How have you practiced cancel culture and in what ways has it been effective or ineffective?
10. In what ways have you expected people to be perfect, the same as you, or able to read your mind?
11. How do you relate to and use your privileges?
12. In what ways do you excuse your unhealthy, oppressive, or toxic behaviors?
13. What is the story held by your neighborhood, community, culture, city, state, or nation about themselves? What is the story about these spaces and groups held by outsiders? What would be a more empowering story and how can you help spread it?
14. In what ways do your ethical or sustainable actions or inactions prevent you from impacting greater change?
15. What are some ways that you feel excited about creating effective change?
16. What does a mass movement look like that you would be excited to participate in?
17. What can you do today to help create a healthy, creative, safe, sustainable, anti-oppressive, and community-driven world?

PART IV

RELEASING TRAPPED EMOTIONS

Chapter 17

How To Release Specific Trapped Emotions

17.1 Where To Start, 17.2 Major Parts To My Healing, 17.3 Pulling Yourself Out Of A Triggered Space, 17.4 Right After You Have A Life-Or-Death Experience, 17.5 Unaddressed Single Past Incidents And PTSD, 17.6 Attachment Wounds And Complex PTSD, 17.7 Stress, Overwhelm, And Anxiety, 17.8 Anger, Judgments, And The Outer Critic, 17.9 Zooming Out And Disrupting Hyperfocus, 17.10 Workaholism, 17.11 Health And Fearing Death, 17.12 Self-Blame And Self-Hatred, 17.13 Loss And Grief, 17.14 Rejection, 17.15 Insecurity And Jealousy, 17.16 Feeling Empty Or Numb, 17.17 Sounds, 17.18 Religious And Spiritual Abuse, 17.19 Ancestral Trapped Emotions, 17.20 Appearance, 17.21 Touch

Now that you have the tools for releasing trapped emotions, we can explore some specific types of suffering in more detail. As a reminder, all trapped emotions share three things in common - unexpressed emotions, self-limiting stories, and wanting resolution. Healing can be accomplished by regulating your nervous system (Part I), releasing emotions (Part I), reframing a story (Part II), and correcting anything reinforcing the trapped emotion such as behaviors, mindsets, relationships, or environments (Part III). Some trapped emotions are also accompanied by attachment wounds which must be healed by building secure attachment as explored in Sections 14.2 and 17.6. Working on any of these will aid you in transforming the others.

The pathway to healing looks different for everyone, but the end result shares some common threads as explored in Section 2.11. Keep in mind that the examples in this chapter are how I personally might go about healing, but you may need to use a different method depending on your unique experiences and circumstances. Adapt the skills shared throughout the book to meet your needs. There are hundreds of ways to relieve suffering, and it is rarely ever a linear pathway, so create a system that works best for you. Sometimes you will take steps backward, and that is okay - it is all learning that can be applied to making progress in the future. Let's begin.

17.1 Where To Start

If you feel overwhelmed about where to begin your healing, I suggest starting with finding an ally to help you such as a therapist or support group as explored in Section 4.7. Then, improve your self-care with the MENDSSS routine that I introduced in Section 4.9. Alongside this, devote to a regular mindfulness and breathing practice as discussed in Chapter 5. This could involve a sitting meditation, but yoga, qigong, and tai chi are all especially potent by combining mindfulness with movement and breathing. If you're dealing with attachment wounds or CPTSD, start learning about the inner family in Chapter 10 or check out Section 17.6.

17.2 Major Parts To My Healing

I want to share the most important moments of my own healing journey from being raised in a stressful family dynamic while simultaneously dealing with a lot of body shame. My healing is still a work in progress after 15 years, but whereas my life was once filled with hatred, depression, and isolation, I now feel fairly decent most days and have a number of healthy friendships. It has been a lot of work, but also a lot of joy. Some of my pivotal moments were:

- Dedicating to a creative practice in drawing, painting, and writing poetry
- Cutting off communication from my family for almost 5 years, and afterward establishing very specific boundaries in how I interacted with them
- Connecting with other activists upset about the state of the world
- Living in cooperative housing with alternatively-minded individuals
- Doing psychedelics several times in a safe and therapeutic setting
- Microdosing psychedelics and listening to what my body needed when in a depressive rut or having suicidal ideations
- Being vulnerable and dating people
- Using an elimination diet to learn what I was allergic to - I ended up cutting out concentrated sweeteners, gluten, and beans, as well as largely limiting my intake of fried food, red meat, alcohol, and restaurant food

- Having a selection of music, movies, and music videos to help pump me up and connect to my emotions
- Finding moldable shoe inserts that allowed me to walk and hike again
- Learning mindfulness through a Buddhist sangha following the teachings of Thich Nhat Hanh
- Tuning into my emotions and learning what I needed when feeling overwhelmed, such as sleep, social connection, communication, or deep breathing
- Improving my quality of sleep by eating my major meals for breakfast and lunch, cutting out proteins and big meals in the evening, limiting screen use at night, using a blue light filter, getting enough physical activity, napping, turning a fan on to block out ambient sounds, using a sleep mask, and using moldable underwater earplugs
- If I ate at night, I also found that drinking at least three quarts of water after eating, but at least an hour before actually going to bed, would help me sleep
- Consuming less media and dedicating to more pro-social activities like board games, dance, support groups, and rock climbing
- Spending more time outside of my house in nature
- Reading *Complex PTSD* by Pete Walker and *The Body Keeps The Score* by Bessel van der Kolk, plus the myriad of other books found in Chapter 19
- Attending *Adult Children of Alcoholic and Dysfunctional Families* online meetings at least once a day for six months straight
- Talking about emotions and drama with friends less, instead reserving social time for activities
- Speaking with my inner child regularly and striving to become my own loving parent
- Learning how to do self-guided EMDR
- Earning enough money to be able to spend it on fun things and not worry about becoming homeless - part of this was through selling art and books, but initially it helped taking on odd jobs, especially with yard maintenance and cleaning houses
- Volunteering for a concert hall and weekly dance group to start meeting more people, dancing, and hearing more music
- Detaching my self-worth from how other people showed up in my life
- Removing toxic and aloof friendships and feeling more okay about spending time alone, which greatly helped break my codependent

urges
- Removing as much stress as possible from my life such as difficult housemates, repetitive work tasks, angry people, and loud environments
- Committing to activities and communities before individuals such as dance, bouldering, potlucks, and *Adult Children of Alcoholics and Dysfunctional Families*
- Getting into ecstatic and partner dancing to overcome a lot of social anxiety, get a cardio workout, and receive healthy platonic touch
- Forming a spiritual connection to nature and the world around me

17.3 Pulling Yourself Out Of A Triggered Space

Sometimes you are going to find yourself in a difficult state of mind that you are unsure how to get out from. Maybe you are depressed, anxious, sad, angry, numb, or judging yourself through the inner critic for several days in a row. While the goal is to slow down, get present, feel your emotions, and change your story, that can be a really big ordeal. Especially when your emotions are being reinforced with your thoughts and coping mechanisms, how do you overcome your mood?

When I recognize I am in a safe space but still spiraling in negativity and dissociation, I start trying random things. Often I begin by reaching out to friends and loved ones. Sometimes this works, especially with those who will cuddle me since physical touch is very regulating for my nervous system by proving closeness, trust, and connection. However, I don't always have access to cuddling. With other friends I recognize that sharing my struggles often only repeats injury and still avoids me from feeling my emotions. Then I might try watching a movie, getting better sleep, going out to nature, complimenting a friend, seeing live music, attending a support group meeting, exercising, or journaling. I also try cutting out things that I know are unhealthy coping mechanisms making me feel worse like sugar, overeating, video games, social media, or television. In the past when things have been especially bad, I have had success with microdosing or taking an anti-anxiety medication as well.

After a few days or weeks of this, there is a moment where I surrender. I can feel my body again. Maybe it was during a meditation, or seeing a concert that reminded me of how beautiful and full of possibilities the world is. Maybe I spoke to someone who I felt some tendrils of new possibility with. Maybe I hit a rock bottom, or maybe I woke up and realized all the ways I've been ignoring myself and that I need to take a real day off.

In this surrender, I don't turn on my phone or try to make plans. I have a general acceptance that maybe everything my inner critic says is true, and that's okay. I stop thinking of the past or trying to seek external validation. Instead, I reconnect to my body with deep and slow breathing. As my physical senses return, I can finally have an emotional release or thoughtful epiphany. I might stay laying in bed while staring out the window, switching between experiencing my sensations, journaling, speaking with my inner child, looking at pictures of friends, recognizing conversations I need to have, writing a gratitude list of things that still feel good, correcting the inner critic, or creating a plan of action to improve my life. This might all take anywhere from thirty minutes to two hours.

Often there are multiple days of this exploration into release as I come to terms with what I am really needing. Sometimes there are steps backward, or momentary periods of relief that get swallowed up by the inner critic or indulging in addictive behaviors. Gradually though, things improve as my willpower, energy, and awareness come back. After the first surrender, things do tend to get easier and more enjoyable. I'll often go back to repeat some of the activities I previously tried that may not have worked the first time, like being in nature or spending time with friends. Just be sure not to do the same thing over and over again and expect results. When you notice it not working, try something else. Life can get better very quickly. This is all a much faster process when you already have a regular mindfulness practice!

17.4 Right After You Have A Life-Or-Death Experience

According to somatic therapist Peter Levine, the goal after having a life-or-death experience, or equally intense situation, is to reduce the heart rate to normal levels as soon as possible.[106B] This can be accomplished with the methods explored in Chapter 5 and Section 7.1. Levine shares that the body inherently knows how to heal, but we often prevent it from doing so.

As soon as you are removed from the danger, allow your body to move, release, or make sounds in any way that it wants to. This includes crying, screaming, twitching, shaking, or moving your arms. If possible medical professionals should not strap people down or otherwise attempt to stop these movements from happening. This is aided by having a trusted ally present who can help you feel safe. As previously mentioned in Chapter 9, recalling distressing memories within 24 hours of a difficult event and playing Tetris shortly afterward can help to further decrease traumatic symptoms.[85] In the following days, seek out support from loved ones, release your emotions as they arise, practice good self-care, and get help from a therapist or support group as necessary.

17.5 Unaddressed Single Past Incidents And PTSD

If 90 days after a single incident you are still experiencing abnormal emotional, behavioral, or bodily symptoms, there are several things you can do. Single incident trapped emotions, or PTSD, can also happen many years prior in childhood, so you may not remember the incident well or who you were before the incident. This includes any intense stress experienced or witnessed by the body, including abuse, injury, or difficult medical procedures. You can refer to Chapter 3 for a list of potential causes and symptoms of trapped emotions.

Start by resourcing yourself through a strong self-care routine with better sleep, time in nature, quality social time, exercise, and the support of a therapist or group. Create a safe environment for yourself. Pick up a mindfulness practice such as meditation or yoga to reconnect to your body. See Chapters 4 and 5. You can also create imagined resources to assist you when confronting a trapped emotion or when you become overwhelmed as explored in Section 6.4. These can either be objects that were important to you from around the time of the incident, or current friends and fictional companions. People will often still have success releasing basic trapped emotions without a good self-care practice though, especially as trapped emotions can make it difficult to do things like get sleep or exercise. The only real requirement is having an environment that is safe from the past difficulty.

There are many effective strategies for single-incident trapped emotions. These include somatic, EMDR, psychedelic, inner family systems, and narrative exposure therapy. Details for these were explored in Part II of the book. I believe that of these, somatic, narrative exposure, and psychedelic therapies are the most straightforward.

17.6 Attachment Wounds And Complex PTSD

According to psychologist Dr. Daniel Brown, complex PTSD (CPTSD) is caused by attachment wounds paired with traumatic incidents, typically repeated over and over again.[218] As previously stated in Section 3.4, attachment wounds can be caused by instability in any close relationship, but are most likely from growing up with your parents. Parents who were abusive, always away at work, poor at communicating, addicted to any substances, or otherwise unavailable tend to create deep insecurity in their children. This shows up in various maladaptive behaviors throughout life, including anxious, avoidant, or disorganized attachment. For instance, small shifts in behavior or inconsistency make you feel rejected, you might spend time with friends but still feel alone, when you become triggered you barely recognize your friends, or you habitually seek out and create relationships that are codependent, unavailable, or abusive. If you are currently experiencing an abandonment spiral in which you suddenly feel disconnected from everyone and unable to experience joy in social connections, see the next section.

The reason why many methods for treating single-incident traumas do not work for CPTSD is because CPTSD is primarily the result of attachment wounds that impact the brain differently than something like a life-or-death experience. For children, parts of the brain don't develop fully or shut down with limited activity. Furthermore, methods of healthy relating are never learned. According to Dr. Daniel Brown, it generally takes at least two years to transform your attachment style into secure and healthy relating.[218] This may sound like a long time, but there will be many incremental improvements along the way. This does not mean you become perfect, but you know how to build secure attachment. You may still react to your traumas, but you also know how to regulate your nervous system, come back to a place of stability, and repair conflicts with loved ones. Brown shares his model, *The Three Pillars of Comprehensive Attachment Repair*, as one method for healing CPTSD and creating secure attachment. These steps can happen simultaneously or in any order:

1. ***Creating idealized parents*** – On at least a weekly basis, visualize through your entire life with idealized parents who model healthy attachment. Essentially you are giving yourself everything that you missed out on growing up. This was explored in Section 10.6 with inner family work and reparenting. Visualization was also introduced in Section 4.6.
2. ***Learning metacognition*** – Brown explains that metacognition is the ability to know your state of mind and what strategies you use to solve problems. In this way, you can self-reflect and alter your behaviors to reach more desirable outcomes. People with attachment wounding have different parts of their metacognition shutoff though, which in extreme cases leads to things like narcissism, sociopathy, or borderline personality disorder. Learning metacognition then involves stimulating the brain with different practices that widen its perspective outside of a hyperfocused state. For instance, becoming mindfully aware of your physical sensations, emotions, thoughts, and external environment as

explored in Chapter 5. You might also identify the inner critic in Section 5.9, understand your self-limiting beliefs in Section 6.3, speak to your future self in Section 10.7, commit to an activist cause after realizing how a thing impacts you in Chapters 15 and 16, learn what you can and cannot control in Section 13.3, learn how to empathize with people in Section 13.7, or journal about an experience and how it impacted yourself and others in the past, present, and future in Section 7.11.

3. **Collaborating** – People who grow up with insecure attachment figures are often highly independent and lack the ability to work as a team. The final pillar then teaches how to collaborate, ask for help, socialize, and be interdependent without falling into codependency. This might involve learning healthy socializing strategies and playing team sports (Chapters 8 and 14), living in a community (Chapter 14), working on a collaborative project, or supporting a social change group (Chapters 15 and 16).

I would also add that this work requires having places of safety and gradually adopting more and more self-care practices. There are many other strategies for healing your attachment wounds that incorporate aspects of these three pillars too. For instance, Laurel Parnell's attachment-focused EMDR is explored in Chapter 9. Inner child work and Richard Schwartz's Internal Family Systems has great benefit as shared in Chapter 10. Section 14.2 introduced many methods for building secure attachment with a partner, even when one or both partners are avoidant, anxious, or disorganized in their attachment style. Then there are free support groups like *Adult Children of Alcoholics And Dysfunctional Families* with workbooks and meetings. These groups work best if you attend meetings multiple times a week, volunteer to be of service in various ways, find people to call and share with outside of the meeting, as well as work with others through the literature and workbooks.

According to CPTSD therapist Pete Walker, part of your healing will require that you experience and integrate unconditional love into your core.[184A] Dr. Daniel Siegal also believes that any healthy connection with a person may help rebuild your ability to create secure attachment in partnership.[157] Of course, this is often easiest when you are in a romantic relationship with someone who is either already secure or willing to co-create a secure relationship. Even just witnessing healthy attachment or imagining being given it can have a positive effect though as explored with the idealized parents.[240] Animal and plant companions will also greatly assist in this process. For me, engaging in communities helped as well since they tend to be more stable than any one individual can be.

With a healthy connection, you can self-reflect through journaling, exploring the positive and negative aspects of your life story in an honest and cohesive narrative. When you can directly see unhealthy patterns and where they began, it becomes easier to transform them. This is much simpler if you put yourself around people with secure attachment styles and create a stable outer world to start creating changes within. That may also require stepping away from insecure attachment styles and people with abusive tendencies such as partners or parents.

Many people also seek out a chosen family that acts as a replacement for their family of origin. While these figures usually cannot quite take on the same roles that a biological family can, it is quite soothing knowing you have people that care for you deeply. Unfortunately, the legal and medical systems usually do not grant rights to chosen family, but you can write a legal will to ensure that your end of life and assets are not controlled by your biological family. You can also be legally adopted into another family, but if you already have a legal guardian, some states may require that guardian give their consent first.

For a more in-depth guide to healing attachment wounds, I highly suggest Pete Walker's *Complex PTSD: From Surviving to Thriving*. Clinicians may also be interested in Dr. Daniel Brown's book, *Attachment Disturbances in Adults: Treatment for Comprehensive Repair*. There are also plenty of articles and podcasts that cover this topic, especially through the *Therapist Uncensored Podcast*.

17.7 Stress, Overwhelm, And Anxiety

Stress, overwhelm, and anxiety are some of the most common feelings that fuel emotions like sadness and anger. In the moment, you can breathe deep and slow with equal timing for the in and out breaths. Use the somatic techniques found in Chapter 5. Mindfully step out of your thoughts and into your body. Check into where the stress is located, which is often around your stomach, heart, throat, forehead, or eyes. Breathe deeply into it, and if possible, allow it to transform into tears. If you can't, fake a crying motion by tensing your abdomen and arms while squeezing your eyes shut. Alternatively, use an intense release like a growl, yell, loud singing, rapid jumping, or tensing your entire body for a few seconds before letting go. Repeat these exercises several times and then pause for several minutes. How do you feel now? Depending on the severity of the situation, you may feel entirely fine, or have a sense of emptiness. If residual emotions are still there, repeat the somatic releases.

If your thoughts are fueling your difficult feelings, consider journaling to break apart the stories and self-limiting beliefs you have. See Chapters 6 and 7. You can also practice thought-stopping by saying that you do not want to think about something, or by redirecting to a different thought as explored in Section 5.9. Use the acronym HALT (hungry, angry, lonely, tired) to identify what action you can take to relieve your feelings. Spend some time doing nothing, staring out the window with a blank mind, or go out to nature and watch the trees and birds. Write out a list of what is going right in your life, or about the things you like or love right now. Ask for reassurance from your partner or friends to know that they care about you. You can also create boundaries with stressful people, or communicate through a conflict. See Chapter 8. For preventative measures against stress, integrate as many aspects of the MENDSSS protocol into your life as possible as discussed in Section 4.9.

17.8 Anger, Judgments, And The Outer Critic

See Section 5.8 about healthy angering and Section 5.9 about the outer critic. In general though, reduce the stress in your life. Regulate your nervous system enough to avoid using violence, judgmental language, or shouting. Practice thought-stopping techniques and reframe self-limiting beliefs. Get mindful of your body and sense into what it needs to feel safe. Is one of your values being contradicted? Do you want someone to change a behavior? Realign your life to better match your values, or use nonviolent communication to ask for what you want. You are also more likely to judge or feel angry toward things you do not understand, so increase your cultural intelligence and try to research why a person might be behaving a certain way. Start filling your life with more positive inputs. Write gratitude lists, compliment people, and focus on things that bring you joy while walking outside. Use a complaining bracelet anytime you complain or make a judgment against someone as explored in Section 8.13. Keep in mind that complaints and judgments are also often hidden inside of comparing things as better or worse than others. Developing compersion, the feeling of joy for the success and happiness of another, will also help as explored in Section 14.2.

17.9 Zooming Out And Disrupting Hyperfocus

An important part of healing trapped emotions is being able to reconnect with the bigger picture and see yourself beyond your pain. Zooming out from the hyperfocus on difficult memories or judgmental thoughts can be accomplished through any of the main techniques for releasing trapped emotions throughout the book. These include finding a place of safety, having an emotional release, exploring your story through journaling, communicating through strife, or doing small or large amounts of psychedelics. However, sometimes you might need something you feel comfortable going to immediately, or create a regular practice of staying connected. Anything that creates a strong feeling or sense of awe typically does the trick. These include:

- Socializing while doing something fun
- Talking with someone you respect, crush on, or find attractive
- Staring at trees or being out in nature with few signs of humanity
- Attending a live music concert or other performance
- Watching a movie in which you resonate with the story or characters
- Being hugged, cuddled, or danced with in a way that shows there is a lot of trust, such as by being held tightly with a lot of pressure
- Sleeping
- Practicing a spirituality or religion which defers some of the reasoning behind an incident to other energies or entities
- Looking at a picture of Earth before and after an incident happened
- Traveling
- Reading, watching, or listening to the lived experiences of others, especially biographies of people who inspire you
- Accomplishing something that you're proud of, like making a piece of artwork in an accessible style
- Any form of diminishing the ego as explored in Section 13.2

17.10 Workaholism

If you find yourself with no free time, guilt yourself over relaxing, struggle to take time off work, or sign up for every optional project suggested, you may be addicted to being busy. Often workaholism is instilled in us by a sense of abandonment that was only slightly alleviated by the affirmation received when performing well enough in school. We may have also had to parent our parents or siblings, growing up much too fast to keep family members safe.

Ask yourself what you are missing out on that you are replacing with work. Perhaps that is fulfillment, romance, rest, or play. Part of overcoming workaholism is learning to assert needs and boundaries, as well as saying no to extra projects. Schedule in free time and relaxation. Talk to your inner child about what they want to be doing with their life and find ways to play. If money is an issue, what can you do to simplify your life or earn more? If possible, consider that working for someone else any more than 40 hours a week is too much. Change your ideas about what success means as explored in Section 13.4.

17.11 Health And Fearing Death

Poor health and impending death are typically highlighted by hyperfocus on the negative. Some of this stems from a culture obsessed with immortality rather than quality of life. Naturally, taking steps to improve your health can be the best route to feeling better, but this may not be possible. Changing this narrative may then involve spending more time in nature, connecting with a higher power, or committing to a community. Speaking to the parts of yourself that are insecure about your health or mortality can also be profoundly healing. Connect to the cycle of life and focus on what you are capable of rather than what you cannot do. As discussed in Chapter 11, psychedelic-assisted therapy has also been shown to be immensely powerful at easing end-of-life suffering. *Death doulas* are becoming more popular as well to support people through their impending end.

17.12 Self-Blame And Self-Hatred

When we are sensitive or were raised with perfectionistic attitudes, it is easy to blame ourselves for just about anything going wrong. We may apologize when something is not our fault or even say sorry to inanimate objects we bump into while alone. Self-blame is especially pervasive in activist groups who collectively guilt themselves and others for the myriad of social and environmental problems in the world. In extreme cases we may even hate ourselves, taking on so much responsibility for the world's problems that we cannot see ourselves as good. Parental figures, partners, or cultural ideas may also instill this within us by how they talk about our appearance, race, intelligence, or abilities.

Identify who instilled this self-blaming or self-hating attitude in you and grieve and anger about their actions. Use thought-correction techniques to identify what is true and if it may not have been your fault as explored in Section 5.9 and Chapter 6. Practice self-love and self-compassion to understand and appreciate your unique gifts in Chapter 13. Develop your personality with new hobbies and transform how you consume media in Chapter 12. Remember that every incident is a complex series of events that typically involves much more than just you. If you are to blame and it is something you can reasonably change, use nonviolent communication to apologize and do

17.13 Loss And Grief

Death of loved ones, fires that burn your home, and other unfortunate events are bound to happen in everyone's life. Take as much time to grieve as necessary, even if that is years longer than it takes other people. According to Andrew Huberman's research, there are ways to heal your heart faster though.[78]

The main thing that hurts is the brain's expectation that the object of your loss will still be around or contact you. It is important to honor and celebrate your connection with this person, animal, or thing, rather than trying to forget or dissociate from them. Feel your attachment to them. Remember the good times and what they meant to you. Set up an altar with a photo of your loved one. Join a grief support group. Host an annual celebration of life and practice communal grieving to help a whole group of people both support each other and move on past the grief.

These actions are most beneficial when you do not blame yourself for the incident. Let go of any guilt you might be having about this loss. Forgive yourself and know that you have no control over the past now as explored in Sections 13.3 and 13.13. You likely did not even have control over the situation when it happened either. Even if you did, all you can do is learn from the event and move forward. You can also practice healthy angering to acknowledge when it was actually institutions such as the health industry and capitalism that failed a person. See Section 5.8.

The efficacy of healing from grief seems to increase the calmer you are when engaging with your attachment and memories of a loss. For instance, deep and slow breathing while journaling about a loss can create better healing outcomes. Getting enough sleep and other basic self-care techniques covered in Chapter 4 will also help.

According to Huberman, all of these practices allow your brain to transition away from expecting the object of your loss to still be around or contact you. This may be further helped with:

1. Using visualization to speak to or visit people or places that once were to resolve anything you are holding onto. The people who impacted your life deeply are a part of you, and can always be spoken with just like any other inner self explored in Chapter 10.
2. Using EMDR to integrate the loss as something that happened in the past. See Chapter 9.

3. Creating new connections and enjoying your hobbies.
4. Remembering that the world is abundant and filled with positive possibilities.
5. Practicing a spiritual tradition or connecting more deeply with a higher power.

17.14 Rejection

Rejection mostly happens when in pursuit of jobs, friends, or lovers, and can be handled in much the same way as described with breakups in Section 14.3. Remember that you are never entitled to a person's time or knowing the reason why they rejected you. An important aspect of getting past the rejection is creating stories that do not demean or catastrophize the situation. Overcoming self-limiting beliefs is covered in Chapter 6, but might specifically include things like noting any red flags you avoided, using a rejection as an opportunity to grow as a person, congratulating yourself on being vulnerable, or accepting that rejection is an entirely normal aspect of life.

Focus on the specific instance that you were rejected from rather than seeing it as an attack on your whole identity, appearance, or personality. You can also thank a person for knowing what they want, or see if they might be interested in meeting you halfway by being friends instead of lovers, or by offering you an internship or some constructive feedback instead of a job. Learning to move on sooner will make the possibility of getting an enthusiastic yes from someone else more likely as you confidently put yourself out there again. At least some self-reflection and journaling is always good though after a rejection, especially if it follows a recurring pattern. Speak to your inner child about how you love them and will not abandon them. Connect with communities that you feel unconditional love from, spaces that you know will not leave you.

17.15 Insecurity And Jealousy

If you are feeling insecure or jealous about a connection, identify and observe that emotion. It is stress that if mindfully held can become tears. Ask yourself where that feeling is coming from. Was there a time in your past that you felt abandoned or did not get what you wanted? Use EMDR to locate the memory and work to renegotiate it. Once you have removed some of the painful emotions, consider what you can do in the future to feel more secure or to get what you want. What would make you feel confident, attractive, or successful? Are you having unrealistic expectations of how other people should treat you? Are you trying to control something that cannot be controlled? Are you relying on just one person to meet all your needs? How can you form a healthier relationship with yourself and make more friendships that will meet your unmet needs?

Instead of worrying about if you're defective, focus on the possibility that you're just incompatible. Remember that each person has their own unique set of interests, desires, and availability. In healthy relationships, it is okay to ask for support or reassurance too. Do not let your feelings explode, open up about them using nonviolent communication. Learning about *compersion* may also help as discussed in Section 14.2.

17.16 Feeling Empty Or Numb

Even if you are otherwise capable of having an emotional release in life, you may not always have access to one. This is especially prevalent when you are disassociated, at rock bottom, or feeling empty and numb. The latter may occur with extreme emotional overwhelm, or shortly after having an emotional release. Motivation may be especially low in these times, but I have found a few tactics that work. These include going on a walk, sleeping, reaching out to a friend, looking at photos of loved ones, or just continuing on with your schedule to the best of your ability. Given time, these states typically pass, but they may also require creating change in your life like a breakup, communicating your needs, finding a better job, or connecting with new friends and communities. See Sections 3.5 and 4.1 for handling dissociation and rock bottoms.

17.17 Sounds

Certain sounds, but most commonly loud ones, may trigger a freeze or flight response in an individual. This is common in war veterans or when there was yelling or doors slamming growing up. Things like barking dogs and hammering can be really difficult for me. I have noticed that it is much easier if I can visually witness or am participating in those loud activities myself. For instance, I do much better if I watch fireworks rather than stay indoors.

If you are actively being triggered, remove yourself from the upsetting sound and then release some of the energies by crying and shaking. If that is not an option, then blocking out the triggering sound can be helpful. I sometimes put in moldable underwater earplugs and then cover my ears with headphones blasting music or white noise. Speak to your inner child, telling them that you know they are scared, but you are confident you can keep them safe from the difficult sounds. Use EMDR to identify and renegotiate the difficult experience that you originally faced with loud sounds. Integrate the belief that you are capable of protecting yourself from harm.

Once while working in the same room as a friend running a loud sewing machine, I became triggered and decided to speak to my inner child. *I know this is scary, but I will keep you safe, this is a tool that makes work easier, it's not going to hurt you. Let me show you, we can make a warm blanket together.* Then I visualized using the sewing machine with my inner child, which calmed them down considerably.

17.18 Religious And Spiritual Abuse

Many people grow up being manipulated and abused by religious or spiritual ideologies. Research and understand the hypocrisy and contradictions of your religious or spiritual upbringing and worship group. Speak to your inner child about their feelings and how they relate to your experiences. Explore religions and spiritualities that do not work from a place of fear-mongering but rather empower you and your community. Speak to your inner ancestors and connect with their Earth-based spiritual beliefs. Connect with a support group or therapist who specializes in recovering from religious abuse and trauma.

17.19 Ancestral Trapped Emotions

As previously mentioned, there is a divide around how ancestral trapped emotions play out in the body. Increased sensitivities and stress are likely. In your immediate life, create a safe space and practice calming techniques. Improve your resilience to stress with meditation, healthy social networks, and positive self-talk. Understand that you may be more sensitive than others, and that is okay. Identify and renegotiate the self-defeating stories you tell yourself. Use EMDR, inner child work, or narrative exposure therapy to reestablish the trigger as actually being safe. The mice mentioned in Section 2.6 were able to be deconditioned from their inherited threat response by simply being given a safe environment while the smell was activated - essentially exposure therapy.[59]

Some therapists like Resmaa Menakem also believe that a person must renegotiate their ancestor's trapped emotions as well.[120] This can be accomplished by creating a history of your ancestors, speaking to those inner hurt selves, and giving them some of the love and kindness they never received. It can also be done in an ancestral trauma group. Grieve for your ancestors. Create a shrine to honor them or write a letter. Figure out what they need to start feeling safe. See Section 10.8.

You can also create rituals or celebrations that honor these unresolved energies from the past. Photos and learning some basic history about wars, religious practices, and diseases might help. Ancestry websites that do DNA testing like <www.ancestry.com> may connect you to information your family never had growing up. Please keep in mind that this does not mean you have to fix or otherwise put yourself around abusive parents or relatives. All of this can be done within your own mental landscape. The renegotiation of your ancestor's pain may involve finding within it the story of strength, survival, and overcoming. Celebrate your culture's or family's resilience.

17.20 Appearance

Within certain environments, you may have had your appearance or clothing stigmatized or altogether ignored. This is especially common in young, elderly, poor, disabled, and marginalized populations. You may have also been called ugly and never felt the desire to even try changing your appearance. On the other hand, you might have had constant pressure on your appearance and are now hyper-aware of your looks. Learning to own your body in ways that feel good can help to find peace in public and your mirror. There are a few ways to do this:

- Dress up in ways that make you feel attractive, safe, magical, comfortable, or powerful
- Let go of unrealistic expectations for yourself and focus on what you can change
- Understand mainstream fashion norms and utilize them when necessary to increase your chance of success
- Understand how mainstream attraction is often based on Eurocentric and racist thought, they are changeable to other forms
- Learn traditional ways that your culture or race has taken care of hair
- Find communities that accept your appearance or support you in healthfully changing your appearance such as in a weight watchers group
- Understand that true love and healthy intimacy require mental attraction much more than physical attraction
- Understand the nuances of gender and how mainstream gender norms have greatly hurt men, women, trans, and non-binary people
- Understand that you are worthy of love, kindness, and respect. It is therefore okay to feel angry when those things have been deprived from you
- Reframe your thinking about your appearance - instead of trying to be physically attractive, go for powerful, magical, wizardly, artful, or

funny

Being practical and poor country folk, yet simultaneously edging around hippie-dom, my parents' sense of fashion was questionable to say the least. I grew up with a mullet that I eventually braided into what others cringingly referred to as a "rattail." Then there were the clothes worn into oblivion and my food allergies that caused me acne and cysts. I hated my appearance and constantly felt ashamed and unworthy of others. While people did accept me regardless, with all the other stresses in my life, I couldn't see that myself. Finally figuring out that I had control over my appearance greatly relieved my anxiety and depression. I got a proper haircut, found a diet that cleared up my face, and started wearing better clothing. While there are still some improvements I could make to fit in with different groups, I generally feel content with my appearance now. I still have scarring on my face, but you know what, it kinda makes me feel like a wizard. Sometimes people I find attractive find me attractive too, so it all works out.

In *The Body Is Not An Apology*, Sonya Renne Taylor explores how a person's body is most frequently shamed based on age, weight, skin color, gender, physical ability, and various notions of attractiveness. The average person's body is nothing like the average model's, but the dominant culture asserts that is what we need to succeed in life and love. Body shaming is largely perpetuated by capitalism, the fashion industry, and politics. When a person's attractiveness requires dozens of makeup products, surgeries, health foods, articles of clothing, and fitness classes, billions of dollars are made. Simultaneously, body shaming helps preserve the dominant power of White heterosexual men and religious organizations who can more easily shun marginalized groups of people.

Natural attraction is typically based upon the qualities of your parents, childhood peers, and shared interests, but discriminatory influences in media and the voices around you push certain characteristics to be more or less attractive. Exploring the conversation around *desirability politics* may interest you. Episode 366 of the *Multiamory* podcast and Tressie McMillan Cottom's essay *In The Name of Beauty* are good places to start. While it can be depressing to become aware of factors that influence what people are attracted to, it is possible to undo these influences by:

- Limiting your exposure to media that pushes body-shaming narratives
- Increasing your time around other types of bodies

- Starting to ask yourself questions about why you find certain bodies more attractive than others
- Releasing the emotions you have trapped regarding your own and others' bodies

I am not saying that you can totally ignore your appearance or personality. Being fun, healthy, and fashionable, whatever those characteristics mean to you or the group you are attracted to, will go a long way in increasing your chances of connecting with them. Please note that these three characteristics have nothing to do with your body type though, they are traits nearly anyone can obtain. You can learn to be playful. You can be healthy regardless of weight, age, or ability. You can thrift shop or go to a clothing swap for clothing that feels good to wear. You can find freedom in movement and dance, such as in ecstatic dance. You can care for your body, love your body, and find ways in which you feel attractive or at least content in your body.

You may be anywhere on this spectrum of body shaming - either toward yourself or toward others, and likely a mix of the two. Perhaps you were born with a body that mostly fits into the fashion industry's narrative and greatly benefit from the privileges it gives you in your dating life and career, or you constantly felt ashamed of your body and do your best to hide it. Taylor quotes Angela Davis saying *I'm no longer accepting the things I cannot change. I'm changing the things I cannot accept.* Some of those unacceptable things involve a society not built for the diversity of bodies that inhabit it including seats that are too small, clothing that does not fit, buildings that are inaccessible to people living with disabilities, and actors who represent only a tiny sliver of what people look like. Regardless of this discrimination, everyone is capable of love and happiness.

If you feel out of touch with the gender you were raised as, it is completely okay to explore other ways to express yourself. You may initially feel some shame or anxiety around this with uncertainty as to how loved ones, family, and society will treat you. Use somatic releases as these feelings arise. Connect with the LGBTQ+ community either online or in-person to bolster the confidence you have in your identity. Some churches and recovery programs specifically support people who identify as LGBTQ+, so surround yourself with these safe spaces. Using healthy communication will go a long way in discovering who is an ally and who is not. You also do not need to divulge your identity to a person who you know does not support you. Some people will need time to accept your authentic identity, and others will be entirely unable to transition their interests into this new personality. You may remove or limit contact with these people knowing that there are a lot of allies out there who will love you for who you are.

17.21 Touch

Insecurity or dislike of touch typically happens in people who were sexually violated, physically harmed, or otherwise inappropriately touched at any point in their life. Release the trapped emotions, use visualization to stop the incident from happening or have help from your mental allies, and understand that you are now capable of saying "no" and protecting yourself. You can also teach your inner child how to fight and defend themselves. Understand the principles of consent explored in Chapter 14 and connect with more people who will respect your boundaries. Ketamine infusions are starting to be used as well to help with touch-related struggles.

Bessel Van Der Kolk discusses several healing modalities for sexual assault survivors in *The Body Keeps The Score*. Animals can help rebuild a person's trust in touch and relational energy.[97W] Animal connection can be found by getting an animal companion, volunteering at an animal shelter, or doing animal therapy such as with horses or dogs. Trauma-informed massage and yoga paired with mindful breathing exercises can help rebuild a person's connection to their body and their ability to discern between safe and dangerous touch.[97X,97Y] Going slow is important. Rhythmic drumming, solo or partner dance, tai chi, qigong, aikido, judo, tae kwon do, kendo, jujitsu, and capoeira are also potential options, some of which can simultaneously empower a person in their ability to protect themselves.[97Z]

How you approach touch is important as well. Dismantle the idea that intimacy requires sex and that sex requires intimacy. Know what abuse and manipulation look like as explored in Chapter 3. Finding sources of safe touch can be very healing. Safe touch involves people who will listen to what you want and you feel comfortable saying no to. It is also entirely okay to be asexual, disinterested in touch, or prioritize other love languages over physical contact. You don't have to hug anyone. You don't have to have sex just because someone wants it. You are allowed to check in with yourself to let others know what will feel safe and nourishing. Maybe that is a handshake instead of a hug, or cuddling instead of sex. I occasionally tell people, "I don't feel like hugging" or "I don't want touch right now." While it sometimes requires an explanation, I feel so much better that I did not force myself. Remember, try to choose feeling guilty over resentment. Respect what you want, and that may require channeling some healthy anger or communicating your needs as we explored in Section 5.8 and Chapter 8.

***
Chapter Reflections

1. What do you want to heal from?
2. Which tools in this book seem the most likely to be able to help you heal your trapped emotions?
3. How do you relate to your appearance?
4. What things, within your control, would make you feel better about your appearance or care less about it?
5. In what ways do you compare yourself to others?
6. What relationships do you want to repair and what steps can you take to begin that repair process?

Chapter 18

Moving Forward With Radical Self-Care

Humans are truly amazing. We are capable of surviving through great difficulty, healing from years of turmoil, and still experiencing amazing joy. Unfortunately, there are not enough quality mental health professionals for everyone wanting support in this healing process. Even if there were, many people do not have access to these supports due to location, income, or lacking representation in race, language, and lived experience. What's more, these professionals typically cannot fix an inequitable society, help a person who lacks basic needs, or repair the natural world. As such, we must decentralize the mental health industry by creating a culture of freely available radical self-care. This might include:

1. Organizing support groups in which members collectively focus on specific trapped emotions, read literature, integrate psychedelic experiences, develop the inner child and loving parent relationship, practice mindfulness, interpret dreams, or learn about self-care. This might also involve teaching people tools like self-hypnosis, solo EMDR, somatic therapy, or co-counseling.
2. Dismantling systems of oppression such as racism, transphobia, sexism, law enforcement, and capitalism.
3. Creating social activities that help people build community such as potlucks, games, and art events.
4. Knowing how to identify dysregulation and how to help a person regulate their nervous system.
5. Co-creating securely attached relationships with lovers, friends, and communities.
6. Destigmatizing psychedelics and creating safe containers for their use.

7. Improving cultural intelligence and celebrating diversity.
8. Practicing healthier ways of communicating through conflict and repairing relationships by learning techniques such as nonviolent communication, conversational receptiveness, Imago, forgiveness, and making amends.
9. Talking with people about their behaviors and communication instead of ostracizing them.
10. Using restorative justice and harm reduction approaches.
11. Talking openly about emotions more.
12. Protecting natural habitats, preventing logging and mining in riparian areas, growing gardens, planting trees, removing lawns, creating parks, and addressing climate change seriously.

The *self* is intricately woven into the people around you and your environment. How can you adopt and share the tools in this book with your community? How can you start to promote equitable solutions and heal the natural world? How can you address your personal trapped emotions and attachment wounds?

Many people are already helping create this cultural shift, and so many resources available to heal trapped emotions and attachment wounds. Although mental health professionals can be quite useful and may expedite your process, humans have been finding ways to heal since the beginning. Keep trying and you will discover success. Changes you begin right now will make the future so much easier. You can overcome adversity and defy the fate that has been laid out before you. Just remember that there will still be hard days, and sometimes your progress will seemingly regress or be quite slow. These are not failures, they are learning opportunities and part of being a healthy person. It's okay if it takes you a few months or even years to incorporate healthier behaviors - you have been living in another reality for quite a while. It is reasonable that just as much time may be needed to undo the difficulties you have experienced. However, just reading this book is proof that you have progressed. You know how to heal.

You also are not alone. Most people are struggling with something and deeply desire a healthy community. The more you transform and reject cultures that propagate suffering, the less power they have to hurt others. As you find a deeper sense of contentment, purpose, and joy, the people around you will feel better as well and understand a pathway forward past their suffering. If it feels safe to do so, help inspire others by talking about your journey openly in music, poetry, painting, or social media updates. Doing so allows others to feel seen in their suffering and gain insights into how they too can begin healing. Be the person who breaks the cycle.

We have covered a lot in these chapters and I want to finish by leaving you some options to start exploring, with or without the assistance of a mental health professional. Remember that healing can take years, so slow down. Different steps to recovery may happen quickly back-to-back, but more often will require a month or longer between each. Integration takes time as well. You may never fully be the person you were prior to your stressful life experiences but know that it is okay to change. You may even grow in profound ways creatively, empathetically, spiritually, and relationally. While difficult, your experiences have taught you much and given you an opportunity to understand how to heal, not only yourself, but those around you too. You can start your journey by:

1. Signing up to see a therapist that practices a trauma-informed therapy such as somatic, EMDR, Internal Family Systems, prolonged exposure, neurofeedback, or psychedelic-assisted therapies. If you cannot afford or find a good therapist, find allies in support groups, co-counseling, or meditation groups.
2. Removing stressful, toxic, immature, and abusive people from your life.
3. Limiting and removing unhealthy coping mechanisms and replacing them with healthier ones. For instance, eat better, spend time in nature, exercise, read more books, engage in pro-social activities, address your addictions, and get a decent amount of sleep.
4. Taking medicines to manage your depression, anxiety, or other mental struggles.
5. Finding community in friends, support groups, religious and spiritual gatherings, volunteer opportunities, dance, meditations, or activist causes.
6. Reconnecting to your body through a mindfulness practice such as sitting meditation, deep breathing, yoga, tai chi, or exercise.
7. Learning how to release trapped emotions with somatic techniques, communal grieving, or communication.
8. Reframing your self-limiting beliefs and stories.
9. Altering the maladaptive behaviors you may have picked up. Develop the habits, skills, and communication techniques you missed out on.
10. Being of service and living for something beyond your own ego by transforming the laws, cultures, and behaviors that cause suffering in

the world.

I suggest re-reading the parts of *Radical Self-Care* that you found particularly useful by referencing the *Table of Contents* or doing further reading from the *Works Referenced*. Beyond my personal experiences, this book came about thanks to dozens of authors and hundreds of researchers who I had the privilege of learning from. Regardless of where you start, start somewhere. Increasing your knowledge will only get you so far because nothing will change unless you practice and dedicate yourself to releasing trapped emotions and transforming society.

Thank you for believing in yourself. I know you are capable of so much and wish you the best on your journey from here. If you found this book helpful, please share it with a friend, write a review online at *The Story Graph*, *Amazon*, or *Goodreads*, or follow my latest adventures and say hi at <www.sageliskey.com> or <www.instagram.com/sage.liskey>. You can also support this work and get some extra goodies by subscribing to my Patreon at <www.patreon.com/sageliskey> or purchasing some art and mental health posters from my Etsy store at <www.etsy.com/shop/radcatpress>. Good luck out there!

Chapter 19

Works Referenced

19.1 Trauma And PTSD, 19.2 The Inner Child And Parts Of Ourselves, 19.3 Psychedelics, 19.4 Meditation, Spirituality, And Buddhism, 19.5 Addiction, Alcohol, And Dysfunctional Families, 19.6 Relationships, 19.7 Money, Business, Creativity, And Finances, 19.8 Gender, Race, And Social Justice, 19.9 Social And Communication, 19.10 Miscellaneous

Beyond my experiences growing up in a dysfunctional family, living in alternative communities, and participating in activist groups, I learned about the contents of these pages by reading many books. This list may appear overwhelming at first, but just read about whatever you are currently focusing on in your healing. For broad overviews, I highly suggest reading in order: *Complex PTSD, My Grandmother's Hands, The Body Keeps The Score*, and *In An Unspoken Voice*. Know that most of these are available through your local library and as audiobooks. I listened to these for free while working odd jobs (at two to four times speed) through my local library's partnership with the Hoopla phone app. There's also the Libby app.

I placed the books that I benefited most from at the top of each section. That does not mean the books at the bottom are bad because I usually did not include the books that I found lacking in quality. This said, some of these books have perspectives I disagree with or find stigmatizing, and it is important to read commentary on each, especially in the ever-changing world of gender, race, social justice, and science. Use your critical thinking, apply what you've learned in this book, know that each topic is actively developing, and check out the reviews online. Starting a self-care book club could be a great way to stay accountable to your education, have meaningful discussions, and get support as well.

19.1 Trauma And PTSD
- Complex PTSD: From Surviving to Thriving - Pete Walker

- The Body Keeps The Score: Brain, Mind, and Body in the Healing of Trauma - Bessel van der Kolk
- In An Unspoken Voice: How the Body Releases Trauma and Restores Goodness - Peter A. Levine
- My Grandmother's Hands: Racialized Trauma and the Pathway to Mending Our Hearts and Bodies - Resmaa Menakem
- Who You Were Before Trauma: The Healing Power of Imagination for Trauma Survivors - Luise Reddermann
- The Polyvagal Theory in Therapy: Engaging the Rhythm of Regulation - Deb Dana
- Adult Children Of Emotionally Immature Parents: How to Heal from Distant, Rejecting, or Self-Involved Parents - Lindsay C. Gibson
- Raising An Emotionally Intelligent Child - John Gottman
- The Heart and Mind of Hypnotherapy: Inviting Connection, Inventing Change – Douglas Flemons
- The Tao Of Fully Feeling: Harvesting Forgiveness Out of Blame - Pete Walker
- A Therapist's Guide To EMDR: Tools and Techniques for Successful Treatment - Laurel Parnell
- Adult Children Of Alcoholics: Alcoholic / Dysfunctional Families (ACA Big Red Book) - ACAWSO
- Twelve Steps Of Adult Children: Steps Workbook - ACAWSO
- What Happened To You? Conversations on Trauma, Resilience, and Healing. Bruce D. Perry and Oprah Winfrey
- The Clinician's Guide to Exposure Therapies for Anxiety Spectrum Disorders - Timothy A. Sisemore
- Prolonged Exposure Therapy for Adolescents with PTSD Emotional Processing of Traumatic Experiences, Therapist Guide - by Edna B. Foa, Kelly R. Chrestman, and Eva Gilboa-Schechtman
- Healing Trauma: Restoring the Wisdom of Your Body (Sounds True audiobook version) - Peter Levine
- Waking The Tiger: Healing Trauma - Peter Levine
- Trauma Stewardship: An Everyday Guide to Caring for Self While Caring for Others - Laura van Dernoot Lipsky with Connie Burk

19.2 The Inner Child And Parts Of Ourselves

- Recovery Of Your Inner Child: The highly acclaimed method for liberating your inner self - Lucia Capacchione
- Reconciliation: Healing The Inner Child - Thich Nhat Hanh

- Greater Than The Sum Of Our Parts: Discovering Your True Self Through Internal Family Systems Therapy - Richard C. Schwartz
- Internal Family Systems: Skills Training Manual - Frank G. Anderson, Martha Sweezy, and Richard C. Schartz

19.3 Psychedelics
- How To Change Your Mind: What the New Science of Psychedelics Teaches Us About Consciousness, Dying, Addiction, Depression, and Transcendence - Michael Pollan
- The Psychedelic Explorer's Guide - Safe, Therapeutic, and Sacred Journeys - James Fadiman
- Food Of The Gods: The Search for the Original Tree of Knowledge - Terrence McKenna

19.4 Meditation, Spirituality, And Buddhism
- Meditations For Emotional Healing: Finding Freedom in the Face of Difficulty - Tara Brach
- Radical Acceptance: Awakening the Love that Heals Fear and Shame - Tara Brach
- The Untethered Soul: The Journey Beyond Yourself - Michael A. Singer
- That Which You Are Seeking Is Causing You To Seek - Cheri Huber
- The Heart Of The Buddha's Teachings: Transforming Suffering into Peace, Joy, and Liberation - Thich Nhat Hanh
- Just So: Money, Materialism, and the Ineffable, Intelligent Universe - Alan Watts
- The Trauma Of Everyday Life - Mark Epstein
- Pronoia Is The Antidote For Paranoia: How the Whole World is Conspiring to Shower You with Blessings.
- Be Here Now - Ram Dass
- The Four Agreements – Don Miguel Ruiz

19.5 Addiction, Alcohol, And Dysfunctional Families
- The Easy Way To Control Alcohol - Allen Carr
- Quit Like A Woman: The Radical Choice to Not Drink in a Culture Obsessed with Alcohol - Holly Whitaker
- Recovery: A Guide for Adult Children of Alcoholics - Herbert L. Gravitz and Julie D. Bowden

19.6 Relationships
- Polysecure: Attachment, Trauma, and Consensual Nonmonogamy - Jessica Fern
- Fierce Intimacy: Standing UP to One Another with Love – Terry Real
- Your Brain On Love: The Neurobiology of Healthy Relationships - Stan Tatkin
- The New Codependency: Help and Guidance for Today's Generation - Melody Beattie
- More Than Two: A Practical Guide to Ethical Polyamory - Eve Rickert and Tatiana Gill
- Mating In Captivity: In Search of Erotic Inteligence – Esther Perel
- All About Love: New Visions - bell hooks

19.7 Money, Business, Creativity, And Finances
- Tools of Titans: The Tactics, Routines, and Habits of Billionaires, Icons, and World-Class Performers - Tim Ferriss
- Creative Calling: Establish a Daily Practice, Infuse Your World with Meaning, and Succeed in Work + Life - Chase Jarvis
- I Will Teach You To Be Rich: No Guilt. No Excuses. No BS. Just a 6-Week Program That Works - Ramit Sethi
- A Cat's Guide To Money: Everything you need to know to master your purrsonal finances, explained by cats - Lillian Karabaic

19.8 Gender, Race, And Social Justice
- My Grandmother's Hands: Racialized Trauma and the Pathway to Mending Our Hearts and Bodies - Resmaa Menakem
- Healing Resistance: A Radically Different Response to Harm - Kazu Haga
- My Body Is Not An Apology: The Power of Radical Self-Love - Sonya Renee Taylor
- Native: Identity, Belonging, and Rediscovering God - Kaitlin B. Curtice
- Patriarchy Blues: reflections on manhood - Frederick Joseph
- The Unapologetic Guide To Black Mental Health - Rheeda Walker
- Black Fatigue: How Racism Erodes the Mind, Body, and Spirit - Mary-Frances Winters
- Healing Racial Trauma: The Road To Resilience - Sheila Wise Rowe
- So You Want to Talk about Race - Ijeoma Oluo

- Emergent Strategy: Shaping Change, Changing Worlds - Adrienne Maree Brown
- Mutual Aid: Building Solidarity During This Crisis (and the Next) - Dean Spade
- Pleasure Activism: The Politics of Feeling Good - Adrienne Maree Brown
- The New Jim Crow: Mass Incarceration In The Age Of Colorblindness - Michelle Alexander
- Leading with Cultural Intelligence: The Real Secret to Success, Second Edition - David Livermore
- We Will Not Cancel Us: And Other Dreams of Transformative Justice - Adrienne Maree Brown
- White Fragility: Why it's So Hard for White People to Talk About Racism - Robin DiAngelo
- Gender Outlaws: The Next Generation - Kate Bornstein
- Trans Like Me: conversations for all of us - CN Lester
- The Antiracist: How To Start the Conversation about Race and Take Action - Kondwani Fidel
- Racism Without Racists - 5th Edition: color-blind racism and the persistence of racial inequality in america - Eduardo Bonilla-Silva
- How To Be An Antiracist - Ibram X. Kendi
- The Autobiography of Malcolm X - Malcolm X
- A People's History of the United States - Howard Zinn
- The Racial Healing Handbook: Practical Activities To Help You Challenge Privilege, Confront Systemic Racism & Engage In Collective Healing - Anneliese A. Singh

19.9 Social And Communication
- Nonviolent Communication: A Language of Compassion - Marshall B. Rosenberg
- Social Empathy: The Art of Understanding Others – Elizabeth Segal
- The Highly Sensitive Person's Complete Learning Program: Essential Insights & Tools for Navigating Your Work, Relationships, & Life - Elaine Aron
- The Power Of Vulnerability: Teachings of Authenticity, Connections and Courage - Brene Brown
- The Dance of Anger: A Woman's Guide to Changing the Patterns of Intimate Relationships - Harriet Lerner
- When Anger Hurts: Quieting The Storm Within Second Edition -

Matthew McKay, Peter D. Rogers, Judith McKay
- Quiet: The Power of Introverts in a World That Can't Stop Talking - Susan Cain
- TED TALKS: The Official TED Guide to Public Speaking - Chris Anderson

19.10 Miscellaneous
- The Power Of Moments: Why Certain Experiences Have Extraordinary Impact - Chip Heath & Dan Heath
- Atomic Habits: An Easy & Proven Way to Build Good Habits & Break Bad Ones - James Clear
- The Subtle Art of Not Giving A F*ck: A Counterintuitive Approach To Living A Good Life - Mark Manson
- The Tipping Point: How Little Things Can Make a Big Difference - Malcolm Gladwell
- The Brain That Changes Itself: Stories of Personal Triumph from the Frontiers of Brain Science - Norman Doidge
- Braving The Wilderness: The Quest for True Belonging and the Courage to Stand Alone - Brené Brown
- Connected: The Surprising Power of Our Social Networks and How They Shape Our Lives - Nicholas A. Christakis and James H. Fowler

Chapter 20

Further Resources

20.1 Finding A Therapist, 20.2 Addiction And Dysfunctional Family Resources, 20.3 Podcasts, 20.4 Meditations, 20.5 Confidential Emergency Hotlines

Beyond books, here are some additional resources for your healing journey. Especially for clinicians, the *National Institute for the Clinical Application of Behavioral Medicine* (NICABM) has some great resources which can earn them continuing education credits. For instance, the *Treating Trauma Master Series: A 5 Module-Series on the Treatment of Trauma*.

20.1 Finding A Therapist

Therapists can be found online. GoodTherapy and PsychologyToday have directories of locally available therapists who are easily searchable. Online therapy is also available through BetterHelp Online Counseling and Talkspace.

20.2 Addiction And Dysfunctional Family Resources

There is a Twelve Step program for almost any addiction or dysfunctional relationship. This includes for alcohol, narcotics, codependency, and dysfunctional families. However, many of these programs have some problematic aspects to them as documented in *Quit Like A Woman* by Holly Whitaker. This said, many of these issues have been resolved in the group *Adult Children of Alcoholics And Dysfunctional Families* (ACA), especially when using Tony A's Twelve Steps. Most people dealing with trapped emotions from youth will benefit from joining online or in-person ACA groups at <https://adultchildren.org>.

You can check out <https://en.wikipedia.org/wiki/List_of_twelve-step_groups> for a fairly comprehensive list of Twelve Step programs. Please keep in mind that the use of God, higher power, and spirituality in these programs is quite flexible in definition - it could be nature, a community, the totality of your life, or even the group you attend. There are also alternatives to programs like *Alcoholics Anonymous* such as *Refuge Recovery* and *The Luckiest Club*, just search online for recovery options.

20.3 Podcasts

Beyond books, a lot of information contained in *Radical Self-Care* was also inspired by several podcasts. These include *Therapist Uncensored*, *Hidden Brain*, *The Science of Psychotherapy*, *Huberman Lab*, and the amazing interviews hosted on *The Chase Jarvis Live Show* and *The Tim Ferriss Show*. Hearing about the journeys of others through struggle to success has been deeply nourishing for me and I cannot thank Tim and Chase enough for their work.

20.4 Meditations

Several apps provide great meditations and reminders. I suggest the free Insight Timer app, but there are many others. There are also thousands of free meditations online. Tara Brach, Jack Kornfield, and Thich Nhat Hanh are some of the most famous. If you're interested in joining a meditation community, search or ask online about sanghas. There are also several figures like Ram Dass and Alan Watts who give phenomenal talks on the ego, love, and materialism.

20.5 Confidential Emergency Hotlines

Domestic Abuse - 800-281-2800
Addiction Treatment - 1-800-662-4357
Suicide Prevention – 800-273-8255
Fireside Psychedelic Peer-Support - Call or text 62-FIRESIDE

Chapter 21

Bibliography

1. Ahmadi N, Moss L, Simon E, Nemeroff CB, Atre-Vaidya N. *EFFICACY AND LONG-TERM CLINICAL OUTCOME OF COMORBID POSTTRAUMATIC STRESS DISORDER AND MAJOR DEPRESSIVE DISORDER AFTER ELECTROCONVULSIVE THERAPY.* Depress Anxiety. 2016 Jul;33(7):640-7. doi: 10.1002/da.22451. Epub 2015 Nov 10. PMID: 26555786.
2. Ahmadizadeh, Mohammad Javad, Mehdi Rezaei, and Paul B. Fitzgerald. *Transcranial direct current stimulation (tDCS) for post-traumatic stress disorder (PTSD): A randomized, double-blinded, controlled trial.* Brain Research Bulletin, Volume 153, 2019. Pages 273-278. ISSN 0361-9230. <https://doi.org/10.1016/j.brainresbull.2019.09.011.>
3. Aleem, Zeeshan. *1 Map Shows How Many Hours You Need to Work Minimum Wage to rent an Apartment in Any State.* Mic.com. 2015 June 10. <https://mic.com/articles/120428>. Web. 2018 Aug. 17.
4. Anderson, Riana E., Monique C. McKenny, and Howard C. Stevenson. *EMBRace: Developing a Racial Socialization Intervention to Reduce Racial Stress and Enhance Racial Coping among Black Parents and Adolescents.* Family Process Institute, Vol. 58, No. 1, 53-67, 2019. doi: 10.1111/famp.12412
5. Andre, Michael, Aliza Aufrichtig, et al. *National Exit Polls: How Different Groups Voted*, 3 Nov. 2020. The New York Times. <www.nytimes.com>. Web. 2022 Jul. 13
6. Aron, Elaine. *The Highly Sensitive Person's Complete Learning Program.* Sounds True. 2019. Narrated by Elaine Aron. Audio.
7. Association for Psychological Science. *Cultural Reactions to Anger Expression can Affect Negotiation Outcomes.* 2010 Jul 10. Web. 2022 Jul. 7. <www.psychologicalscience.org>.
8. Association for Psychological Science. *The "Warm Glow" of Giving May Overshadow Doing the Greatest Good.* Association for Psychological Science. 2018 May 29. Web. 2022 Jul. 15. <www.psychologicalscience.org>
9. Balcetis, Emily and David Dunning. *See What You Want to See: Motivational*

Influences on Visual Perception. Journal of Personality and Social Psychology. 2006, Vol. 91, No. 4, 612-625. DOI: 10.1037/0022-3514.91.4.612

10. Bashir N., et al. "The ironic impact of activists: Negative stereotypes reduce social change influence." European Journal of Social Psychology 43.7 (Dec. 2013): 614-626. Wiley Online Library. Web. 30 Jun. 2014. doi: 10.1002/ejsp.1983

11. Basso, Julia C., et al. *Brief, daily meditation enhances attention, memory, mood, and emotional regulation in non-experienced meditators*. Behavioural Brain Research. 2019. Volume 356. P 208-220, ISSN 0166-4328. Science Direct. Web. 2022 Jun. 24. <https://doi.org/10.1016/j.bbr.2018.08.023>.

12. Bastos, Silvia. *How To Master Communication in Open, Polyamorous and Other Relationships*. 19 Dec. 2018. Better Humans. Web. 29 Mar. 2022. <https://betterhumans.pub>.

13. Borresen, Kelsey. *Can't Resolve Fights With Your Partner? 'Emotional Flooding' May Be To Blame*. Huffpost. 2022 Sep. 20. Web. 2022 Sep. 21.

14. Brandt, Andrea. *Is Our Culture to Blame for Our Unhealthy Anger?* 2019 May 1. <www.psychologytoday.com>. Web.

15. Brittany K. Lannert, et al. *Relational trauma in the context of intimate partner violence*. Child Abuse & Neglect, 2014; 38 (12): 1966. Web. 2022 May 12. DOI: 10.1016/j.chiabu.2014.10.002

16. Brittle, Zach. *Turn Towards Instead of Away*. The Gottman Institute. No date. Web. 2022 Jul. 19. <www.gottman.com>.

17. Burkus, David. *You're NOT The Average Of The Five People You Surround Yourself With*. Medium. 2018 May 23. Web. 2022 Jun. 21. <https://medium.com>.

18. Cain, Susan. *Quiet: The Power of Introverts in a World That can't Stop Talking*. New York: Broadway Paperbacks, 2013. Print. A(p.136)

19. Capacchione, Lucia PH. D. *Recovery of Your Inner Child: The highly acclaimed method for liberating your inner self*. Simon & Schuster / Fireside, 1991.

20. Carloni, Sara, et al. *Identification of a choroid plexus vascular barrier closing during intestinal inflammation*. Science 22 Oct 2021. Vol 374. Issue 6566. pp 439-448. Web. DOI: 10.1126/science.abc6108

21. Carr, Allen. *The Easy Way to Control Alcohol*. Narrated by Richard Mitchley. Arcturus Publishing. 2013. Audio.

22. Castleman, Michael. *Masturbation: Will the Controversy Never Cease?* Psychology Today. 2015 Jun. 15. Web. 2022 Jun. 10.

23. Conkle, Ann. Serious Research on Happiness. Association for Psychological Science. 2008 Aug. 1. Web. 2022 Jun. 20. <www.psychologicalscience.org/>

24. Curtice, Kaitlin B. *Native*. Christianaudio.com. 2020. Narrated by Kaitlin B. Curtice. Audiobook.

25. Dana, Deb. *The Polyvagal Theory in Therapy*. Narrated by Coleen Marlo. Tan-

tor Media, Inc. 2019. Audiobook.
26. Dashorst, Patricia et al. "Intergenerational consequences of the Holocaust on offspring mental health: a systematic review of associated factors and mechanisms." *European journal of psychotraumatology* vol. 10,1 1654065. 30 Aug. 2019, doi:10.1080/20008198.2019.1654065
27. Dedeker Winston, Jase Lindgren, and Emily Matlack. *245 - Your Ex's Social Media*. Multiamory. 2019 Nov. 5. Podcast.
28. Dedeker Winston, Jase Lindgren, and Emily Matlack. *271 - The Power of Receiving "No"*. Multiamory. 2020 May 12. Podcast.
29. Dedeker Winston, Jase Lindgren, and Emily Matlack. *285 - Compersion Research with Marie Thouin*. Multiamory. 2020 Aug. 18. Podcast.
30. Dedeker Winston, Jase Lindgren, and Emily Matlack. *355 - Singlism and the Truth About Being Single*. Multiamory. 2022 Jan. 18. Podcast.
31. Dedeker Winston, Jase Lindgren, and Emily Matlack. *371 - Repeating Unhealthy Relationship Patterns Part 2 of 2*. Multiamory. 2022 May 10. Podcast.
32. Delude, Cathryn M. "Brain researchers explain why old habits die hard." MIT News. 19 Oct 2005. Web. 20 Jun 2013.
33. Dias, Brian G, and Kerry J Ressler. "Parental olfactory experience influences behavior and neural structure in subsequent generations." *Nature neuroscience* vol. 17,1 (2014): 89-96. doi:10.1038/nn.3594
34. Dunn, Elizabeth, et al. *Prosocial Spending and Happiness: Using Money to Benefit Others Pays Off*. Association for Psychological Science. Current Directions in Psychological Science. 2014 Feb. 3. Web. Jul. 15 2022. <https://doi.org/10.1177/0963721413512503>.
35. Dwyer, Anna, V., Dawn, L. Whitten, and Jason, A. Hawrelak. "Herbal Medicines, Other Than St. John's Wort, In The Treatment Of Depression: A Systematic Review."*Alternative Medicine Review* 16.1 (2011): 40-49. *CINAHL with Full Text*. Web. 22 Feb. 2012.
36. Evans, Dr. Mike. *23 and 1/2 Hours*. Online Video. YouTube. 2 Dec 2011. Web. 20 Feb 2012.
37. Fadiman, James, PhD. *The Psychedelic Explorer's Guide: Safe, Therapeutic, and Sacred Journeys*. Chapter 19. Narrated by Steven Jay Cohen, Tantor Audio, 2018.
38. Feduccia et al. *Breakthrough for Trauma Treatment: Safety and Efficacy of MDMA-Assisted Psychotherapy Compared to Paroxetine and Sertraline*. Frontiers in Psychiatry. 2019 12 Sep. Vol. 10. Web. <https://doi.org/10.3389/fpsyt.2019.00650>.
39. Ferriss, Tim. #615: Dr. Andrew Weil. The Tim Ferriss Show. 2022 Aug. 17. Podcast.
40. Ferriss, Tim. *#521: Dr. Andrew Huberman*. The Tim Ferriss Show. 7 July 2021.

Podcast.
41. Fern, Jessica. *Polysecure: Attachment, Trauma, and Consensual Nonmonogamy*. Narrated by Jessica Fern. Thorntree Press, 2020. Audiobook.
42. Forbes, Malcolm, et al. *Placebo and Nocebo Effects and Why They Matter in Clinical Practice*. Psych Scene Hub. Posted 2021 Oct. 11. Updated 2022 Jan. 4. Web. 2022 May 5.
43. Fritscher, Lisa. *The 5 Stages of Courtship*. The Anatomy of Love. No date. Web. 2022 Jun. 6. <https://theanatomyoflove.com/>.
44. Gabrielle I. Liverant, Stefan G. Hofmann & Brett T. Litz. *Coping and anxiety in college students after the September 11th terrorist attacks*. Anxiety, Stress & Coping. 2004. 17:2, 127-139. Published online 2007 Jan 25. DOI: 10.1080/00033790420000221412
45. Gerderman, Dina. *Minorities Who 'Whiten' Job Resumes Get More Interviews*. 2017 May 17. Web. 2022 Aug. 11. <https://hbswk.hbs.edu/>
46. Gibson, Lindsay C. *Adult Children of Emotionally Immature Parents*. New Harper Publications, Inc., 2015. A(p.38), B(p.88)
47. Gilbert, Dan. *The surprising science of happiness*. TED. 2012 Apr. 26. Web Video. 2022 Jul. 13. <www.youtube.com>.
48. Gomez, L E, and Patrick Bernet. "Diversity improves performance and outcomes." *Journal of the National Medical Association* vol. 111,4 (2019): 383-392. doi:10.1016/j.jnma.2019.01.006
49. Gottman, John. *Raising An Emotionally Intelligent Child*. Narrated by Roy Worley. Macmillan Audio, 2018. Audiobook.
50. Gramlich, John. The gap between the number of blacks and whites in prison is shrinking. 2019 Apr. 30. Web. 2022 Aug. 11. <www.pewresearch.org>
51. Gravitz, Herbert L. and Julie D. Bowden. Recovery: A Guide for Adult Children of Alcoholics. Simon & Schuster 1985.
52. Grohol, John M., Psy.D. *15 Common Cognitive Distortions*. PsychCentral. Healthline Media. Web. 17 May 2016.
53. Gross, Terry. "Habits: How They Form And How To Break Them." NPR Fresh Air from WHYY. 5 Mar. 2012. Web. 24 Jun. 2013.
54. Guschanski, Alexander and Özlem Onaran. *The decline in the wage share: falling bargaining power of labour or technological progress? Industry-level evidence from the OECD, Socio-Economic Review*, 2021;, mwaa031, https://doi.org/10.1093/ser/mwaa031
55. Haga, Kazu. Healing Resistance. Tantor Media, Inc. 2020. Narrated by Tom Parks. Audiobook.
56. Harrington, Rebecca. *One Quality In Men Might Be Even More Attractive Than Good Looks And Sense Of Humor*. IFLScience. 2016 Aug. 18. Web. 2022 Sep. 26.
57. Head, KA, and GS Kelly. "Nutrients And Botanicals For Treatment Of Stress:

Adrenal Fatigue, Neurotransmitter Imbalance, Anxiety, And Restless Sleep." *Alternative Medicine Review* 14.2 (2009): 114-140. *CINAHL with Full Text.* Web. 22 Feb. 2012.

58. Heath, Chip and Dan Death. *The Power of Moments.* New York: Simon & Schuster, 2017. Print.
59. Henriques, Martha. *Can the legacy of trauma be passed down the generations?* BBC. 2019 Mar. 26. Web. 2022 May. 5. <www.bbc.com>
60. Hill, Richard and Matthew Dahlitz. *Babette Rothschild talks about revolutionizing trauma treatment.* The Science of Psychotherapy, Babette Rothschild. 2021 May 5. Podcast. <www.thescienceofpsychotherapy.com>.
61. Hill, Richard and Matthew Dahlitz. *Brian Quinn Talks Bipolar Disorder and Depression.* The Science of Psychotherapy, Dr. Brian Quinn. 2022 Jan 28. Podcast. <www.thescienceofpsychotherapy.com>.
62. Hill, Richard and Matthew Dahlitz. *Dr Johanna Lynch talks about integration and whole person wellbeing.* The Science of Psychotherapy, Dr. Johanna Lynch. 2022 Jul. 4. Podcast. <www.thescienceofpsychotherapy.com>.
63. Hill, Richard and Matthew Dahlitz. *Dr Moshe Perl Talks Neurofeedback.* The Science of Psychotherapy, Dr. Moshe Perl. 2021 May 16. Podcast. <www.thescienceofpsychotherapy.com>.
64. Hill, Richard and Matthew Dahlitz. *Loretta Breuning talks about habits of a happy brain.* The Science of Psychotherapy, Loretta Breuning. 2022 Aug. 22. Podcast.
65. Hill, Richard and Matthew Dahlitz. *Omar Reda Talks about the Wounded Healer.* The Science of Psychotherapy, Omar Reda. 2022 May 16. Podcast.
66. Hill, Richard and Matthew Dahlitz. *Stephen Porges talks about Polyvagal Safety.* The Science of Psychotherapy, Stephen Porges. 2021 Sep. 26. Podcast. <www.thescienceofpsychotherapy.com>.
67. Hill, Richard and Matthew Dahlitz. *Thomas Verny talks about the embodied mind.* The Science of Psychotherapy Podcast, Verny, Thomas. 2022 Apr. 4. Podcast.
68. Hill, Richard and Matthew Dahlitz. *Victor Yalom talks about psychotherapy.* The Science of Psychotherapy Podcast, Verny, Thomas. 2022 Aug 8. Podcast.
69. Huberman, Andrew. *Controlling Your Dopamine For Motivation, Focus & Satisfaction.* Huberman Lab. Episode 39. 2021 Sep. 27. Podcast.
70. Huberman, Andrew. *Dr. David Anderson: The Biology of Aggression, Mating, & Arousal.* Huberman Lab. Episode 89. 2022 Sep. 12. Podcast.
71. Huberman, Andrew. *Dr. Emily Balcetis: Tools for Setting & Achieving Goals.* Huberman Lab. Episode 83. 2022 Aug. 1. Podcast.
72. Huberman, Andrew. *Dr. Matthew Walker: The Science & Practice of Perfecting Your Sleep.* Huberman Lab. Episode 31. 2021 Aug. 2. Podcast.
73. Huberman, Andrew. *Dr. Rhonda Patrick: Micronutrients for Health &*

Longevity. Huberman Lab. Episode 70. 2022 May 5. Podcast.
74. Huberman, Andrew. *Erasing Fears & Traumas Based on the Modern Neuroscience of Fear*. Huberman Lab. Episode 49. 2021 Jun. 12. Podcast.
75. Huberman, Andrew. *Focus Toolkit: Tools to Improve Your Focus & Concentration*. Huberman Lab. Episode 88. 2022 Sep. 5. Podcast.
76. Huberman, Andrew. *How to Enhance Your Gut Microbiome for Brain & Overall Health*. Huberman Lab. Episode 61. 2022 Feb. 28. Podcast.
77. Huberman, Andrew. *Optimize & Control Your Brain Chemistry to Improve Health & Performance*. Huberman Lab. Episode 80. 2022 Jul. 11. Podcast.
78. Huberman, Andrew. *The Science & Process of Healing from Grief*. Huberman Lab. Episode 74. 2022 May 30. Podcast.
79. Huberman, Andrew. *The Science of Love, Desire and Attachment*. Huberman Lab. Episode 59. 2022 Feb. 14. Podcast.
80. Huberman, Andrew. *Understand & Improve Memory Using Science-Based Tools*. Huberman Lab, Episode 72. 2022 May 16. Podcast.
81. Huberman, Andrew. *Understanding & Controlling Aggression*. Huberman Lab, Episode 71. 2022 May 9. Podcast.
82. Huberman, Andrew. *Using Light (Sunlight, Blue Light & Red Light) to Optimize Health*. Huberman Lab. Episode 68. 2022 Apr 18. Podcast.
83. IESE Business School. *Why You Need Cultural Intelligence (And How To Develop It)*. 2015 Mar. 24. Web. 2022 Aug. 9. <www.forbes.com>
84. *Is the Idea of Manifesting Change Bad for Mental Health?* Newport Institute. 2021 Dec. 2. Web. 2022 May 18. <https://www.newportinstitute.com>.
85. James, Ella L et al. "Computer Game Play Reduces Intrusive Memories of Experimental Trauma via Reconsolidation-Update Mechanisms." *Psychological science* vol. 26,8 (2015): 1201-15. doi:10.1177/0956797615583071
86. Jarvis, Chase. *Happiness is an Inside Job with Dr. Rangan Chatterjee*. The Chase Jarvis Live Show, Rangan Chatterjee. 2022 Jun. 15. Podcast.
87. Johnson JM, Nachtigall Lb, and Stern TA. "The effect of testosterone levels on mood in men: a review." Psychosomatics 54.6 (2013 Nov-Dec): 509-14. US National Library of Medicine. PubMed. Web. 9 Jan. 2015. doi: 10.1016/j.psym.2013.06.018.
88. Johnson, Kara. *If You've Always Wondered if You're "Black Enough," You're Not Alone*. The EverGirl. 2021 Apr. 3. Web. 2022 Jul. 18. <https://theeverygirl.com/black-enough-stereotype/>.
89. Joseph, Frederick. *Patriarchy Blues*. Harper Perennial, 2022. Print.
90. Kanu, Hassan. 'Exclusionary and classist': Why the legal profession is getting whiter. Reuters. 10 Aug. 2021.
91. Kaufman, Scott Barry. *Post-Traumatic Growth: Finding Meaning and Creativity in Adversity*. Scientific American. 2020 Apr. 20. Web. 2022 Sep. 18. <https://blogs.scientificamerican.com>.

92. Kay, Katty and Claire Shipman. *The Confidence Gap*. The Atlantic. 2014. May. Web. 2022 Jun. 28. <www.theatlantic.com>
93. Kendi, Ibram X. *How To Be An Antiracist*. One World. 1st Edition. 2019. Print.
94. Kennon M. Sheldon & Sonja Lyubomirsky. *Revisiting the Sustainable Happiness Model and Pie Chart: Can Happiness Be Successfully Pursued?* The Journal of Positive Psychology. 2019 Nov. 7. Web. 2022 Jun. 6. DOI: 10.1080/17439760.2019.1689421
95. Killingsworth, Matthew A. *Experienced well-being rises with income, even above $75,000 per year*. The Proceedings of the National Academy of Sciences. 2021 Jan. 18. Volume 118 (4) e2016976118. <https://doi.org/10.1073/pnas.201697611>
96. Kingsland, James. *IBD may disrupt mental health by breaking gut-brain link*. 26 Oct 2021. Medical News Today. Web. 4 Nov 2021.
97. Kolk, Bessel Van Der. *The Body Keeps The Score*. Penguin Books, 2015. A(p.166), B(p.*268-271*), C(p.*127*), D(p.81), E(p.94), F(p.123), G(p.226), H(p.81), I(p.*298-310*), J(p.*242-245*), K(p.*258*), L(p.*240-245*), M(p.*254-256*), N(p.*254-255*), O(p.*215*), P(p.*114*), Q(p.*329*), R(p.*64*), S(p.222), T(p.*196*), U(p.*300-301*), V(p.*114*), W(p.*215*), X(p.94), Y(p.*273-274*), Z(p.*209-210*), AZ(p.*162-163*), BZ(p.*121*), CZ(p.87), DZ(p.215)
98. Korb, Alex. *Calm Your Face, Calm Your Mind*. Psychology Today. 2012 Aug. 21. Web. 2022 Jun. 8. <www.psychologytoday.com/us/>.
99. Lanzoni, Susan. *How Role-Playing Can Enhance Empathy*. Psychology Today. 2021 Apr. 8. Web. 2022 Jun. 26. <www.psychologytoday.com>.
100. Layton, Julia. "Is it true that if you do anything for three weeks it will become a habit?" howstuffworks. No date. Web. 20 Jun. 2013
101. Lemig, Chris. *Hypnosis for PTSD: How It Works, Effectiveness, and Examples*. Choosing Therapy. 2022 May 17. Web. 2022 Jun. 23. <www.choosingtherapy.com>
102. Lepore, Jill. *The Invention of the Police*. The New Yorker. 2020 Jul. 13. Web. 2022 Aug. 16. <www.newyorker.com/>
103. Lester, CN. *Trans Like Me*. Tantor Media, Inc. 2018. Narrated by CN Lester. Audiobook.
104. Levine, Nick. What Is 'Radical Monogamy'? 8 Mar 2022. Vice Media Group. Web. 29 Mar 2022. <www.vice.com>
105. Levine, Peter. *Healing Trauma: Restoring the Wisdom of Your Body*. Narrated by Peter Levine. Sounds True, 2007. Audiobook.
106. Levine, Peter. *In An Unspoken Voice: How the Body Releases Trauma and Restores Goodness*. North Atlantic Books. Berkeley, California 2010. Print. A(p.59), B(p.8), C(p.43-46), D(p.56-58)
107. Li, Wendy Wen, et al. *Novelty Seeking and Mental Health in Chinese University Students Before, During, and After the COVID-19 Pandemic Lockdown: A*

Longitudinal Study. Front. Psychol. 2020 Dec. 3. Sec. Organizational Psychology. Web. 2022 Aug. 31. https://doi.org/10.3389/fpsyg.2020.600739
108. Lilienfeld, Scott O. *Microaggressions: Strong Claims, Inadequate Evidence*. Perspectives on Psychological Science, 2017, Vol. 12(1) 138-169. Web. 2022 Aug. 8. DOI: 10.1177/1745691616659391
109. Lim, Chaeyoon and Robert D. Putnam. *Religion, Social Networks, and Life Satisfaction*. American Sociological Review. 2010 Dec. 13. Volume: 75 Issue: 6, page(s): 914-933. https://doi.org/10.1177/0003122410386686
110. Lipsky, Laura Van Dernroot and Connie Burk. *Trauma Stewardship: An Everyday Guide to Caring for Self While Caring for Others*. Narrated by Laura Van Dernoot Lipsky. Berrett-Hoehler Publishers. 2009. Audiobook.
111. Livermore, David. *Leading with Cultural Intelligence*. Second Edition. Gildan Audio. 2015. Audio Book.
112. Luckiest Club, The. *Our sober community mission*. No date. Web. 2022 Aug. 5. <www.theluckiestclub.com/mission>.
113. Lyubomirsky, Sonja et al. *Becoming happier takes both a will and a proper way: an experimental longitudinal intervention to boost well-being*. Emotion (Washington, D.C.) vol. 11,2 (2011): 391-402. doi:10.1037/a0022575
114. Margaret Shih, Todd L. Pittinsky & Amy Trahan (2006) Domain-specific effects of stereotypes on performance, Self and Identity, 5:1, 1-14, DOI: 10.1080/15298860500338534
115. María Carmen Cenit, Yolanda Sanz, and Pilar Codoñer-Franch. *Influence of gut microbiota on neuropsychiatric disorders*. World J Gastroenterol. 2017 Aug 14; 23(30): 5486–5498. Published online 2017 Aug 14. doi: 10.3748/wjg.v23.i30.5486
116. McKay, Matthew, Peter D. Rogers, and Judith McKay. *When Anger Hurts: Second Edition*. Narrated by Emmanuel Chumaceiro. Tantor Media, Inc. 2021. Audiobook.
117. Maria Shaflender talks about nutrition for mental health. The Science of Psychotherapy. 19 Nov. 2020. Podcast.
118. Martin, Michael. *Who Is Native American, And Who Decides That?* Interview with Anton Treuer. NPR. 2012 Nov. 1. Web. 2022 Jul. 29. <www.npr.org>.
119. Medications and Health Conditions that Pose Considerable Risk to MDMA Users. Dance Safe. No date. Web. 2022 Apr. 4. <https://dancesafe.org>
120. Menakem, Resmaa. *My Grandmother's Hands*. Central Recovery Press, Las Vegas 2017. Print.
121. McKenna, Terence. *Food of the Gods*. Narrated by Jeffrey Kafer. Tantor Media, Inc., 2012. Audiobook.
122. Mineo, Liz. *Good genes are nice, but joy is better*. The Harvard Gazette. 2017 Apr. 11. Web. 2022 Jun. 20. <https://news.harvard.edu/gazette/>.
123. Musick, Kelly, and Ann Meier. *Are both parents always better than one?*

Parental conflict and young adult well-being. Social science research vol. 39,5 (2010): 814-30. Web. 2022 Jun. 22. doi:10.1016/j.ssresearch.2010.03.002

124. Myhrstad, Mari C W et al. *Dietary Fiber, Gut Microbiota, and Metabolic Regulation-Current Status in Human Randomized Trials. Nutrients* vol. 12,3 859. 23 Mar. 2020, doi:10.3390/nu12030859

125. National Institute of Mental Health. *What is post-traumatic stress disorder, or PTSD?* NIMH. Revised 2020. Web. 2022 Jul. 13. NIH Publication No. 20-MH-8124.

126. Newman, Tim. *The fitness placebo: Can you really think yourself fit?* Medical News Today. 2017 Jul. 22. Web. 2022 Jul. 29. <https://www.medicalnewstoday.com>.

127. *Nonviolent Communication Training Course.* Dir. Marshall B. Rosenberg. The Center For Nonviolent Communication, 2010. Audio CD. CD #3.

128. Oluo, Ijeoma. *So You Want to Talk about Race.* Blackstone Publishing. 2018. Narrated by Bahni Turpin. Audiobook.

129. Okereke OI, Reynolds CF, Mischoulon D, et al. Effect of Long-term Vitamin D3 Supplementation vs Placebo on Risk of Depression or Clinically Relevant Depressive Symptoms and on Change in Mood Scores: A Randomized Clinical Trial. *JAMA.* 2020;324(5):471–480. doi:10.1001/jama.2020.10224

130. Parnell, Laurel. *A Therapist's Guide to EMDR: Tools and Techniques for Successful Treatment.* Narrated by Wendy Tremont King. Tantor Audio, 2020. Audiobook.

131. Paula Goolkasian, et al. "Effects Of Brief And Sham Mindfulness Meditation On Mood And Cardiovascular Variables." Journal Of Alternative & Complementary Medicine 16.8 (2010): 867-873. CINAHL with Full Text. Web. 22 Feb. 2012.

132. Perry, Bruce and Oprah Winfrey. *What Happened To You?* Flatiron Books, 2021. United States of America. A(p.*119*), B(p.*248*), C(p.*200*), D(p.*279-281*), E(p.*217*), F(p.*108*), G(p.36), H(p.*31-36*), I(p.*164-165*), J(p.*142-151*), K(p.*85-86*), L(p.*145*), M(p.*114-115*), N(p.*199*), O(p.*230*), P(p.*85-86*), Q(p.*148*), R(p.*142-151*), S(p.*178-179*), T(p.197), U(p.*179-183*)

133. Pierson, E., Simoiu, C., Overgoor, J. et al. *A large-scale analysis of racial disparities in police stops across the United States.* Nat Hum Behav **4,** 736–745 (2020). https://doi.org/10.1038/s41562-020-0858-1

134. Pollan, Michael. *How To Change Your Mind.* Penguin Books, 2018. Print.

135. Pollan, Michael. *This Is Your Mind On Plants.* Penguin Books, 2021. Print.

136. Power, R., Pluess, M. *Heritability estimates of the Big Five personality traits based on common genetic variants.* Transl Psychiatry 5, e604 (2015). https://doi.org/10.1038/tp.2015.96

137. *Prolonged Exposure (PE).* American Psychological Association. Updated June 2020. Web. 2021 May 1.

138. Rae Olmsted KL, Bartoszek M, Mulvaney S, et al. Effect of Stellate Ganglion Block Treatment on Posttraumatic Stress Disorder Symptoms: A Randomized Clinical Trial. *JAMA Psychiatry.* 2020;77(2):130–138. doi:10.1001/jamapsychiatry.2019.3474
139. Rao, Ankita. *To Some, Mindfulness Feels too Whitewashed to Embrace.* VICE Media Group. Jun. 29. 2018. Web. Apr. 4 2022. <www.vice.com>.
140. Raypole, Crystal. *Yes, Self-Hypnosis Can Really Work — Here's How to Give It a Try.* Health Line. 2021 Aug. 16. Web. 2022 Jun. 23. <www.healthline.com>.
141. Reavis JA, Looman J, Franco KA, Rojas B. *Adverse childhood experiences and adult criminality: how long must we live before we possess our own lives?* Perm J. 2013 Spring;17(2):44-8. doi: 10.7812/TPP/12-072. PMID: 23704843; PMCID: PMC3662280.
142. Reddermann, Luise. *Who You Were Before Trauma.* Narrated by Christa Lewis. Tantor Audio, 2020. Audiobook.
143. Robinson, Bryan. *The 90-Second Rule That Builds Self-Control.* Psychology Today. Apr 26 2020. Web. Apr. 4 2022.
144. RollSafe. MDMA (Molly/Ecstasy) Dosage. RollSafe. No Date. Web. <https://rollsafe.org>. 2022 Apr. 19.
145. Rosenberg, Marshall. *Nonviolent Communication: A Language of Compassion.* Encinitas: Puddle Dancer Press, 2002. Print.
146. Rosenzweig, Laney. *The ART of Rapid Recovery.* YouTube, uploaded by TedX Talks, 24, Nov. 2015. https://www.youtube.com/watch?v=vP7dx03arxI
147. Rowe, Sheila Wise. *Healing Racial Trauma.* Christianaudio.com. 2020. Narrated by Sheila Wise Rowe. Audiobook.
148. Rui Du, et al. *The Multivariate Effect of Ketamine on PTSD: Systematic Review and Meta-Analysis.* Front. Psychiatry. 2022 Mar. 9. Web. 2022 Jun. 15. <https://doi.org/10.3389/fpsyt.2022.813103>.
149. Russell, Stephen T. and Jessica N. Fish. *Mental Health in Lesbian, Gay, Bisexual, and Transgender (LGBT) Youth.* National Library of Medicine. Annu Rev Clin Psychol. 2016 Mar 28; 12: 465–487. Web. 2016. Jan. 14. doi: 10.1146/annurev-clinpsy-021815-093153
150. Scangos, K.W., Khambhati, A.N., Daly, P.M. et al. Closed-loop neuromodulation in an individual with treatment-resistant depression. Nat Med 27, 1696–1700 (2021). https://doi.org/10.1038/s41591-021-01480-w
151. Schwartz, Richard C. *Greater Than The Sum Of Our Parts.* Narrated by Richard C. Schwartz. Sounds True, 2018. Audiobook.
152. Segerstrom, Suzanne C, and Gregory E Miller. *Psychological stress and the human immune system: a meta-analytic study of 30 years of inquiry.* Psychological bulletin. Vol. 130,4 (2004): 601-30. doi:10.1037/0033-2909.130.4.601
153. Sentencing Project, The. *Report to the United Nations on Racial Disparities in the U.S. Criminal Justice System.* 2018 Apr. 19. Web. 2022 Aug. 11. <www.sen-

tencingproject.org>
154. Shakeshaft, Nicholas G., Et al. *Strong Genetic Influence on a UK Nationwide Test of Educational Achievement at the End of Compulsory Education at Age 16*. PLOS ONE. 2013 Dec. 11. Web. 2022 Jul. 15. https://doi.org/10.1371/journal.pone.0080341
155. Shellenbarger, Sue. *Use Mirroring to Connect With Others*. The Wall Street Journal. 2016 Sep. 20. Web. 2022 May 6. <www.wsj.com>.
156. Shih, Margaret, et al. "Stereotype Susceptibility: Identity Salience and Shifts in Quantitative Performance." *Psychological Science*, vol. 10, no. 1, 1999, pp. 80–83, http://www.jstor.org/stable/40063382. Accessed 5 May 2022.
157. Siegel, Daniel. *Making Sense of Your Past by Daniel Siegel, M.D*. PsychAlive. 2010/2011. Web. 2022 Jun. 27. <www.psychalive.org>
158. Sinha R, Jastreboff AM. "Stress as a common risk factor for obesity and addiction." Biol Psychiatry. 2013;73(9):827–835.
159. Sinusoid, Darya. *The Confidence Gap: Why Men Have More Self-Esteem*. Shortform. 2021 Sep. 4. Web. 2022 Jun. 28. <www.shortform.com>.
160. Sisemore, Timothy. *The Clinician's Guide to Exposure Therapies for Anxiety Spectrum Disorders*. Chapter: *Three Other Adaptations of Exposure Therapy*. New Harbinger Publications, 2012. E-book.
161. Spade, Dean. *Mutual Aid*. Tantor Media, Inc. 2021. Narrated by Stephen R. Thorne. Audiobook.
162. Stein, Murray B. and Naomi M. Simon. *Ketamine for PTSD: Well, Isn't That Special*. The American Journal of Psychiatry. 2021 Feb. 1. <https://doi.org/10.1176/appi.ajp.2020.20121677>.
163. Steiner, Susie. *Top five regrets of the dying*. The Guardian. 2012 Feb. 1. Web. 2022 Jun. 17. <www.theguardian.com>.
164. Stevens, Ann Huff. *Climbing out of Poverty, Falling Back in: Measuring the Persistence of Poverty Over Multiple Spells*. The Journal of Human Resources. Vol. 34, No. 3 (Summer, 1999). 557-588. Pub by University of Wisconsin Press. https://doi.org/10.2307/146380
165. Szabadi, E. "St. John's Wort And Its Active Principles In Depression And Anxiety." *British Journal Of Clinical Pharmacology* 62.3 (2006): 377-378. *Academic Search Premier*. Web. 20 Feb. 2012.
166. Tafra, Karla. *Stop Guessing What Your Shrooms Dosage Should Be And Start Following This Guide*. Healing Maps. 2021 Sep. 20. Web. 2022 Apr. 19.
167. Taylor, Ralph. Breaking Away From Broken Windows: Baltimore Neighborhoods And The Nationwide Fight Against Crime, Grime, Fear, And Decline. Avalon Publishing, 2001. Print.
168. Taylor, Sonya. *The Body Is not An Apology: The Power of Radical Self-Love*. Narrated by Sonya Renee Taylor. Berrett-Koehler Publishers, 2021. Audiobook.
169. *The 5 F's: fight, flight, freeze, flop and friend*. Rape Crisis England & Wales. No

date. Web. 2022 May 16. <https://rapecrisis.org.uk>
170. Thompson, Andrea. *Black Birders Call Out Racism, Say Nature Should Be for Everyone*. Scientific American. 2020 Jun. 5. Web. 2022 Aug. 15. <www.scientificamerican.com>
171. Thouin, Marie. *Beyond Monogamy and Polyamory: The Freedom of Novogamy*. What Is Compersion. Apr. 7 2022. Web. Apr. 12 2022. <www.whatiscompersion.com>.
172. Thouin, Marie. *Compersion in Consensually Non-monogamous relationships: A Grounded Theory Investigation*. No Date. Web. 2022 Jun. 8. <www.whatiscompersion.com/research>.
173. Treurer, Anton. *Everything You Wanted to Know About Indians But Were Afraid to Ask*. Tantor Media, Inc. 2017. Narrated by Kaipo Schwab. Audiobook.
174. Tudor-Ștefan Rotaru & Andrei Rusu. *A Meta-Analysis for the Efficacy of Hypnotherapy in Alleviating PTSD Symptoms*. International Journal of Clinical and Experimental Hypnosis. 2016. Published online 2015 Nov. 24. 64:1, 116-136, DOI: 10.1080/00207144.2015.1099406
175. Vaknin, Sam. Closure is Bad for You. Youtube. Prof. Sam Vaknin. Sep. 3 2021. Web. Apr. 6 2022. <https://www.youtube.com/watch?v=lk7b5duM0f4>.
176. Vedantam, Shankar. *All The World's A Stage-Including The Doctor's Office*. 2019 Apr. 29. Hidden Brain. <https://www.npr.org/transcripts/718227789>.
177. Vedantam, Shankar. *How to Really Know Another Person*. Hidden Brain. NPR. 2022 Sep. 19. Interview with Tessa West. Podcast.
178. Vedantam, Shankar. *How Labels Can Affect People's Personalities and Potential*. 2017 Dec. 11. Hidden Brain. NPR. Online.
179. Vedantam, Shankar. *Nature, Nurture And Your Politics*. 2018 Oct. 4. Web/Audio. Hidden Brain. NPR. <www.npr.org>.
180. Vedantam, Shankar. *Reframing Your Reality: Part 1; Part 2*. 2022 Jul. 18 and 2022 Jul. 25. Hidden Brain. NPR. Podcast.
181. Vedantam, Shankar. *Separating Yourself from the Pack*. 2022 Jul. 11. Hidden Brain. NPR. Online.
182. Vedantam, Shankar. *You 2.0: How to Open Your Mind*. 2022 Aug. 29. Hidden Brain. Interview with Adam Grant. NPR. Podcast.
183. Veenstra L, Schneider IK, Koole SL. Embodied mood regulation: the impact of body posture on mood recovery, negative thoughts, and mood-congruent recall. Cogn Emot. 2017 Nov;31(7):1361-1376. doi: 10.1080/02699931.2016.1225003. Epub 2016 Sep 14. PMID: 27626675.
184. Walker, Pete. *Complex PTSD: From Surviving to Thriving*. Published by Azure Coyote. 2014. Print. A(p.59), B(p.53-54), C(p.57), D(p.61), E(p.167), F(p.194), G(p.207-213)
185. Walker, Pete. *The Tao of Fully Feeling*. Narrated by Christopher Grove. Tantor

Media, Inc., 2019. Audiobook.
186. Walker, Rheeda. *The Unapologetic Guide To Black Mental Health*. New Harbinger Publications. 2020. Narrated by Janina Edwards. Audiobook.
187. Walsh, Bryan. *Does Spirituality Make You Happy?* Time. 2017 Aug. 7. Web. 2022 Jul. 12. <https://time.com>
188. Walum, Hasse, et al. *Genetic variation in the vasopressin receptor 1a gene (AVPR1A) associates with pair-bonding behavior in humans*. PNAS. 2008 Sep. 16. 105 (37) 14153-14156. Web. Jul. 5. <https://doi.org/10.1073/pnas.0803081105>.
189. Wastyk, Hannah C., et al. *Gut-microbiota-targeted diets modulate human immune status*. Cell, Volume 184, ISSUE 16, P4137-4153.e14, August 05, 2021. Published July 12, 2021. DOI: https://doi.org/10.1016/j.cell.2021.06.019. Web.
190. Weiss, Suzannah. *Can Orange Juice Really Improve a Psychedelic Trip?* Double-Blind Mag 2020 Dec. 28. Web. <https://doubleblindmag.com/can-orange-juice-really-improve-a-psychedelic-trip/>.
191. West, Lindsey M., Roxanne A. Donovan, and Lizabeth Roemer. *Coping With Racism: What Works and Doesn't Work for Black Women?* Journal of Black Psychology. 2009 Nov. 17. Web. <https://doi.org/10.1177/0095798409353755>.
192. *What's the Best Temperature for Sleep?* Cleveland Clinic. Healthessentials. 2021 Nov. 16. Web. 2022 Jun. 15.
193. What We Know Project. *What Does the Scholarly Research Say about the Effect of Gender Transition on Transgender Well-Being?* Cornell University. 2018. Web. 2022 Jul. 29. <https://whatweknow.inequality.cornell.edu>.
194. Whitaker, Holly. *Quit Like A Woman*. The Dial Press 2021. Print.
195. Winters, Mary-Frances. *Black Fatigue*. Berrett-Koehler Publishers. 2020. Narrated by Robin Miles. Audiobook.
196. Woolfe, Sam. *Understanding The Proper LSD Dosage For You*. Healing Maps. 2021 Sep. 27. Web. 2022 Apr. 19.
197. Xianglong Zeng, et al. *The effect of loving-kindness meditation on positive emotions: a meta-analytic review*. Frontiers in Psychology. 2015 Nov. 3. <https://doi.org/10.3389/fpsyg.2015.01693>.
198. Xiao Ma, Zi-Qui Yue, Zhu-Quing Gong, et al. *The Effect of Diaphragmatic Breathing on Attention, Negative Affect and Stress in Healthy Adults*. Frontiers In Psychology 2017; 8: 874. NCBI 2017 Jun 6. doi: 10.3389/fpsyg.2017.00874
199. Asare, Janice Gassam. 4 Ways That White Supremacy Harms White People. Forbes. 2020 Sep. 18. Web. 2022 Sep. 29. <www.forbes.com>
200. Felton, James. One Flirting Technique Almost Always Works, According To Psychologists. IFLScience. 2022 May 5. Web. 2022 Oct. 7. <www.iflscience.com>

201. Vedantam, Shankar. *Watch Your Mouth*. 2022 Oct. 3. Hidden Brain. Interview with Lera Boroditsky and John McWhorter. NPR. Podcast.
202. Hill, Richard and Matthew Dahlitz. *Dr Dan Siegel talks IntraConnected - MWe (Me + We)*. The Science of Psychotherapy, Dr. Dan Siegel. 2022 Nov. 4. Podcast. <www.thescienceofpsychotherapy.com>.
203. Beadle, Alexander. *MDMA Reopens Child-like "Critical Periods" in the Brains of Mice to Promote Mental Healing*. Analytical Cannabis. 2021 Sep. 2. Web. 2023 Jan. 1.
204. Segal, Elizabeth. Social Empathy. Tantor Media, Inc. 2018. Audiobook. Narrated by Celeste Oliva.
205. van Honk J, Schutter DJ, Bos PA, Kruijt AW, Lentjes EG, Baron-Cohen S. *Testosterone administration impairs cognitive empathy in women depending on second-to-fourth digit ratio*. Proc Natl Acad Sci U S A. 2011 Feb 22;108(8):3448-52. doi: 10.1073/pnas.1011891108. Epub 2011 Feb 7. Erratum in: Proc Natl Acad Sci U S A. 2013 Jul 9;110(28):1660-1. PMID: 21300863; PMCID: PMC3044405.
206. Vedantam, Shankar. *How to Complain Productively*. 2022 Dec. 19. Podcast. Hidden Brain. NPR. <www.npr.org>.
207. Netz Y. Is the Comparison between Exercise and Pharmacologic Treatment of Depression in the Clinical Practice Guideline of the American College of Physicians Evidence-Based? Front Pharmacol. 2017 May 15;8:257. doi: 10.3389/fphar.2017.00257. PMID: 28555108; PMCID: PMC5430071.
208. Ferriss, Tim. *#648: James Clear, Atomic Habits*. The Tim Ferriss Show. Podcast. 2023 Jan. 4.
209. Real, Terry. *Fierce Intimacy*. Sound True. 2018. Narrated by Terry Real. Audiobook.
210. Vedantam, Shankar. *Relationships 2.0: How To Keep Conflict From Spiraling*. 2022 Nov. 31. Hidden Brain. NPR. Podcast.
211. Huberman, Andrew. *How Meditation Works & Science-Based Effective Meditations*. Huberman Lab. Episode 96. 2022 Oct. 31. Podcast.
212. Huberman, Andrew. *The Effects of Cannabis (Marijuna) on the Brain & Body*. Huberman Lab. Episode 92. 2022 Nov. 3. Podcast.
213. Huberman, Andrew. *AMA #3: Adoptogens, Fasting & Fertility, Bluetooth/EMF Risks, Cognitive Load Limits & More*. Huberman Lab. 2023 Jan. 13. Podcast.
214. Vedantam, Shankar. *Who's In Your Inner Circle?* 2023 Jan. 9. Hidden Brain. NPR. Podcast.
215. Ferriss, Tim. *#625: Dr. John Krystal – All Things Ketamine*. The Tim Ferriss Show. Podcast. 2022 Sep. 29.
216. Huberman, Andrew. *Dr. Nolan Williams: Psychedelics & Neurostimulation for Brain Rewiring*. Huberman Lab. 2022 Nov. 10. Episode 93. Podcast.
217. Erkoreka L, Zumarraga M, et al. *Genetics of adult attachment: An updated*

review of the literature. World J Psychiatry. 2021 Sep 19;11(9):530-542. doi: 10.5498/wjp.v11.i9.530. PMID: 34631458; PMCID: PMC8474999.
218. Mariott, Sue and Ann Kelley. *Treating Complex Trauma and Attachment with Guest Dr. Daniel Brown REPLAY (157)*. The Therapist Uncensored Podcast. Episode 157. 2021 Sep. 24. Podcast.
219. Davis C, Cohen A, Davids M, Rabindranath A. *Attention-deficit/hyperactivity disorder in relation to addictive behaviors: a moderated-mediation analysis of personality-risk factors and sex*. Front Psychiatry. 2015 Apr 20;6:47. doi: 10.3389/fpsyt.2015.00047. PMID: 25941494; PMCID: PMC4403287.
220. NIDA. "Genetics and Epigenetics of Addiction DrugFacts." *National Institute on Drug Abuse*, 5 Aug. 2019, https://nida.nih.gov/publications/drugfacts/genetics-epigenetics-addiction Accessed 18 Feb. 2023.
221. Vedantam, Shankar. *Persuasion: Part 1* and *Part 2*. 2023 Jan. 16 / Jan. 23. Hidden Brain. NPR. Podcast.
222. Influence At Work. *The Science of Persuasion: Seven Principles of Persuasion*. No date. Web. 2023 Feb. 18. <www.influenceatwork.com>.
223. Kashtan, Mika. *Basic Pitfalls of Using NVC*. The Fearless Heart. 2012 Jun. 14. Web. 2023 Feb. 19. <https://thefearlessheart.org/basic-pitfalls-of-using-nvc/>.
224. Odell, Shannon. *A Neuroscientist Explains What Conspiracy Theories Do To Your Brain*. Inverse. 2019 Jan. 15. Youtube Video. 2023 Feb. 19. <www.youtube.com>.
225. Manotas, Manuel A. *Mindfulness Meditation and Trauma: Proceed with Caution*. 2015 Oct. 21. Web. 2023 Feb. 22. <www.goodtherapy.org/>
226. Mariott, Sue and Ann Kelley. *Attachment-Focused EMDR – Tools & Techniques to Heal Trauma with Dr. Laurel Parnell (170)*. The Therapist Uncensored Podcast. Episode 170. 2022 Jan. 3. Podcast.
227. Nuys, David Van. Working with Attachment and Trauma, with Daniel Brown, PhD. Transcribed from Shrink Rap Radio #649. 2019 Jul. 4. Web. 2023 Feb. 23. <https://medium.com/@shrink/>
228. Hopper, Elizabeth. *Can You Cultivate a More Secure Attachment Style?* Greater Good Magazine. 2017 Sep. 19. Web. 2023 Feb. 26. <https://greatergood.berkeley.edu/>.
229. Park Y, Johnson MD, MacDonald G, Impett EA. *Perceiving gratitude from a romantic partner predicts decreases in attachment anxiety*. Dev Psychol. 2019 Dec;55(12):2692-2700. doi: 10.1037/dev0000830. Epub 2019 Sep 12. PMID: 31512890.
230. Aizenman, Nurith. *How The 3 Nobel Winners For Economics Upended The Fight Against Poverty*. NPR. 2019 Oct. 15. Web. 2023 Feb. 27. <www.npr.org>
231. Alloway, Tracy P. What 20 Seconds of Hugging Can Do for You. 2022 Jan. 19. Web. 2023 Feb. 27. <www.psychologytoday.com>.

232. Huberman, Andrew. *Dr. Oded Rechavi: Genes & the Inheritance of Memories Across Generations*. Huberman Lab. 2023 Feb. 27. Podcast.
233. Vedantam, Shankar. *Happiness 2.0: The Only Way Out Is Through*. 2023 Feb. 13. Hidden Brain. Interview with Todd Kashdan. NPR. Podcast.
234. Merck KGaA. A closer Look At Distress Tolerance. Merck KGaA. No Date. Web. 2023 Mar. 6. <www.emdgroup.com/>.
235. Sunrisertc. DBT Distress Tolerance Skills: Your 6-Skill Guide to Navigate Emotional Crises. Sunrise Residential Treatment Program. No date. Web. 2023 Mar. 6. <https://sunrisertc.com/distress-tolerance-skills/>
236. Vedantam, Shankar. *Happiness 2.0: The Path to Contentment*. 2023 Feb. 6. Hidden Brain. Interview with Iris Mauss. NPR. Podcast.
237. Mariott, Sue and Ann Kelley. *Exploring Internal Working Models with Ann & Sue (199)*. The Therapist Uncensored Podcast. Episode 199. 2023 Mar. 7. Podcast.
238. Mariott, Sue and Ann Kelley. *Our Friend the Hippocampus: Disarming Human Defenses with Ann & Sue, Session 2 of 5 (184)*. The Therapist Uncensored Podcast. Episode 184. 2022 Sep. 1. Podcast.
239. Mariott, Sue and Ann Kelley. *Whole Brain Living, Psychology + Neuroanatomy + Spirit with Dr. Jill Bolte-Taylor – REPLAY (195)*. The Therapist Uncensored Podcast. Episode 199. 2023 Jan. 10. Podcast.
240. Mariott, Sue and Ann Kelley. *Sue and Ann Explore Self Criticism and Internal Scripts (Ep.169)*. The Therapist Uncensored Podcast. Episode 169. 2022 Feb. 16. Podcast.
241. Pat Ogden, Peter Levine, Bessel van der Kolk, and Ruth Lanius. *How to Work with the Limbic System to Reverse the Physiological Imprint of Trauma*. NICABM. The Treating Trauma Master Series: A 5-Module Series on the Treatment of Trauma. 2023 Mar. 10. Webinar.
242. Pat Ogden, Peter Levine, and Bessel van der Kolk. *How to Work with Traumatic Memory That is Embedded in the Nervous System*. NICABM. The Treating Trauma Master Series: A 5-Module Series on the Treatment of Trauma. 2023 Mar. 8. Webinar.
243. Pat Ogden, Dan Siegal, Bessel van der Kolk, Ruth Lanius, Allan Schore. *The Neurobiology of Attachment*. NICABM. The Treating Trauma Master Series: A 5-Module Series on the Treatment of Trauma. 2023 Mar. 7. Webinar.
244. Kidera, Jeannie. *How reading fiction can make you a better person*. Big Think. 2023 Feb. 13. Web. 2023 Mar. 15. <https://bigthink.com/neuropsych/>
245. Pat Ogden, Bessel van der Kolk, Ruth Lanius, Stephen Porges. *How to Help Clients Tolerate Dysregulation and Come Back from Hypoarousal*. NICABM. The Treating Trauma Master Series: A 5-Module Series on the Treatment of Trauma. 2023 Mar. 9. Webinar.
246. Vedantam, Shankar. *Revealing Your Unconscious: Part 1 & Part 2*. 2023 Mar.

13 & 14. Hidden Brain. Interview with Mahzarin Banaji. NPR. Podcast.
247. Vedantam, Shankar. *How Your Beliefs Shape Reality*. 2023 Mar. 6. Hidden Brain. Interview with Jer Clifton. NPR. Podcast.
248. Vedantam, Shankar. *Happiness 2.0: The Reset Button*. 2023 Feb. 27. Hidden Brain. Interview with Dacher Keltner. NPR. Podcast.
249. *Why We Disagree So Often*. Neuroscience News. 2023 Mar. 17. Web. 2023 Mar. 18. <neurosciencenews.com>
250. *The 26 Primal World Beliefs*. My Primals. No date. Web. 2023 Mar. 20. <https://myprimals.com/the26beliefs/>
251. Hill, Richard and Matthew Dahlitz. *Imago Relationship Therapy*. The Science of Psychotherapy, Harville Hendrix and Helen Hunt. 2023 Mar. 13. Podcast.
252. Hougaard, Rasmus. *Four Reasons Why Compassion Is Better For Humanity Than Empathy*. Forbes. 2020 Jul. 8. Web. 2023 Mar. 30. <Forbes.com>
253. Team Tony. *A Guide to Empathy and Compassion*. Tony Robbins. No Date. 2023 Mar. 30. <tonyrobbins.com>
254. Invisibilia. *Emotions*. 2017 Jun. 22. Podcast.
255. Jarvis, Chase. *6 Types of Magic Words That Will Help You Get Your Way with Jonah Berger*. The Chase Jarvis Live Show. 2023. Mar. 29. Podcast.
256. Huberman, Andrew. *Leverage Dopamine to Overcome Procastination & Optimize Effort*. Huberman Lab. 2023 Mar. 27. Podcast.
257. Mariott, Sue and Ann Kelley. Dreams: What do they really mean? An open discussion with Ann & Sue *(200)*. The Therapist Uncensored Podcast. Episode 200. 2023 Mar. 21. Podcast.
258. Mecking, Olga and Ruth Terry. *Why Doing Nothing Is Good For You*. Yes! 2022 Aug. 17. Web. 2023 Apr. 18. <www.yesmagazine.org>
259. Perel, Esther. *Mating In Captivity*. HarperAudio, 2006. Narrated by Esther Perel. Audiobook.

About The Author

Sage Liskey is an Oregon-born author, artist, designer, poet, event organizer, and public speaker. He is the founder of the Rad Cat Press and writes books about uplifting lives and reimagining society. Past works include *The Happiest Choice: Essential Tools For Everyone's Brain Feelings*, *You Are A Great And Powerful Wizard: Self-Care Magic For Modern Mortals*, and *You're A Snarky Darkness: Illustrated Poems For Radical Empowerment*. Please say hello at www.sageliskey.com or radcatpress@gmail.com!

About The Artist

Tara Chávez is a Latinx illustrator born and raised in the mountains of Southern Oregon. After graduating from the California College of the Arts, she moved to France and now resides in Normandy. She spends her time cooking, gardening, and creating art that explores the human relationship to the environment and self. Tara's illustrations aim to empower people to share their experiences and continue learning about life. You can follow Tara at <instagram.com/tchavezillustration> or see her website at <tarachavez.com>.

Made in the USA
Monee, IL
04 May 2023